Your Google® Game Plan for Success

Increasing Your Web Presence with Google AdWords, Analytics, and Website Optimizer

Joe Teixeira

WILEY

Wiley Publishing, Inc.

Your Google® Game Plan for Success: Increasing Your Web Presence with Google AdWords, Analytics, and Website Optimizer

Published by
Wiley Publishing, Inc.
10475 Crosspoint Boulevard
Indianapolis, IN 46256
www.wiley.com

Copyright © 2010 by Wiley Publishing, Inc., Indianapolis, Indiana
Published simultaneously in Canada

ISBN: 978-0-470-64164-4

Manufactured in the United States of America

10 9 8 7 6 5 4 3 2 1

For general information on our other products and services please contact our Customer Care Department within the United States at (877) 762-2974, outside the United States at (317) 572-3993 or fax (317) 572-4002.

Wiley also publishes its books in a variety of electronic formats. Some content that appears in print may not be available in electronic books.

Library of Congress Control Number: 2010932416

To my beautiful fiancée, Francine. Every little thing that you do is magic!

Credits

Acquisitions Editor
Scott Meyers

Project Editor
William Bridges

Technical Editor
Todd Meister

Production Editor
Daniel Scribner

Copy Editor
Sadie Kleinman

Editorial Director
Robyn B. Siesky

Editorial Manager
Mary Beth Wakefield

Marketing Manager
David Mayhew

Production Manager
Tim Tate

Vice President and Executive Group Publisher
Richard Swadley

Vice President and Executive Publisher
Barry Pruett

Associate Publisher
Jim Minatel

Project Coordinator, Cover
Lynsey Stanford

Proofreader
Candace English

Indexer
Ron Strauss

Cover Designer
Michael E. Trent

Cover Image
©istockphoto.com/Tom Nulens

About the Author

Joe Teixeira is the director of web intelligence at MoreVisibility, a Google Analytics Certified Partner (GACP). Joe is a leader in the field of web analytics and is Google Analytics Individually Qualified (GAIQ), as well as Google AdWords, Yahoo! Search Marketing, and MSN AdCenter Certified. He has presented more than 100 online webinars on a variety of topics, including web analytics, pay-per-click marketing, and SEO, as well as webinars focusing on user experience and testing. In 2009, Joe co-authored *Google Analytics, 3rd Edition* (Wiley, ISBN 978-0-470-53128-0), and he has appeared as a guest blogger on the official Google Analytics blog. Joe has also spoken at industry events about web analytics and online marketing for the Direct Marketing Association and PubCon by WebmasterWorld. He blogs on MoreVisibility's "Analytics and Site Intelligence" blog at www.morevisibility.com/analyticsblog, and can be found on both Twitter (@jtex316) and LinkedIn (linkedin.com/in/joeteixeira).

About the Technical Editor

Todd Meister has been developing with Microsoft technologies for more than 15 years. He's been a technical editor on more than 75 titles, ranging from SQL Server to the .NET Framework. Besides doing technical editing, he is an assistant director for computing services at Ball State University in Muncie, Indiana. He lives in central Indiana with his wife, Kimberly, and their four children.

Acknowledgments

Your Google Game Plan for Success is my first solo gig. I co-authored *Google Analytics, 3rd Edition* with Jerri Ledford in 2009, and felt as though I had it in me to author my own book. Now it's in the hands of people like you!

There is just no possible way I could have done all this hard work alone. There are a few individuals I'd like to thank, because without them this book would not be in your hands today.

The first person is my beautiful fiancée, Francine. She supported me and stood by me throughout the entire process of putting this book together. Without her moral and emotional support, I truly don't know where I'd be today. She also makes a mean banana pudding. I love you, Francine.

I also want to thank my future in-laws, Ronnie and Ira. Anytime I talk about this book, I can tell that you are just so proud of me and can't wait to have a signed copy of it in your hands. I'm touched that I make you so proud of me. I love you two very much.

An extra-special thank-you goes to my brother Fausto and my sister-in-law Katie for being my No. 1 fans.

Finally, there is a group of hard-working, dedicated, thorough, motivated, bright, awesome people who have really rolled up their collective sleeves and put in long hours to make sure that this book is first-class material for you, the reader. These folks never get thanked enough, so I'm happy to acknowledge the entire team at Wiley Publishing for everything they've done to get this project off the ground and running. Specifically, I'd like to thank my project editor, Bill Bridges; my sharp tech editor and copyeditor, Todd Meister and Sadie Kleinman; and my acquisitions editor, Scott Meyers. Special thanks to Mary Beth Wakefield for stepping in for a few weeks while Bill was on vacation. You guys *made* this book.

And to you, reader, thank you, and enjoy *Your Google Game Plan for Success!*

Contents at a Glance

Contents

Introduction

Welcome to *Your Google Game Plan for Success*! My name is Joe Teixeira, and I am honored to be the author of a book on this fantastic, rich, deep, and insightful subject. I hope it will help you expand your knowledge of some of Google's greatest products.

Whether you just started doing online marketing yesterday or have been doing it for 20 years, I believe — no, I *know* — you can get a lot from this book. If you're fairly new to the Internet and have just started as a marketing manager or web designer, or have even started your own business, you'll be able to learn how to get comfortable (and good) with Google AdWords, Google Analytics, and Google Website Optimizer. You'll learn a boatload of techniques and tactics for using these great tools, obtaining insights from them, and, of course, significantly increasing your chances of making money.

If you've been doing business online for a number of years, either on your own or for your organization — small, medium, or large — this book is going to serve two purposes. First, it's going to serve as a very handy desk guide: as you'll see by flipping through the pages, there's lots of information gathered from lots of different places, including a healthy amount of my own personal experiences and ideas that are not available anywhere online. This book is going to give you insights, knowledge, and angles that you may not have considered before.

If all those who read *Your Google Game Plan for Success* can learn at least three new tactics, techniques, or pieces of useful information that they can apply to their own business, organization, or personal knowledge, this book will have completed its mission. Of course, you can learn many more than three things And if you see me at a conference or catch me at a local bookstore somewhere, feel free to ask me a question or two. At the end of this book I've provided some ways for you to reach out to me online, because I feel that the ability to connect with me via LinkedIn or Twitter is the best "add-on" feature that I can provide.

About 'Your Google Game Plan for Success'

The idea behind *Your Google Game Plan for Success* is to take three of Google's most successful products, show you how to use them, and explain how to draw significant insights from them. Each of the three programs — Google AdWords, Google Analytics, and Google Website Optimizer — is at the top of its class and is used by the majority of businessmen and -women who do anything online.

Google AdWords is the most successful online advertising program in history. It specializes in pay-per-click advertising programs for people just like you who are looking to promote, sell, or announce their products, services, or content. Unlike traditional means of advertising, AdWords is fast, cheap, and extremely detailed. And you — the website owner — are in full control.

Google Analytics is the most popular web-analytics tool in the industry. Hundreds of reports and thousands of segmenting possibilities and enterprise-level features allow anyone who has or is building a website to access rich information about that site's visitors. It's also completely free of charge, and may always be. Web analytics is the best way to measure success online, and Google Analytics is simply the best in the industry.

Google Website Optimizer allows website owners to conduct scientific experiments on their site pages to improve conversion rates (referring to successes, such as a visitor's buying something from your online store or filling out an inquiry form). In a matter of days you'll be able to allow the most important audience — your website's visitors — to determine which content/color/call to action appeals to them, and which website elements don't. Like Google Analytics, Google Website Optimizer is free — you can conduct as many controlled website experiments as you want.

While the "Big Three" Google products are the core focus of this book, I also cover some other Google programs, like Insights for Search, Ad Planner, AdSense, and Webmaster Tools. Each of these programs plays its own role in helping you deliver your message to your audience, and each should be tried at least once in your website's lifetime. They're all free and easy to use, so your operating costs are low, and AdSense even gives you money for using it! You probably won't be able to retire on your AdSense revenue, but hey, every bit helps.

How This Book Is Organized

I've divided this book into six parts:

Part I: Getting Started. This is one of a few chapters in this book that is "vendor-neutral." In other words, it isn't geared toward Google, Yahoo!, Microsoft, or any other vendor. Instead, Chapter 1 focuses on organizing a plan of attack for your online marketing, and asks important questions about whatever it is you're currently doing. I dive deep into how you may be measuring success currently, and how marketing and conducting business online really differs from offline efforts.

Part II: Google AdWords. In Chapters 2 through 6, you'll gain a deep understanding of the new Google AdWords user interface, the Google Content Network, and cost-per-click advertising online. If you're already the world's foremost expert in all things AdWords, you can use these chapters as a reference guide for the future, or as a good refresher course. Everyone else will learn not just how to use AdWords, but how to pay per click like a professional.

Part III: Google Analytics. My personal area of expertise will become your most trusted resource, and the key to unlocking your understanding of your website's visitors. I'll not only cover the most popular web-analytics program, but will also talk about the web-analytics industry as a whole, provide a technical guide to Google Analytics, and explore some of the more sophisticated features available. If you like numbers, data, and insights, you're going to love Chapters 7 through 10.

Part IV: Google Website Optimizer. To truly optimize your website for conversions and increase the number of leads, phone calls, and sales, you'll need to start using Google Website Optimizer immediately. I'm going to go through the entire process of opening, creating, and analyzing your experiment data in Google Website Optimizer, and set a good foundation for understanding how the program works by discussing elementary statistical concepts. There's also a technical side to Google Website Optimizer, which I'll also cover.

Part V: Executing Your Game Plan. Chapters 14, 15, and 16 will show the sheer power of using the aforementioned three Google programs together. You'll learn how to sync Google AdWords and Google Analytics, how to use Google AdWords and Google Website Optimizer in tandem, and how to analyze experiments from Google Website Optimizer in Google Analytics. As you'll see, you're going to need to use the combined strength of multiple programs to really succeed online.

Part VI: Wrapping It Up. The final section of *Your Google Game Plan for Success* will provide you with a potpourri of other awesome programs out there that are just waiting for you to take advantage of them. Programs like Insights for Search, FeedBurner, Merchant Center, and even Yahoo! Search Marketing are all there to further help you succeed. I then wrap everything up in a nice summary in the book's final chapter, and provide you with a solid appendix of links to popular industry blogs and significant Twitter accounts.

What You're Not Going to Get Out of This Book

It should be clear from the previous pages what you'll be getting out of *Your Google Game Plan for Success*. You're going to receive a deep knowledge of the "Big Three" Google programs, and a great reference guide.

However, there are two major things that you're *not* going to get out of this book:

Product-bashing: This book features a big section on Google Analytics, but that doesn't mean that I hate or dislike Omniture Site Catalyst, WebTrends, or Yahoo! Web Analytics. In fact I like those products very much — specifically Omniture's Test&Target, the new WebTrends Live UI, and Yahoo!'s Path Analysis reports. The title of this book has the word "Google" in it, but that doesn't mean I won't talk about non-Google products, or that I dislike them.

Vendor hype: In the same breath, let me say that I'll try to keep my "Google love" to a bare minimum. Do I love Google Analytics? Yes, absolutely. Are there things that suck about Google Analytics? Yes, absolutely. So when something isn't useful, I'll point this out to you so you don't have to waste your time on it.

And as I indicated earlier, you'll get a unique and (I hope) colorful perspective on using these Google products. However, I wouldn't feel right about asking you to pay hard-earned money without offering something further. I want to be able to answer any questions that you may have during or after your reading of this book, and I most definitely want to hear your feedback and comments. You can contact me at jtex316@gmail.com. My Twitter handle is @tex316 and my LinkedIn profile is at http://linkedin.com/in/joeteixeira. Again, I probably can't reply to you instantaneously, but I'll get back as quickly as I possibly can.

Getting Started

In This Part

What's Your Game Plan for Success?

In high school I was in a program called the Junior Reserve Officers Training Corps (JROTC). Our senior Army instructor was a retired U.S. Army colonel (a "full-bird" colonel, as he would emphasize). He was a tough, no-nonsense leader who preached the values of teamwork against the backdrop of our own motto: "Leadership. Citizenship. Challenge. Responsibility."

One of the colonel's pet peeves in life was a poorly designed lesson plan. The only thing worse than a poorly designed lesson plan was no lesson plan at all. He would vent to us about how frustrated he was made by the horribly inadequate lesson plans of some of the school's faculty. We even had lesson-plan workshops, where we outlined our own plans and executed them to judge their effectiveness. When you're exposed to something like this at age 14, it kind of sticks with you for the rest of your life.

It always amazes, confuses, and intrigues me when businesspeople don't have some kind of plan of action — some kind of direction. You can hear it in the way they speak to you, you can see it in the way their website or marketing material is designed, and you can just feel it in your bones. You would think that having a game plan would be the most obvious and first thing a business owner would want to do — I mean, how can you start doing business without one? Unfortunately, lots and lots of website owners don't have any plan or any direction whatsoever, and some who do are going on a cross-country road trip without a GPS device.

Before you dive into Google AdWords, Google Analytics, and Google Website Optimizer, I highly recommend that you digest this first chapter, especially if you're thinking about or are in the middle of your first foray into doing business on the World Wide Web. You're going to get a good sense of how you should be thinking as an owner or marketer of a website, or even as someone who performs technical updates to a website.

What's Your Current Plan of Online Action?

Whether you've just finished designing and uploading your first website or are on your 15th different redesign since 1993, there are some high-level philosophical and introspective questions that you really should be asking yourself.

When I talk about having a "game plan," I'm not suggesting that you start creating accurately organized spreadsheets outlining every single second of your business life. The "Type A" brain in me would love to have you do just that, but my more abstract side wants you just to have an awareness at this time of what your answers would be to the questions in the following five sections. These questions are very simple, yet often forgotten, and they really need to be addressed before you do anything else. If you've never thought about or been posed these questions, then I have already accomplished one of the personal goals I have regarding you, the reader, in this book — and we're only a few pages in!

Why Did You Build a Website?

You wouldn't think that a question this simple would be one of the most difficult to answer, but it's true. Why did you — the soon-to-be-master of all things Google — spend all that money and invest all that time? Was it just because having a website is something everyone else was doing? Do you have a product to sell that will change the course of history? Are you a multinational conglomerate or nonprofit organization that wishes to spread its message to the masses? Did you build your e-business five years ago for one reason, but now find this has evolved into a completely new set of reasons?

Answering this fundamental website question will actually help you put your entire online presence in perspective, and you'll be a better person for it, guaranteed.

What Does Your Website Look Like?

People in general have very short attention spans and even less in the way of patience. They want websites to load faster than electronically possible and they want the best deals and discount codes available on the Net. When they visit your website for the very first time, they are subconsciously determining if they like your site or not, and in that same fraction of time, they're deciding whether to continue or go back to Google and try another search result.

So let's say that your website passes that first mental checkpoint for the typical visitor. Now, your website also has to do something apart from just being visually attractive. It has to be enticing. It has to be engaging. It has to be persuasive.

If you're trying to sell a product online, you'd better be really engaging; otherwise visitors to your site will not want to continue with you after the initial impression. Take a quick peek at Figure 1-1 from DIRECTV's homepage. DIRECTV has some satellite television service to sell you, and it makes sure you know about it without totally overwhelming you and rubbing it in your face. The company isn't passive about it, since it doesn't want to be confused with an informational type of site, but the approach is also not incredibly aggressive, so you won't confuse DIRECTV with a get-rich-quick scheme or some late-night infomercial.

The question "What does your website look like?" doesn't ask only about aesthetically pleasing qualities (which I will cover in depth in the Google Website Optimizer chapters of the book). It also asks what you are doing on the website to keep the attention of visitors so they'll hang around for more than just a few seconds.

Figure 1-1: DIRECTV's homepage

What Does Your Website Do?

Currently, most sites on the Web don't do much of anything, except provide the visitor with content (a lot of websites don't even do that). However, with the influx of more and more technologically advanced websites, visitors are beginning to expect any website they visit to do more and more for them. What was acceptable in 1999 or 2004 is now passé, and what was yesterday's news is today's history. Throw in the social-media explosion of the last decade, and you get a fusion of all sorts of different websites scattered throughout the Internet, all doing an array of different things.

Understand what it is your website does before opening up an AdWords account and sending a bunch of traffic to your landing pages. Also understand what it doesn't do, and if it's something that you feel your web constituency doesn't need. There's nothing wrong at all with a "basic" website (e.g., one with no "Web 2.0" – based interactive applications, complex Flash pieces, or studio-quality videos). Just make sure that you're getting your message across clearly to your site visitors, engage your visitors properly to start to do business with them, and don't force your website to pretend to be something it's not.

How Does Someone Benefit from Your Website?

On the Web, especially with a new site, you're going to have to be extremely good to make a profit. Depending on what your online business model is, this question may have added importance for you.

Whatever you do online, there's a good chance someone else is already doing it much better. Your great idea may be already in motion and being executed by someone else. And your "can't live without" revolutionary product of the century may not be as good as the "really can't live without" product of the millennium that your competitor is all over. However, that doesn't mean you can't still be really good at what you do, and have one of the best sites on the Web. It takes a lot of work and it may not come easy for you. You'll need to do market research, learn about your industry vertical, perform continuous testing to improve your website, and, most importantly, offer your visitors a benefit that they will appreciate and tell all their friends about.

Part of being great online is having the uncanny skill to make visitors feel as if they're getting an inside deal, a very special offer, or the inside track on the best product or service known to man. Take Figure 1-2, for example, which is eHarmony's homepage. The two things that you should immediately notice are the "Curious about how eHarmony works?" message at the top right, and then the word "FREE" followed by "to Review Your Matches" on the left-hand side (eHarmony also mentions this toward the bottom of the page). So not only is eHarmony trying to give you an inside look at how its system works, but it also presents an advantage to joining — the ability to review your matches for free. This is the kind of thing your website needs to do in order to attract visitors at a deeper level.

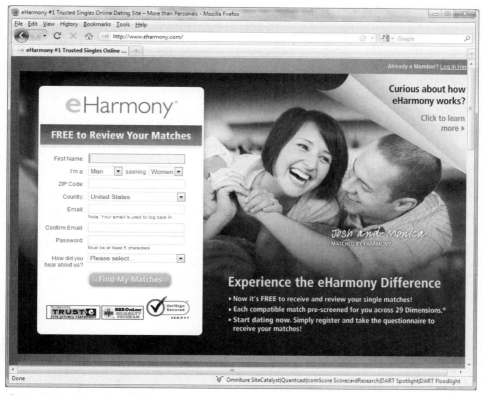

Figure 1-2: eHarmony's homepage

If you're not doing it, there are a dozen other websites out there that will do it instead. You really can't afford not to provide some kind of benefit to your site's traffic that no other site can match. If you can do that and market it better than anyone, all of a sudden your bright orange background and cheesy horizontal banner ad don't seem that annoying. And what's more, your asking price doesn't seem as high. See where this is going?

How Do You Plan on Marketing Your Website?

Finally we get to the point where we ask ourselves, "How in the world am I going to get eyeballs and clicks on my site?" Because you're reading this book, you're either using or interested in using Google AdWords, which is an excellent, cost-effective choice. But what else are you going to do to keep the traffic coming and coming?

On the Web, there are no rules saying that if you've had a website since 2000, you're automatically entitled to free traffic that will convert at the same high rate of success a kid fresh out of college is getting. Just because you've been around for a decade and your tagline says you're the best, that doesn't mean you have a right to the traffic and transactions that the kid with a six-month-old site is "stealing" from you. The Web doesn't care how long you've been doing it — it cares only about how well you're doing it.

How you plan your marketing strategy as you move forward can't be about ego or a sense of entitlement. It has to be about a consistent, dedicated effort to continue to optimize your marketing campaigns, your website's marketing message, and your website as a whole for search engine optimization.

But it doesn't even end there. Your offline marketing affects your online marketing, and vice versa. Your TV, radio, and print ads have a big-time effect on the ultimate success of your website, and your website can mean the difference between success and failure for your offline efforts. Let's try to avoid the latter by making sure that your ads are in sync with each other across different marketing channels and different marketing media for optimal results. You'll definitely read more about this as the book progresses.

Now that you've digested these five baseline questions a little bit, let's switch gears and talk about something else that's very important and unfortunately often mired in ignorance: how success is measured online.

How Are You Measuring Success?

Let's hope you already have an answer at the ready when you think about this next subsection of Chapter 1. It doesn't have to be the perfect answer, a right answer, or even a fully qualified answer. You should be able to come up with *something* that is useful for you to measure success. Perhaps this is what you did when you originally launched your site way back in the day, or maybe your boss asked you some questions and you had to dig deep and provide some kind of answer.

The good news is that you're measuring success. Or at least someone asked you to compile some figures so that that person can attempt to measure success. The bad news is that most people don't know how to measure success. But that's OK — everyone has to start somewhere. A lot of website owners don't even care about measuring success, which sends chills up my spine.

Measuring success isn't a right or wrong answer, or a true-or-false question. You can be measuring success excellently, you can be doing a halfhearted job, or perhaps you just couldn't care less. Most people use one or more of the next five "groups" to do their measurements.

Visits, Hits, and Page Views

You probably know one of these terms already — hits. This term has been around for a long time, and it used to be in the form of a counter on a lot of websites in the early to mid-1990s. It was also used in those prehistoric Internet days to measure success. If your site had 30,000 hits a month, you were winning. If your hit counter below the "Sign My Guestbook" link and above the animated "E-mail" icon was large, you were in charge. Boy, have we come a long, long way from those times.

Or have we? I recently spoke to someone who kept referring to "hits" and "visits" and how he wanted as many of those as possible, because he read some article or spoke to some "guru friend" who told him that getting as many hits and visits as possible was the way to succeed online. Let's hope this individual will heed the suggestions that I gave, and that this mentality is the exception, not the rule.

Hits and visits are basically the same thing — I won't go into semantics about the differences between the two. Page views are pretty much what they sound like — views of pages on your site. They're the foundation for most of the important web analytics and online-marketing metrics that are used to measure success, and they do serve their purposes in the grand scheme of things. However, they are in no way, shape, or form a reliable, intelligent, or worthy group of metrics to measure success with. There are no additional insights, no additional information, and no additional actions that you can take from knowing how many visits or hits your site has received. Figure 1-3 shows a piece of the dashboard report from Google Analytics. This particular website has received almost 300,000 visits and well over a million page views in this time frame . . . but who cares? Where did these visits come from? What pages did these people view? Did they request quotes? Did they buy something from the store? What were their average order values? How many visits did it take most people to purchase an item?

These are the questions that need answering if you are to begin to measure success online — hits, visits, and page views cannot answer these questions or provide any help beyond simply telling you how many pairs of eyeballs viewed your site.

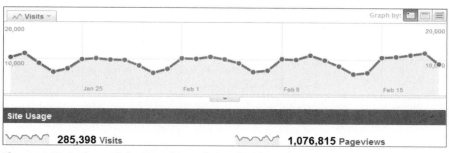

Figure 1-3: A piece of the Google Analytics dashboard

Time on Site, New vs. Returning Visitors, and Events

I like to group these potential success measurement metrics together because they are very tricky and slippery. Yes, slippery! Let me explain.

Time on Site is usually reported as an average, and it's the average amount of time, in minutes, that all visitors spend on your site. So it goes one step beyond a metric like Visits, because Average Time on Site takes all the time that all the visitors spent on your site, and reports back a ratio to you. It's an improvement upon Visits and Page Views, and for some websites it can be of a higher importance, but it's nowhere near where we want to be. It's a start, at best.

Something like Average Time on Site, which you see in Figure 1-4, doesn't allow you to evaluate performance. In Figure 1-4, you can clearly see in the upper-left corner that the Average Time on Site is two minutes and forty-eight seconds. You can also see a distribution by day of the same metric. But what you can't take away from this metric or this screenshot is whether two minutes and forty-eight seconds is good for you, bad for you, or neutral. Did visitors spend only that average amount of time on your site before they were frustrated with it and left? Did they spend all that time trying to figure out how to use your search function? Did they visit 10 different pages and then place a rush order with gift wrapping and next-day shipping? We cannot infer any of that, but in general, the more time visitors spend on your site, the higher the chances that they will convert (but not always — there are a lot of exceptions to that general rule).

Figure 1-4: Average Time on Site graph

Similar challenges for measuring success arise when you look at a report like the New vs. Returning Visitor report. Here, Google Analytics (or whatever web-analytics program you're using) can determine the percentage of visitors who have visited your site only once, and the percentage who have visited twice or more. Figure 1-5 shows this very popular pie chart found within the Visitors section of Google Analytics; it's also found prominently in nearly every web-analytics package.

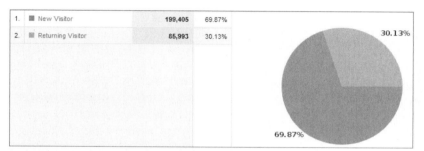

Figure 1-5: New vs. Returning Visitor report

Figure 1-5 shows a breakdown between new and returning visitors that's as nearly "classic" as you can get — a 70/30 percentage split. But as with Average Time on Site, where do you go from here? Without segmenting, applying a date-range comparison, or digging any further, you can't really do much with this report other than add it to your own knowledge of what is happening with your website. Great for your knowledge and understanding, not so great for measuring online success.

Events — interactions with special website objects or functionalities that do not generate page views — are also very tricky to measure for success, because again they are simply counts of raw things that happen on your site, without much meaningful weight associated with them. Is it important to track events from your video players or your brand-new Web 2.0 – based artwork designer? It definitely is — you need to know what people are using and what you can optimize and improve upon. Can knowing the number of clicks on your play button help you measure success on your website? Probably not, unless you're somehow charging money for every minute that's viewed on your videos, or if visitors can somehow get to a brochure download or lead-generation form from your advanced website functionality.

Conversions, Goals, and Successes

Now we're really cooking! If you're looking to improve your rate of form submissions, the number of times someone downloads your services brochure, or the number of items ordered from your online store, you're definitely on the right path to measuring success!

You see, it doesn't matter how long visitors spend on our sites or how many visitors there are, or how many pages they viewed. The question that should always hang over your website is, "Did these visitors perform specific important tasks on my site?" Visiting your homepage, viewing your "About Us" page, and looking at your executive bios are nowhere near as important or special as submitting a form to receive a white paper or contacting you to receive more information about product X, Y, or Z. All your marketing efforts — be they online or offline — should be geared toward continually improving these highly important website actions.

If you don't currently think about what actions you want your website's visitors to perform, log on to your site today and think about three or four very important things you'd want a visitor to do. Sometimes these actions will be very obvious, like the action of buying something. But a lot of websites aren't e-commerce storefronts, so sometimes they aren't obvious. Another general rule of thumb: If visitors have to use their keyboards on your site, chances are extremely high that whatever they had to use those keyboards for is something really important — and you should consider that a success point of your site.

Customer/Visitor Feedback

Do you take feedback from your website visitors? Do you ask them about their visit to your site, much as bed-and-breakfast hosts will ask you about your stay? If you don't have any way to listen to the voice of your most important person, the website visitor, you should listen up.

When I used to work for Publix Supermarkets, straight out of high school, a pie chart in the break room showed what feedback shoppers would usually give to a friend or family member about their shopping experience. It showed that 8 of 10 people would give negative feedback, 1 of 10 would give no feedback, and 1 of 10 people would give positive feedback. People in general are much more likely to give you feedback about the things that you're doing wrong or poorly than they are to give you feedback about how awesome you are and what a great product or service you provide. So when you see books on Amazon or reviews on Expedia and there are dozens and dozens of five-star reviews, you know you've found something good.

Since no website, including yours, is perfect, you should provide some type of customer feedback tool on your site. Collect enough feedback pieces and you'll probably see similarities in the problems that visitors are having on your site. A lot of times, these problems are not obvious to you or people who are very close to the site, and you need outside opinions and voices to help you figure out a better way. It's a great, inexpensive, and intelligent way to improve your website for everyone.

In Chapter 17, I'll talk about some of the better tools that you can use to collect this very important visitor feedback.

Key Performance Indicators (KPI)

OK, if you're doing this already, then you are at a higher level of measurement knowledge than most people. Congratulations to you!

Key Performance Indicators are the solutions to the mini-equations that you've built to measure how your website is performing. They are not metrics, like Average Time on Site or Bounce Rate, and they are not counts of things, like Transactions or Goal Conversions. KPIs, as they are abbreviated, help you understand your website's performance at both a macro and a micro level. Something like Returning Customer Average Order Value or Google AdWords per Visit Value can be a KPI for your website, since you can dissect and segment that number in many ways. Two or three particular KPIs are very important, no matter what type of website you own or work for. KPIs are so important that numerous blogs and articles are written about them, and there is a *Big Book of Key Performance Indicators*, by Eric Peterson, one of this field's outstanding contributors.

You can also flip the KPI concept upside down and come up with what's known as a *Key Risk Indicator*, or KRI. For example, if your New Visitor White Paper Download Rate drops below a certain level, you will know quickly that the marketing effort or change you made is putting you at risk of losing a lot of money. It's like an early-warning system, sounding a general alarm to you to make changes ASAP or pull the plug.

Doing It Online Is Different from Doing It Offline

That headline is probably the biggest understatement of the entire book! Online marketing, branding, and presence is a completely different beast than offline marketing, branding, and presence.

Many of you may be thinking about advertising online for the first time, and you may have backgrounds in traditional media (radio, TV, or print). I'm not going to debate whether online media is better or worse than offline media, and I'm not going to ask you to choose between them. I think more and more online marketers are starting to realize that offline marketing isn't "dead" and that it is still — and probably always will be — a powerful and effective form of marketing. Online marketing is simply a different medium, reaching some of the same offline audience but a whole other slice of the population pie that won't hear, see, or read your traditional advertisement.

I also feel that traditional marketers are beginning to be influenced by what's going on with their online counterparts, which is (I hope) leading to some updates, changes in the ways things are done, and, of course, more competitive prices for us online folks!

Online marketing is currently doing three things that really differentiate it from offline advertising.

Fast, Faster, Fastest!

Let's say that I've just launched my brand-new AdWords campaign, targeted to the state of Florida and running during business hours only, Monday through Friday, with a cost per lead of $25. It's chock-full of different ad groups, keywords, and negatives. It took a lot of work to put all this together and it's finally up and running!

But — oh, no! — there's a misspelled word in my top branding ad, and it's very embarrassing! Heaven forbid anyone should see this shameful error; I will be laughed right off the Internet!

Ahh . . . all better! In the time it took you to read those last two paragraphs, the misspelled ad has been corrected and the correction is live on Google and its Search Partners. Even though the campaign went live, you caught the error and fixed it instantly. No embarrassing typo, no lost business, no smudge on your brand.

Try making a change that fast with a television commercial. Try making a change at all in a print flyer or magazine. Changes and updates can happen instantaneously online — not so much offline.

No Charge for Changes

Oh, by the way, I almost forgot to mention that the instantaneous change I just made didn't cost me anything whatsoever. In the cost-per-click online marketing world, you're charged only for the clicks on your ads — nothing else. You're not charged operating costs (unless you work with an agency running your campaigns for you), you're not charged for making any changes or creating any new campaigns, and in most cases you're not even charged for impressions (eyeballs) that view your ads. Isn't that wonderful?

With a traditional marketing contract you may not be so lucky.

Much Higher Level of Accountability

Just launched a campaign at eight in the morning? You should have preliminary data on it by 10 a.m. in Google AdWords. Need to know how many visitors have visited your site today? Simply sign on to Google Analytics and bring up today's visitors up to the hour. Need to know how your A/B experiment is performing before the results are complete? Log on to your Google Website Optimizer account and see its progress so far.

In the offline marketing world you're considered a lucky advertiser if you are able to get an estimate on your share of impressions by the end of the month. You can't log in to an interface, you can't call your agent, and you can't download a report. That technology isn't available offline — yet.

But online marketers aren't the beneficiaries only of faster reporting speeds — they enjoy a much higher level of accuracy as well. When you sign on to your Google AdWords account, you can see that your local Products campaign received a total of 1,092 clicks for the month of July. That's not an estimate or a guess — that's 1,092 clicks on the dot. Google is even able to remove invalid clicks (from spammers and competitors who are bad sports) before you see them, and of course you're not charged for said invalid clicks.

Can you know for certain how many actual views there were on your television commercial in the month of July? Do you know for certain how many listeners heard your 30-second spot on Big 105.9? And how many readers saw your half-page color ad in *Better Homes and Gardens* magazine?

You really don't know, and there really isn't a way to know, just how effective your offline advertisements are. You're leaving it in the hands of the media gods, and it's up to them to decide your fate. Online marketing doesn't do things on a wing and a prayer.

Getting Started on Your Journey to Success

OK, so you've made it this far, which means that you're now fully ready to tackle the world of Google and become a successful online marketer/website owner. You now know the major differences between online and offline marketing, you have a good idea of what it takes to measure success online, and you have decided upon a plan of action by asking yourself five basic questions about your website. You couldn't be more prepared to begin your journey to success!

Remember a few pages back when I said that no matter what type of website you have or are thinking about having, there is probably one out there already doing it better than you? Well, the opposite is also true. No matter what, there is someone out there doing it much worse than you are right now. You never hear anything about them because . . . well . . . they're not very good. So just keep in mind as you're reading my book that you're probably going to make some mistakes, forget to code a page or tag a URL, and have an ad group or a campaign that fails. Everyone has screwed something up before, myself definitely included. With online marketing and Google's awesome products you'll learn invaluable lessons from your mistakes, just as you do in other areas of life. Don't be afraid to swing for the fences, and don't let the negative customer feedback that may come your way stifle your progress. Fix the mistakes, optimize the campaigns, listen to your customers, keep your head down, and move on. You CAN do this!

So let's start diving deep into *Your Google Game Plan for Success* by exploring the wonderful world of online marketing with Google AdWords.

Google AdWords

In This Part

Welcome to Google AdWords!

Google AdWords is the gold standard of online cost-per-click advertising. In fact, it's arguably the gold standard in any form of online marketing. Google AdWords and the cost-per-click advertising model is a multibillion-dollar-per-year industry. It's fast, cheap, easy to set up, and a lot of the other things that we talked about in the previous chapter.

This chapter is dedicated to opening up a Google AdWords account, learning its structure, and explaining how things work. Depending on how well you know Google AdWords, this chapter may seem basic, but it's important to lay the foundation for things to come later in this book. If you are familiar with Google AdWords but haven't logged in or worked in it for a while, you may want to review this chapter, since a lot has changed recently. There is now an entirely new and updated user interface with many more bells and whistles than the previous model.

This chapter also includes lots of pictures, which should be welcome to those of you who are more apt to learn through images.

NOTE **Google AdWords is constantly and rapidly evolving. Seemingly every week there are updates and new features added in. It's impossible to be 100 percent up to date with every feature in a printed book like this one. Your version of Google AdWords may have slightly different features or possibly a slightly different look and feel from what is presented in this book. But the heart of the AdWords user interface will most likely be the same.**

Creating a Google AdWords Account

Obviously, before you can start advertising in AdWords you'll need your own Google AdWords account. Before you can even get that, you'll need to make sure that the e-mail address you're planning on using to log in to Google AdWords is also a Google account. A few steps are required to create a Google account, but after you do it once you can use the same e-mail address for all other Google products, like Analytics and Website Optimizer. Let me first show you how to create a Google account, even though the chances are very high that you already have one (a Gmail account is a Google account, but you can also use a Yahoo!, Hotmail, or corporate e-mail account to create a Google account).

Creating a Google Account

The first place you'll want to go is www.google.com, and you'll want to look on the upper right-hand corner of the page for the "Sign in" link — you may have to move your mouse to make the links visible. After clicking "Sign in" you'll see a login screen, and you should see a link below the login area on the right-hand side of the page that says Create an Account Now (or an equivalent directive). Click that link to reach the first page of the Google account-creation screen. Figure 2-1 shows the top half of that account-creation screen.

Google accounts

Create an Account

If you already have a Google Account, you can sign in here.

Required information for Google account

Your current email address:

    e.g. myname@example.com. This will be used to sign-in to your account.

Choose a password: Password strength:

    Minimum of 8 characters in length.

Re-enter password:

☐ Stay signed in

Creating a Google Account will enable Web History. Web History is a feature that will provide you with a more personalized experience on Google that includes more relevant search results and recommendations. Learn More
☑ Enable Web History.

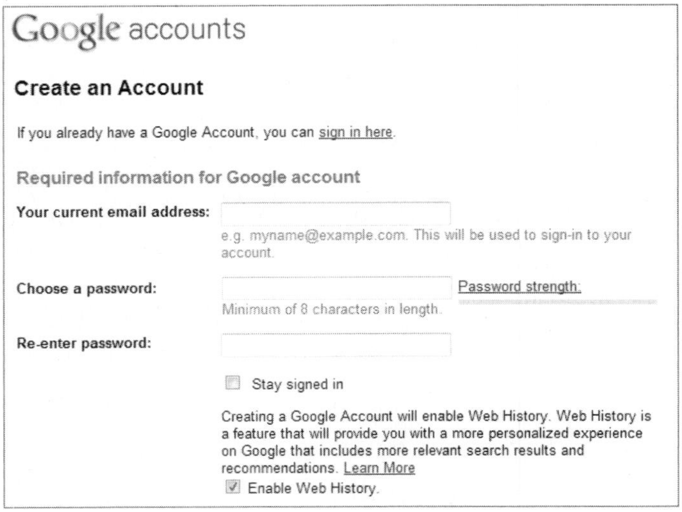

Figure 2-1: Google account-creation process, step 1

An interesting note: enabling web history will enhance your personalized search results from Google. You'll experience different search results when you're logged in to your Google Account from when you're not logged in.

After inserting your e-mail address and creating your password, scroll down to fill out the Location, Birthday, and Word Verification fields. Once you're done, click "I accept. Create my account." Figure 2-2 shows you what this bottom half looks like.

Figure 2-2: Google account-creation process, step 2

Once you have created your Google account you'll need to take a few additional steps. You'll first be taken to a screen that will ask you to provide your cell-phone number, so you can receive a six-digit SMS text message that you'll need for verification. After entering the six-digit code you'll be redirected to a confirmation page, informing you that you will be receiving an e-mail from Google with a verification link that will look something like this: `https://www.google.com/accounts/VE?c=CKOM48yWp_nmZhD-ncL85JyPwc0B&hl=en`

Click the URL to activate your Google account and have access to any Google product.

Opening a Google AdWords Account

Now you'll want to visit `www.google.com/adwords` to start the process of creating your AdWords account. If you haven't closed your browser or logged out of your new Google account before visiting the preceding URL, you should see some kind of message notifying you that your e-mail address isn't a valid AdWords log-in. That's OK — simply look above it and click the Get Started button (it may say something different — AdWords typically runs Google Website Optimizer experiments including that call to action to improve sign-up rates).

Figure 2-3 shows the first screen of the AdWords account-creation process. I recommend that you select the first radio button in each section. Selecting "I do *not* use these other services" will prompt you to create a new Google account (which would be redundant, as you already have a Google account), and selecting "I'd like to choose a new login name and password just for AdWords" will allow you to create a second Google account (which can be confusing, especially if you plan on using Google Analytics and Google Website Optimizer). Ultimately, it's your choice, and your choice doesn't influence anything.

Next you'll be required to select your permanent time zone, your country or territory, your actual time zone, and your account's currency. Please use caution when selecting these four options — they are permanent and cannot be modified after you click Continue. You are provided with a link to review the payment options for local currencies, and you'll also notice the two forms of payment that AdWords offers its customers: Postpay (automatic payments) and Prepay (manual payments). We'll talk more about these in just a little bit.

Figure 2-3: Creating your Google AdWords account

Now your AdWords account is officially created, and you should see a confirmation screen. Click the Sign In to Your AdWords Account link and you'll be taken to your Home tab within your AdWords account. You'll see a screen resembling the one in Figure 2-4 before creating your first campaign, which I highly recommend that you do right away. This way you can get used to the AdWords interface, and you can take care of entering your billing information, which needs to be verified before you can start running any ads with Google.

Creating Your First AdWords Campaign

On your new account's homepage you will right away notice the big Create Your First Campaign button on the upper left-hand side of the screen. You can click that right away, or you can get familiar with the tabs and all the links that are now available to you throughout this interface. There is even a video on the Home tab, and a search function so you can search the Google Help Center for all AdWords-related topics. Figure 2-4 shows what's underneath the Home tab before you create your first campaign and before you enter your billing information. Once you perform those two tasks you'll find a different set of items under your Home tab, which you'll see an example of in a few pages.

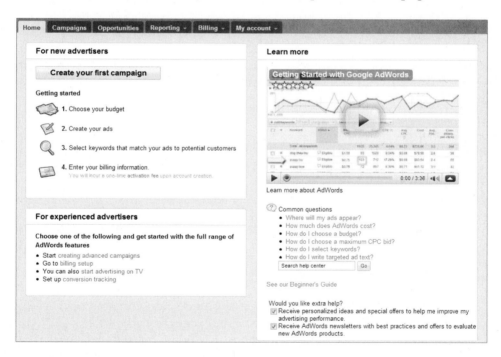

Figure 2-4: The first Home tab in Google AdWords

After clicking the silver Create Your First Campaign button, you'll see the campaign settings screen that you'll become very familiar with over time.

There are a number of options to choose from on this screen, which we will dive deeper into later in this chapter, but for right now you'll want to just make sure that the location, language, bidding, and daily budget options are to your liking. Set a low daily budget and a low bidding option just for now so that you can move on to the next step. Google AdWords allows you to set a manual cost-per-click bid for all keywords (or set each cost-per-click bid individually), and allows you to set automatic cost-per-click bids (Google will take your daily budget and create the cost-per-click bids for you). Click Save and then continue to creating your ads and keywords.

In the next step you'll create at least one ad and be asked to create at least one keyword for your ad group. You can create a text ad or image ad, use the display-ad builder, or create a mobile ad. If you're creating a text ad you'll be required to enter a headline for it (25 characters maximum), two description lines (35 characters maximum each), a display URL (35 characters maximum), and a destination URL. You can preview your ad on the right-hand side, or you can click the Help Me Write an Effective Text Ad link to learn more about writing an ad (or wait until Chapter 3, where I'll show you some ways to write effective ad copy). Below the ad creator you'll be able to enter keywords that you'd like your text ads to be triggered by when someone performs a query on Google. You can add as many keywords to your ad group as you wish on the left-hand side, and you should have noticed sample keywords that appeared after you entered your website's display URL in the preceding text ad. One best practice for keywords (also covered in Chapter 3) is to include only a few very relevant keywords per ad group. You can also estimate the search volume of your selected keywords to get an idea of how many clicks and impressions you expect to receive. Figure 2-5 shows an example of the Create Ad and Keywords screen.

Your first campaign, ad group, ad, and keywords have now been created, but they won't be displayed on Google unless you complete the next step, which is setting up your billing options and entering your payment information. Clicking Save and Continue to Billing will redirect you to the Billing tab.

Choosing a Billing Method and Entering Billing Information

First, select your billing country and hit Continue. Once you do, you'll see the two billing options, Postpay and Prepay, that I mentioned earlier. Take your time in deciding between these two options — you will probably have to create a brand-new AdWords account if you decide you want to change this setting in the future.

- **Postpay billing:** This allows AdWords to charge your bank account or credit card after you receive clicks. If you have a lot of budget allocated to cost-per-click advertising and you know you're going to be very cautious about how you spend your money, postpay billing may be a good option for you. For U.S. advertisers only, you can enter bank-account information via direct debit, and AdWords will automatically withdraw funds from your account. For everyone else, you'll have to use the credit-card option (debit cards with the credit-card logos on them will also work).

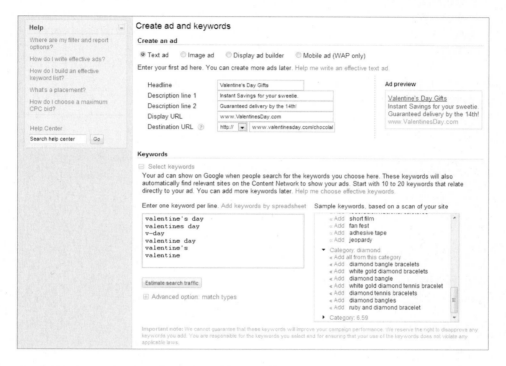

Figure 2-5: Creating your first ads and keywords

■ **Prepay billing:** This allows AdWords to deduct funds from a prepaid balance as clicks accrue. If you have a set amount of money allocated to cost-per-click advertising each month, prepay billing may be your best bet. It's also a good idea if you are not sure about advertising with Google AdWords — you can prepay a balance and use it as a test to see whether or not you like AdWords. Prepay billing also requires a credit card, and debit cards with the credit-card logos on them will also work in prepay billing.

After selecting your desired billing method, you'll be asked to review Google's advertising program terms, which can be printed out or saved if desired. Check "Yes, I agree" to continue. On the next screen you'll finally be asked to select your credit card and provide your full billing information.

Please note that AdWords will charge you a small one-time activation fee to begin running your AdWords ads on Google. This small fee covers the costs of providing you with an AdWords account and entering ads and keywords before you are charged for any clicks. It's a negligible charge: five dollars in the United States or five euros in Europe, for example.

You're now finished with the initial setup of AdWords, and you can go back and make changes to your campaigns and interact with the AdWords interface. Let's learn about the different tabs, and what you can do within each one.

Becoming Familiar with the Google AdWords Interface

Google AdWords has a virtually limitless number of options to select from. Geo-targeting, keyword match types, position preferences, display-ad builder, opportunities, reporting, and various tools just scratch the surface of this great cost-per-click program.

AdWords organizes everything into six tabs lying horizontally toward the very top of the interface. The six tabs are designated Home, Campaigns, Opportunities, Reporting, Billing, and My Account.

The Home Tab

The Home tab is the top-level overview of your AdWords account performance. Consider it your "homepage," where you can review the basic statistics, statuses, and campaign performance. On the left-hand side of this Account Snapshot you can set up custom alerts, view your account financial status, read recent announcements from the AdWords team, add up to 10 campaigns to your watch list, and view a summary of your top keywords' performance. On the right you'll receive a summary of all active online and television campaigns, a campaign performance report, and some help and tips from the AdWords Help Center. It's a great dashboard for obtaining high-level insights into your AdWords campaigns, and it's also customizable: you can move each box to a position of your liking, or minimize it if you don't wish to see it any longer.

It may be more convenient for you to start at the Campaigns tab instead of the Home tab when you log in to AdWords. If this is the case, you can click a link found toward the very bottom of the Home tab to switch the starting page to the Campaigns tab when you log in to AdWords.

Figure 2-6 shows an example of what you may find under your Home tab.

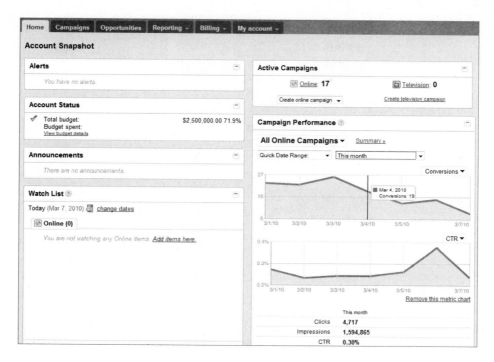

Figure 2-6: The Home tab (Account Snapshot)

The Campaigns Tab

You'll spend most of your time within the AdWords interface in the Campaigns tab. This is where all campaign information, settings, and statistics are available, and where you'll do your day-to-day work. There's a mountain of options within the Campaigns tab. On the left-hand side of the screen you'll find an alphabetized list of all your online campaigns, which you can click to access individually. Below that list are links for the AdWords help section, answering common questions asked by advertisers.

The middle portion of the Campaigns tab starts with a date-range slider toward the very top, which is clickable and editable, allowing you to view campaign performance for any date range desired. Below the date range are several sub-tabs, where you can access Campaigns, Ad Groups, Settings, Ads, Keywords, Networks, and Audiences. Immediately below that are additional options to further drill down into your AdWords campaigns. These include the ability to display offline (paused or deleted) campaigns, segmenting options, a filter-creation tool, and a column-customization feature, allowing metrics to be added to or removed from the main data table. Toward the right-hand side of these options you'll find a search function, which helps if you have several campaigns at once, a show/hide trending chart toggle, and an export function, allowing you to download your campaign data in several different file formats.

The graph that's found below these ancillary options is editable — you can change what metrics appear here. Below this graph you'll find buttons to create a new campaign, change a campaign's status, and perform other actions. Finally, below all of this, you'll see each one of your campaigns listed, with corresponding metrics for each campaign. Clicking any campaign name will let you drill down into the campaign to the ad-group level, and clicking any ad group within your campaign displays its keywords. You'll notice as you drill down that the order of the sub-tabs above the trending graph and the available options around the trending graph will update and make sense with where you are in the interface. You'll always know where you are in AdWords by a breadcrumb trail that appears toward the very top of the screen, right underneath the main AdWords tabs. Figure 2-7 shows an example of the Campaigns tab and its many different options.

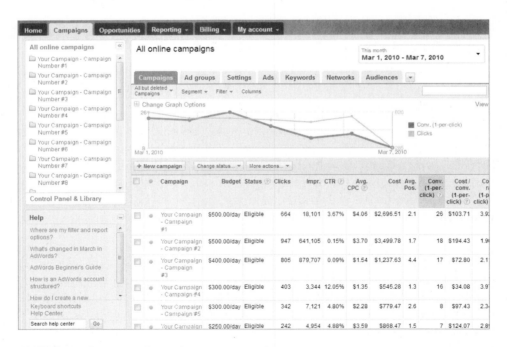

Figure 2-7: The Campaigns tab

The Opportunities Tab

A relatively new feature in AdWords, the Opportunities tab analyzes your campaign performance and provides recommendations for you. It's like having your own account representative watching your campaigns and providing guidance along the way.

The two main types of opportunities that AdWords will suggest to advertisers are keyword bid ideas and keyword ideas, which will be stacked on top of one another within the Opportunities tab. You may also receive some campaign budget ideas if Google decides that your budget isn't being used to its fullest potential. The keyword bid ideas table will show you the impact you should expect to experience on each suggested keyword if you increase its cost per click. Google also provides you with a link to view the estimates for each keyword's performance if you were to decrease costs. Clicking a keyword suggested in the Opportunities tab pops open a window, shown in Figure 2-8.

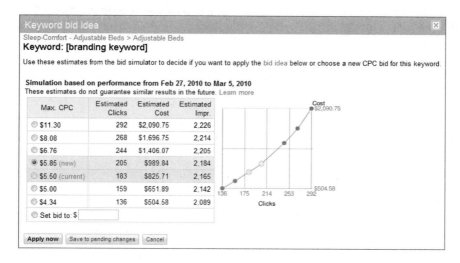

Figure 2-8: Keyword bid ideas (Opportunities tab)

The keyword ideas table will analyze your current keyword list and identify growth opportunities that make sense based on your campaign and ad-group structure. The better your campaign structure, the more accurate Google can be in providing these keyword recommendations to you. Each suggested keyword will be shown alongside its estimated monthly search volume, and when any keyword is clicked, a pop-up window appears, showing you each suggested keyword, which ad group it should be placed in, the advertiser competition for each keyword, and a rating system that will help improve how AdWords returns suggestions to you in the future. You can even download this keyword suggestion list into a CSV file to analyze offline. Figure 2-9 shows you what keyword suggestions will look like:

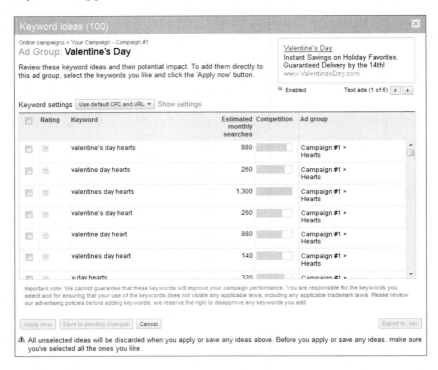

Figure 2-9: Keyword Ideas (Opportunities tab)

The Reporting Tab

The Reporting tab is the first to have its own drop-down menu with its own subsections. There are five subsections within the Reporting tab:

- **Reports:** The report center is the place to create and view custom reports. The last 15 reports you created will be listed here, as well as any report templates created for future use. I'll show you how to create a report and what it looks like later in this chapter.

- **Change history:** Everything you do in AdWords is recorded and stored in the My Change History section. This information can be retrieved as far back as January 1, 2006. Chapter 5 goes deep into the My Change History tool.

- **Conversions:** AdWords advertisers can add a piece of JavaScript code to their most important (conversion) pages. This code is available from within the Conversion Tracking section. It's accessible via this sub-section, and I'll also cover it in depth in Chapter 6.

- **Google Analytics:** As you'll learn in later chapters, you can access your Google Analytics account from within your Google AdWords account. This sub-section is the place to do that.

- **Website Optimizer:** Ditto for Website Optimizer. Access your experiment data right from within the AdWords interface via this sub-section.

The Billing Tab

The Billing tab also has its own drop-down menu, with two subsections:

- **Billing summary:** A complete summary of all of your billing activity will be reported on this page. You can view the details of your last payment, your primary payment method, and your current AdWords balance, all from within this easy-to-use report. You can also view a list of payments and billing activities toward the bottom of this page.

- **Billing preferences:** An overview of the preferences that you selected when you first set up your AdWords account will be found here. You should see your credit-card type, billing, and other personal information.

NOTE If you work for an agency or manage a "My Client Center" AdWords account, your billing options will most likely be different from the ones just described. You'll possibly see an "Invoice" section, showing you the details of your invoicing terms, and a "Budget" section, showing you the details of your monthly budget. However, chances are that you won't need to worry about the Billing tab if you work for an agency or work within an MCC AdWords Account.

The My Account Tab

The last of the six tabs in Google AdWords is reserved for information about your AdWords account. It is broken up into three subsections:

- **Account access:** This shows all the e-mail addresses that have access to your Google AdWords account, and their roles. Normally only one e-mail address (yours) has access to your AdWords account, but you can invite anyone to your account from within this section.

- **Notification settings:** AdWords can send you a variety of e-mail notifications, from serious ones like billing alerts to performance suggestions.

I advise you to enable as many of these alerts as you possibly can, especially if you are very new to Google AdWords. Figure 2-10 shows the Notification Settings window.

▪ **Preferences:** This page will review for you the preferences that you selected when you first created your AdWords account, such as time zone and language. This simple page will become extremely important in later chapters, as this will be the place to edit your destination-URL auto-tagging, which we'll cover later on in the book.

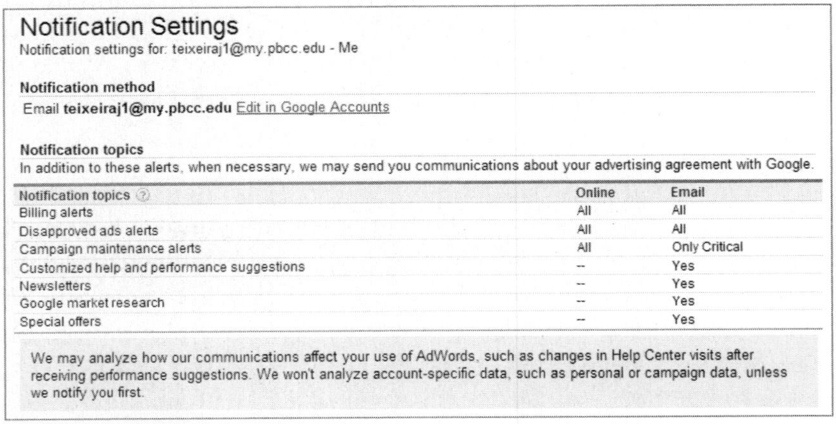

Notification Settings
Notification settings for: teixeiraj1@my.pbcc.edu - Me

Notification method
Email **teixeiraj1@my.pbcc.edu** Edit in Google Accounts

Notification topics
In addition to these alerts, when necessary, we may send you communications about your advertising agreement with Google.

Notification topics ⓘ	Online	Email
Billing alerts	All	All
Disapproved ads alerts	All	All
Campaign maintenance alerts	All	Only Critical
Customized help and performance suggestions	--	Yes
Newsletters	--	Yes
Google market research	--	Yes
Special offers	--	Yes

We may analyze how our communications affect your use of AdWords, such as changes in Help Center visits after receiving performance suggestions. We won't analyze account-specific data, such as personal or campaign data, unless we notify you first.

Figure 2-10: Notification settings (My Account tab)

A high-level walk-through of Google AdWords is nice to get you familiar with the interface, but we really need to be more thorough in order to truly learn what AdWords can do. There still are many nuances to show and explain. The rest of this chapter will focus on digging deeper within each tab, and showing examples of how everything works.

The Home Tab

As we reviewed earlier, the Home tab — also known as the Account Snapshot page — is the dashboard for your Google AdWords account. It's one of my personal favorite things in all of online marketing, and I am surprised at how underrated it is. (This is ironic, considering that I'm always suggesting that the user segment everything and "dive deep" into campaigns and data. This Account Snapshot page is a high-level overview.)

There are eight elements within the Account Snapshot page and, as mentioned before, these can be rearranged to your individual liking.

Alerts

If you have any disapproved ads or keywords, budget shortfalls, payment issues, or any other issues that are very important and require your immediate attention, the Alerts element will tell you about them. Some alerts, like those having to do with disapproved ads, must be taken care of right away to ensure that your ads continue running on Google and its search partners. Alerts can be very valuable and force you to take important action when necessary.

On the other hand, alerts may become irritating and you may wish to stop certain ones from appearing. Go back and view Figure 2-10, where you'll see the Notification Settings page within the My Account tab. The status in the Online column will indicate which alerts appear on your Account Snapshot page and which don't.

Account Status

Your total budget, the percentage of your budget spent, and a green checkmark are the three things you should always see on the Account Status element. This area just keeps you abreast of your budget situation, and the green checkmark notifies you that your account is active and ready to go. If you have a brand-new AdWords account you may see "You have no status messages," which is not necessarily a bad thing.

Announcements

When Google AdWords launches a new feature, or when you have some important message from Google, your Announcements element will indicate it to you. It's great for keeping up with the latest development news on AdWords, but it can also become bothersome. You can once again visit the Notification Settings page to enable or disable any announcements as you see fit.

Watch List

Now we get into some of the "meat" of the Account Snapshot page. Your Watch List can show you up to 10 selected campaigns that you've deemed critical. You won't have to go very far to analyze your most important campaigns' performance with the Watch List.

You should have a "No items here" message in the Watch List window. Click Manage Your Watch List, which is at the bottom of this window, to open up a new window that looks like the one in Figure 2-11. All your campaigns — including paused or deleted ones — will be listed here. Simply click Add to add them to the right-hand side, or Remove to clear them off your Watch List. Once added, your selected campaigns appear on your Account Snapshot page, which shows you impressions, clicks, click-through rates, and cost-per-click metrics for each. You can also change the date range of your Watch List: you should see a small calendar icon above the list of campaigns.

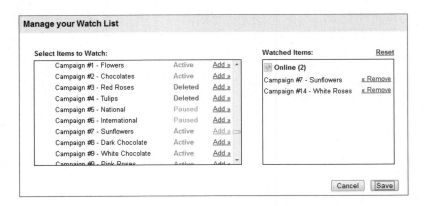

Figure 2-11: Managing your Watch List

Keyword Performance

The Keyword Performance element of the Account Snapshot page is quite robust. By default, your top 10 "Best Performing Keywords" by click-through rate will be shown to you, with links for viewing keywords beyond the top 10. However, you can heavily customize this window. First, you're given six separate keyword-performance choices:

- **View all keywords:** Shows every keyword in your account.
- **Best-performing keywords:** Shows the keywords with the highest click-through rates.
- **Worst-performing keywords:** Shows the keywords with the lowest click-through rates.
- **Keywords with no clicks:** Shows any keyword without a click in the specified date range.
- **Expensive keywords:** Shows the keywords with the highest average cost per click.
- **Competitive keywords:** Shows the keywords for which there is the most competition among advertisers on AdWords.

Each metric column that appears for each keyword is sortable, and each keyword is clickable: clicking a keyword will take you within that keyword's campaign, where you can edit it. Mousing over any keyword will pop open a small box showing that keyword's status and within which campaign it is nested. Like the Watch List element, the date range can be modified to your liking, but unlike the Watch List, the list of keywords can be exported into a CSV file.

This quick Keyword Performance report may very well become one of your favorite reports over time. Check out Figure 2-12 for an example of the Keyword Performance window.

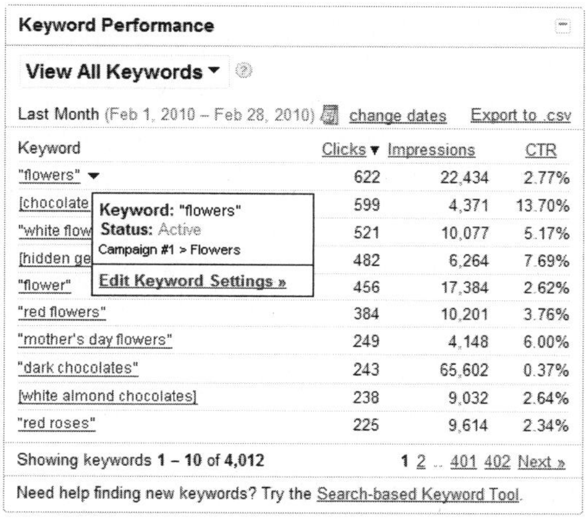

Figure 2-12: Keyword performance

Active Campaigns

This is a simple element of your Account Snapshot page. It simply lists the number of online campaigns in your account, and the number of television campaigns. You are provided with some quick links to create a keyword-targeted or placement-targeted campaign, as well as a new television campaign.

Campaign Performance

Here in the Campaign Performance window you can view multiple metrics against each other, or perform a date-range comparison between two separate time periods. You can view campaign performance for all online campaigns, or for individual campaigns by choosing them from the large drop-down menu toward the top of this element. Furthermore, the metrics that show in the trending graph can also be changed — the default metric is usually Conversions.

Below the graphs are a line-item summary of the selected campaigns' activity from your selected date range. When you have a date-range comparison applied you'll see each date range's metrics and a Difference column on the far right, showing you either the increase or the decrease over time for that particular metric. The focus of this element is performance, so a heavy emphasis is placed on conversions and success-oriented metrics. Figure 2-13 shows a good example of the Campaign Performance element with a date-range comparison applied.

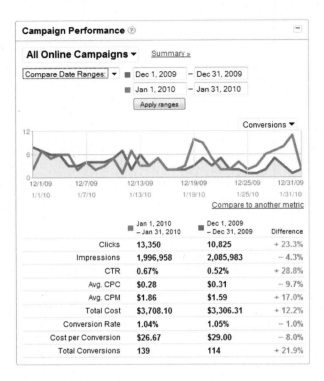

Figure 2-13: Campaign performance

Help and Tips

Finally, you can search for articles within the AdWords Help Center and for answers to commonly asked questions in this final element, Help and Tips. There may be a question that you don't know the answer to, or a time when you're simply looking for a refresher in a particular area. This will be the place to go in such cases.

The Campaigns Tab

As I mentioned earlier, the bulk of your time in AdWords is going to be spent within the Campaigns tab. This is where all statistics about your campaigns, ad groups, ads, and keywords are located, and this is where you can make any changes to bid prices, geo-targeting, and ad copy, and do any kind of work. I'll first cover what you can do within the Campaigns tab, and after that I'll discuss what's found underneath each individual sub-tab.

Functions and Features within the Campaigns Tab

Within this first sub-tab you'll notice some functions that will be available in all the other sub-tabs within the main Campaigns tab. They are:

- **Date-range slider:** This will be available on the top right of all sub-tabs within the main Campaigns tab. You can view today's campaign data, yesterday's data, last month's, this month's, all-time, and even a custom date range. Your date-range option will be saved so that the next time you log in to AdWords you'll see data for the same date range as on your last login.

- **All enabled campaigns:** This is a small drop-down directly underneath the Campaigns sub-tab. It allows you to toggle between viewing all enabled campaigns, all but deleted campaigns, and all campaigns regardless of status.

- **Segment:** Segmenting your campaigns, ads, and keywords will become critical to the success of your AdWords account, so you should become very familiar with this button, located next to the All Enabled Campaigns button. You can segment anything in AdWords by network type, click type, device, or a number of different date ranges. Each campaign, ad group, ad, and keyword will contain additional rows of segmented information when a segment is applied, as shown in Figure 2-14. Here a campaign is segmented by week, so the performance of this campaign is broken down by each week in the month of February. Notice the vastly different conversion figures, while cost and average position remain virtually identical.

		Campaign	Budget	Status ?	Clicks	Impr.	CTR ?	Avg. CPC ?	Cost	Avg. Pos.	Conv. (1-per-click) ?	Cost / conv. (1-per-click) ?	Conv. rate (1-per-click) ?
☐	●	Campaign #1 - Chocolates	$100.00/day	Eligible	2,438	79,371	3.07%	$0.46	$1,120.10	1.4	95	$11.79	3.90%
		Week of Feb 1, 2010			606	20,034	3.02%	$0.43	$261.42	1.4	29	$9.01	4.79%
		Week of Feb 8, 2010			580	18,255	3.18%	$0.46	$267.67	1.4	13	$20.59	2.24%
		Week of Feb 15, 2010			631	20,454	3.08%	$0.47	$295.25	1.4	31	$9.52	4.91%
		Week of Feb 22, 2010			621	20,628	3.01%	$0.48	$295.76	1.4	22	$13.44	3.54%

Figure 2-14: Segmenting a campaign by week

■ **Filter:** Filtering is another powerful segmentation option in AdWords. The Filter button is located right next to the Segment button, and allows you to view campaigns, ads, and keywords that meet certain criteria. For example, in Figure 2-15 I have created a filter that shows all the campaigns with 35,000 impressions or more, 500 or more clicks, and less than $2,000 in total cost. This filter can be saved for use the next time you log in to AdWords.

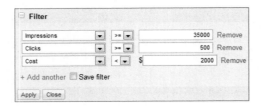

Figure 2-15: An example of a filter being created

■ **Columns:** The Columns button offers yet another great customization function within the Campaigns section. When this button is clicked, a menu will appear of all available metrics to display in AdWords. You'll notice that almost half the metrics are not checked. Interesting bits of information, like impression share and many-per-click conversions, are unchecked by default. Figure 2-16 shows the full menu, and all the different metrics options that you should definitely explore within your own account.

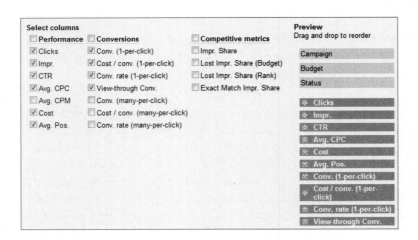

Figure 2-16: Columns with all available metrics

- **Search function:** Every sub-tab comes equipped with a search tool for your convenience. It's located on the far right-hand side of the screen.

- **Show/hide graph:** The trending graph can be toggled off or on. Its button is located directly to the right of the search function.

- **Download report:** You'll find this button next to the Show/Hide Graph toggle button. You can download reports in a variety of different file formats.

- **Change graph options:** The two metrics that you see on the trending graph can be changed to any two metrics you feel like viewing. Figure 2-17 shows the menu you'll see when you want to change the graphing options for your own campaigns.

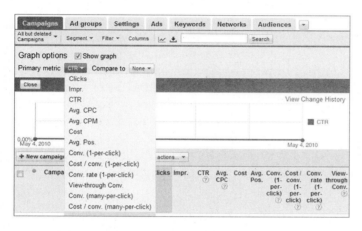

Figure 2-17: Available graphing options

The Campaigns Sub-Tab

As you saw in earlier images, every campaign that you have ever created will be listed here and ready for you to analyze and work on. Clicking an individual campaign in this list will show you all the ad groups, ads, and keywords associated with it, and you'll be able to change bid prices and many other settings.

Within the Campaigns sub-tab you can edit each campaign's daily budget and status. If you wish to increase or decrease a daily budget, or to pause, enable, or delete a campaign, you can do so from within this tab. All the functions and features that we just covered are available in this sub-tab. Each column heading, including those of the columns that you add in with the Columns feature, is sortable, which will help your analysis efforts greatly. Finally, you can edit the name of any campaign here as well — mouse over any campaign name to see a small pencil image appear, and click on that to edit a campaign's name.

> **NOTE** The action of deleting a campaign doesn't really delete it as you'd expect. "Deleted" is simply a status for a campaign. You can un-delete it at any time.

The Ad Groups Sub-Tab

Each ad group from every campaign you've ever created is listed here in this sub-tab. You can edit each ad group's name, and pause or delete any ad group, just as you can in the Campaigns sub-tab. (There is also a main Campaigns tab.) However, in this tab three editable items are available to you.

The default maximum cost per click, the managed placements maximum cost per click, and the Content Network maximum cost per click bid prices can all be edited here on the fly. These default bids that you can edit are safety nets in the event that you don't set a bid for any ad or keyword within an ad group. In Google AdWords, bids at the keyword level override any bids at the ad or ad-group level, and in campaigns without keywords, the ad bid overrides the ad-group bid. We'll also go deeper into placement targeting and the Content Network in Chapter 5.

Clicking any ad group that's listed will show you all the ads and keywords associated with that group.

The Settings Sub-Tab

Each campaign in Google AdWords has its own unique settings that apply to that campaign (and only that campaign). You can click any campaign name to view and edit that campaign's settings, and, as you'll quickly notice, there are a lot of settings to choose from!

We'll cover the basic ones in this chapter, and save some of the advanced settings for Chapters 4, 5, and 6. Starting from the top and working your way down the page, you'll see the following settings options:

- **Campaign name:** You can edit your campaign name here, as you can from the Campaigns sub-tab.

- **Locations:** This is one of the most important settings in AdWords and cost-per-click advertising, which I also talk about in Chapter 3. This shows the locations around the world where your ads will be displayed. Clicking the Edit link will pop open a window that allows you to choose your countries, regions, states, and cities, or to draw your own custom radius. Metro areas, predefined bundles, and radius targeting are also available for each campaign. Geo-targeting such as this in AdWords is available only at the campaign level — any ads and keywords within a campaign will have the campaign's settings applied to them. You'll also be able to show relevant addresses with your ads if you have a Google Places account.

■ **Languages:** It's important to note that AdWords won't automatically translate your cost-per-click ads. If you're targeting a country that does not speak your native language, your ads will be shown to visitors from that country in your language, untranslated. Ensure that the language settings match the audience you're targeting.

■ **Demographic targeting:** This is available only for Content Network campaigns, and we'll cover it later in the book. For now, just know that this is where you'll be able to edit demographic targeting settings.

■ **Networks:** Another important campaign setting is the Networks setting, where you define the places your ads will appear. By default your ads will be shown on every network available. However, most (if not all) of the time, this is suboptimal. Selecting the Let Me Choose radio button will allow you to select the Google.com site, Google.com Search Partners, the Google Content Network, or managed placements. As a best practice, you'll want to create different campaigns for different networks, and set different bids for different networks (as we talked about earlier in the chapter).

■ **Devices:** You can choose to show your ads to all types of devices, which is the AdWords default setting. If that doesn't work for you, you have the ability to show your ads only to desktop/laptop computers, or only to mobile devices. There are also some advanced options specifically for mobile devices, as shown in Figure 2-18.

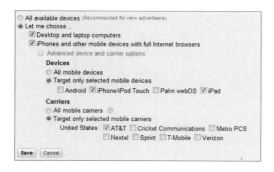

Figure 2-18: Advanced mobile-device options

- **Ad extensions:** Google AdWords has recently introduced additional business information for your online ads. Product images from your Google merchant account, click-to-call phone numbers, and Sitelinks can extend your ad and make it more appealing to a potential customer. We'll cover these advanced options in greater detail in Chapter 4.

- **Bidding option:** Your bidding option is also available to be edited for your campaigns. There are three focused bidding options available: Focus on Clicks, Focus on Conversions, and Focus on Impressions. We'll also cover this in greater detail in Chapter 4.

- **Budget:** The daily budget is how AdWords knows how much money it has to allocate throughout the course of each day. You can enter a budget manually, or use the View Recommended Budget tool to view the AdWords recommendations.

- **Advanced settings:** For brand-new Google AdWords advertisers, these advanced settings should be left alone, at least for the time being. For anyone with experience in cost-per-click advertising, this will be the place to manage advanced settings, such as Position Preference, Ad Scheduling, Ad Rotation, Frequency Capping, and more. Once again, Chapter 4 will cover all the advanced campaign settings available in AdWords.

The Ads Sub-Tab

In this sub-tab (Figure 2-19) every ad from every campaign will be listed. Ads that appear here will look as they would on a search engine results page, which is a nice feature. You can edit from within this sub-tab, as from within the other tabs covered so far, but you'll want to exercise caution when editing an ad here and within the AdWords interface in general.

AdWords allows you to create and delete ads at will, but editing an existing ad is a bit of a different story. Editing an ad actually deletes the existing ad and creates a new one. This is important because with a new ad come new statistics, which will be reset for the new ad that you edit. The deleted ad gets stored away in the Deleted Ads row, which is available if you click the All Ads button, which is the very first button on the left-hand side, directly underneath the Campaigns sub-tab.

The Keywords Sub-Tab

The fifth sub-tab within the main Campaigns tab is the home for all keywords across all AdWords campaigns. As with its Ads sub-tab neighbor, editing keywords within this tab will delete the existing keyword and add a new keyword in its place. This also resets all statistics, and the old keyword will be stored in the Deleted Keywords column. The keyword's match type is considered a part of the keyword and cannot be edited.

Figure 2-19: The Ads sub-tab

You can edit the keyword's status (enabled or paused), bid price, and destination URL without deleting it and creating a new keyword in its place. Keep in mind when editing keywords that the bid price and destination URL that you use will override the ad bid price and destination URL, as well as the ad-group bid price and destination URL. The keyword's bids and URLs take priority over everything else.

Toward the very bottom of the keywords sub-tab (you may have to scroll very far down) you'll notice a link titled Negative Keywords. These are words that, if used in a person's search query, will disqualify your ads from being displayed. You'll be able to add, edit, or delete ad-group-level and campaign-level negative keywords by clicking on the link. With AdWords you can create negative keywords at the campaign level (so all ad groups have the same negative keywords applied to them) and at the ad-group level (so select ad groups have the same negative keywords applied to them).

Using negative keywords is an extremely helpful optimization technique to keep costs down and increase your return on investment. I cover negative keywords in Chapter 3.

The Networks Sub-Tab

Figure 2-20 shows the Networks sub-tab, where a statistical breakdown of your advertised networks is displayed. The Search Network is made up of the Google search engine's result pages and Search Partners, which are websites, like AOL. The Content Network is made up of managed placements and automatic placements. Remember that you can always edit the networks in which your ads appear within the Settings sub-tab inside the main Campaigns tab.

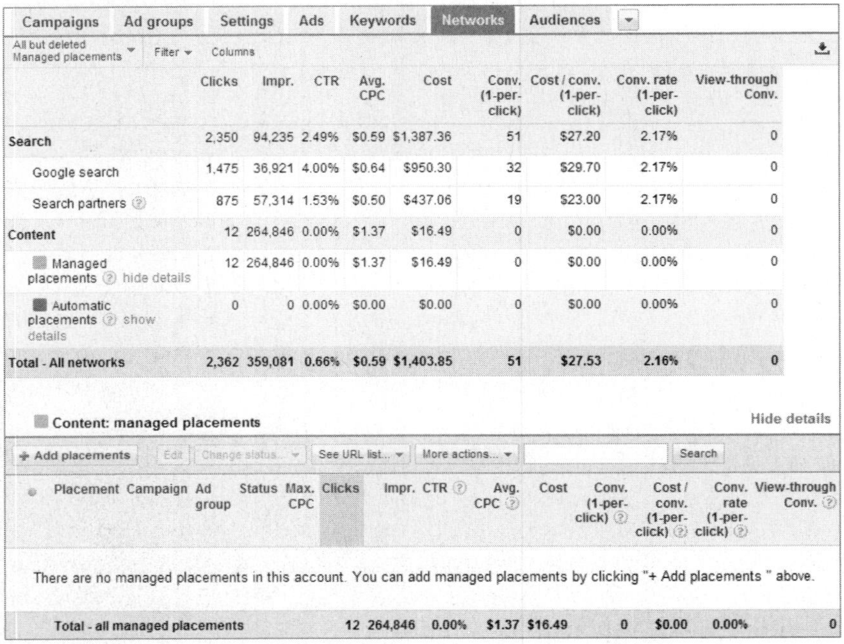

	Campaigns	Ad groups	Settings	Ads	Keywords	Networks	Audiences	▾	

All but deleted Managed placements ▾   Filter ▾   Columns

	Clicks	Impr.	CTR	Avg. CPC	Cost	Conv. (1-per-click)	Cost / conv. (1-per-click)	Conv. rate (1-per-click)	View-through Conv.
Search	2,350	94,235	2.49%	$0.59	$1,387.36	51	$27.20	2.17%	0
Google search	1,475	36,921	4.00%	$0.64	$950.30	32	$29.70	2.17%	0
Search partners ⑦	875	57,314	1.53%	$0.50	$437.06	19	$23.00	2.17%	0
Content	12	264,846	0.00%	$1.37	$16.49	0	$0.00	0.00%	0
■ Managed placements ⑦ hide details	12	264,846	0.00%	$1.37	$16.49	0	$0.00	0.00%	0
■ Automatic placements ⑦ show details	0	0	0.00%	$0.00	$0.00	0	$0.00	0.00%	0
Total - All networks	2,362	359,081	0.66%	$0.59	$1,403.85	51	$27.53	2.16%	**0**

■ **Content: managed placements**   Hide details

+ Add placements | Edit | Change status ▾ | See URL list... ▾ | More actions... ▾ | | Search |

●	Placement	Campaign	Ad group	Status	Max. CPC	Clicks	Impr.	CTR ⑦	Avg. CPC ⑦	Cost	Conv. (1-per-click) ⑦	Cost / conv. (1-per-click) ⑦	Conv. rate (1-per-click) ⑦	View-through Conv. ⑦

There are no managed placements in this account. You can add managed placements by clicking "+ Add placements " above.

| Total - all managed placements | | | | | | 12 | 264,846 | 0.00% | $1.37 | $16.49 | 0 | $0.00 | 0.00% | 0 |

Figure 2-20: The Networks sub-tab

The Audiences Sub-Tab

The final sub-tab within the main Campaigns tab is the Audiences tab. I'll spend some time talking about placement targeting and remarketing in later chapters, but for now just know that this final tab is where you'll be able to manage, edit, and create audience lists and remarketing campaigns. This type of advanced advertising can really expand your reach and target the appropriate segments for your business.

We've covered all the sub-tabs within the Campaigns tab, and now we'll take a better look at the next main tab in AdWords as we move from left to right on the screen: the Opportunities tab.

The Opportunities Tab

Google AdWords automatically analyzes your budget, your keywords, and your overall campaign performance and provides recommendations for you within this tab. As I mentioned earlier in this section, the Opportunities tab is like a personal consultant at your disposal. Every few weeks the AdWords system will review your account and provide recommendations (or "ideas") that are statistically significant, and that will improve your traffic and campaign performance.

You may log in to your account and find no ideas; this tends to happen with new AdWords accounts or those with very limited daily budgets. But normally you'll find one of three types of opportunity ideas from Google:

- **Keyword ideas:** Google will scan your ad-group structure and generate some keywords for you that you're not currently bidding on. As I mentioned earlier in the chapter, if you have a tight, well-organized account structure, the keywords that Google will suggest for you are going to be very accurate. If you have a poorly organized account, Google may be very inaccurate with its keyword ideas. Clicking an idea will bring up all the keywords that Google recommends inserting in that keyword's ad group — but don't just take Google's word for it. Use your common sense and make sure that you can afford these keywords first before adding them to your ad groups.

- **Keyword-bid ideas:** Similar to the keyword ideas, Google will provide specific bid ranges plotted on an (x/y) coordinate graph. As you increase your bids, the number of impressions increases, but so does your total cost; your costs will be lower as your impressions decrease. Applying keyword-bid ideas to your keywords should meet your goals. If you want more impressions and possibly more clicks, increase your bid prices (but keep in mind that your daily budget won't be changed; the more you raise your keyword bids, the more they will "hog" the available impressions against your daily budget, which means some of your other keywords will be left in the dark).

- **Campaign budget ideas:** Google's Opportunities tab will also analyze your daily budget, and inform you if you've been hitting your daily budget frequently. If you have been, Google will suggest to you that you may be missing out on available impressions and clicks, and will show you some rather advanced forecasting. Google takes a look at the last 15 days of activity within your account, and calculates the best possible daily budget to reach as many customers as possible. Figure 2-21 shows a campaign budget idea in action. To the right there is a sliding bar/scale that will show you where your current daily budget is, where the Google recommended daily budget is, and any point in between. Sliding the bar up or down will change the forecasting intelligence displayed on the left-hand side of the pop-up. The number of impressions, clicks, and other items of statistical information are available for you to digest, and you can toggle between viewing these stacked bar graphs by either impressions or clicks. Obviously, these suggestions are truly valuable only if you can afford to raise your daily budget to the recommended amounts, but even if you can't afford it, you can always use this area to get an idea of what could be.

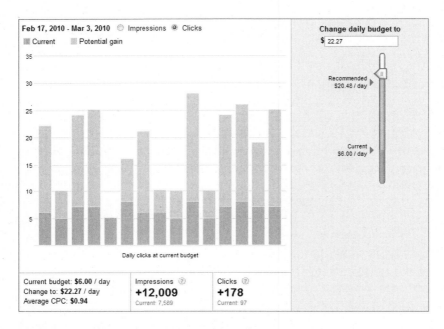

Figure 2-21: Campaign budget ideas (Opportunities tab)

I highly recommend that you check your Opportunities tab every few weeks to view what Google's automated Opportunities tab system has in store for you.

The Reporting Tab

The Reporting tab is home to the Report Center, where we'll focus our attention in this section. You can access Conversion Tracking, My Change History, Google Analytics, and Google Website Optimizer from this tab, but I want to walk through the steps of creating a report and accessing reports for future use. Creating a customizable report in AdWords enhances your analysis efforts, and can shed some light on a certain data set that may not have been readily visible up to this point. Reports are also easier to integrate with a CRM system or database that you may manage, versus manually entering information.

Once you're in the Report Center you should see a link reading Create a New Report on the upper middle portion of the page. Click that link to start the report-creation process. You can save up to 15 reports at any one time in your AdWords account.

Report Types

Your first decision in creating your report will be to select a report type. At the time of this writing, Google AdWords offers 10 different report types, depending on the type of information that you're looking to retrieve. These types are as follows:

- **Placement/keyword performance:** This report type will show you performance data for keywords or placements that you're targeting.

- **Ad performance:** Here you can view performance data for each of your ads.

- **URL performance:** Here you'll see the performance for each destination URL (not to be confused with display URL).

- **Ad-group performance:** This shows ad group reporting for one or more campaigns.

- **Campaign performance:** This reports data at the campaign level.

- **Account performance:** Your entire account's performance can be reported on.

- **Demographic performance:** Here you view data for sites by demographic.

- **Geographic performance:** This report is broken down by the location of your visitors.

- **Search-query performance:** This shows performance for the actual search queries that triggered ad impressions (not the keywords that you're bidding for, but the actual search terms visitors use on Google).

- **Placement performance:** This shows Content Network performance on the sites on which you're advertising.

You can select only one report type per report. If you need multiple reports, finish creating one report and create another new report.

Settings

Next you'll select some basic settings for your report. This naturally includes selecting your unit of time. Twelve separate units of time are available, and if those default units don't suit your needs, you can always create a custom date range. In Figure 2-22 you'll see that you can either select to have your report run for all campaigns and ad groups, or manually select them one by one.

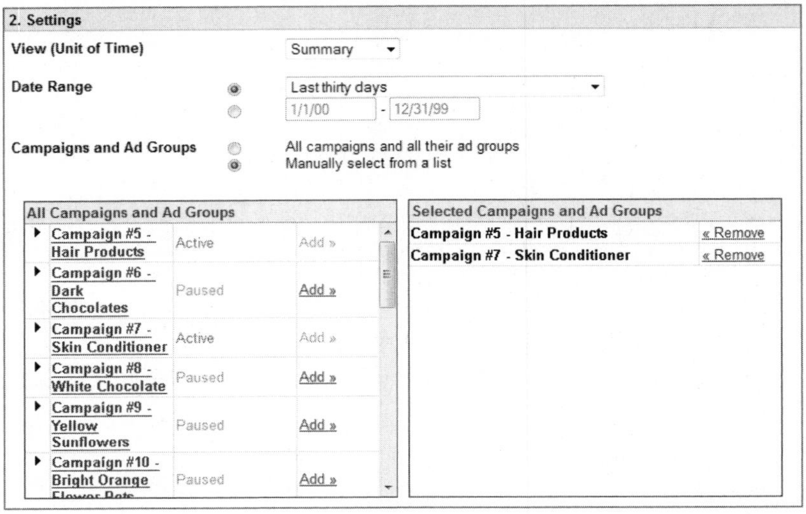

Figure 2-22: Basic reporting settings

Advanced Settings

While completely optional, advanced settings are critical to getting your report to look the way you want it to. There are two links in this section to click on: Add or Remove Columns, and Filter Your Results.

Clicking Add or Remove Columns will reveal a rather large layer of column options with a lot of metrics that are not available anywhere else in the AdWords interface. By default your report will contain 15 data columns, but you can select as many as 49! Check out Figure 2-23 for the full menu of available reporting columns.

The Filter Your Results link allows you to perform a set of operations similar to the Filter function from within the main Campaigns tab. You can select up to 12 different criteria, and enter restrictions for each criterion as you see fit. This filtering option can really help clean up the report that you eventually create, as it can either eliminate a lot of "junk" or it can be specifically targeted to your reporting needs. Figure 2-24 displays an example of some filter restrictions being applied to a report.

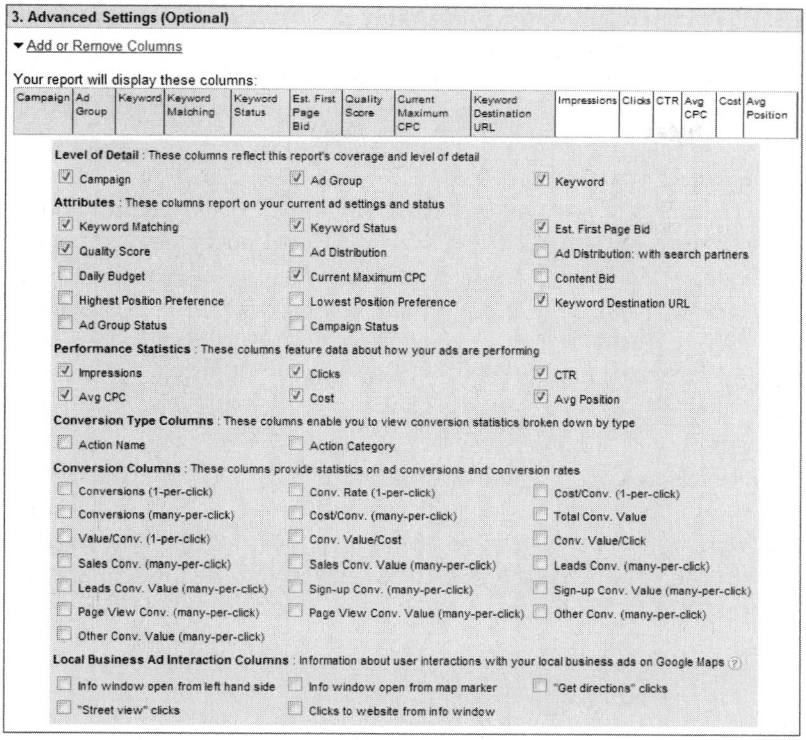

Figure 2-23: Available reporting columns

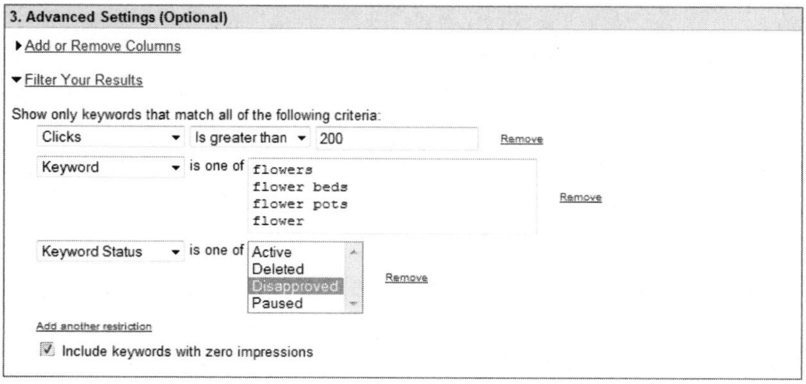

Figure 2-24: Available reporting columns

Templates, Scheduling, and E-Mail

The final sections of the report-creating process are naming your report and scheduling your report's delivery options. First you'll want to give your report a name that you'll be able to easily identify when you go back to look it up in the Report Center.

Next you can save the report as a template, which allows you to quickly reuse the settings for another new report in the future. After that, you can schedule the report to run every day (daily), every Monday (weekly), or every first day of the month (monthly). Finally, you can set up this report to be e-mailed at your scheduled delivery times to one or more e-mail addresses. You can send your report as a file attachment in a CSV, CSV for Excel, TSV, XML, or HTML file format.

Once you're finished with this section it is time to create your report by clicking the silver Create Report button at the bottom of the page. You'll be redirected to the Report Center, where you'll see your created report status eventually change to Completed. The report settings and the requested date will appear, and if you've saved the report as a template, it will be listed underneath the report, as in Figure 2-25.

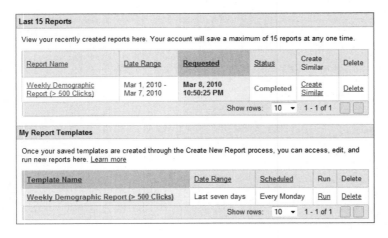

Figure 2-25: Reports listed in the Report Center

Viewing Your Report

Clicking the name of the report will pop open a new tab or window on your browser, and show you your data in an easy-to-read and -understand report format. If you've ever seen a report from Google Analytics or remember what some of the images from AdWords from within this chapter look like, you'll see similarities between the style of Google AdWords reports and that of Google Analytics.

Within this report you can view detailed statistics (generated date of report, date range, and such). You can export the report on the fly in many of the file formats just mentioned, and you can create a similar report to the one you just created. You can open this report as a Google Spreadsheet (helpful for non–Excel owners and for online collaboration). Any of the column headings are sortable, and you can view more rows by scrolling all the way down the report and clicking the arrows on the bottom right-hand side.

Figure 2-26 shows the final product: an example of a created report.

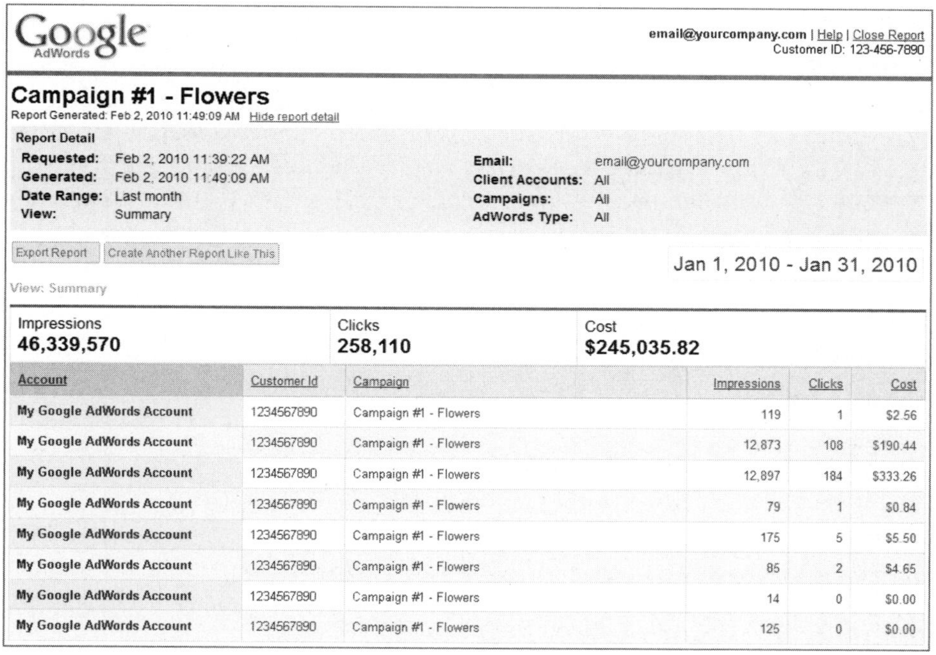

Account	Customer Id	Campaign	Impressions	Clicks	Cost
My Google AdWords Account	1234567890	Campaign #1 - Flowers	119	1	$2.56
My Google AdWords Account	1234567890	Campaign #1 - Flowers	12,873	108	$190.44
My Google AdWords Account	1234567890	Campaign #1 - Flowers	12,897	184	$333.26
My Google AdWords Account	1234567890	Campaign #1 - Flowers	79	1	$0.84
My Google AdWords Account	1234567890	Campaign #1 - Flowers	175	5	$5.50
My Google AdWords Account	1234567890	Campaign #1 - Flowers	85	2	$4.65
My Google AdWords Account	1234567890	Campaign #1 - Flowers	14	0	$0.00
My Google AdWords Account	1234567890	Campaign #1 - Flowers	125	0	$0.00

Figure 2-26: A created report from the Report Center

The Billing Tab

For most AdWords advertisers the second-to-last tab within the AdWords interface will include two reports: a Billing Summary and a Billing Preferences report. If you manage an MCC (a "My Client Center" containing multiple AdWords accounts), or have an agency account, you'll see an Invoice Summary report and a Budget report.

Billing Summary

Just as with any other report in Google AdWords, you can view top-level data and apply a custom date range to it. Your last payment, with the amount paid, date, and payment method, is shown at the far left of the scorecard going across the top of the summary screen. Your primary payment method is also shown, along with the status of the payment method. A "valid" status means that your credit card was processed without errors. An "expired" or "declined" status message requires immediate action if you are to continue advertising with AdWords. You may also see a "pending" status, indicating that your payment may already have been made and is just processing. The item on the far right of the scorecard is your current balance, showing your total unpaid advertising costs and billing threshold. Naturally, as with all things AdWords, the Billing Summary page can be downloaded into a CSV file or opened as a Google document. Figure 2-27 shows the Billing Summary page.

Figure 2-27: The Billing Summary report

Billing Preferences

The Billing Preferences page is a sensitive one, as it carries all your personal billing and payment information. Check this page before you start advertising with AdWords to ensure that all the information is up to date. Here you can edit your billing and payment information and edit your primary and secondary (backup) payment details.

Agency/MCC Billing

The Invoice Summary and Budget tabs appear for those with MCC or Agency AdWords accounts. In the agency advertising world, credit is typically extended to the agency of record, and an unlimited amount of funds can be spent with AdWords at any one time. The agency of record is invoiced and required to pay a lump sum for all cost-per-click charges that it owes AdWords. This privilege is usually granted to agencies only after a successful trial period including a good history of payment and high spending.

In almost all situations you, the online marketer, won't need to worry about any Agency/MCC billing reports or settings, as these are set up by your finance/accounting department before you even start setting up your first campaigns.

The My Account Tab

The final tab and final part of Chapter 2 is the My Account tab. There are three reports in this drop-down menu, where you'll be able to edit the notifications that AdWords delivers to your inbox and also be able to invite other users to share your AdWords account.

Account Access

Situations may arise where you'll need to allow someone else to have access to your AdWords account. This could be a friend, a colleague, or an agency helping you out with your campaigns. Regardless of the situation, you can invite anyone with an e-mail address to have access to your AdWords account. However, the type of access you grant is important, and you have a few options to choose from:

- **E-mail-Only Access:** All that users can do with this type of access is receive e-mail notifications and messages in their inboxes from AdWords. These users cannot do anything at all within your account — they can't even sign in. Clearly, this is the most restrictive access available in AdWords.

- **Reports-Only Access:** These users can view the Campaigns tab in a view-only mode, and they can view the Reports tab (and run reports within it). This is not as restrictive as E-mail-Only Access, but it still keeps a very tight rein on a user.

- **Standard Access:** A Standard Access user can create campaigns, edit settings, run reports, and do almost everything that an account's owner can do. The only thing a Standard Access user cannot do is manage access levels or disable access to the account.

- **Administrative Access:** Administrators can do everything that you can do within your account. This is the least restrictive type of access. Depending on the necessary task (API functions), the user may need to be an administrator and have the same controls as you.

Choose your user's access level carefully, and never give out your own login information to anyone for any reason. Trust me on that last statement.

Notification Settings

As you saw way back in Figure 2-10, your notification settings, which are the e-mails that AdWords sends you and the announcements it sends to your Account Snapshot page, can be edited from this page. As I said before, you should probably enable as many of these settings as you can, especially if you are new to Google AdWords or to cost-per-click marketing. You can always go back and disable them later, but for now it's probably a good idea to keep as many notifications active as possible.

Preferences

High-level account preferences are editable from this final report in Google AdWords. Your display language, number preference, and destination-URL auto-tagging are editable from this screen. Remember that your time zone country/territory and your billing preference (prepay or postpay) cannot be edited at all. In Chapter 14 we'll come back to this page to ensure that destination-URL auto-tagging is enabled, which is a critical part of allowing Google AdWords data to appear in Google Analytics.

We covered a whole lot in this chapter, and I hope you've learned where everything is located in Google AdWords and how things are organized. We went from the very start of the Google account creation process to the very end, covering all the many points in between. You'll notice that I didn't talk too much strategy or philosophy about cost-per-click advertising here in Chapter 2. That's completely reserved for the next chapter in *Your Google Game Plan for Success*, the chapter titled "Cost-per-Click Advertising." This is where I explain how the industry as a whole functions and some of the essential strategies that you'll need to know (and that if you already know, it's a good idea to review while you're here).

I hope that you've enjoyed our book thus far! Don't go anywhere, because we have a lot more material to cover.

CHAPTER 3

Cost-per-Click Advertising

Knowing how to do everything within the Google AdWords interface is great, but it's usually a good idea to have a solid foundation in the basics of cost-per-click advertising before you get too far into your advertising budget.

Advertising online has definitely come a long way in just the last four or five years, but some of the basics are still very much the same. There are some strategies you'll want to use to maximize your dollars. Some of them are self-explanatory and probably obvious, while others may not be so obvious. In this chapter I'll talk about some of the core concepts of cost-per-click advertising, different keyword match types, geo-targeting, and some good examples of different ad variations that you could use in your ad groups.

A Brief Review of Cost-per-Click Advertising Online

You've opened up your Google AdWords account and have created your first campaign. The green "active" text appears next to your Campaign, Ad Group, and Keyword lists and you've established your daily budget. You're now ready for thousands of qualified, ready-to-convert visitors to come to your site.

Before you even get your very first visitor, a lot of things are happening behind the scenes to ensure a level playing field between you and your competitors, and to ensure that AdWords' policies are being followed to the letter. Your ads are going to go through editorial review, which will look at the keywords you're bidding for, the ads you've written, and other account settings that may influence the delivery and schedule of your ads. At the same time, your ads and keywords are being assigned rankings (Quality Score), and your account is developing a history. The spelling of your ads is being analyzed, the family-friendliness of your ads is being evaluated, and your destination URLs are being checked for validity. Your cost-per-click bids, your preferences, and your Geo-Targeting settings are applied so that your ads appear where you want them to appear. Your delivery methods and your delivery schedules are being applied so that your ads appear when you want them to appear. And since you're probably not the only advertiser bidding for your chosen keywords, your campaign is being graded and evaluated against those of other competitors trying to earn that web surfer's click. All of this is happening simultaneously, and your daily budget is being taken into consideration (which is extremely helpful for advertisers with limited budgets, as it avoids a situation in which the richer you are, the better you perform).

In a matter of minutes, sometimes an hour or two, your ads start showing up on Google, as well as Google's Search Network Partners and the Content Network if you've opted in to those networks. As you're collecting impressions and people start to see your ads, Google starts optimizing its search results to provide the end user with the best possible search experience. If your ads start receiving clicks, Google starts to show your ad higher up on the page, and, depending on your daily budget, it may start showing your ads more often. If Google notices that you're not getting very many clicks, it starts cutting back your impressions, and your ads get shown less and less. Even if you're doing well so far, that doesn't guarantee that you will be doing well tomorrow or the day after. New competitors may start challenging you for clicks, and they may start driving up the prices for keywords, which means you will have to step it up a notch and optimize your ads and keyword bids and your account's structure to win back those visitor clicks. By next week this cycle will have repeated itself with every new campaign, ad group, and keyword that you create in AdWords. Lather, rinse, repeat. Welcome to cost-per-click advertising online!

What You're Actually Charged For

Unless you're paying "per thousand impressions" (The "CPM" billing model), you're going to be paying each time someone actually clicks on your ad. As noted in Chapter 1, you won't be charged for impressions, and you won't be charged for making changes to your campaigns. But what a good number of advertisers don't even realize is that you're not necessarily charged the dollar amount that you bid.

Let's say that your maximum cost-per-click bid is $0.50 for a particular keyword. But the minimum cost-per-click that you see in AdWords is $0.10. If no one else is bidding on that keyword (which usually happens with branding keywords, but not always), you'll only pay $0.10 for that click. However, you'd be willing to pay up to $0.50 if need be.

Another example: Two advertisers, Logitech and Kensington, are bidding on the same keyword: "optical wireless mouse." The minimum cost per click for that keyword is a whopping $6.50! Kensington throws down a bid of $8.25, but Logitech outbids its competitor at $8.50. Both advertisers receive one click each. Kensington, which bid at $8.25, will actually pay $8.25 and not $6.50, because there is another competitor outbidding it. Logitech will pay one cent above the next-highest bid, which winds up being $8.26, even though it is willing to go as high as $8.50. As you'll read later in the chapter, this sometimes is the nucleus for a potential all-out bidding war between two competitors.

As you'll also learn, it's not all about money and how much of it you have to spend. Your ad or keyword's cost per click plays one part in the grand scheme of things.

Where Your Ads Actually Appear

Figures 3-1, 3-2, and 3-3 show three different examples of where your cost-per-click ads will actually appear online. Figure 3-1 shows ads on top of "natural" or "organic" search engine results, and also shows ads that appear on the right-hand side of such results. Contrary to popular belief, Google doesn't select the ads that appear in this prime real estate — users do.

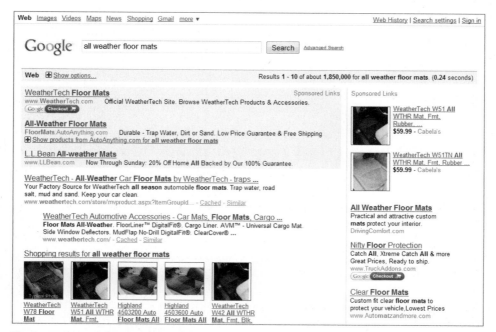

Figure 3-1: Google search results

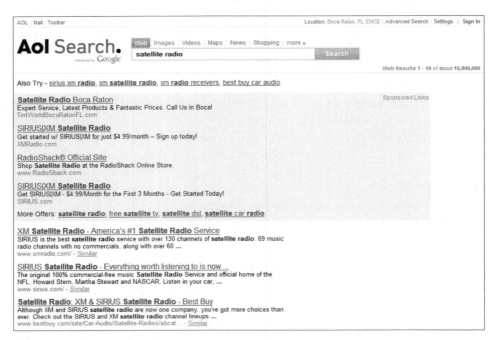

Figure 3-2: AOL search results

Figure 3-2 shows one of Google's most important Search Network Partners, AOL, and shows text ads on that website's search results page. These ads are the exact same ones that appear on Google for almost all advertisers.

Figure 3-3 shows some text ads on one of About.com's website pages, thanks to Google's Content Network. This is a ancillary network of partners for Google for which text ads appear within website content, and do not require a search result to generate an impression. I dedicate Chapter 5 of this book entirely to the Google Content Network and Placement-Targeted Campaigns.

The Critical Role that Landing Pages Play

Enticing a person to click your pay-per-click ad is only one piece of the online success puzzle. After this person makes that click on your paid advertisement, what he or she sees next needs to be even more engaging, persuasive, and demanding of attention. I'm of course talking about your landing pages, and the critical role that they play in the success of your online efforts.

As you'll read in Chapters 11 and 12, the average web visitor has an extremely short attention span. He or she needs to focus attention on the task at hand, or chances are extremely high that this person will simply close the browser or go back to the search results page to look for something else — no matter how well your ad is written. When you log in to your Google Analytics account and view the Loyalty: Length of Visit report within the Visitors section, you'll see that the highest percentage of visitors spends between zero and 10 seconds on your site. In the same Visitors section, the Loyalty: Depth of Visit report will most likely show you that most visitors visit only one page of your site per visit. So, basically, your website has a window of opportunity of one page and between zero and 10 seconds to convince a visitor to continue to another page or section, and not go back to Google or close the browser.

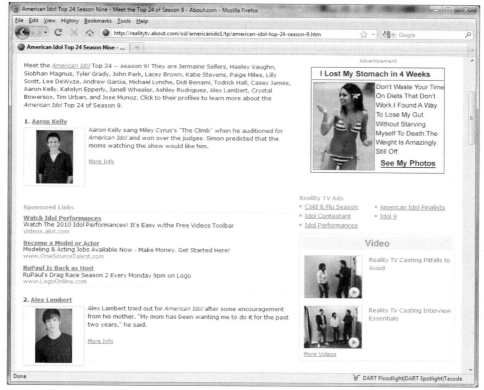

Figure 3-3: About.com web page

How do you maximize your "window of opportunity" on your website? It's a simple question whose answer may seem complicated, but it's not that complicated at all. Using an A/B or multivariate testing tool, like Google Website Optimizer or Omniture's Test&Target, can help you answer the original question and optimize your conversion rate at the same time. Professionals with excellent track records know that spending time optimizing their AdWords campaigns isn't enough anymore. Running controlled experiments on their

AdWords campaigns' landing pages and allowing visitors to decide what they like best by their actions is another important piece to online success.

A good example of an attractive, engaging, and welcoming landing page is the one in Figure 3-4 from VisiStat, a hybrid web-analytics/lead-generation tool. When I click one of its pay-per-click ads, I am assured that this company is a solid and reputable one, and that it takes its business seriously. I'm immediately enticed by both the Sign-Up Free button on the right-hand side and the Live Demo button at the top of the page. The page is clean and neat, has a simple color scheme, and clearly explains what the company does. The text that I read in its pay-per-click ad is in line with what I'm reading on its landing page, and the call to action (the Sign-Up Free and Live Demo buttons) stands out and is appealing to me. This landing page has done a good job of earning my attention, and I reward it by diving deeper into the site and learning more about VisiStat. I may even give its free program a try!

Figure 3-4: VisiStat's pay-per-click landing page

It's apparent to me that VisiStat has carefully selected this landing page to use in pay-per-click advertising, and it knows what it's doing. I'm quite confident that other visitors to this landing page will also be interested in looking further into the site.

Landing pages are a key component in online success, and we'll talk much more about them in the upcoming chapters, as well as in the next section of this chapter.

The Google AdWords Quality Score

Contrary to popular belief, you don't need to be the richest person or have the largest budget in online advertising to hold the top position in paid search results. Whether you're spending a hundred dollars or a million dollars a month, you are judged by the same standards as everyone else. Each paid vendor accomplishes this differently, and Google uses what it calls the Quality Score to rank your keywords. The higher your Quality Score, the higher the likelihood that your ads will appear toward the top of a search engine results page for a particular keyword, and the less it will cost you. The lower your Quality Score, the higher the likelihood that your ads *won't* appear toward the top of a search engine results page for a particular keyword, and the more it will cost you. It's really that simple.

As we glossed over in Chapter 2, the Quality Score is given to your ads and keywords in the form of a ranking between 1/10 and 10/10, with 1/10 being the lowest score you can get and 10/10 being the highest. Clicking the Status icon in your Keywords tab will show you your keywords' current Quality Score.

Each time a keyword you're bidding for matches a search query, the Quality Score is calculated, which means that you don't have to wait weeks or months after making changes to your keywords in order to receive a better Quality Score. Your keywords' Quality Score directly influences your actual cost per click, your first-page bid estimate, and even how highly your ads will be ranked, which are all things that remain to be covered in this chapter.

Google uses two different Quality Scores: one for Google and Search Partners, and one exclusively for the Content Network. Each one is different, so take some time to learn about each network's Quality Score to have successful campaigns on both network types.

Quality Score for Google and Search Partners

Several different factors affect your Quality Score for search queries on Google and Search Partner sites, like AOL. They are as follows:

- **Historical click-through rate:** The history of each individual keyword's click-through rate (performance).
- **Your account history:** The click-through rate of both your keywords and your ads.

- **Display URLs:** The click-through-rate history of the display URLs in each ad group.

- **Landing-page quality:** How user-friendly, original, and content-rich your landing pages are, as well as how fast they load.

- **Keyword relevance:** How relevant your keywords are to both your ads and the matched ads from a user's search query.

- **Geo-targeting performance:** This shows how your entire account has historically performed in the target area in which your ads are displayed.

- **Other factors:** Google has other Quality Score measurement factors that it does not release to the public.

There are two minor things to point out. When Google attempts to calculate the ad position for a keyword-targeted ad, it does not take into account landing-page quality, and when calculating the first-page bid estimates, it doesn't consider the matched ad or search query.

You probably noticed a recurring word in the previous list: *history*. The history of your account is permanent, so anything you've ever done in AdWords will have an impact on your Quality Score. But don't worry if you haven't had a successful AdWords campaign in the past — there are many different ways to quickly improve your keywords' Quality Score, as you'll see in what follows.

Quality Score for the Google Content Network

With the Google Content Network, keywords aren't matched to a search query or used to serve ads to the website's visitors. Ads are matched to a page's content and targeted demographic, and a user is presented with the ads by default. So the Quality Score for the Content Network focuses on an ad's eligibility to appear on a Content Network website. The factors that determine the score are as follows:

- **Ad performance:** The ad's historical performance on the desired site and on similar sites.

- **Ad relevance:** The relevance of the ads and the keywords in that AdWords ad group to the site where the ad will appear.

- **Landing-page quality:** The quality of the page that users are taken to when they click on your ad.

There are other factors determining Quality Score that Google does not make public. Keep in mind that the Quality Score algorithm is always being optimized and is constantly evolving.

Optimizing Your Quality Score

Everyone wants a Quality Score of 10/10, but not everyone wants to put in the work that's required to get as close to a perfect score as possible. Depending on the size of your account, the tips that follow may mean a lot of work hours for you, but if any task is deserving of your time, this is it. It's virtually impossible to succeed in AdWords (or any other pay-per-click channel, for that matter) without following these guidelines.

The Google AdWords help section has a really good article called "Tips for Success" about optimizing your Quality Score, so I have summarized that article here for you.

- **Identify your advertising goals:** You, the advertiser, can probably find yourself saying one of these three things: "I want more clicks," "I want to increase my click-through rate," or "I want to improve my ROI." If you find yourself saying at least two of those three things, that's great! If you find yourself saying all three, that's even better. Focus on attracting the right audience for you with the techniques that I'll talk about in a little while.

- **Organize your AdWords account:** This is probably one of the most under-rated Quality Score improvement techniques ever — perhaps because not many advertisers are aware that an account's organization is a key component in Quality Scores. Organizing your campaigns by topic helps you manage your AdWords campaigns more efficiently and helps your Quality Score — see Figure 3-5 for a diagram that shows how your Google AdWords account should be structured. Targeting the proper language and locations and creating highly specific ad groups are two more great organizational techniques. Finally, avoid using duplicate keywords across ad groups, as Google can show only one ad per advertiser on a particular keyword at a time. Having identical keywords across different ad groups means that you are competing against yourself!

- **Carefully choose relevant keywords and placements:** The higher the relevancy of your keywords and your placement-targeted campaigns, the easier it is for your future customers to find you, and the higher your Quality Score is likely to be. It's very easy to get into the habit of adding lots of keywords from one of Google's keyword tools or selecting lots of Content Network websites on which to display your ads, but quantity doesn't equal quality. Become your own campaign's biggest critic and be excruciatingly analytical of each and every single keyword and website involved with your campaigns. The time you take to do this now will reward you tenfold later as you're flying past your competitors.

- **Create straightforward, targeted ads:** You never want to confuse, trick, frustrate, or alienate any of your target audience while it's clicking on your ad. Shockingly, this happens all the time on Google! "Simpler and more straightforward" should be your motto when you're writing ads, especially since you have such little room to work with in the first place. Include relevant keywords and a strong call to action, and be sure to test multiple ads in each ad group to see what works best and what's most effective for your audience.

■ **Optimize your website for conversions:** As you've learned so far, your landing page quality is a big component of your AdWords Quality Score. Using Google Website Optimizer you'll be able to optimize for conversions without breaking a sweat, but you'll want to make sure that your users are going to the correct landing page (with the right category, service offering, etc.), and that the user experience/user friendliness of your landing page isn't compromised by attempts to get a visitor to become your customer. Reduce the number of clicks it takes users to find what they want. Place the important information towards the top left or top center of the page. Have a simple lead-generation/e-commerce process. Use your own common sense and ask yourself if you'd engage with your own website.

■ **Track results; test often:** Doing both of these isn't going to directly affect your Quality Score, but you are going to have a rough time raising your Quality Score if you aren't tracking your results, keeping track of your progress, and testing different ads, keywords, targets, placements, and settings often. You can't "set it and forget it" in pay-per-click marketing and hope for the best, or rest on your laurels if everything is running well now. Track, test, track some more, test some more, and track and test some more again. It's not a one- or two-time thing: it's an advertiser's lifestyle.

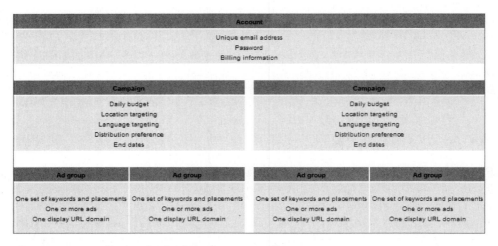

Figure 3-5: A well-organized AdWords account diagram

Keyword Match Types

Ever since I started doing pay-per-click advertising, keyword match types have been a hot topic of debate. As they should be: each keyword match type serves its own unique purpose for both your keywords and your advertising goals. The standard options that you have in pay-per-click advertising for your keywords are Broad Match, Phrase Match, Exact Match, and Negative Match.

Let's review each match type.

"Broad Match" Keywords

Broad Match gives you the widest possible reach with each and every one of your keywords. When a user types a search query into Google, it will display back to the user results that match the user's query as loosely as possible. For example, let's say that you have the keyword "green iPod" set to Broad Match. Any time this search query is used on Google, you have a chance to have your ads appear. You also have a chance of your ads appearing for "green iPod" if any of the words within your keyword are searched for, in any order.

With Broad Match, if someone searches for "iPod green," your ad may appear. If someone searches for "red iPod," you ad may also appear, because the search query contains "iPod," which is a part of one of your keywords set to Broad Match. "iPod repair," "green hats," "going green," "I'm green with envy," "iPod is not as good as Zune," or "green aliens with iPods" may also cause your ad to appear on Google. If you have a limited budget or a very specific target audience, this can get scary fast!

If you specifically want as many clicks as possible immediately, and if you have the money for it, Broad Match is definitely the way to go for you — especially if you're bidding on keywords that are your own company name or trademarked brand, or any other protected identity. However, chances are that for almost any other situation the next two match types will be more suited to your needs and produce a higher quality of lead for your business.

"Phrase Match" Keywords

Phrase Match narrows down your audience considerably from Broad Match, as its requirements are stricter for allowing your ad to appear for a search query. With Phrase Match, the keyword that you're bidding on must have its words appear in the sequence which you dictate in order for your ad to appear in a search result. Other words can appear behind or in front of your keyword, but your keyword must remain intact with Phrase Match.

Let's again use our "green iPod" example. If a user enters "green iPod" into Google, your ad is eligible to appear. If someone types in "I love my green iPod" or "green iPod for sale," your ad is also eligible to appear, as the keyword "green iPod" appears intact regardless of what words come before or after it.

If someone types in "green 16gb iPod," your ad will not appear, because a separate word occurs in the middle of your Phrase Match keyword. Your ads also won't appear for searches on "iPod green," because in Phrase Match "green iPod" and "iPod green" are different keywords — the order of the individual words of a search phrase must be intact.

Phrase Match is well liked by most advertisers, as it gives you a good balance between a targeted audience and enough reach to be effective in pay-per-click. It's not as inclusive as Broad Match, so it will help filter out irrelevant visitors, and it's not as rigid as Exact Match, so it will still allow new customers to find your products and services without their having to be exact with their search queries.

"Exact Match" Keywords

Exact Match is pretty much what it sounds like. Your keyword must exactly match the search query typed into Google, or your ad won't appear. There are no exceptions with Exact Match, which significantly narrows your audience, giving you the smallest, most segmented audience possible.

In our "green iPod" example, the only possible way that your ad can appear with Exact Match is if someone types in "green iPod" exactly. No words can come before, after, or in the middle of your exact keyword and the order of the words within your keyword also have to match. Any deviation from "green iPod," and your ad will not appear (match types on Google are not case-sensitive — someone can type in "green ipod" without capitalizing the "P" in "iPod," and even with Exact Match your ad will still be eligible to appear).

Exact Match is perfect for advertisers with very limited budgets, and those looking for the highest possible cost-per-lead or return-on-investment numbers. However, there's a much slower turnaround time in getting this highly qualified traffic to your site, because Exact Match does severely limit your exposure. With Phrase Match you have a chance to appear for possibly relevant search queries that you didn't think of bidding for, while with Exact Match you take that variable out of the equation. Exact Match should be used with a specific intent or goals in mind.

"Negative Match" Keywords

Using negative matching is an extremely helpful way to optimize your AdWords campaigns, as well as a great way to refine the audience that sees your ads. Negative Match allows you to add words to your ad groups or campaigns that, when used in a search query, make your ads ineligible to be displayed.

"Green iPod" is a good example of a term that you'd want to use some keywords for in the ad group or possibly the campaign where the keyword resides. If you are using Broad Match, any of the words in the keyword make your ad eligible to appear, so your ad could appear for anyone who searches for "green apple," "green hat," or "green eggs and ham." Using "apple," "hat," "eggs," and "ham" as negative keywords will allow you to continue using Broad Match while simultaneously excluding your ads from appearing for any searches using those undesired words.

It's also an excellent idea to use negative keywords when using Phrase Match. Let's say that you don't repair iPods; you only sell them. Having your ad appear for a query for "green iPod repairs" or "green iPod problems" wouldn't be a good fit for your business, and it wouldn't be a wise way to spend your money. Entering in negatives of "repairs" and "problems" will also help optimize your keyword list by excluding even more undesirables.

You can apply negative keywords to Exact Match keywords, but it's redundant, as Exact Match requires that your keyword match the search query exactly. Using "apple" as a negative keyword for an ad group containing Exact Match keywords won't make a difference because, by default, you're already excluding "apple" and everything else except your exact keyword.

Negative keywords also come in "Broad," "Phrase," and "Exact," just like regular keywords. These are helpful for negative search terms that are two or more words in length, and they are the opposites of their keyword counterparts. For example, using "repair store" as an Exact Match negative for the ad group containing a Broad or Phrase Match "green iPod" keyword would not allow your ad to be shown for "green iPod repair store" or "repair store green iPod." Because it's an exact negative, "repair store" would need to be typed in just as you see it before, after, or in the middle of your keyword in order to prevent your ad from appearing for that search query — if "repair" or "store" is used in the query by itself, your ad would still be eligible to appear.

Negative keyword matching is a technique that should be used by every cost-per-click advertiser, and is a standard option across the paid-search industry.

The Great Debate: Keyword Match Types

Read any number of industry-related blogs or articles on the Web, and you'll be sure to find staunch supporters of one keyword match type, and their opponents who love a different match type for any number of reasons. Forums, blogs, Twitter, and the pay-per-click industry have been filled with great information and dialogue about this topic.

Ultimately, it's up to you and your business objectives. I can't tell you, "Do not use any Broad Match keywords!" or "Change all your Exact Match keywords to Phrase Match!" because there isn't one blanket statement that will cover every desired outcome, including your own. Now that you understand what the different match types do, how they work, what the pros and cons are, and what negative keyword matching is, you should be able to make a very educated decision for your online efforts. If you want never-ending streams of clicks and impressions to spread the word to every human being on the Web, use Broad Match. If you have a limited budget and have to stick to a specific cost per conversion and don't want any irrelevant searches at all, use Exact Match. Not sure what to use? Try Phrase Match and see what happens.

Test different match types and analyze their results, and then compare those to your bottom line. The match types that match your goals are the match types that you should use.

Cost-per-Click Ads

At the end of the day, when users type a search term into Google or their favorite search engine, a cost-per-click ad is what they'll see. Most of the ads you see online are text ads, and most of them appear in a search engine result. There are also other types of ads, like the ones that appear on a Content Network, such as image and video ads. There are limitless possibilities with online cost-per-click ads.

Because of size and space limitations on a search results page, and to provide a level playing field for all advertisers across the board, Google and other pay-per-click vendors employ some strict rules about what you can and can't do with your ads. Let's start this section by reviewing what those restrictions are.

Standard Text Ads and Restrictions

Figure 3-6 should look very familiar to you: it's what the average, everyday cost-per-click ad on Google looks like in a search engine result. You have up to three ads at the top of the page, and as many as eight ads going down the right-hand side. The former are usually in a light-colored box, and are wider than their right-hand-side counterparts. Some ads can include badges, like one for Google Checkout, and some can include local information, like the right-hand ad second from the bottom in Figure 3-6. In the last few months ads have started to include listings from multiple sources, such as Google's Merchant Center (formerly Google Product Submit).

When you start to build ads on Google, as we reviewed in Chapter 2, you'll encounter some technical and other restrictions on how your ads can appear. Some of these restrictions are fairly standard across most search engine–based cost-per-click vendors. They include:

- **A 25-character limit for your headline:** You have only 25 characters to grab the attention of a potential visitor. Characters include spaces and punctuation marks.

■ **A 70-character limit for your description:** In Google AdWords you're allowed two lines for a description for your ad, which is broken up into two 35-character-limit lines. Some search engines, like Yahoo!, also allow you 70 characters, but will not force you to write your ad in two 35-character segments.

■ **A 35-character limit for your display URL:** The green URL of your website that appears on the bottom of your ad must be 35 characters in length. This includes www and .com (or your website's domain extension). *Note: The display URL isn't necessarily the URL to which the visitor is taken on your site.*

■ **A 1,024-character limit for your destination URL:** The destination URL is not visible to anyone, unless he or she clicks on your ad and looks at the URL in the browser's address bar. This URL is the actual page on your site to which a visitor is taken. The character limit — 1,024 — is made long on purpose to accommodate any type of tracking that you wish to install, as well as to make more than enough room for any URL your website may have.

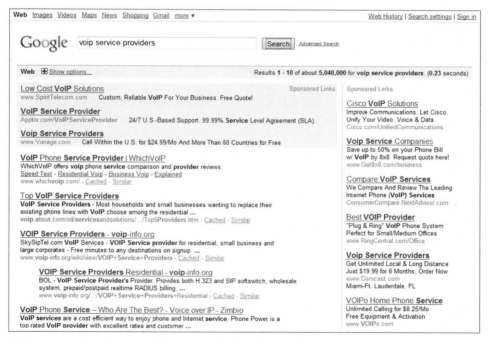

Figure 3-6: Pay-per-click ads appearing on Google

There are also some other general rules, fairly standard across the industry, that you should be aware of. They include, but are not limited to:

■ **Illegal content:** Almost every paid advertiser frowns heavily upon illegal or "not-family-safe" content. These almost always include alcohol, tobacco, firearms, pornography, gambling, handicapping sports, illegal drugs, or, of course, spam. Any hint of any of these topics will definitely get your ad disapproved, and may even get your account deactivated.

- **Truthfulness/honesty:** Google doesn't like it when advertisers use scams or bait-and-switch techniques on their ads. You'll suffer from very low Quality Scores and have higher-than-normal cost-per-click prices (if your ad is even approved) if you use shady, underhanded tactics in your ads. If you say "20% off" on your ad, your landing page must also say "20% off" (or the equivalent).

- **Unsubstantiated claims:** All businesses want to promote themselves as leaders in their industries or the best in the world. Unless it's verified by a reputable third-party organization that you are indeed the very best, you should leave these claims out of your ads. If you actually are number one, you'll need to have a link to an article or the website of the third-party source that can verify your statement within one or two clicks of your landing page.

- **Trademarked terms:** Not only are you not allowed to use trademarked terms unless you have explicit authorization to do so, but you may get into some legal trouble as well. This is tricky to avoid if you are a reseller of virtually any product, but you must follow this rule to advertise online. (The search engines do not want to be held liable for your improper usage of someone else's trademark, so it's highly enforced.) Make sure you have written permission and that Google knows about it before you use a trademarked term.

- **Improper language:** Google is a family-safe search engine, and therefore its ads must also be suitable for families. I definitely understand that your target audience may find it "cool" to see a curse word in your ad, and it may even appeal to them. But it's not allowed, so you'll need to find another way to write to your audience.

Using the "Keyword Insertion" Function

Figure 3-7 shows an ad being created in Google AdWords, and the preview of that ad. Notice what's in the Headline field: {KeyWord:401k Rollover}. This is called the Keyword Insertion function, and using it is one of the most popular techniques in paid-search-ad creation.

Keyword Insertion will insert the user's search query into your headline, provided the user's search query is 25 characters or less. If it is longer your "default" headline will be used. Having a user's search query appear in your ad magnifies the chances that the user will click it, and when a user's search query appears in your ad, that part is bolded, making it more prominent.

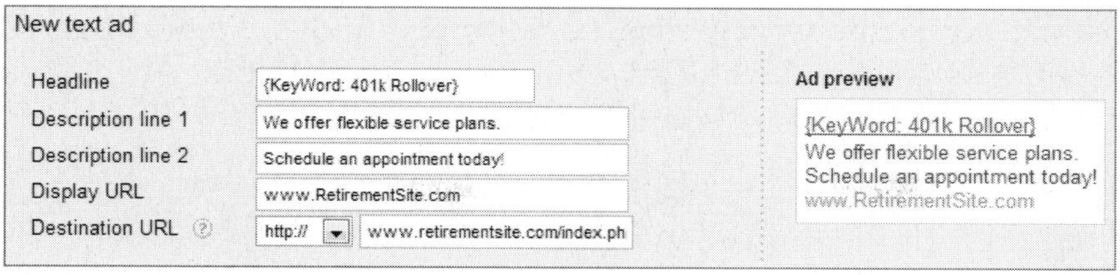

Figure 3-7: Using Keyword Insertion

For example, let's say that your ad group contains the keywords "401k rollover" and "401k plans." A user types in "401k plans" and your ad is using Keyword Insertion. The term "401k plans" will appear as the headline for that user. The same applies if the user types in "401k Rollover." Now let's say that you also have "401k matching contributions" as a keyword, and someone types that into Google. Your ad using Keyword Insertion will show the default text that you used when creating the ad, because "401k matching contributions" is more than 25 characters long. The default keyword in Figure 3-7 is "401k Rollover."

The way the Keyword Insertion function looks in Figure 3-7, with the *K* and the *W* in "KeyWord" capitalized, tells Google to capitalize the first letter of each word in the user's search query. The way you use capitals in the Keyword Insertion function will dictate to Google how to capitalize the user's query in the headline of your ad. Figure 3-8 shows a table of all possible examples of Keyword Insertion capitalization.

Your ad's title	How the ad title appears to users	What part of the keyword is capitalized?
Buy {keyword:Puppies}	Buy golden retrievers	No part
Buy {Keyword:Puppies}	Buy Golden retrievers	The first letter of the first word only (sentence capitalization)
Buy {KeyWord:Puppies}	Buy Golden Retrievers	The first letter of each word (initial capitalization)
Buy {KEYWord:Puppies}	Buy GOLDEN Retrievers	The entire first word and the first letter of each additional word
Buy {KeyWORD:Puppies}	Buy Golden RETRIEVERS	The first letter of the first word and the entirety of each additional word
Buy {KEYWORD:Puppies}	Buy Golden Retrievers	The first letter of each word (initial capitalization)

Figure 3-8: Keyword Insertion capitalization

Typically, ads using Keyword Insertion convert at higher rates and rake in higher average order values than ads that don't.

Testing and Experimenting with Different Ads

In order to succeed at online advertising you'll have to experiment continually with different ads in each ad group. Google can automatically rotate any ad variations you create for your audience, showing you with their click-through and conversion rates which ads are more effective than others. You can't do this by simply creating one ad per ad group and letting it run its course. You'll need to test, test, and test some more. Typically, you'll want to have as many as three or four ads running simultaneously, and you'll want to disable or edit any ads that are not performing well, and come up with some more ideas for another ad.

There are an infinite number of things to test with your cost-per-click ads. You already know of one — Keyword Insertion. What else can you test? Here are some great ideas for you:

- **Price vs. % off:** Which is more appealing to your visitors: "$10 off" or "5% off"?

- **Features vs. safety:** "High Quality, Durable," or "Strong UV Protection"?

- **Calls to action:** "Buy Now," "Shop Today," "Order Online," "Act Now," and a host of other imperative statements can (and should) be tested.

- **Two sentences vs. one:** Try writing the same ad twice, but vary the punctuation so that one ad features one 70-character sentence while the other features two 35-character sentences, and analyze the results.

- **Display-URL case:** What impact would www.WebSite.com have over www.website.com? The answer may surprise you!

- **Display-URL sub-folder:** If your display URL is www.WebSite.com, try www.WebSite.com/Offer and note how that affects your click-through rate.

- **Online vs. offline:** Do you take leads over the phone? Try inserting your phone number in one ad and track the increase or decrease in phone calls.

- **Free vs. complimentary:** They mean the same thing, but they may perform very differently.

- **Question vs. answer:** Which headline works better for your visitors: "Got Engine Problems?" or "We Fix Engines!"?

- **Quantity in stock:** Will you get more sales if you use "Limited Number in Stock" or "Every Item Fully Stocked"?

- **Punctuation:** "Sign up for our free demo" with a period at the end is good, but will "Sign up for our free demo!" work better?

As you can tell, the number of ad variations is as large as your imagination. Remember, there is no additional cost for creating as many ad variations as you please!

Other Types of Ad Formats

We'll go much deeper into different ad formats in Chapter 4, but it's good to point out now that cost-per-click vendors have been introducing different types of ad formats in the cost-per-click bidding model. Specifically, they've been allowing image ads and video ads to be created and placed on their Network Partner websites.

Typically, image ads are more expensive than text ads, and you have to create more than one size of the same ad to accommodate different Network Partner sites. Depending on the website, you may need to provide a 125 × 125 image or a 200 × 600 image. Google does make it easy for you by providing you with its Display Ad Builder tool, right within AdWords, which we'll also cover in Chapter 4. The Display Ad Builder tool is great for anyone without access to a professional graphic designer.

Some websites even accept video ads, which can also be managed and advertised from Google AdWords. These are typically very expensive, and require a lot more maintenance than either text or image ads. There are also strict rules and guidelines for both image and video ads that we'll cover in depth in the next chapter.

Geo-Targeting

The final big piece of the cost-per-click advertising puzzle is the geo-targeting options that you select for your campaigns. These are heavily dependent on your business model, your budget, your goals, and how well you can advertise in different regions of the country and the world.

Google and the major cost-per-click vendors allow you to geo-target your ads in similar ways, but once again Google is at the front of the technology curve, allowing you to easily select your targets for each campaign. And, typically, geo-targeting is applied at the campaign level. If you want your United States audience to receive different ads and bid on different keywords from your Canada audience, the wisest choice would be to create two different campaigns, one targeted to the United States and another one targeted to Canada.

Selecting a Country, State/Region, or City

Figure 3-9 shows the Google AdWords Geo-Targeting tool that appears to you when you click Edit from within your Settings tab. If you're in the United States, you'll by default be opted in to show your ads to the United States. As you can see in Figure 3-9, the United States, including Alaska and Hawaii, is highlighted, and a Google Maps–style pin is placed on the mainland. And, just as from within Google Maps, you can view your geo-targeting options with this standard Map view, the Satellite view, or a Hybrid view that will show you the satellite view with map details overlaid.

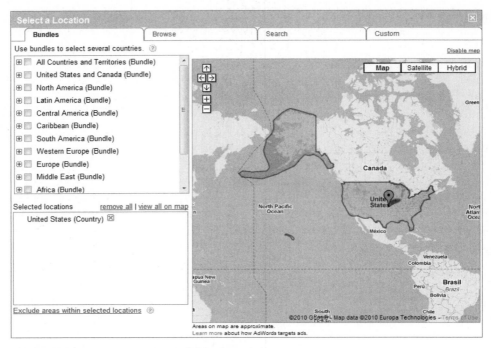

Figure 3-9: Geo-targeting in Google AdWords

To select any country or country "bundle," simply click it on the left-hand side of the Geo-Targeting tool, and Google will take care of the rest for you. Clicking the small plus sign to the left of any country or bundle will expand the selection to show you any state or region. With Google AdWords you can also select individual cities or designated market areas (DMAs), such as metro areas. Figure 3-10 shows that I've selected only the Denver, Colorado, metro area, which would be perfect for a local campaign, such as one for a festival or an outlet mall.

If I were an electrician, tax attorney, or owner of a movie theater or brick-and-mortar bicycle shop in the city of Denver, I'd want a tightly targeted area for advertising my business, which I could get by continuing to drill down on the menu on the left-hand side and selecting individual cities.

Creating a Custom Targeted Area

When you click the Custom tab within the Geo-Targeting tool, you're afforded the opportunity to select a custom targeted area for your ads to appear in. The two major options that you'll need to know about are the Radius targeting option and the Custom Shape targeting option.

With the Radius targeting option, it's fairly simple. You enter a radius in either miles or kilometers within which you'd like your ads to appear, and you're pretty much done. If your service area is inside a 10-mile radius, simply enter 10; Google will draw a circle with a radius of 10 miles, and your ads will be shown to any visitor within that 10-mile radius who is searching for your keywords.

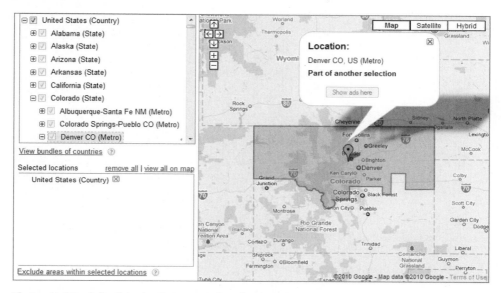

Figure 3-10: Selecting the Denver, Colorado, metro area

However, radii often don't translate well into the real world, and you'll wind up having to draw a custom-targeted area. For example, I live in South Florida, a few miles from the Atlantic Ocean. Drawing a 10-mile radius around my area would mean that I'd be targeting the ocean with almost half of it, which would be useless, and it could miss potential customers to the west. So, as shown in Figure 3-11, I designed a custom shape that fit my needs, and didn't waste any targeting space by showing my ads to anyone in either the Atlantic Ocean or the Everglades. As you can see, this area also encroaches upon cities in Broward County, even though I live and work in Palm Beach County.

Actually, drawing the shape is extremely easy to do, and can prove to be a fun exercise!

Who Actually Sees My Geo-Targeted Ads?

Before you hit Save and start showing your geo-targeted ads to your intended audience, you should be aware of who is actually going to see your ads, and who won't see them.

Google AdWords uses IP address matching to determine a user's physical location in the world. When a user enters a search query into Google, before it shows the user any ads Google will cross-check each eligible ad with its Geo-Targeting settings, and make a decision as to whether or not to show a user the ad.

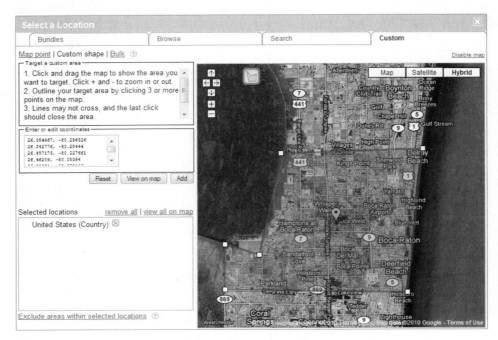

Figure 3-11: A custom-targeted shape for South Florida

Take a close look at Figure 3-11, and find the city Coral Springs on the very bottom left of the map. Coral Springs is outside my selected region, so no one searching from Coral Springs should be able to see my ads from within this particular campaign, right? Not so fast. If users in Coral Springs have their Internet service providers (ISPs) in Boca Raton (where there are countless ISPs), those users — who are outside my own custom-targeted shape — will be able to see my campaign's ads.

But the reverse is also true. Anyone receiving Internet service from Coral Springs but living in Boca Raton won't be able to see this campaign's ads, no matter how much this person might try. This is normally how it works with geo-targeting, so you should expect a few clicks and visits to appear from outside your targeted area from time to time, regardless of whether you're drawing a custom shape, entering a radius, or selecting individual countries and territories from the main list.

As far as cost-per-click advertising goes, you should now have a good understanding of some of its core elements. As far as Google AdWords is concerned, you're just getting started! As you're about to learn in Chapter 4, AdWords goes way beyond any other pay-per-click vendor by providing you with even more "advanced" opportunities, such as different bidding options, Sitelinks Display Builder, and lots more.

Advanced Opportunities within Google AdWords

In Chapter 2 I walked you through the new Google AdWords interface. I gave you a tour showing where everything is located, how everything is organized, and how to perform the basic operations necessary to use the interface. However, I purposely left some parts out and saved them for this chapter. If you're a newbie to cost-per-click advertising, you wouldn't appreciate being bombarded with things like placement targeting, remarketing, ad extensions, or display builder. It can be overwhelming to place everything about AdWords in one chapter, so I decided to divvy up the information between Chapter 2, this chapter, and Chapter 5.

The first — and possibly most obvious — omission from Chapter 2 is the launching pad for this chapter of the book. The Google Content Network has become a big part of AdWords over recent years, working a little bit differently from the Google Search Network. Let's start there.

As noted in earlier chapters, a Search Network is Google, AOL, or any "engine" where a user types in a search query. A Content Network is a network of websites that in this case serves ads from Google.

The Google Content Network

Google has designed and refined a technology in which your ads can appear on sites and on page placements throughout the Web based upon the page's content and keywords that you're bidding on. This technology, known as the

Google Content Network, reaches more than 80 percent of global Internet users, with a 76 percent unique reach (that is, non-repeated visitors) in the United States alone (Source: comScore Networks machine-based panel). A visitor performing a search on Google can type in a search query and visit a site that comes up within a search engine result. That site may show relevant text, image, or video ads based upon that original search query. Your ad may be clicked on, and it may generate additional conversions and sales for you.

Within the Settings sub-tab under the main Campaigns tab, you can put any current Search Network campaign into the Google Content Network and begin to display your ads instantly. However, doing so may seriously deplete your budget and your available impression share from AdWords. Usually, the Google Content Network generates several thousand impressions daily, even for low-yield advertisers pushing niche products. What you'll want to do is create a new, separate campaign for your Content Network ads and keywords. When you do this, ensure that this new campaign isn't also added to the Search Network as your original campaign would be; otherwise, you could be duplicating bids on keywords and ads and competing against yourself. You can use the same keywords and ads that you use for your search campaign in your Content Network campaign, and in a lot of cases this is the most convenient and efficient way to manage it.

The Google Content Network allows you to create three different types of ads to display on Content Network sites: text ads, image ads, and video ads. It is up to the publisher (owner) of the website to determine what types of ads will be available to advertise with — I'll show you an image later to illustrate how you'll know which websites accept which ad formats. (With Google AdSense, site owners are paid by Google to place Content Network ads on their site's pages.) This means that you also have to follow best-practices guidelines and meet editorial review guidelines here.

Text Ads

Text ads on the Content Network are exactly like the ones you create for search campaigns in AdWords, but Content Network publishers have the right to change the shape, font size, and color of your text ads. Text ads do have to follow the same character-length restrictions as search text ads, and must also meet editorial guidelines. They can also appear within videos and feeds, but they don't always — again, it depends on what the website's publisher allows.

Figure 4-1 shows a good example of a publisher within the Google Content Network, and of how text ads may appear different on a website as opposed to a search engine results page. This page, on the Healthy Eating Recipes blog, has Content Network text ads within the top-left header image, as well as four ads going down the page on the right-hand side. You can't tell it from Figure 4-1, but the two ads on the top left have a dark yellow font color for links and a white font color for the description. The shape of the top-left ads is also different, as there are three lines, not two as in Search Network ads. The ads on the bottom right have long first lines and short second lines, because each is one long sentence (which can't be done in the Google Search Network). The display URLs in both sets of ads have very small font sizes and are different colors, which have also been customized.

Figure 4-1: Example of Content Network publisher with text ads

These ads were created right within AdWords, just like any other Search Network ads that these particular advertisers may have within their campaigns. Let's hope they've separated their Content Network ads from their search ads by creating separate campaigns in AdWords for both.

Image Ads

Image ads are interesting because they allow for a lot more creativity than the standard 70-character-limit text ads. An estimated 95 percent of all Content Network websites accept image ads today in a variety of IAB-standard sizes.

IAB is the acronym for the Internet Advertising Bureau, which sets forth guidelines for things such as the size at which publishers should expect advertisers to create their image ads.

Image ads, just like text ads, are matched to a page's content. You must have good ad copy and a good message, and comply with all editorial guidelines from Google, or you will not be able to run image ads on its Content Network. With image ads you can upload your already-created image right into the AdWords interface by navigating to the Ads sub-tab within the Campaigns main tab, and then clicking on Create a New Ad from the farthest-left drop-down menu about two inches down from the Campaigns sub-tab. You can also create images for use in the Content Network by using the Display Builder tool, which we'll discuss in Chapter 6.

Figure 4-2 shows the portion of the page that appears when you want to upload your image ad into an ad group. You can browse for your image locally, give it a unique name, and enter in a display and a destination URL. Looking to the right of Figure 4-2 will inform you of the file formats and sizes that Google Content Network sites accept. A few things that this right-hand area won't tell you are that Google accepts animated .gif files and that Google cannot accept CMYK-format images. If you upload an image in CMYK, it may appear as a broken link or as an error message on the publisher's website. To be sure this doesn't happen to you, ensure that your image designer (or you, if you're creating the images) saves any Content Network image ads in the Web-standard RGB color format.

Figure 4-2: Image-ad-creation menu within Google AdWords

A couple of other details about image ads will be helpful for you to know. Google allows you to create as many image ads per campaign as you'd like to. At this time, there are no limits on the number of ads that you can create via the Display Builder tool or upload from within your campaign. Image ads are almost always more expensive (have a higher cost per click) than text ads, so be sure to set your campaign's daily budget higher to accommodate your image ads. Also, you'll want to give your images a descriptive name that doesn't exceed 50 characters. This helps the Google engineer who will eventually be looking at your image ad to approve it.

Here's some food for thought. As I mentioned a little bit ago, website owners who are Content Network partners can accept text, image, and video ads. Some accept all three ad formats, most accept image and text ads, and all Content Network partner websites accept text ads. Let's hypothetically assume that you have an ad group that contains both an image ad and a text ad, and the campaign is added to the Content Network. How does Google know which ad, the image ad or the text ad, to display on any given Content Network site?

What Google AdWords does is show the most relevant ad, either your image ad or your text ad. It will look at your selected keywords, your daily campaign budget, and the quality of the ads themselves in order to determine which ad it should show on any given Content Network partner website. If you want to show only your image ads (or video ads for that matter) for a particular campaign, your best bet is to create an ad group that contains only image ads — but be sure that you're not competing against yourself by having a second ad group containing only text ads for the same list of bidded keywords. About 5 percent of all Content Network websites do not accept image ads, so you'll be missing out on an impression and possible customer roughly one out of 20 times if you don't have at least one text ad with your image ads.

Video Ads

For maximum exposure you can create video ads that will display on select Content Network partner websites that accept video ad formats. Today there are far fewer Content Network partners that accept video ads, so the chances of your ads appearing on the Content Network are not as high as if you were using an image or a standard text ad. There are also a lot of differences between video ads and image or text ads, as well as much more robust specification requirements.

Google offers three different types of video ads to advertisers: click-to-play video ads, in-stream video ads, and InVideo ads. Click-to-play video ads allow the site visitor to control clicking the video ad in order to play it. In-stream video ads will play for either a minimum of 15 seconds or a maximum of 60 seconds as soon as the web page loads. InVideo ads appear within the bottom 20 percent of the video's stream-play space and are more prominent on YouTube and what Google considers "premium" partner network sites.

Click-to-play video ads can be stopped or skipped, while in-stream video ads or InVideo ads cannot. Click-to-play video ads and inVideo ads are eligible for both the cost-per-click pricing and the cost-per-impression pricing models, while in-stream video ads can be paid for only within the cost-per-impression pricing model. (We'll talk about pricing models in a few more pages.) All three types of video ads are required to have a working destination URL that, if clicked by a visitor, will take that visitor to the advertiser's website.

With click-to-play video ads, a static opening image (which you can also create) is first shown to a web browser. Click-to-play video ads on the

AdWords Content Network are available in either a medium rectangle shape (300 × 250 pixels) or a large rectangle shape (336 × 280 pixels). In-stream video ads do not require a static opening image but have their own set of technical specifications. They do not have a set pixel size, but must be created with a standard 4:3 aspect ratio. InVideo ads can be either Flash overlays or videos, with each file format containing its own laundry list of tech specs. When you're uploading or ready to create a video ad in AdWords, your best bet is to visit the following three URLs, which outline all technical specifications that you need to be aware of:

- **Click-to-play** video-ad technical specifications:

  ```
  https://adwords.google.com/support/aw/bin/answer
  .py?hl=en&answer=66788
  ```

- **In-stream** video-ad technical specifications:

  ```
  https://adwords.google.com/support/aw/bin/answer
  .py?hl=en&answer=153708
  ```

- **InVideo** ad technical specifications:

  ```
  https://adwords.google.com/support/aw/bin/answer
  .py?hl=en&answer=90377
  ```

Figure 4-3 shows an example of an inVideo ad on a YouTube video for a *Mr. Bean* episode. The episode is entitled "Mr. Bean — Army Cadets," and while the video is playing, an ad for Quaker Oatmeal scrolls on the bottom 20 percent of the video, with a call to "vote now!" and participate in the ad's challenge.

Figure 4-3: InVideo ad from Quaker Oatmeal

InVideo ads can also appear as full-screen advertisements that begin 15 seconds before your video starts (like the ones on every video on www.hulu.com). The image ad on the right-hand side is also from Quaker and it matches the InVideo ad, but it's not a part of video advertising. In this situation, Quaker spent a good chunk of change to advertise in this fashion. You can also expect to spend a lot not only on video advertising, but on creating the video as well.

Automatic and Managed Placements

Regardless of the type of ads that you decide to run on the Content Network, you'll have the choice between running automatic placements and managed placements within AdWords. Automatic placements will select websites for your Content Network ads to appear on, based upon your ad group's keywords. To enable automatic placements you'll need to click on the Relevant Pages across the Entire Network radio button within the Settings sub-tab of the main Campaign tab. Managed placements are websites on which you specifically choose to advertise. You can enable your managed placements by selecting the Relevant Pages Only on the Placements I Manage radio button within that same Settings sub-tab.

You really want to think about which option you're selecting and why you're selecting it. Using automatic placements is a very "hands-off" approach to advertising on the Content Network. You're basically allowing Google to determine the websites suitable to display your ads, while using your ad group's maximum cost-per-click bid price to charge you per click or per thousand impressions. Managed placements are the sites where your ads are appearing that you'd like more control over. Any site that is a managed placement can have its bids changed, providing you with much greater flexibility with a more ROI-intelligent spend of your money.

If you're looking for as many eyeballs as possible as soon as possible, and you have a high or unlimited advertising budget, you can probably use the Content Network with automatic placements and not worry. For all other advertisers, spend your money wisely and choose the managed placements option to control the bid prices for each website. If you need to remove a website entirely, you can exclude it by using the Site and Category Exclusions tool, which will be discussed at the end of Chapter 5.

Tips for Success on the Content Network

You'll notice a lot of similarities between the following list of tips for success and the tips for success I covered in Chapter 3. However, there are some differences, most notably the placements and the sites that your ads appear on or are excluded from appearing on.

Search for "tips for success on the Google Content Network" on Google, and you should find an article that will include these five tips:

- **Campaign structure:** Tightly themed ad groups within a campaign are one of the key determinants of Quality Score on the Search Network as well as on the Content Network. Keep your Content Network ad groups as focused as possible for optimal results.

- **Keywords:** As a general rule, you'll want to have anywhere from 5 to 20 keywords for ad groups that share the same topic. Don't combine keywords for different services or products, and don't overload your ad groups with an endless list of keywords. Take the 10 or 12 most important keywords for you and run with them. Delete keywords that don't perform and replace them with new ones (avoid adding keywords without deleting poor ones first).

- **Ads:** Your ads are obviously the most important piece of data that will determine whether or not a user visits your website from a Google Content Network partner. First, keep the network that you're advertising in mind. In the Google Search Network, a user types in a search query, and ads that are relevant to that search query are displayed. The end user *wants* to find the information that he or she is searching for, and your ads are competing against other cost-per-click ads and organic search engine results for that user's click. In the Content Network, the user has already made at least that first click at some point in time, and needs to be strongly persuaded to click another ad from within a website. It's critical to be able to relate the product or service on the website to the ad in the Content Network, be it a text, image, or video ad. Users in this network may even think that your ad is spam (because it's not on www.google.com), so you have to be ultra-persuasive here. Clear offers, strong calls to action, dedicated landing pages, and all the other smart ideas from the Search Network world also apply.

- **Content bids:** If you remember from just a few pages ago, selecting the Managed Placements option from within your campaign's Settings sub-tab allows you to control the bid for each Content Network site on which you're advertising. The Automatic Placements option takes the average of your keyword- and ad-group-level cost-per-click bids and uses that average as the bid price. As I've said before, if you're a "hands-off" type of marketer who's interested in reaching as many eyeballs as possible, automatic placements are probably the way to go. If return on investment and quality traffic are top priorities, you'll want to enable managed placements (and remove nonperforming sites by excluding them via the Site and Category Exclusion tool). Bid preferences should be checked against the goals that you're looking to meet with the Content Network.

- **Negative keywords:** As explained in Chapter 3, negative keywords also can be applied to the Content Network. This really is a great way to exclude users performing irrelevant searches and what could be unqualified traffic. Even if you just want as many people as possible to see your message, adding negative keywords to your Content Network campaigns can ensure that you're spending your money wisely and that your message doesn't fall on deaf ears. For most advertisers, using negative keywords is yet another trick up their sleeve to further improve ROI and conversion rates.

Keep in mind that your ad will or won't be shown on a Content Network site based upon the Quality Score and the bid price. Content Network sites can show as few as one ad to as many as four or five ads on one page. Will your ad be one of them?

Display Builder

Images are expensive. Ask any design company for a quote to create the simplest .gif image, and you'll feel as if you quality for a government bailout. But you need images, because they're very attractive and can be used on the Google Content Network that I just covered. So how do you, the hard-working advertiser, afford to create the multiple image sizes and formats that you need in today's digital world? Enter Google's Display Ad Builder.

You'll be able to create image ads from a growing library of hundreds of image templates, sorted by category and popularity. Pick any image and edit its headline, font colors, and text, and within a few short minutes you will have saved yourself a lot of money and time, while simultaneously launching image advertisements on the Content Network. Did I mention that Display Ad Builder is free to use?

To get started, find your Ads sub-tab within the main Campaigns tab and click the New Ad drop-down menu, which is the farthest-left drop-down menu under the graph. The menu will provide you a link to the Display Ad Builder, which will expand the table and show you all the available ad templates.

Selecting Your Ad Template

Once you arrive at this screen, you should see a laundry list of categories down the left-hand side of the page. Everything from seasonal and educational to rich media and audio/video image templates is available, including interesting sortable options like "most popular" and "highest click-through." A good number of these templates are animated, but several are static, for your convenience if you prefer static ones. The image template that you choose will dictate what information you'll need to provide, so there's no standard display ad template. However, you should be prepared to write a headline, a few lines of descriptive text, the text that the clickable button (call to action) will have, a display URL, and a destination URL. You could be asked to insert logos, product images, or a link to your YouTube video. Figure 4-4 shows an example of the template selection screen.

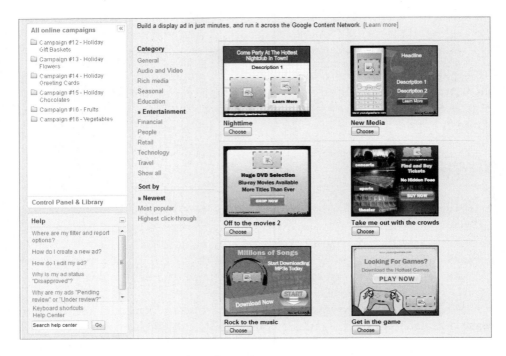

Figure 4-4: Selecting your display-ad template

Editing and Launching Your Display Ad

Once you select your template you'll have plenty of editing options to customize your new image ad. Figure 4-5 shows an example of what you'll see by picking one of the ads in the Entertainment category. You can insert an ad name, a ticket stub text (this image starts by scrolling small ticket stub images for which you can edit the text and font type), a headline, description lines, and lower, on this page but not shown, a display URL and a destination URL. To the right of the editing options are the ad variation options. You can create your ad in any one of the listed sizes — there's no cost to do so. Depending on the scope of your Content Network campaign(s), you should create your image in enough size variations to cover all possible size requirements of a potential website that you'd like your ads to appear on.

Once you create your image and it starts displaying on a Content Network site, you'll be able to see statistics for it just as you would for a text or video ad. Optimize accordingly with the tips you've learned in this chapter and Chapter 3.

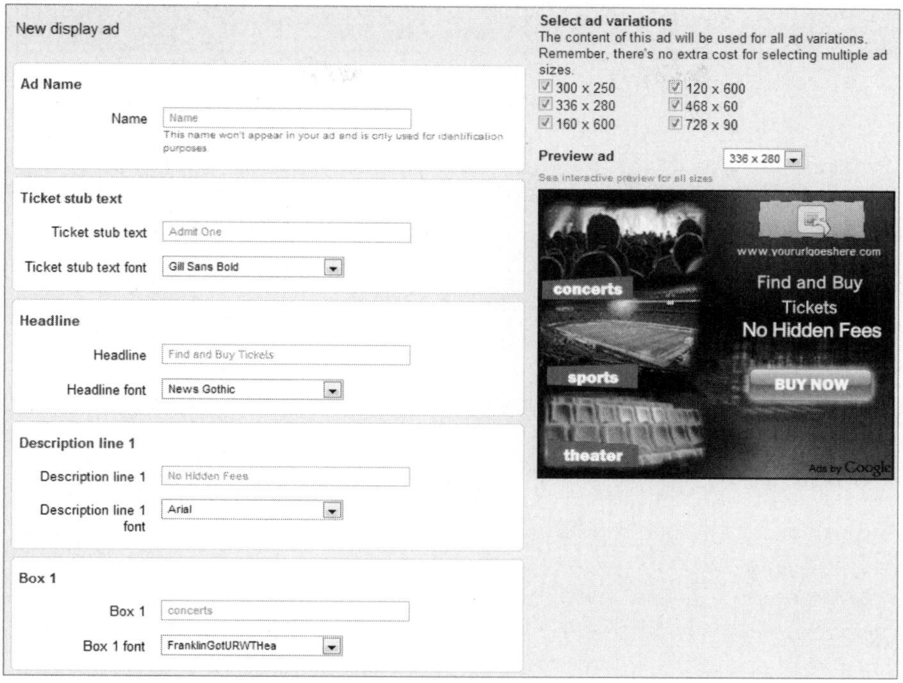

Figure 4-5: Editing your display-ad image: ad variations

You don't necessarily *have* to use the Display Ad Builder. You may be good at graphic design, or you may already have images created. If this is the case, simply click Image Ad instead of Display Ad Builder in the drop-down menu mentioned earlier to bring up the dialog box shown in Figure 4-6. You'll need to name it and provide both a display URL and a destination URL. Your uploaded image cannot exceed 50K in size, but this feature supports more image types and sizes than are available in the Display Ad Builder. Your uploaded image will have to comply with all the standard terms, conditions, and trademark/copyright laws, so be careful.

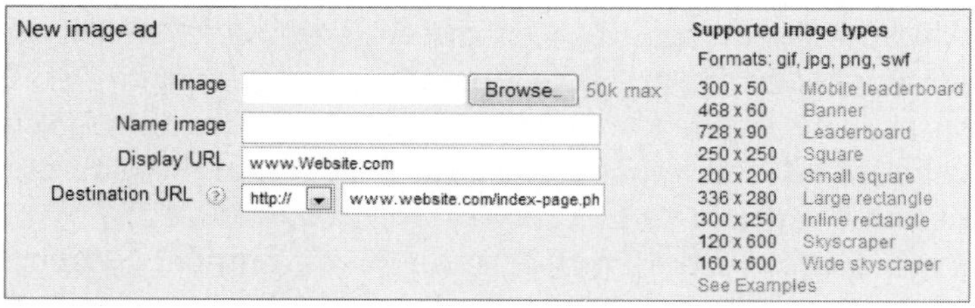

Figure 4-6: Options for uploading your own image ad

AdWords Bidding Options

Up until now, we've talked about only one AdWords bidding model: the cost-per-click bidding system. It's as straightforward as it gets; you set a bid, a user clicks your ad, and you pay one cent more than the next-highest bid from your maximum cost-per-click bid. I haven't mentioned two other types of bidding, and I have yet to tell you how Google groups your advertising goals with your bidding options.

There are three types of AdWords bidding options: cost-per-click (CPC), cost-per-thousand-impressions (CPM), and cost-per-acquisition (CPA).

Bidding Focus on Clicks (CPC)

You're already familiar with the standard traditional bidding model used globally. In AdWords, you can set either manual bids (for ad groups, ads, or keywords) or automatic bids, an option that takes your daily budget and evenly disperses it throughout the day.

I encourage you to use manual bidding whenever possible. Manual bidding gives you complete control over each ad's or keyword's bid price, which is something you really need complete control over. Automatic bidding sounds like an easy "hands-off" approach to managing your bids, but there are drawbacks you need to be aware of. First, automatic bidding will disable ad scheduling, which is an important advanced feature to be introduced later. Second, you will not be able to control your maximum cost-per-click bids, leaving Google's automated system to decide how to bid for you and how to spend your daily budget. You're more than welcome to give automatic bidding a try, but you'll most likely want the control that comes with manual bidding. Even if you set one bid for your entire ad group, and every ad or keyword within that ad group is the same bid, at least you're in control of how your money is spent.

Bidding Focus on Impressions (CPM)

If you're thinking about the Content Network, and you're thinking about all the potential eyeballs staring at your ads, you may want to look into cost-per-thousand-impressions bidding, also known as CPM bidding. Instead of paying for clicks (meaning the visitor has actually gone to your site), you'll pay just for each thousand impressions your ad receives. A thousand may not sound like many, but on the Content Network you may consistently receive several thousand or more impressions daily. Just as with cost-per-click bidding, you'll select a maximum CPM bid for the ads that you'll be displaying, but you'll want to consider a higher CPM bid (in comparison to a CPC bid). CPM-bidded ads always occupy the entire ad space available on a Content Network site with an image, video, or expanded text ad. There will be fewer advertisers competing against you, but the competition will be much tougher to win a placement on a site, especially when you use a lower bid.

In case you're wondering, there's no advantage on the Content Network in using CPM bidding over CPC bidding. They both compete in the same auction, and one bidding type doesn't trump the other. It's about what fits your goals, budget, and performance.

Bidding Focus on Conversions (CPA)

Cost-per-acquisition bidding is all about one acronym: ROI. Using the CPA option once again puts the AdWords system in the driver's seat, just as automatic CPC bidding does. Google will look at your account's historical performance, your daily budget, and the cost per acquisition that you set within AdWords. It will take this data and set cost-per-click bids on your ads and keywords in an attempt to stay below your CPA bid. Google can set high cost-per-click bids at times for ads it deems more valuable, and lower the bids when it deems the time and ads less valuable.

Using CPA bidding may actually lower your conversion rate a bit, and will affect other metrics, so you want to make sure that you know exactly what your cost-per-acquisition really is, or that you know how to calculate it. Furthermore, your campaign must have received 30 conversions within the last 30 days and must be receiving conversions at a consistent rate for a few days in order for you to use the CPA bidding model

NOTE The cost-per-acquisition bidding model requires that you install the Google AdWords Conversion Tracking code on the key conversion pages of your website. You cannot use CPA bidding without this code, and you really won't know what your CPA bid might be unless you have a clear idea of where you'd like your site visitors to go and what you want them to do when they get there. I cover conversion tracking in Chapter 5.

Once you decide on a bidding option, all ad groups, ads, and keywords within that campaign will be instantaneously updated to reflect your new settings. If you feel you've made a mistake and the bidding option is not working out for you, you can always edit it by returning to the Settings sub-tab within the main Campaigns tab.

Advanced Campaign Settings

I've been purposely holding out on you so that you could get the basics of Google AdWords and cost-per-click advertising down. I've been hinting in the previous chapters that AdWords has some "advanced" settings, like Position

Preference, Ad Scheduling, and Frequency Capping within the Settings sub-tab of the main Campaigns tab. Now that I've covered all the basics and some of the more in-depth AdWords topics, it's a perfect time to introduce you to the advanced features that can definitely help your campaign's overall performance.

Let's begin the second half of this chapter by digging into each individual feature.

Languages

I mentioned in Chapters 2 and 3 that AdWords won't translate your text, image, or video ads for you — this is something you'll have to do on your own if you're interested in targeting potential customers outside your native language. In AdWords you can select which languages to display your ads in; the selection is made within the Settings sub-tab of any AdWords campaign.

By looking at Figure 4-7, you'll see that you can choose among about three dozen language options simply by clicking on checkboxes in front of the languages. However, because AdWords doesn't translate your ads, any ads written in, say, English, will be shown to Spanish users. Needless to say, showing ads to customers speaking another language won't result in very high click-through or conversion rates.

To advertise in another language you actually need to write the ad in that language. If you don't have access to a translator, you can try using one of the many free translation tools online, but I'll warn you that they're not 100 percent accurate. I can vouch for that, since Portuguese is my second language. The user's browser language option is what determines the language in which the Google search engine will be displayed, and in what language users see your search and content ads. Languages are separate from locations, so a user in France could have an English-language setting and see your ads in English, not French. So if you have an international business model and live in the United States, you can advertise to the entire world without worrying whether your customers can read your ads — it's completely dependent upon their browsers' language settings. (Conversely, users in your native country could have different browser language settings, which could exclude them from seeing your ads.)

Position Preference

Available only on the Search Network for keyword-targeted campaigns, Position Preference allows you to select a preference for the actual numerical position in which you want your ads to be displayed. This is gold for advertisers who need a strong brand presence and need to have their ads displayed only in top positions. It's copper for advertisers who are looking for high volumes of impressions and clicks.

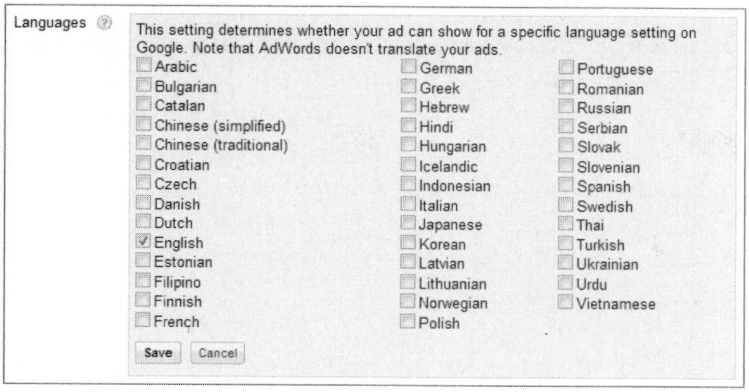

Figure 4-7: Available language options for your AdWords campaigns

When you enable Position Preference within the Settings sub-tab of any campaign, a new column will appear in your Keywords tab, allowing you to manually edit the position preferences for each individual keyword. Suppose you want your ads to show only in the top position, which is Position 1. You'll select From 1 in the first drop-down menu and To 1 in the second drop-down menu, and hit Save. From that moment on, the keyword's ad (when matched to a Google search query) will potentially appear only in Position 1, which is the shaded box in the top middle of a search engine result. Suppose you want a range of positions, say Positions 1 through 5. You'll select From 1 in the first drop-down menu and To 5 in the second, and click Save. Your ads will potentially appear only in Positions 1 through 5. I just used an important word — "potentially." Google can't guarantee that your position preference will be awarded to you on any impression. It will try its best to ensure that your ads match your position preference, but your ad won't always be displayed in the position that you want it in. If you want an ad for a specific keyword to appear in Position 1 and in no other position, your ad still could appear in Position 2 or 3. Even if you want ads to display on the right-hand side of the page (usually Positions 4 through 10), your ad may pop up in Positions 1 through 3 from time to time. Position Preference is simply not an exact system, but in my experience it works well enough that your ads will be shown based on your preferences most of the time.

Another thing to consider is that with Position Preference enabled, your reach (volume) will take a serious hit, especially if you want to display ads in only one or two positions. A lot of impressions and clicks can accrue from all the other positions combined, so if traffic volume from AdWords is a priority for you, think twice before enabling Position Preference. If you want a high volume of both impressions and clicks, and never to be displayed in a low position, you'll have to find the right balance between the Position Preference range and the volume of impressions and clicks you receive from that preference. My best advice for you: Test out Position Preference and continue to tweak it until it's just right for you.

You can select a preference for an exact position, below a certain position, above a certain position, and within a range of positions. Position Preference is a campaign-level setting, but it must be edited individually at the keyword level. Remember, being number one isn't automatically the most successful position. Don't use Position Preference to fall into the trap of being number one just to be number one without any good reason.

Delivery Method

You have two ad-delivery options for each campaign: standard delivery and accelerated delivery.

Standard delivery, the default option, will show your ads evenly over the course of a 24-hour day. The AdWords system will automatically divide your daily budget into equal parts and distribute your ads throughout the day as smoothly as possible without interruption. It can do this because AdWords isn't allowed to substantially exceed your daily budget, and it's able to forecast the impression and click volume that your campaigns will receive. This is a good solid option for most advertisers.

If you need to do some aggressive advertising, such as to promote a last-minute sale or a limited-time offer, accelerated delivery is your best bet. As soon as the clock strikes 12 midnight in your local area, the floodgates will open and the AdWords system will start to display your ads. Like diners at an all-you-can-eat buffet, your campaigns devour as many impressions and clicks as your daily budget can allow for. However, once your daily budget has been reached, your campaigns stop showing ads until the next day, or until you raise your daily budget. I've seen many a campaign get burned with accelerated delivery (i.e., the campaign runs out of funds before 9 a.m. — not a pretty situation, especially if it's someone else's money, like a client's).

If you have enough funds, you could probably get away with accelerated delivery on a campaign that contains only your branding keywords or your top-performing keywords, because you can never have enough traffic from those two types of campaigns. But be careful using accelerated delivery on other campaigns — play it safe at first if you're not sure or if you have a limited budget to spend.

Ad Scheduling

Ad Scheduling has got to be one of the most requested and used features in Google AdWords.

It's easy to see why it's so popular. You tell AdWords on which days and at what times of day to display your ads. By default, your ads get shown 24 hours a day, seven days a week. This is clearly suboptimal for a lot of businesses.

Why would you run ads at 11 p.m. on a Saturday encouraging customers to call your office?

From within any Settings sub-tab, you'll find Ad Scheduling as a link toward the bottom of the screen. Click the link to bring up the window that is shown in Figure 4-8. The gray boxes are the time slots of each individual day your ads are not being shown. The other boxes represent the times that your ad is running. AdWords provides ad scheduling options for each 15-minute interval. Click a time under the Time Period column to bring up the pop-up box shown at the bottom of Figure 4-8; then you can edit that day's time schedule. You can pause the day entirely by clicking Not Running, and you can copy that day's settings to another day by clicking the Copy drop-down menu at the bottom of that pop-up.

You can also edit something very interesting. Notice the field on the far-right of the pop-up window, with a % symbol and the word Remove to the right of the field. You can use this field to edit the bids for a particular time of day. Let's say that the morning (8 a.m. to noon) is normally your business's slow time. You can, for example, bid at 50 percent of your maximum cost per click during that period, by entering in "50" and setting your time schedule to 8 a.m. to noon. You can then click the Add Another Time Period link and complete your desired time schedule with a bid setting of 100 percent. This is a great way to maximize your daily budget and refine your spends to an even greater, more intelligent degree.

Ad Scheduling is another campaign-level option, applied to all ads and keywords across your entire campaign.

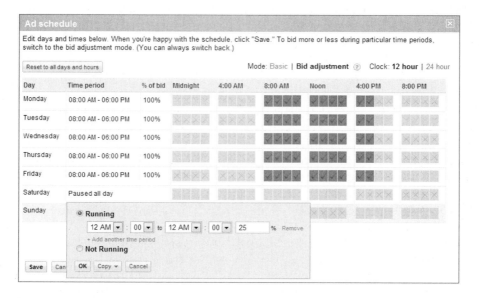

Figure 4-8: Ad Scheduling for AdWords campaigns

Ad Rotation

Toward the very bottom of any Settings sub-tab for any campaign is a link titled Ad Delivery. When you click that link you'll see an option for Ad Rotation. AdWords provides you with two options for Ad Rotation: Optimize and Rotate.

Optimize is the default option, and the most widely used Ad Rotation option for most advertisers. Optimize starts by showing all your ads, and then works to show the ads that perform the best more frequently than the ads that don't perform as well. For example, let's say one of your ad groups has three ads. The first has a click-through rate of 1 percent, the second a rate of 2 percent, and the third a rate of 5 percent. With the Optimize option enabled, AdWords will show the ad with a 5 percent click-through rate far more often than the other two. In a lot of cases, AdWords will almost entirely give up on the other two ads and show the best-performing ad almost exclusively. In my opinion, this is one of the best "hands-off" options AdWords offers.

But my opinion isn't necessarily shared by everyone. As I am writing about this feature, I am thinking of a colleague of mine who makes a strong case for the Rotate option, and prefers to use that over the Optimize option. The Rotate option evenly rotates all the ads within an ad group, forcing you to manually pause or edit under-performing ads. If your ad group with three ads receives 900 impressions in one day, AdWords will show exactly 300 impressions for each of the three ads within the group.

I honestly feel that this even rotation is not a good idea for you. There are some benefits to allowing AdWords to do some of the work for you, and this is one of them. Why put some of your customers through ads that aren't as good as other ads they could be seeing? Why take the risk of a lower click-through rate and possibly a lower conversion rate? Still, my colleague swears by even rotation. As she points out, AdWords doesn't run a statistically significant number of impressions or clicks in order to determine which ads are performing the best. AdWords very quickly starts to identify an ad that is performing well and starts serving up that ad more often with the Optimize feature. Depending on when the ads are created and launched (time of day, day of the week, or season), and depending on the volume of impressions and clicks, one ad may look invincible in comparison to the others, but may not be when presented to a larger sample size. In other words, AdWords doesn't survey enough visitors before it starts showing an ad more often — what could prove to be the worst ad over the course of time could be the one that AdWords starts displaying more frequently right away, which means that the ads that are actually better will receive less volume and take longer to beat an opposing ad.

Which option you choose is entirely up to you. If you do select the Optimize option, your best-performing ad will (eventually) be shown more frequently. If you select the Rotate option, you will have to remember to go back into the ad group, analyze performance, and pause the other ads. Ad Scheduling is a campaign-wide setting.

Frequency Capping

The AdWords Content Network can take you by surprise. I'm not kidding when I say that your ads may receive several thousand impressions daily from a Content Network site. You may not even receive many clicks, which means you'll have comparatively low click-through rates. In some cases, a 0.05 percent (i.e., five hundredths of a percent) click-through rate can be considered great. Don't worry — your click-through rates for the Content Network are judged separately from your click-through rates for the Search Network, and thus don't affect your Quality Scores.

To place a cap or a "hard stop" on the number of impressions your Content Network campaigns receive on either a daily, weekly, or monthly basis, the Frequency Capping option is your friend. You can cap the number of impressions per unique user on a site, so that the same unique user sees your ad only a certain number of times per time period. This is very helpful, because the same unique user can visit the same website multiple times a day and hundreds of times in one month. This happens on sites with message boards or other interactive elements, like fantasy sports sites. If the users aren't interested in your ad, they may never click it, so you're wasting impressions on users who have no interest in you. Setting a cap of 50, for example, provides each unique user a fair chance at clicking your ad. If after 50 visits users still haven't clicked your ad, it's probably a safe bet that they are not interested.

Frequency Capping can be applied at the ad-group level or at the individual ad level, and is available only on the Content Network (not the Search Network — would be nice if it were).

Demographic Bidding

Finally, Demographic Bidding allows you to set bid percentages based upon users' gender and age brackets. Certain websites on the Content Network are able to collect this information. Usually these are social-networking sites like Facebook, sites with message boards, or any sites that store personal user information. This information is very private: Personal names, addresses, ZIP codes, and other sensitive info are never shared. Instead, users are aggregated (for example, I'm male and between 25 and 34 years old).

The link for Demographic Bidding is the very last link at the very bottom of the Settings tab. When you click this link, the dialog box in Figure 4-9 opens up. You can exclude users based on gender or age bracket by clicking the checkbox corresponding to the option you desire. Even though my example doesn't show any statistics, your Content Network campaign will show clicks, impressions, click-through rate, average cost per click, and total cost segmented out. If I actually did want to start running this campaign in the Content Network, you can see from Figure 4-9 that my ads would be shown only to users that I'm not excluding, which are the users in the 18–24 bracket and the 25–34 bracket. Looking above that, you'll see that for males I'm willing to bid 75 percent *more* than my original bid, and for females I'm willing to bid a full 100 percent *more* than my original bid. You can bid more aggressively for specific age brackets as well.

The Demographic Bidding window doesn't show data on specific websites. You can use the Report Center that I displayed in Chapter 2 and select the Demographic Performance report to see a full list of all Content Network sites and statistics for each individual site. Also, when two demographic bid increases overlap each other, the percentages will be added together. The example that appears in the Demographic Bidding window is perfect. If your female increased bid is 10 percent, and your 18–24 age bracket increased bid is 15 percent, your bid will be increased by 25 percent for females between the ages of 18–24 (10 percent from the gender preference and 15 percent from the age-bracket preference).

Sites that don't collect demographic information will not be able to have your settings applied to delivery and distribution. Demographic Bidding settings apply to all ads and ad groups within a campaign.

Demographic bidding ⊠

This summary shows how your ads have performed on sites that offer demographic data. Click any row to adjust your bid for that demographic group. You can also use the exclude checkboxes to hide your ad from that group.
0.00% of total impressions are from sites with demographic data. ⓘ

Traffic Reports by Gender and Age (for last 7 days)

Gender	Exclude	Modify bid	Clicks	Impr.	CTR	Avg. CPC	Cost
Male	☐	Bid + 75%	0	0	0.00%	$0.00	$0.00
Female	☐	Bid + 100%	0	0	0.00%	$0.00	$0.00
Unspecified			0	0	0.00%	$0.00	$0.00
Total			**0**	**0**	**0.00%**	**$0.00**	**$0.00**

Age	Exclude	Modify bid	Clicks	Impr.	CTR ⓘ	Avg. CPC ⓘ	Cost
0-17	☑		0	0	0.00%	$0.00	$0.00
18-24	☐	Bid + 100%	0	0	0.00%	$0.00	$0.00
25-34	☐	Bid + 100%	0	0	0.00%	$0.00	$0.00
35-44	☑	Bid + 0%	0	0	0.00%	$0.00	$0.00
45-54	☑	Bid + 0%	0	0	0.00%	$0.00	$0.00
55-64	☑	Bid + 0%	0	0	0.00%	$0.00	$0.00
65+	☑	Bid + 0%	0	0	0.00%	$0.00	$0.00
Unspecified			0	0	0.00%	$0.00	$0.00
Total			**0**	**0**	**0.00%**	**$0.00**	**$0.00**

Figure 4-9: Demographic bidding options

Ad Extensions

In this final section of Chapter 4 I'll take you beyond the regular text, image, and video ads that I've been talking about up to this point. Ad Extensions are a relatively new feature within AdWords that allow you to augment your current ads to provide your customers with more information about your business. Ad Extensions "extends" your ad text to potentially include your location, address, or phone number, additional links, or product images. Certain extensions, like location and product extensions, can appear on Google Maps or Google Product Search.

Ad Extensions are edited within each Settings sub-tab in any campaign, just like all the advanced features mentioned earlier. You'll find Ad Extensions toward the bottom of the tab, where you may see up to five different options. Ad Extensions are a newer AdWords feature, which means that they may not be available in your country or in your account. (You may see a few but not all Ad Extensions possibilities.) You don't have to pay anything extra to use Ad Extensions on your ads — you simply pay each time any user clicks your ad or any ad extension link, like Sitelinks. Users can click your ads in Google Maps using the local business ad extensions, and you still won't be charged as long as the user doesn't click a link to visit your site directly. This could be beneficial, as you could advertise a lot for free.

Location Extensions: Business Owners

If you're the owner of a local restaurant, ice cream shop, or veterinary business, you can link your Google Local Business Center account and have your address appear within cost-per-click ads on Google and Google Maps. A Local Business Center account allows your local business to have valuable information appear within Google Maps listings, such as your address, your phone number, directions, and more. This is a phenomenal feature for anyone using a mobile device and searching locally on Google, as well as anyone searching from a regular desktop or laptop computer. Creating a Local Business Center account is easy: simply go to www.google.com/maps and click the Put Your Business On Google Maps link on the left-hand side of the map page. Follow the simple instructions from that point forward to add your listing. You will need to be signed in with your Google account in order to proceed.

In fact, your business may already be listed, even if you've never gone through this process before. There will be a Claim Listing button if your address and business name are returned to you during the setup process. If your business isn't there, you will be able to click Add Listing to insert it. There's no shortage of details to enter: you can put in business hours, photos, videos, menu and payment options, and lots more. Be aware that Google will need to verify your business to make sure it's legit. You'll be given a few verification options at the end of the Local Business Center sign-up process.

Look closely at Figure 4-10. I've performed a search on Google Maps for *Chicago deep dish pizza*, which is delicious beyond words. The first and clearly most prominent sponsored ad, on the top left, is from Renaldi's Pizza and takes full advantage of local business ad extensions. Both within the map itself and on the top left, the cost-per-click text ad appears, along with a map icon and address. The map's sponsored link within the dialog box includes the business's full mailing address, website URL, and phone number. Because it's on Google Maps, you are also provided with links for Directions, Search Nearby, and more, which are not being charged to Renaldi's Pizza.

The other listings below the sponsored listing on the left-hand side are what you would consider "organic" Google Maps listings. These other pizzerias have their addresses and phone numbers pulled in from the results that the Google Local Business Center has for them, which may or may not have been entered manually.

Figure 4-10: Ad extensions on Google Maps

Location Extensions: Non-Business Owners

Franchise partners, shift managers, and even agency employees can enter up to nine separate business locations for their company or clients by selecting the non-business option from the Ad Extensions section of the Settings sub-tab. Here verification that you own a business is not required, and you can enter your information on the fly, without a Local Business Center account.

Figure 4-11 shows the small pop-up window that appears when you add an address as a non-business owner.

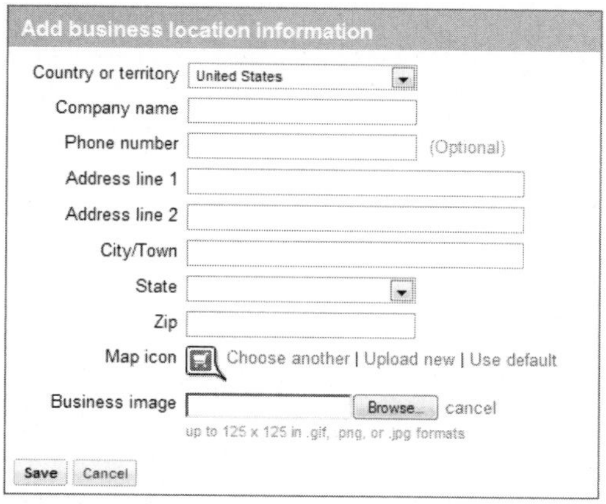

Figure 4-11: Adding business location information

Phone Extensions

If phone extensions are enabled within your AdWords campaign, and any user on an iPhone or Nexus One is searching on Google, that user will be able to click your business phone number to call you directly. Your business phone number appears as a hyperlink, just as a link appears in your desktop browser, and will connect that person to you. Any click a user makes on your hyperlinked phone number from a mobile phone will be charged to you at the same rate as a standard cost-per-click ad, which is one cent above the next-highest bid from your maximum cost-per-click.

To be eligible for phone extensions you'll need to make sure that you're targeting ads to iPhones and other mobile devices with full Internet browsers in the Settings sub-tab, within the Devices section. From this section you'll be able to enter your business phone number and start displaying phone extensions to mobile customers. Figure 4-12 is a screenshot from my iPhone, showing what happens after I click the phone number in the ad for the Dial 7 New York Taxi Service.

Ad Sitelinks

For ads that meet the criteria for high quality, advertisers have the ability to add up to four additional links to their cost-per-click ads on Google and

Search Partner sites by using Ad Sitelinks. If your campaign is a branding campaign, or another high-quality campaign, you'll see an Additional Links link in your Ad Extensions Settings section, where you'll be able to enter up to 10 names and URLs for important links on your site. Depending on the user's search query, AdWords will display up to four Sitelinks below your ad's original display URL.

Figure 4-12: A phone extension as it appears on an iPhone

Each click on an ad Sitelink will incur a cost-per-click charge, just like a click on any other link on your ad or other site extension. Figure 4-13 shows an example of Sitelinks when a search is performed on the query *old navy*, which no doubt brings up an ad from Old Navy's high-quality branding campaign. As you can see, four Sitelinks appear within the ad in Position 1, where each Sitelink takes me to a specific department within the store.

Product Extensions

Product extensions allow for image and product data from your Google Merchant Center account to be displayed within text ads on Google-sponsored search results. If you are an e-commerce merchant who uses Google Merchant Center to upload product data feeds for Google's Product Search, you can sync with your AdWords account for your ad's benefit.

Figure 4-13: Ad Sitelinks for an Old Navy cost-per-click text ad

At the time of writing, the Product Extensions feature is available only to U.S. advertisers. However, it shouldn't be long before this feature is rolled out in Europe and other markets as well. Also, product extensions aren't shown on Search Network sites, like AOL.

Your images, prices, titles, and other data from products that closely match a user's search query may appear on the right-hand side of the search engine results page, usually trumping other sponsored ads.

Figure 4-14 shows an example of product extensions in action, for a query for *noise-canceling headphones*. The top two results on the right-hand side are product extensions, pulled directly from these merchants' Google Merchant Center accounts. Also, notice what's in the middle portion of the search result. The second sponsored ad, from eBay, shows several noise-canceling headphones currently on eBay's auction system. I accessed them by clicking a plus-sign symbol to show products from eBay for my search term. Google is referring to this feature as a "plusbox," and has made it available to high-end advertisers like eBay so they can further expand their sponsored ads. Now *that* is an ad extension!

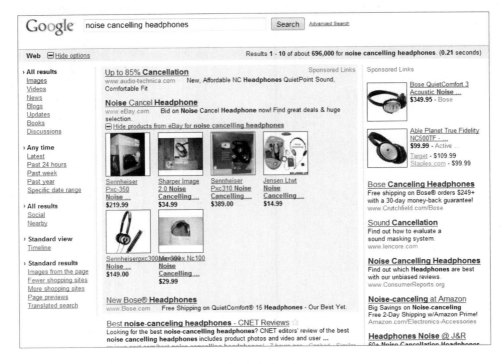

Figure 4-14: Product extensions and the "plusbox"

We've covered quite a bit of advanced material in this chapter, and I hope that I was able to show you several options to enhance, optimize, and increase your campaign's reach. The next chapter talks about specific AdWords tools that you can use to manage your account, and also about unique reporting features like the My Change History tool. I'll also cover conversion tracking and the Google Ad Planner tool, two essential pieces of the AdWords success puzzle.

CHAPTER 5

AdWords Tools of the Trade

A carpenter, a dentist, and an auto mechanic are all good with their hands. They've been tutored and mentored, and have mastered their skills to perfection. Most have the certifications to back it up. Some carpenters are just naturals and can do anything with their hands. A top auto mechanic knows about all there is to know about cars. *All* these folks use the tools of their trade to do their jobs. As an online marketer, you also need to use the tools of your trade to become the very best there is, and make yourself and your clients lots of money.

In this chapter I'll demo a number of tools available both within and outside AdWords. You'll learn about the critical Conversion Tracking tool, the My Change History tool, and Google Ad Planner. The first tool I'll cover is one you could very well use as often as the AdWords online interface; this is Google AdWords Editor.

Google AdWords Editor

AdWords Editor is a free downloadable program that enables you to manage your AdWords account offline and from your desktop. With it you can make bulk changes across multiple campaigns, including budget changes, keyword bid adjustments, and new ads. You can write notes, download bulk spreadsheets, and propose changes to other colleagues who may work together with you.

The best feature of AdWords Editor is that all the changes happen locally, on your computer. Only when you are good and ready will your changes be posted live to your account, and you don't have to worry about losing changes if your Internet connection is lost or your computer crashes — AdWords Editor saves your work as you go along.

AdWords Editor is available for both Windows (Windows 2000 and newer) and Mac OS X (10.4 and newer). It's available to be downloaded and installed from `http://www.google.com/intl/en/adwordseditor/index.html`. Click Download AdWords Editor on the top right-hand side of the page, which will take you to a Thank You page and begin the file download. Once the download is complete, find it on your computer and double-click the installation file. This process should take about a minute, and you'll be ready to download your first campaign from AdWords.

Downloading Your Campaigns

When you open AdWords Editor for the very first time, you'll need to accept the terms and conditions before proceeding. You'll need to scroll down to the bottom of the pop-up box in order to click I Accept to move forward. Next you'll be asked to set your default language and location targeting options for any new campaigns that you create from within AdWords Editor. You'll also be asked to enable or disable usage tracking. Google collects anonymous usage information from your sessions if you enable usage tracking. The information is not personally identifiable, but the choice of whether to enable tracking is entirely up to you. Click OK to open up AdWords Editor for the very first time.

The next thing to appear should look like Figure 5-1. The AdWords Editor window should be open, along with an Open Account window in front of it. Click Add Account at the bottom of the Open Account window to bring up the third window you see in Figure 5-1, which asks you to sign in to your AdWords account. Enter your username and password and click Next to begin downloading your campaigns. A new dialog box should appear, asking you if you'd like to download all campaigns or only selected campaigns. Once you have made this choice a progress bar will appear in a new window, showing you statistics of campaigns, ad groups, and other campaign details downloaded. When the download is done you'll finally be able to start using AdWords Editor!

Working within AdWords Editor

Your campaigns are now downloaded, and it's time to start getting familiar with the AdWords Editor interface. I'll run through the options much as I did in Chapter 2 with the online version of AdWords, but I won't be going as deep — we do have other very important programs to cover in this section.

If you're still new to AdWords, it's my recommendation that you continue using the online version until you have a solid grasp of the interface. If you're already at that level, continue reading!

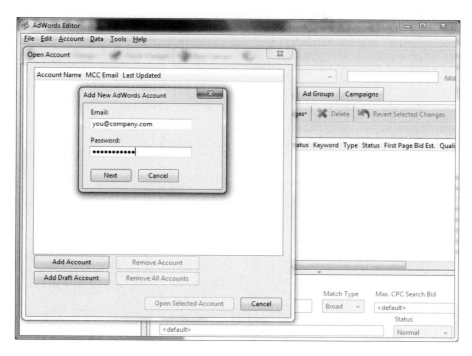

Figure 5-1: Adding a new AdWords account to AdWords Editor

Figure 5-2 shows the standard view of AdWords Editor. At the very top left, options to download files in Excel and to open another account, as well as tools, data options, and a menu, are available. Immediately below that top row, you can download recent changes, check selected campaigns for accuracy, post selected campaigns live, and view AdWords-oriented statistics for your campaigns. Below that second row are the main panels you'll be working with, including a navigation menu on the left-hand side and the editing screen in the middle, with six tabs featuring commands below them. The bottom half of the middle portion of the screen shows you all the settings of your campaign (or selected items, according to the tab you're on).

If you start using AdWords Editor regularly, you'll want to make it a habit to click Get Recent Changes on the upper left-hand side. This will save you a lot of pain by downloading the most recent version of your account. This way, any updates you make to your AdWords campaigns online will be downloaded, so you won't wind up doubling your work or overwriting anything.

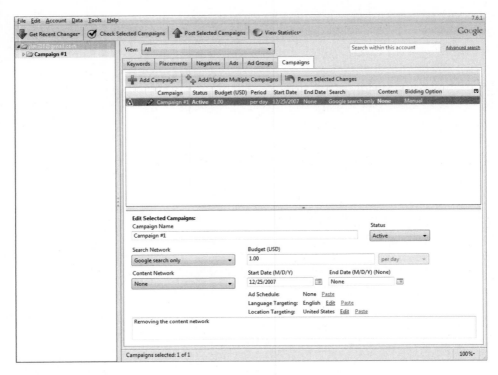

Figure 5-2: The standard AdWords Editor screen

Clicking the File menu button will display options for downloading and backing up your AdWords account. You can export in a CSV file; a ZIP file that includes any uploaded images from image ads, backup, and sharing file formats if you use multiple accounts; and an HTML-friendly version to view your AdWords account in a local web browser. Each menu option enables you to download the entire account or only selected campaigns.

A second interesting menu option is the Tools button. The first one is a Duplicate Keywords tool, which is shown in Figure 5-3. You can find duplicate keywords between ad groups, between campaigns, or over your entire account. You can search by match type, through deleted keywords, and by word order. As your AdWords account grows, it will become increasingly important for you to keep tight control over everything within your account, and it's all too easy to create duplicate keywords unknowingly. The AdWords interface online will let you create and activate a duplicate keyword, which would result in your bidding (competing) against yourself, possibly within the same campaign. With AdWords Editor you can seek out duplicates.

There are two other important tools in this menu. Keyword Grouper scans your campaigns and provides suggestions about how to better organize your ad groups by grouping like-worded keywords together. Remember that a critical component of your keyword's Quality Score is your account structure, which makes this tool invaluable for you to use regularly, especially when you first start working in AdWords Editor.

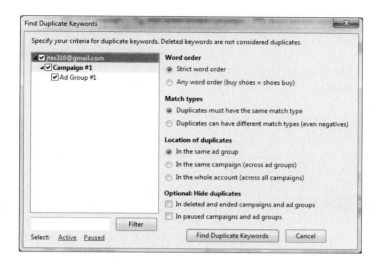

Figure 5-3: Finding keyword duplicates in AdWords Editor

There is also a beta version of the Opportunities tab from AdWords called Keyword Opportunities. Google can find related keywords based on your current account keywords or based on the content of your website. Another key component of a successful AdWords campaign is having a good fit between your ads, the keywords in your ad groups, and the content on the destination URL (landing page) of your ads. Keyword Opportunities can help by suggesting keywords that you may not have thought of to help increase your performance. Of course, neither Google nor I can guarantee that any suggested keyword will in itself automatically improve performance. You can check out the keyword opportunities report by clicking the Tools menu and selecting Keyword Opportunities from the drop-down menu.

Most of your time in AdWords Editor will be spent within the six tabs in the middle portion of the screen. Looking from right to left on your screen, each campaign, active or paused, will be listed here when you download recent changes. AdWords Editor won't download deleted campaigns — you'll have to go to the online interface and switch the status of deleted campaigns for AdWords Editor to be able to download them. Below the Campaigns tab you have options to add a campaign or to add or edit multiple campaigns. There's also a Revert Selected Changes button, which performs an undo for any highlighted element. The same holds true for the other five tabs. Within the Ads tab you are given four sub-tabs, one for each ad type (text, image, local business, and mobile).

At this time AdWords Editor cannot support video ads. Ad previews become available when you select any type of ad in the bottom panel of the program.

The Keywords tab is what I'll use to show you a few more screenshots that demonstrate work within AdWords Editor. Figure 5-4 shows some of the keywords from a few of the campaigns in my AdWords account. If I want to see keywords from only one or two campaigns, I select them from the left-hand navigation menu. Usually, as a default, all your active and paused campaigns will appear together in the six main tabs. Toward the bottom of Figure 5-4 you can see individual keyword details, including the keyword itself, match type, maximum cost per click, destination URL, status (normal, paused, or deleted), and an area for entering comments. Comments are available only in AdWords Editor — they are not available online.

At the very bottom of the screenshot you'll see additional tools at your disposal, including an Advanced Bid Changes tool and an Advanced URL Changes tool. These are like the search and replace functions in Microsoft Office or the Ctrl+F function in your browser. These two tools — especially the Advanced URL Changes tool — can be a total lifesaver if you need to make a sweeping change, for instance because a page was updated or a landing page's URL was changed. It's not as easy to change your URLs like this in the online version of AdWords, and it's not possible to change bid prices at the keyword level across ad groups and campaigns in one shot, so you should become familiar with those two tools.

When you click the Make Multiple Changes button under the row of tabs, you'll be able to add or edit multiple keywords or ads across campaigns. This is a go-to feature in AdWords, especially when collaboration or client approval is required. Normally you either download a desired campaign or ad group in a CSV file format from the File menu, or you start creating a new list of keywords, match types, bids, and destination URLs in Microsoft Excel. You can do all your work in this spreadsheet, show it to your colleague for input or quality control, show it to your business partner or client for approval, and then use the Make Multiple Changes feature to upload your bulk spreadsheet into AdWords Editor. You can also enter the campaign and ad-group names into your bulk spreadsheet.

Figure 5-5 is an image of a fake bulk list of keywords uploaded into the pop-up window that you'll see after clicking the aforementioned button. If you follow the onscreen instructions and create the required column headings, when you paste your work from your spreadsheet program into AdWords Editor, the fields should be tab-delimited (you'll see blank spaces between fields as in Figure 5-5). When you click the Next button below the pane shown in the figure, AdWords Editor will check your new or edited keywords for errors or inconsistencies. If there are none, you'll be good to go by pressing OK. If not, you can cancel and make adjustments as necessary.

If you enter a keyword that is already within your specified campaigns and ad groups, you'll be updating (editing) the corresponding current keyword, not creating a new keyword.

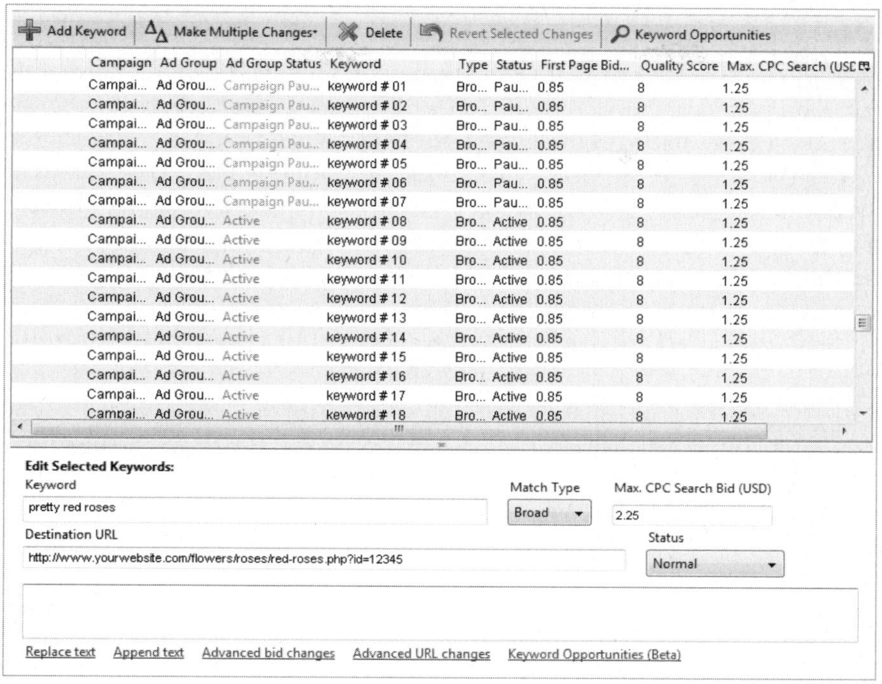

Figure 5-4: The Keywords tab in AdWords Editor

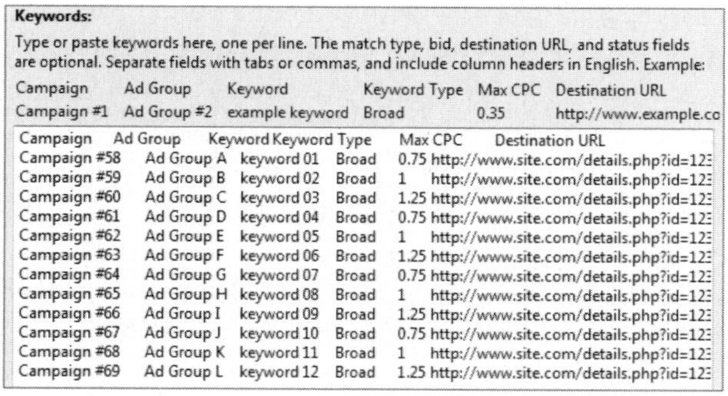

Figure 5-5: Pasting keywords from a bulk spreadsheet

Most of the other functions within AdWords Editor are extremely easy to use. They operate either as menu functions or as pop-up windows, or within the main AdWords Editor panel. As I mentioned in the beginning of the chapter, you'll want to be very familiar with the online interface before delving into the offline software tool. You'll find yourself picking up AdWords Editor in a matter of minutes if you know how the online AdWords interface works.

Posting Changes Live

Once you've completed your work for the day (or for any period), it's time to make your changes live within AdWords. Until you press the large Post Changes button at the very top of the program, all your new, edited, or deleted campaigns, ad groups, negatives, and keywords will be offline. You'll get a chance to review high-level informational statistics about the number of edits or changes you've made, but the best way to make sure AdWords will accept everything is to pay attention to the navigation and the main editing area. You'll notice as you edit items that a purple triangle image will appear next to anything you edit. This lets you know that you've edited something within that campaign, ad group, or keyword. It won't appear when you enter in a new campaign; it will only appear when you make edits to an existing campaign. You should also watch out for red and yellow warning signs that may pop up as you're working within AdWords Editor. If you see a line item with a red or yellow warning symbol, click it to find out what the error is (it will be listed in the bottom half of the main editing panel). Make sure that all the red and yellow warning signs are taken care of before you upload.

Once you hit the Post button, all your work will be uploaded and simultaneously made live in your actual account. It's never a bad idea to double-check that your work is indeed in the interface and set as you want it.

NOTE Just as in the online version, aspects of the offline AdWords Editor program may look slightly different from the images you see in this chapter. Google is constantly pushing out new updates for both the online and offline versions of its programs, so there may be features so new that I wasn't able to cover them here.

Google (DoubleClick) Ad Planner

Google Ad Planner, also known as *DoubleClick Ad Planner by Google*, allows any advertiser to create a robust media plan for sites on which he or she wishes to advertise. With Ad Planner you can define desired target audiences by demographic, language, interests, or geography; you can search for relevant websites that fit your target audience; and you can view detailed website statistics for millions of sites that are not available anywhere else online.

Google also offers Ad Planner for Publishers. If you're a site administrator or owner, you can keep your site information current and up to date, so that would-be advertisers have a higher chance of selecting your site, which in turn increases the possibility that you'll make money.

This innovative tool is available at www.google.com/adplanner. You can also find it by doing a search within AdWords or within the AdWords Help

Center. It's not attached directly to the AdWords interface, and you'll need to be logged in to your Google account in order to create a media plan. Your best bet is to open up a new tab and visit www.google.com/adplanner. Before you create a media plan, you can get a taste of what Ad Planner has in store for you right off its homepage.

Viewing a Site Listing

As you reach the Ad Planner homepage you'll be able to view any site's listing right off the bat, in the upper portion of the screen. Enter a URL for any site and click the arrow button or press the Enter key to view that site's profile. You don't have to log in to your Google account or create a media plan to do this. This site listing enables you to obtain some baseline statistics on any site you wish, and will give you a taste of what the media plan has in store. You can also use it to check out your own site, and view its listing as others will view it.

Figure 5-6 shows you the site profile for www.thedailyplate.com. Starting from the top and working our way down, a thumbnail, a category, and description text are available. If you look closely at Figure 5-6, you'll notice that this site does not have a description in Ad Planner — the site's owner will need to log in to his or her Google account, verify that this site is indeed the owner's, and add a description. A checkmark, indicating that the site is accepting advertising, is also shown.

Below the top part, site-level statistics are available, along with the estimated volume of daily unique visitors plotted on a chart. Statistics on the left-hand side are all estimates, and do not represent actual counts. They are displayed in millions or thousands, depending on the volume of traffic that the site receives. Counts of cookies, visitors, site reach, page views, total visits, average visits per visitor, and average time on site are all available.

If demographic data is available, it will be displayed below the Traffic Statistics area shown in the middle of Figure 5-6. (This particular website does not have demographic data, and this may be the case for most sites that you view in this site listing tool.) Toward the very bottom, you can begin to see the sites that visitors to The Daily Plate also visited, as well as the keywords that were searched for. The interesting metric to note in this area is *affinity*, which is an estimate of how likely a visitor is to visit a site and/or use a keyword that appears on this report. Let's use the example on the bottom of Figure 5-6 to elaborate. The second website (the last visible line on Figure 5-6) is Diet Facts (www.dietfacts.com), and it has an affinity score of 827.8x. This means that a user of the original site, The Daily Plate, is 827.8 times more likely to be found on Diet Facts. Clearly, Diet Facts is a site that The Daily Plate would want to advertise on, as its audience is incredibly likely to be on this site. Conversely, a Diet Facts visitor is also 827.8 times more likely to be found on The Daily Plate.

Keywords work similarly. The second keyword, *applebees nutrition*, has an affinity score of 1,419.8x. Google Ad Planner is suggesting that a user searching for *applebees nutrition* is 1,419.8 times more likely to visit The Daily Plate. It's a no-brainer — The Daily Plate should seriously consider using that keyword on a Content Network targeted campaign, because it provides a great chance to reach the target audience.

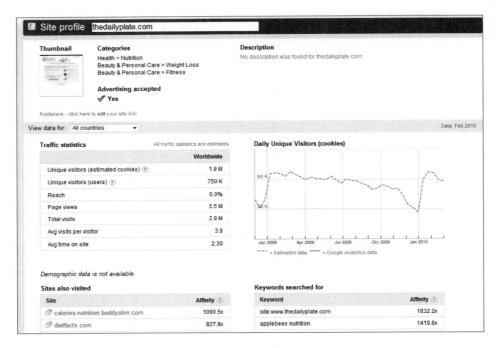

Figure 5-6: Viewing a site listing in Google Ad Planner

Creating a Media Plan

Start creating your media plan by signing in to your Google account from the Ad Planner homepage. You'll need to accept Ad Planner's program terms in order to continue. Check the appropriate checkboxes and hit Continue to begin creating your first media plan.

When you first arrive at the media-planning page, you'll instantly see two main tabs and two sub-tabs. The tabs at the very top of the page are labeled Research and Media Plan. On the Research tab you'll find a website to evaluate statistical data and demographic information; there you'll also be able to add a site to your media plan. The Media Plan tab will show you a full listing of all added sites, as well as some top-level information. Because you must create a media plan before you can add sites, let's go ahead and do that, starting from right to left.

Under the Media Plan tab you'll see a row of silver buttons at the end of the table, along with some command links. If this is your first time using Ad Planner, your tab should be completely blank. Click Create Media Plan to assign your new media plan a name, a country, and a brief description. Save it, and you'll see a screen matching the one in Figure 5-7. Two new sub-tabs will appear, labeled Details and Profile. Each placement and its category will appear within the Details sub-tab, and demographic data will appear under the Profile sub-tab.

Figure 5-7: A blank Media Plan tab in Google Ad Planner

Now it's time to add sites to your media plan. You can do this in one of three ways. You can add sites directly by using the text area and clicking the Add Placements button at the very bottom of Figure 5-7. You can enter as many website URLs as you want, and view the sites' details. On this Details tab you'll see each site's placement (URL), vertical (Category), daily unique visitors (UV), reach, page views, impressions per day, and, most importantly, ad specifications.

Check out Figure 5-8. I've manually added to my media plan placements on which I might want to run a Content Network campaign. I remembered these website URLs and entered them one by one in that bottom-left text area. Each site is listed on the left, and when you click any site's name you'll see its site profile (we'll do this in just a little bit). You can also visit the site directly by clicking that "double window" icon to the left of the site URL. The Category column to the right of the site URLs reveals to me what category each item falls under. Notice that the first URL — cars.com — is listed under Vehicle Shopping. Because I wanted sites that are travel-oriented, I can remove the cars.com placement from my media plan. Now look to the far right of Figure 5-8 and notice the Ad Specs column. This tells me what ad types, if any, each website supports. Any site on the Google Content Network can support text, image, video, and Flash/rich-media ads, and you may see those logos appear from left to right, as you can see for `www.priceline.com`. Because I want to be able to advertise on sites, I can also remove sites that don't accept any ads, like `www.southwest.com` and the bottom three sites.

Roll your mouse over any logo in the Ad Specs column to view the ad-format sizes that particular website accepts.

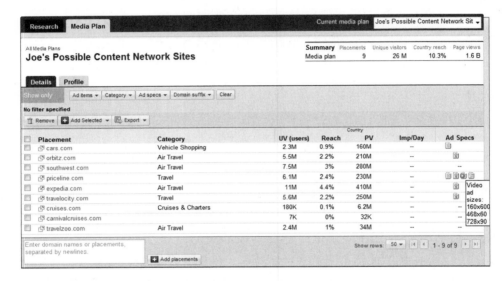

Figure 5-8: Adding sites (manually) to your media plan

The second way you can add sites to your media plan is by first doing some in-depth research by clicking the main Research tab at the very top left of Ad Planner. Here, by default, you should see `www.wikipedia.org` and a full page of analytical and demographic statistics. However, because `www.wikipedia.org` does not accept advertising on its website, it's no good to us at this time. We need to add sites to our media plan that we can possibly advertise on in the future. Therefore, I am going to change the site to `www.priceline.com`, because I already have it in my media plan and we already know from Figure 5-8 that it supports all ad-format types.

When you change your site to `www.priceline.com`, you'll be able to evaluate the site and make a more intelligent, more informed business decision, which should help you decide whether or not you'd like to advertise on the site. You can view graphs, demographic data, a unique-visitor (cookie) trending graph, and the ad-format types the site accepts, just as we talked about in the "Viewing a Site Listing" section a few pages ago.

In that section we didn't cover a few interesting pieces of data that can further help you in your decision-making process:

- **Sites also visited:** The top 10 other sites visited by www.priceline.com visitors listed and ranked by affinity score. For example, at the time of this writing, for www.priceline.com, a site named www.trip.com has an affinity score of 38.0x. This means that visitors visiting www.priceline.com are 38.0 times more likely to visit www.trip.com. This information equals opportunity for you. If the demographic information from www.priceline.com satisfies your target audience, you could also add www.trip.com to your media plan.

- **Keywords searched for:** The top 10 keywords that lead people to the website in question also appear ranked by affinity score. You might want to bid for high-affinity keywords in your Content Network campaigns in Google AdWords.

- **Top sub-domains:** The top sub-domains that the site owns will be listed, along with the number of monthly worldwide unique visitors (unduplicated visitors). You'll see each sub-domain's potential reach and possibly add them to your media plan as well.

The third possible way to search for sites with Ad Planner is by audience type. This is the second sub-tab within the Research main tab, where you'll find a great many options to choose from. Going across the top of the screen, right below the Search by Audience sub-tab you'll see an Audience row and a Filter row, where you can refine the listing of sites that appear. As you can see in Figure 5-9, in the Audience row you can filter the preselected sites by geography, language, demographics (gender, income, education, and age), online activity (which other sites visitors also visit), and something called *load audience*, whereby you load in sites based upon audience type (for example Auto Enthusiasts, Brides-to-be, or Affluent 100K +).

The Filter row allows you to further refine the contents of this Audience sub-tab by filtering according to ranking method, ad items (domains, sub-domains, placements), category (sports, entertainment, health), ad specifications, and domain suffix (.net, .edu, .org). The Ranking method button (when selected) provides you with three options: Comp (for Composition) Index, which displays smaller (lower-volume) sites geared toward your target audience; Best Match, which displays a balance between small and large websites; and Audience Reach, which displays larger but less-targeted sites for the widest possible reach. The default option is Audience Reach, and it takes into account your Filter and Audience row options to provide you with this list of sites and data.

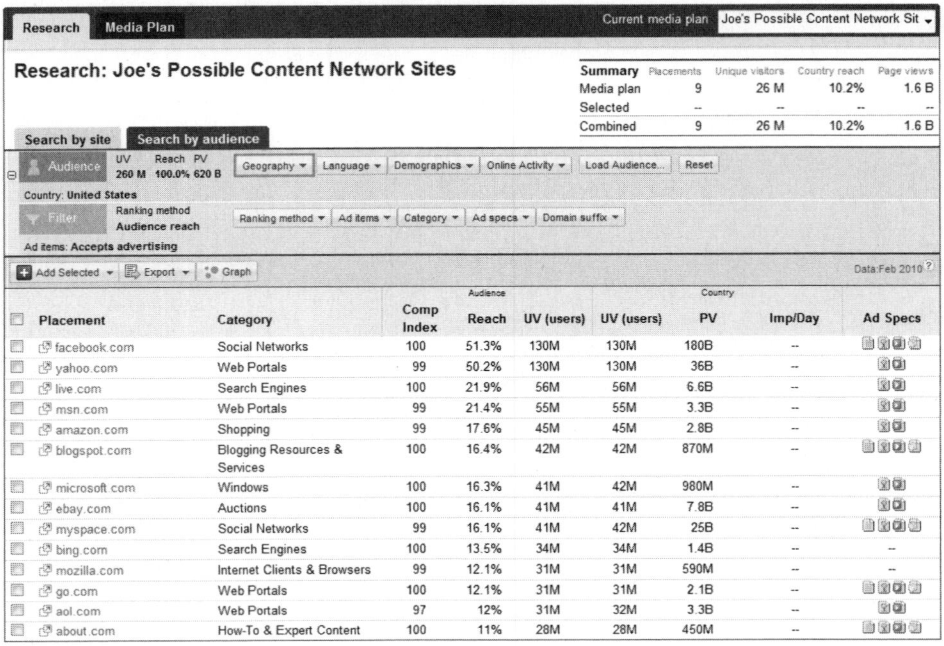

	Placement	Category	Comp Index	Audience Reach	UV (users)	Country UV (users)	PV	Imp/Day	Ad Specs
	facebook.com	Social Networks	100	51.3%	130M	130M	180B	--	
	yahoo.com	Web Portals	99	50.2%	130M	130M	36B	--	
	live.com	Search Engines	100	21.9%	56M	56M	6.6B	--	
	msn.com	Web Portals	99	21.4%	55M	55M	3.3B	--	
	amazon.com	Shopping	99	17.6%	45M	45M	2.8B	--	
	blogspot.com	Blogging Resources & Services	100	16.4%	42M	42M	870M	--	
	microsoft.com	Windows	100	16.3%	41M	42M	980M	--	
	ebay.com	Auctions	100	16.1%	41M	41M	7.8B	--	
	myspace.com	Social Networks	99	16.1%	41M	42M	25B	--	
	bing.com	Search Engines	100	13.5%	34M	34M	1.4B	--	--
	mozilla.com	Internet Clients & Browsers	99	12.1%	31M	31M	590M	--	--
	go.com	Web Portals	100	12.1%	31M	31M	2.1B	--	
	aol.com	Web Portals	97	12%	31M	32M	3.3B	--	
	about.com	How-To & Expert Content	100	11%	28M	28M	450M	--	

Figure 5-9: The Search by Audience sub-tab in Ad Planner

As you are refining this list, you can add any site to your media plan by clicking the checkbox next to the site's URL and clicking the Add Selected button at the very top. You can also export your selected sites into a CSV file (important if you wish to drop these sites into your manual placement targeted campaign in Google AdWords).

If it is helpful, graph these sites by clicking the Graph button. This will open a new pop-up window and show you an interactive bubble chart, which uses the same front-end technology as motion charts in Google Analytics, which I'll demonstrate in later chapters. You can customize the x and y axes (determining which metric each axis represents), the color, and the shape of the bubbles. If you scroll over any bubble you'll see the site's name and date. Mouse over any bubble to see its x-, y-, and z-axis data. Figure 5-10 shows an example of the Ad Planner graphing option.

Finally, click the Media Plan main tab again and click the Profile sub-tab. This contains aggregated demographic data for all selected sites in your media plan. You can view the gender distribution, age brackets, education levels, and household income figures in four horizontal bar graphs. You also get to see a summary of the number of placements selected and the reach of the selected sites, toward the top right of the screen.

Figure 5-11 shows what my Profile sub-tab looks like.

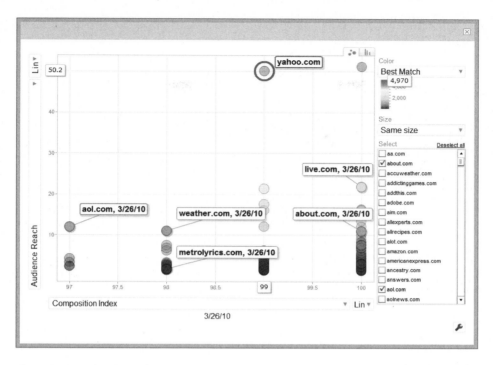

Figure 5-10: Graphing data in Ad Planner

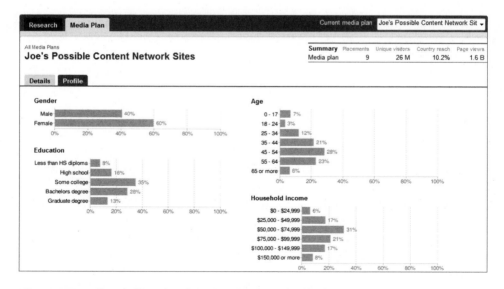

Figure 5-11: The Profile sub-tab within the main Media Plan tab

Google Ad Planner is a must if you plan on advertising in the Content Network. This type of information is not available within the AdWords interface or within AdWords Editor, so you'll need to visit the Ad Planner site to create your media plan and perform your research.

Ad Planner for Publishers

On the very top right-hand side of the Ad Planner interface is a Publishers link. This is where you'll want to go to verify your site and edit the content that appears for your site in Ad Planner.

Before you can do any editing, you'll need to first verify that you own the site in question. You can do this in one of two ways: you can log in to your Google Webmaster Tools account and upload a verification file, or, if you're a DoubleClick MediaVisor client, you can sign in to that account and select the sites you'll want to include in Ad Planner. For Webmaster Tools you'll need to have FTP (*file transfer protocol*, which gives you the ability to upload/download files from your host server) access and the ability to perform basic HTML edits. From within Google Webmaster Tools, you'll be able to click on a link to download your verification file, which is a simple text file that you upload to the root directory of your website. Google often checks for this verification file for search engine spiders, local business listings (Google Places), and other programs, including Ad Planner for publishers.

Once your site is verified and appears listed in the Ad Planner publisher center, you'll be able to edit its category and the ad formats that your site accepts, and to share your Google Analytics data. If you're an administrator of your Google Analytics account, you'll be able to share unique visitors (cookies), page views, total visits, average visits per visitor, and average time on site. This could be advantageous, as the more information you share, the better other advertisers can place their ads on your site. Contact the administrator of your Google Analytics account if it's someone other than you, and ask to be made an administrator in order to share these statistics with Ad Planner.

The AdWords Conversion Tracking Tool

I've been hitting you over the head with words like *insights* and *outcomes* and *analysis* for four and a half chapters now. It's about time I started talking about the AdWords Conversion Tracking tool. When you enable conversion tracking in your AdWords account, you'll activate performance-oriented metrics, which will enable you to make intelligent decisions about how to manage your AdWords campaigns, ad groups, ads, and keywords. You'll be able to assign numerical and financial values that will show you how wisely or frivolously your advertising dollars are being spent.

How Conversion Tracking Works

When a visitor clicks an AdWords ad from an account that has conversion tracking enabled, the visitor will reach the landing page of that particular ad. In the meantime a cookie will be placed on the visitor's computer, identifying the user as originating from an AdWords account with conversion tracking enabled. The campaign, ad group, ad, and keyword information, as well as a date/time stamp are also stored within this cookie. It has a shelf life of exactly 30 days (keep that in the back of your mind for now).

During that browser session, the visitor sees several pages and eventually reaches a key page of that website, such as a "thank you" page after filling out a form, or a "receipt" page after purchasing something from the online store. A snippet of JavaScript tracking code that's placed on this page will send data to Google AdWords, signaling a conversion. In no more than 24 hours this information will be credited back to the keyword that the user originally clicked, and you'll see a conversion appear for that keyword in the AdWords interface. AdWords will also calculate the conversion rate (the percentage of visitors who convert) and the cost per conversion (how much each individual conversion costs, on average), which are two critical metrics for any serious advertiser.

Now, let's say that, for example, a user enters the term *new balance sneakers* in AdWords, clicks an ad for the New Balance website, and does not reach the page on the site that has the AdWords conversion-tracking script. Then let's assume that the same visitor, 15 days later, comes back to Google and performs a search for *new balance running shoes*. She finds another paid search advertisement for New Balance's website, clicks it, and this time converts, purchasing running shoes from the New Balance website. Now, which keyword should receive the credit for the sale? In AdWords, which of the two keywords should receive the conversion statistic? If you said the keyword *new balance sneakers*, you'd be correct.

AdWords uses what is known as a *first-click attribution* model for measuring conversions. The first click's keyword, regardless of how many other clicks occur after it, will receive the conversion credit. Furthermore, Google will "backfill" this data when the conversion occurs. In the previous example there was a 15-day period between the first click and the second (last) click. This 15-day period may not necessarily happen within the same month; the first click could have happened March 25 and the second April 9. This is extremely important to remember if you run any type of monthly or weekly reporting out of AdWords.

One more quick quiz: A visitor searches for *structured settlement* and clicks a paid ad for a particular website. The same visitor comes back 45 days later and uses the same *structured settlement* search query, and clicks an organic listing in the regular search engine results. During this second visit, the visitor converts. Does the *structured settlement* keyword get credit for the conversion in AdWords? The answer this time is no.

The AdWords conversion cookie has a 30-day shelf life. After 30 days the cookie expires, which means AdWords cannot receive credit for that conversion. It would have received credit had that same visitor converted within 30 days, even though the user's second visit to the site was from an organic search engine result.

If a visitor has cookies disabled or is blocking JavaScript, Google cannot collect conversion data from that visitor.

NOTE In Chapter 14 I cover AdWords search funnels. This report shows the keyword paths that visitors take to reach a point of conversion on your site. If a visitor clicks three different ads within a 30-day period, using three different search queries, the Search Funnels report will show you which keyword directly led to a conversion, as well as what other keywords get partial credit for the conversion — called an *assist*. Flip to Chapter 14 to learn how this first-click attribution model can be enhanced, providing you with more intelligent data.

Creating and Installing Conversion Tracking

Log in to your AdWords account and click the main Reporting tab. You should see a drop-down menu appear below the tab. Find the Conversions link and click it. Once there, you'll see an empty table with three sub-tabs. You'll see some links to Google help files on the left-hand side (if you want to learn even more about conversion tracking), and a place for a navigation menu.

Find and click New Conversion from within the Conversions sub-tab to create a conversion action for your account. You can create multiple conversion actions if you have multiple conversion points on your website, but for now I'll just create one to show you how it's done.

Once the New Conversion button is clicked, you'll be asked to enter a name for your conversion and to select a conversion type. This is simply for information purposes, but can be used to organize this section of AdWords if you plan on creating multiple conversion actions. Choose the type of conversion that most closely matches your conversion, and click Save and Continue below. You can choose to select a purchase/sale, a sign-up, a lead, or a view of a key page. There is also an "other" option, in case you're not sure which tracking purpose type to select from.

You should now be redirected to the Code sub-tab, where you'll see some options for your conversion tracking snippet. You can select the page security type (HTTP or HTTPS), an optional revenue figure (to attach a numerical value that will be used to calculate your cost per conversion), the page language that the script will be placed in, the text format for a small notification that will appear to users after a conversion (you can choose here not to show it), and, finally, the color background for the aforementioned notification.

Once you've gone through the list of options, it's time to grab your conversion tracking script. Click Save and Get Code to do just that. Once you do, the JavaScript tracking code will appear. You can either copy/paste it in yourself or send it your web developer, who can insert it. The conversion-tracking script should be placed on the page where you want a conversion to be counted, and it should be placed anywhere within the `<body>` tag of the document.

From here you can click All Conversion Types, which is a link at the very top left of the page. You'll then see your freshly created action listed in the table, with the word *unverified* below the Tracking Status column. You'll need to wait until the tracking code is installed on your site, and for at least one conversion to be credited to this conversion action in order to see a *verified* status for your conversion action.

Conversion Tracking Data and Reporting

Fast-forwarding some weeks into the future, let's return to your AdWords account and click the Campaigns tab. As you've probably noticed in your account, you'll see four new columns on the far right of the main table, where your campaigns will be listed. They appear in Figure 5-12.

Conv. (1-per-click) ⑦	Cost / conv. (1-per-click) ⑦	Conv. rate (1-per-click) ⑦	View-through Conv. ⑦
5	$110.00	3.27%	0
3	$47.09	8.33%	0
1	$44.85	4.17%	0

Figure 5-12: Four conversion columns in standard AdWords reports

From left to right, the first column shows the total number of recorded conversions per campaign (or ad group, ad, or keyword, depending on where you are within AdWords). The second column shows the cost per conversion, on average, for each campaign. The lower the cost, the better your return on investment will be. The third column is the conversion rate. A higher conversion rate indicates a higher likelihood that the campaign, ad group, ad, or keyword will convert and be successful for you. The fourth column shows the number of view-through conversions. A view-through conversion occurs when a visitor views your display ad, but doesn't click it, when on a Content Network site. View-through conversions are available only for campaigns in the Content Network, excluding text ads.

If you click your Reporting tab and click on the Conversions link, you should see conversion data here at the aggregate account level. If you have any unverified tracking scripts, they will appear without any conversions, but the scripts that are verified will have statistics enabled for them. Figure 5-13 shows the Conversions sub-tab for the two conversion types within my account for one day. The "lead" conversion action is reporting, and it shows 16 conversions for this day.

The 16 conversions that you see in Figure 5-13 include what Google considers *many-per-click* conversions. Many-per-click conversions count the number of conversions that occur in a single click. More than one conversion per click can occur if a user converts twice (or more) by only clicking once on an AdWords ad. For example, someone clicks on an ad and converts on one place on the site (one conversion), but then finds another form or another key page of the site where conversion tracking is also installed, and the person converts again. That's two conversions for only one click; hence the name "many-per-click" conversions. Any time a conversion is made within the 30-day cookie shelf-life period, AdWords will add a many-per-click conversion to the overall count.

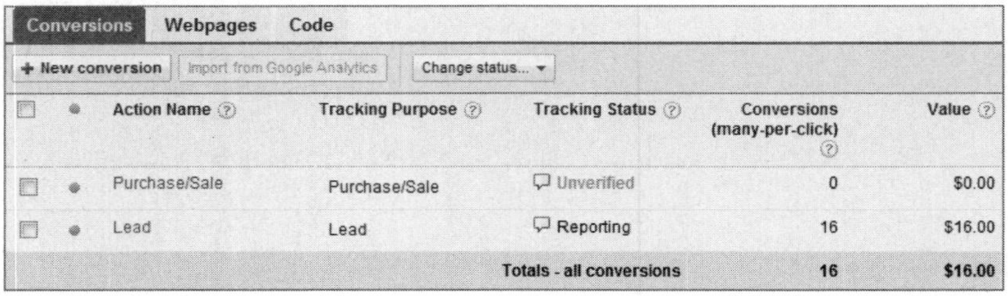

		Action Name ⑦	Tracking Purpose ⑦	Tracking Status ⑦	Conversions (many-per-click) ⑦	Value ⑦
	●	Purchase/Sale	Purchase/Sale	🗩 Unverified	0	$0.00
	●	Lead	Lead	🗩 Reporting	16	$16.00
				Totals - all conversions	16	$16.00

Conversions │ Webpages │ Code
+ New conversion │ Import from Google Analytics │ Change status... ▾

Figure 5-13: The Conversions sub-tab under the main Reporting tab

In Figure 5-12, a screenshot from within the standard AdWords Reporting tab, you see 1-per-click conversions. In Figure 5-13, a screenshot from the Conversions sub-tab within the main Reporting tab, you see many-per-click conversions, which incorporate the total conversions per click. Google keeps these metrics separate by default in order to avoid confusion. However, you can click the Columns button within the main Campaigns tab, as demonstrated in Chapter 2, and add the many-per-click conversion metric to your standard report table.

You can also run reports out of the regular reporting center that focus on conversions. When you create a report, select any report type, and when you get to the Advanced Settings portion of the page, make sure to select Add or Remove Columns, find the appropriate conversion checkboxes, and run your report.

I'll talk about how to evaluate and optimize your campaigns with a conversion-oriented focus in Chapter 6.

The Search-Based Keyword Tool

Almost always, advertisers will walk in the AdWords door with a list of keywords already in mind, on a piece of paper or in a Word document or Excel file. They feel that they have the pulse of their audience at their fingertips, and they believe that they know exactly which search terms their target audience is using to find what it's looking for. But how do they *really* know? If they haven't used tools like Ad Planner or the Search-Based Keyword tool from Google, they really don't know for sure.

The Search-Based Keyword tool from Google AdWords allows you to search for keywords by comparing them to your site's content. It specializes in highlighting keywords that are relevant to your campaigns, but that you are not currently bidding for. It will show you impression share, possible traffic volumes, and average bid prices for each keyword idea that it delivers to you.

The Search-Based Keyword tool is available at www.google.com/sktool. You can also search for it in the AdWords Help Center within your AdWords account.

Start by entering your website URL and words or phrases that are relevant to your marketing efforts. Your website URL should already appear within the Keyword Ideas tab, if you're signed in to your Google account. You can take a shortcut and see all top keywords across all categories by clicking a text link toward the bottom of the page; the Search-Based Keyword tool will find relevant unused keywords for your account.

You can also search for keywords on any site online. Take a look at what I've done in Figure 5-14. I've searched www.apple.com and entered a keyword of *iphone*, just to see what type of search results and data I can expect to see from the Search-Based Keyword tool. You can apply filters to your search by clicking More Filters at the top of the page. You can filter your search results by monthly search volume, competition, ad and search share, suggested bid price, and URL. You can also restrict your queries to seasonal periods (e.g., keywords like *holiday iphone*).

You can segment your search query by category type (on the right-hand side of the page) and by brand name, and you can edit your geo-location by clicking Edit in the upper-middle portion of the screen. A list of keyword ideas will be displayed in the middle of the page based on your search query and filter preferences. Monthly search volume, competition, suggested bid prices, and the page from which the keyword was extracted are all available.

You can collect any keyword that makes sense for you by checking it off and adding it to your Draft Keywords tab, giving you an easy layout for all selected keywords.

You'll notice in Figure 5-14 that the column sizes seem squished when you are looking at either the Keyword column or the Extracted from Webpage column. At the time of this writing these columns are not expandable, so your best bet is to export your keywords. Clicking the Export button will allow you to download a CSV file, where you'll be able to read the content within the columns more clearly. You'll probably want to do this anyway if you want to import your keywords into your AdWords campaigns after you're done working in the Search-Based Keyword tool.

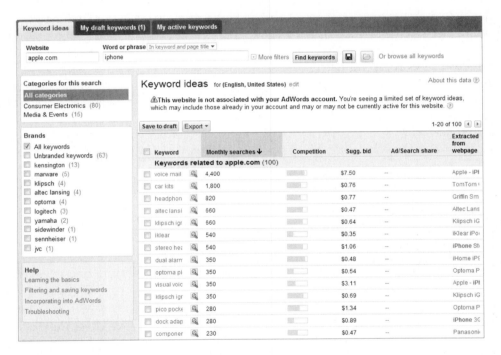

Figure 5-14: The Search-Based Keyword tool

If you are logged in to your Google account, you'll be able to use the third tab, My Active Keywords. This will show you the active keywords you have within AdWords, so that you can compare and contrast the keywords you select from the Search-Based Keyword tool with your current AdWords keywords.

You're an intelligent advertiser, and you know how to build up your AdWords account for a higher return on investment, so there's no reason not to use the Search-Based Keyword, too.

Other Available AdWords Tools

AdWords offers its advertisers a handful of useful tools, scattered across the online interface. These tools can be of great value and help to you along the way as you manage, refine, and optimize your AdWords campaigns. Let's take a look at the tools, what they mean, and where they're located.

My Change History Tool

Google understands that advertisers make a lot of changes over the course of weeks, months, and even years. Even for the best in the game, it's very difficult to keep up with every change, edit, and optimization technique that has been developed. It's tough to go back in time and remember what worked, what didn't work, and what was tried in the past.

With the My Change History tool, you don't need to worry about making a record of everything that you do. Each and every action you take within AdWords, down to the smallest bid change, is recorded and accessible. When you access this tool you'll see filter options, a chart, and a detailed listing of all the changes within your AdWords account since January 1, 2006. Figure 5-15 shows you what the My Change History tool looks like. The My Change History tool is available as the second link within the Reporting tab's drop-down menu.

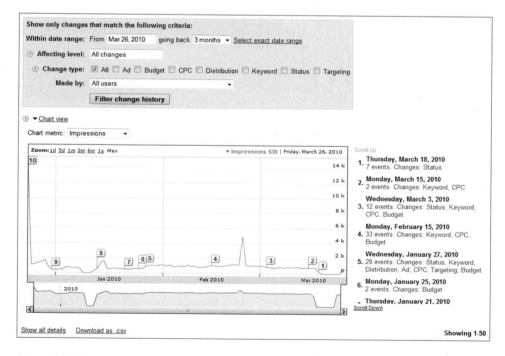

Figure 5-15: The My Change History tool

To summarize, here are some things you need to know about the My Change History tool:

- **Tool location:** Immediately above the trending graph within the main Campaigns tab, and available within any sub-tab.
- **Restrictions:** Data previous to January 1, 2006, is not available.
- **Options:** Exportable into a CSV file.
- **Availability:** All AdWords campaigns.

Ads Diagnostic Tool

If you're concerned that ads are not appearing for certain keyword queries, or if you want to perform a diagnostic test on your AdWords ads, you can use the Ads Diagnostic tool to help you resolve any possible issues with your ads, or to put your worries to rest.

With this tool you can diagnose either a select keyword or all keywords within any selected campaigns in your account. You can select your domain, display language, and user location, based on either IP address or geo-location. If this doesn't satisfy you, you can copy the URL that appears in your browser's address bar after you perform a search on Google, and paste it directly into the Ads Diagnostic tool. Clicking Continue will show you what's wrong with your ads, and the tool will recommend a way to fix it. Check out Figure 5-16 for a screenshot of the Ads Diagnostic tool.

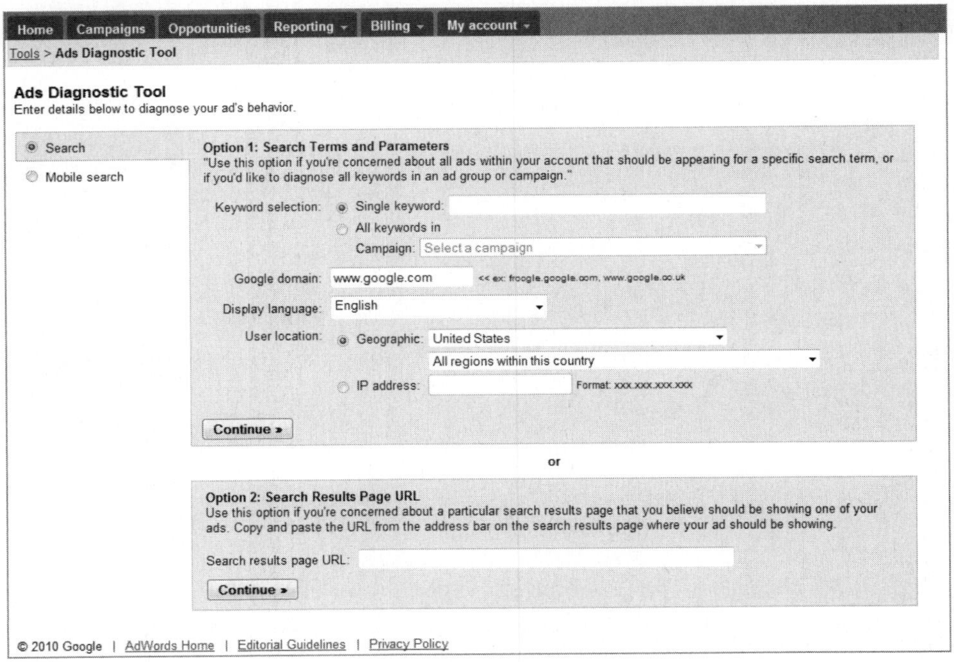

Figure 5-16: The Ads Diagnostic tool

- **Tool location:** Within the Tools section (search for *ads diagnostic tool* in the help section of AdWords)
- **Restrictions:** Available only for text ads on Google
- **Options:** Diagnostics via search terms or search results page URL
- **Availability:** Search and mobile campaigns

Ad Preview Tool

Nothing beats being able to preview your ads as they would appear online. However, doing so will cost you an impression each time you check Google to see how your ads look, which costs you money and pollutes your AdWords statistics.

With the Ad Preview tool at www.google.com/adpreview, you can view your AdWords ads as they would look on a Google search engine results page, without interfering with your impressions or budget. Enter a keyword that will bring up your AdWords ad, select the Google domain and language, and choose your geographical location. Click Preview Ads to show a Google search engine result in preview mode. Now you can see what your ad looks like — and see who else is coming up for that same search term! Look at Figure 5-17 for a screenshot of the Ad Preview tool.

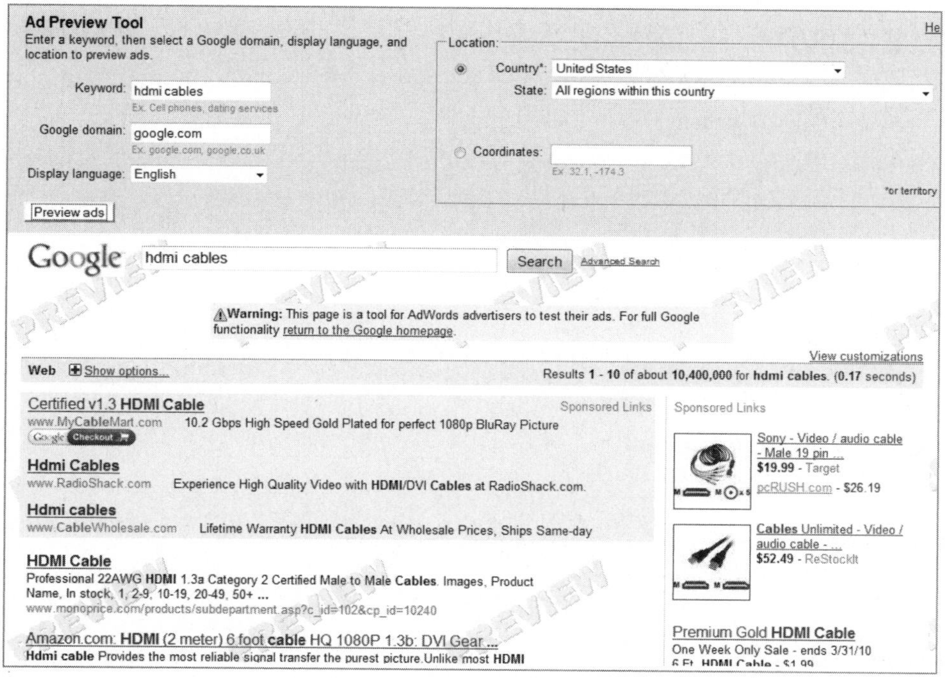

Figure 5-17: The Ad Preview tool

- **Tool location:** Within the Tools section (search for *ad preview tool* in the help section of AdWords).
- **Restrictions:** Available only on Google domains.
- **Options:** Select your keyword, domain, geo-location, and display language.
- **Availability:** All Google targeted campaigns.

Keyword Discovery Tool

You can (and should) use the Search-Based Keyword tool I talked about some pages ago, but if you want some quick and easy keywords to build your AdWords campaigns with, try the Keyword Discovery tool located within your AdWords account.

From within this tool, enter keywords or a website to base your search off of. You have advanced options, such as geo-location, language, and traffic estimation, as well as filters that will help narrow your search results to your possible future keywords. Toward the bottom of the tool you can sort your keyword search results by category, alphabetically, by volume, or by match type. If you find a keyword you like based on its statistics, you can click the checkbox next to that individual keyword to add it to your campaign directly. For each keyword a competitive analysis, monthly volume, and search trends are displayed. You can also sort the table by relevance and customize the columns, much as you can with AdWords.

Figure 5-18 shows an example of the Keyword Discovery tool being used for *brown sock*–type keywords.

- **Tool location:** Within the Add Keyword button in the Keywords sub-tab of the main Campaigns tab, and from within the Tools section (search for *keyword tool* in the help section of AdWords)
- **Restrictions:** Keyword-based data only (no image or video)
- **Options:** Adding your keyword, domain, geo-location, and match type, directly to your AdWords campaign
- **Availability:** Any keyword-targeted campaign

Traffic Estimator

Keyword tools like the Search-Based Keyword tool and the Keyword Discovery tool are awesome resources to help you become an equally awesome advertiser. Augment this level of greatness by using the Traffic Estimator tool before activating any keywords in your AdWords account.

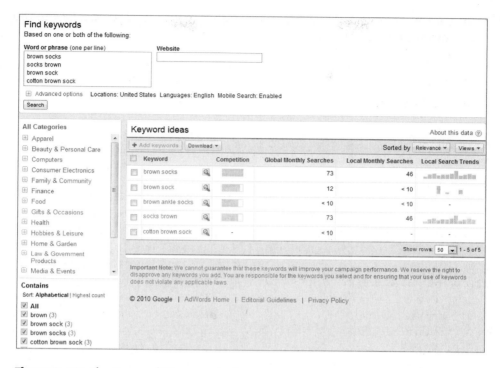

Figure 5-18: The Keyword Discovery tool

On the first Traffic Estimator page, enter keywords line by line. If you want traffic estimates on phrase or exact match too, use quotation marks or brackets to denote phrase or exact, respectively. Choose a currency and a maximum cost per click, enter a daily budget, and select your targeting options. When you hit Continue you'll be taken to the second page, which looks like Figure 5-19. You'll be able to judge each keyword's search volume, estimated average cost-per-click bid prices, estimated ad positions, and estimated daily clicks and costs. You can revise your estimates on the fly or download the keyword list as a CSV file (great for agencies with clients).

- **Tool location:** Within the Tools section (search for *traffic estimator* in the help section of AdWords)
- **Restrictions:** Keyword-based data only (no image or video). Figures raw estimates only
- **Options:** Estimating keyword traffic volumes and exporting into a CSV file
- **Availability:** Any keyword-targeted campaign

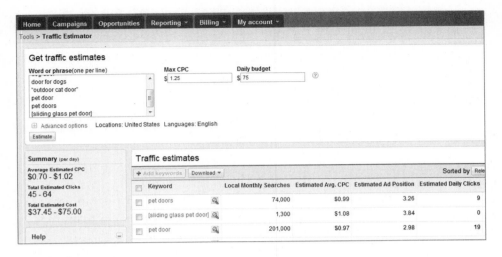

Figure 5-19: The Traffic Estimator tool

IP Address Exclusion Tool

Not everyone uses the Ad Preview tool that I discussed a little bit ago. Lots of people don't know of its existence, so they'll search for their own ads on Google and drive up the impression counts while lowering the click-through rates. This is especially troublesome for those working with people in different office locations or colleagues around the world.

With the IP Address Exclusion tool you can force AdWords to not show your ads to users from a certain IP address. If you know your IP address or the IP address(es) of your colleagues, find the IP Address Exclusion tool from the AdWords help section, and select your campaign. You're allowed to enter up to 20 IP addresses or IP ranges to block from each campaign. After you select your campaign, enter your IP addresses line by line, as shown in Figure 5-20, and click Exclude IP Addresses to apply the exclusions to your campaign.

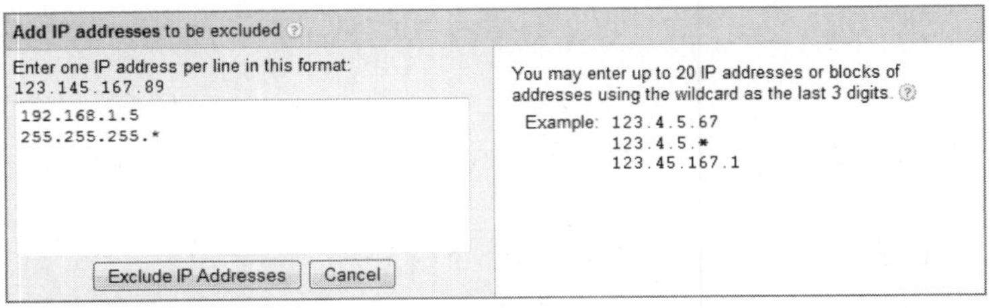

Figure 5-20: IP Address Exclusion tool

- **Tool location:** Within the Tools section (search for *ip address exclusion* in the help section of AdWords)

- **Restrictions:** Up to 20 IP addresses per individual campaign

- **Options:** Wildcards allowed for IP-address ranges

- **Availability:** Any AdWords campaign

Site and Category Exclusion Tool

As you know by now, when you're running automatic placements for your Content Network campaigns, it will show your ads to what it feels are the relevant websites. You can view what websites it runs your ads on, but you can't tell it what websites *not* to run your ads on (before you start your campaign). Until now, that is.

Find this tool from the help section within AdWords, and select the Content Network campaign for which you want site or category exclusions to be applied. Then choose to exclude individual sites, sites by topic or theme, media types (for video and Flash ads), and page types (error pages, parked domains, message boards). Save your changes at the bottom left of the screen, and don't forget to ensure that your date range is what you want it to be on the bottom right-hand side. Figure 5-21 shows an example.

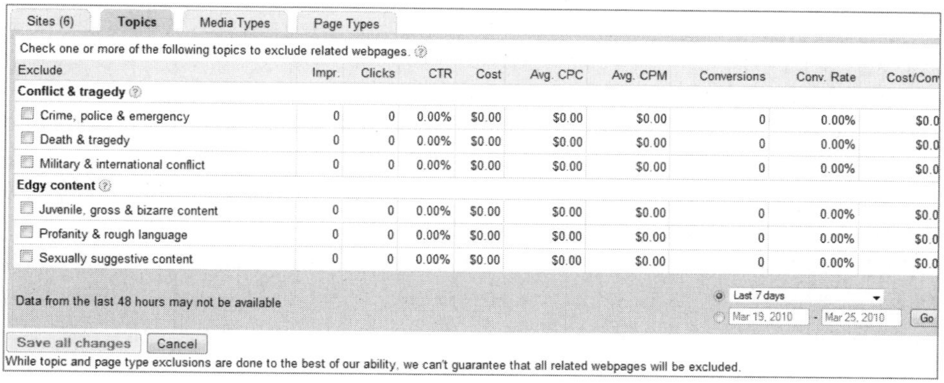

		Impr.	Clicks	CTR	Cost	Avg. CPC	Avg. CPM	Conversions	Conv. Rate	Cost/Con
Sites (6)	Topics	Media Types		Page Types						
Check one or more of the following topics to exclude related webpages.										
Exclude		Impr.	Clicks	CTR	Cost	Avg. CPC	Avg. CPM	Conversions	Conv. Rate	Cost/Con
Conflict & tragedy										
☐ Crime, police & emergency		0	0	0.00%	$0.00	$0.00	$0.00	0	0.00%	$0.0
☐ Death & tragedy		0	0	0.00%	$0.00	$0.00	$0.00	0	0.00%	$0.0
☐ Military & international conflict		0	0	0.00%	$0.00	$0.00	$0.00	0	0.00%	$0.0
Edgy content										
☐ Juvenile, gross & bizarre content		0	0	0.00%	$0.00	$0.00	$0.00	0	0.00%	$0.0
☐ Profanity & rough language		0	0	0.00%	$0.00	$0.00	$0.00	0	0.00%	$0.0
☐ Sexually suggestive content		0	0	0.00%	$0.00	$0.00	$0.00	0	0.00%	$0.0

Data from the last 48 hours may not be available

⦿ Last 7 days ▾
◯ Mar 19, 2010 – Mar 25, 2010   Go

Save all changes   Cancel

While topic and page type exclusions are done to the best of our ability, we can't guarantee that all related webpages will be excluded.

Figure 5-21: The Site and Category Exclusion tool

- **Tool location:** Within the Tools section (search for *site exclusion* in the help section of AdWords)

- **Restrictions:** Maximum of 5,000 sites per campaign

- **Options:** Site-, category-, and theme-based exclusions allowed

- **Availability:** Any Content Network campaign

There you have it — tools that will allow you to take your regular AdWords campaign and turn it into a great AdWords campaign. In addition, another "tool" that will put you far ahead of your competitors and please your customers is your ability to extract insights and take appropriate action continually. This is what really separates the winners from the losers, and if you want to be on the winning side I hope you'll continue to Chapter 6, which is all about insights.

Google AdWords: Analysis and Insights

How do you possibly tie everything together that you've learned in the first five chapters of *Your Google Game Plan for Success*? Well, in this final chapter of Part II, I'll come up with some hypothetical situations, possible solutions, and thoughts based on my years of expertise in this field. By no means will we be finished talking about extracting insights, taking action, and being successful online. However, since AdWords is where your money is spent and your visitors and conversions are gained, it's appropriate to dedicate a chapter to it at this point.

Measuring Success and Taking Actions

If that subhead sounds familiar to you, you've read Chapter 1 of this book, where I talk about what signals, metrics, and key performance indicators you use to measure effectiveness. It's the equivalent of the meaning of life, but in online terms. You can't possibly run a successful AdWords campaign without knowing how to measure success and, subsequently, how to take actions as you deem appropriate.

Notice that I wrote "as you deem appropriate." A lot of the self-proclaimed experts whom you'll see blogging or tweeting about what you should or shouldn't be doing are looking at things in general terms, which don't always apply to your specific situation. In their defense, they don't know what your online marketing goals are, what your boss's goals are, or what your boss's boss's goals are. So when they lay down their 10 commandments of expert pay-per-click marketing tactics or their five triple-platinum rules for success, always think about your goals first and decide whether their advice works for you. Keep an open mind, though, because sometimes there are a few "experts" who do know what they're talking about.

Back in Chapter 4 I showed you that you have three bidding options to choose from for each campaign. You can focus on impressions (which apply to content-network campaigns), you can focus on clicks, or you can focus on conversions (if you have conversion tracking enabled and have received a certain number of conversions within the last 30 days — the "certain number" is always different). These three foci make a good starting point for us as we're thinking about how to measure the success of your campaigns. You don't have to label yourself as "focusing on impressions," because chances are very high that you will want to focus also on clicks or conversions (or all three).

Focus on Impressions

You're running campaigns in the Content Network because you want a high number of impressions — eyeballs seeing your ads. You don't necessarily care whether visitors click your text, image, or video ads, as long as they're seeing them.

It's hardest to measure success when your primary goal is eyeballs, because you require very little effort from your potential audience. You don't care whether visitors click your ad, much less what they do on your site if they get there, and you can't even be sure that they're paying attention to your ad in the first place. Remember that an impression is counted when the page that the ad is on loads, not when a user mouses over the ad or scrolls down the page to where the ad is placed.

Does this mean that you should change your focus? No. Keep sending ads to as many eyeballs as possible, if that's one of your goals. However, you'll want to maximize the dollars you spend by applying advanced AdWords features like *frequency capping*, which limits the number of times a unique visitor can see your ad without clicking it. If you're using the CPM bidding model on your Content Network campaign, a safe bet is to set your cap at no more than 20 per unique visitor. If visitors are exposed to your ad more than 20 times and still haven't clicked it, chances are good that they're simply not interested, and there's no need to waste your money on uninterested eyeballs.

If you're using a standard cost-per-click (CPC) bidding model, try using the Site and Category Exclusion tool to remove manual placements that just aren't working out. This means placements on any Content Network sites with lower-than-average click-through rates (take the average click-through rate of all

Content Network sites, and remove the ones that don't cut the mustard). Keep in mind that a click-through rate should be evaluated in terms of its network — a one-tenth of 1 percent click-through rate is probably very bad for the Search Network, but for the Content Network it is probably very good. Excluding sites with low click-through rates allows your impressions to be directed to websites that seem more interested in your ad, as indicated by the volume of clicks they receive. That way you're not just showing your ads to as many eyeballs as possible; you're showing them to as many *interested* eyeballs as possible. The same rules apply if you also created a conversion action and are tracking conversion rates and cost-per-conversion figures.

Since there is no shortage of impressions on the Content Network, it won't hurt you to perform some searches on the sites you're advertising on to see what your ads are looking like on those sites. Google Content Network Partners, as I discussed in earlier chapters, have the freedom to modify your ads as they deem appropriate to fit their websites. This can be a scary thought, but I will say that little by little, the number of really bad practices has been declining. However, a change that a Content Network site owner made or the placement of your ads on a site may be reasons they aren't performing as well as they should. Or this particular website could be one that you're still trying to decide about. Just keep in mind that you are in control of which sites show your ads. If you're not comfortable with the way your ad looks or where it's positioned, exclude the site in AdWords or contact the site owner to see if he or she will listen to your request (but brace yourself for a rejection). There are plenty of fish in the Content Network sea and plenty of other Internet browsers out there — use tools like Ad Planner to see what other sites you can advertise on and what other sites users visit.

Text ads on the Content Network may only get you so far. Remember that 95 percent of Content Network websites accept image ads, and more and more Content Network sites are accepting video and rich-media ads. When you win a placement for an image, video, or rich-media ad, your ad is the only one shown in that partner's ad space; text ads, on the other hand, appear alongside those from other advertisers. So it may be to your benefit to create some image ads and possibly some video ads to gain even more impressions and really expose your ad to the masses. You can easily create image ads using the Display Builder tool within the Ads sub-tab within any AdWords campaign, so you don't need to break the bank to make an eye-catching image ad. But, just as with text ads, you'll want to cut image, video, or rich media ads with higher CPM prices, and keep the ads that work on the websites that get you maximum exposure and the best bang for your buck.

The Content Network isn't the only place within Google AdWords to accrue impressions: you can spread the word on the standard Search Network as well. You're not going to get anywhere near the volume of impressions you do on the

Content Network, but you'll reach an audience that is searching for a specific product or service directly. On the Content Network, visitors are going about their business visiting their favorite sites, shopping, doing research, or discovering new sites when they basically stumble across your ad. On the Search Network, they're expecting (and possibly demanding) ads, so this audience is prequalified because it wants to be engaged. All you have to do is enable the Search Network, and you're sure to have visitors reading your text ads more carefully than they would read an ad on the Content Network. They may even be able to spare a click, and who knows; they may wind up converting on your site!

On the Search Network, you'll want to pay attention to the volume of impressions on particular ads and keywords. Usually the more impressions you get, the more clicks you'll get, which forces you to raise your ad and keyword bids and decrease bids on other ads or keywords, or to remove ads or keywords that aren't generating impressions. This way you're able to make better use of your daily budget and spend less money on ads and keywords that don't get shown as much. If you really want to get the most bang for your impression buck, place your phone number on your ad, and possibly in the headline of your ad. Some searchers may just call you instead of clicking, which saves you a cost-per-click. However, be careful here, because this will also lower your cost-per-click rate, which may drop your keyword Quality Scores, thereby lowering the number of impressions you receive. Closely monitor calls you get from users who saw your phone number on Google search results, and try to maintain a balance.

To recap, when you focus on impressions, you'll want to do the following:

- Use **frequency capping** when bidding by cost per impression to limit the number of times unique people see your ad without clicking it.

- Add **site and category exclusions** to block unwanted Content Network sites from displaying your ads.

- Visit some sites that you're advertising on to see what your ads look like and where they're placed.

- Create a profile on **Ad Planner** to find new Content Network sites with high impression volumes.

- Make the **Display Builder** your friend, as you can create image ads easily and at no additional cost.

- Reach out to the standard Google Search Network for an even broader impression share.

Focus on Clicks

You're running campaigns across the search or Content Network, or both, and you want people to click your ads to visit your site. You have a special message, offer, or brand to promote to interested web surfers, and getting them to see or read the ad simply isn't enough.

When you focus on clicks, you're able to better measure performance and success compared to when you focus only on impressions. Metrics like cost per click and click-through rate, which I introduced in Chapters 2 and 3, allow you to quantify your efforts and stack them up against your bottom line. Metrics like Quality Score for keywords and ad position for ads allow a rich analysis of your campaign performances. In Chapter 7 you'll begin to see how you can take your analysis efforts even deeper when you see how traffic that comes to your website via an AdWords ad performs.

I have yet to meet an advertiser who did not want to be on the first position for any ad. Almost everyone wants to be number one, but most advertisers shouldn't try to be number one at all costs. As I noted in Chapter 3, it's far too easy to get yourself involved in a bidding war with a competitor (and there will be competitors, guaranteed), which can very quickly drive up your cost per click and eventually reach a point at which you're spending too much. When you consider raising your bids in hopes of leapfrogging over a competitor or inching closer to the number-one position for a keyword or ad, it's important that you practice a conservative approach. In other words, don't raise your bids just to beat out the next advertiser today when you can save your money for other ads, keywords, campaigns, and landing pages tomorrow. Focus on your AdWords account structure, your target audience, writing great ads, and sending users to content-rich, relevant landing pages, and your cost per click will start to come down.

Your landing page is just as important as the ads you write. When users see your ad, whether on the search or Content Network, they're going to read the headline and possibly the description lines before making a decision about whether or not to click. If they do click your ad, you've won only half the battle. You now need to prove to your new website visitors that your ad wasn't just telling them what they wanted to be told — your landing page must reflect or "sync with" your ad in order not only to keep visitors engaged with your site, but also to lower your cost-per-click price and raise your keyword's Quality Score. What you should do is perform some test searches using the Ad Preview tool (covered in Chapter 5) and then visit your ad's landing pages, putting yourself in the visitor's shoes. And as I wrote in earlier chapters, it's really simple: if your ad mentions "20% off," your landing page needs to clearly state "20% off." It's a very simple practice that gets overlooked so often.

Unlike when you focus your efforts on obtaining impressions, when you focus on clicks, volume shouldn't always be your priority. As with impressions, you may get uninterested clicks on your ad from visitors who are just browsing around without a specific intent in mind. You'll also get searchers on Google and other partners who perform searches that bring up your ads, but who won't give you that click. These will inflate the ratio of impressions to clicks, lowering your click-through rate. Low click-through rates are poisonous to Quality Score and cost-per-click bid prices, and when your Quality Scores start dropping, so does your ad exposure. You'll need to be sure that your location and language targeting are suited to the audience you're trying to reach, that your keyword match types and negative keywords help eliminate irrelevant traffic, and that you're using tools like the Search-Based Keyword tool to find new, relevant keywords that your visitors are searching for.

The Content Network may not be your best friend if your focus is on clicks. As I observed a few pages earlier, people who see ads on sites can be frustrated with them, can ignore them, or even if interested may be reluctant to click them. Any advertiser who ever ran a Content Network campaign will tell you stories of 0.02-percent click-through rates and hundreds of thousands of impressions across a vast network of sites. If your focus is on obtaining clicks, play the Content Network cautiously in order to avoid "wasting" thousands of impressions. Use demographic targeting options to refine the audience that may be relevant for your ads, and create separate bids for Content Network placements. Again, advertising on the Content Network really needs to be done with its own dedicated campaign(s), not lumped in with a search campaign. You wouldn't feed both your dog and your cat the same food, and you shouldn't run the same campaign on both the search and Content Networks.

To recap, focusing on clicks means that you should do the following:

- Focus on your **cost-per-click** and **click-through rate** metrics, using best-practice techniques discussed throughout this book to lower costs and raise click-through rates.

- Pay attention to your keyword's **Quality Score** so that you can work on lower-scored keywords and allocate more budget to higher-scored keywords.

- Avoid getting into bidding wars with competitors in an attempt to be in the number-one position at any cost.

- Use tools like **Ad Preview** to ensure that the message in your ads is the message on your website.

- Add more relevant keywords that your users are searching for with the **Search-Based Keyword tool**, while simultaneously pausing or removing keywords that don't bring in clicks.

- Watch the Content Network carefully, and remove irrelevant click possibilities with **demographic targeting**.

- Restructure your AdWords account so that Content Network efforts are in separate campaigns from Search Network efforts.

Focus on Conversions

You have a specific mindset when you focus on conversions. You have a product to sell, a service to offer, or a white paper to give out. You're asking an awful lot from your visitors, and with good reason — you have a business to run and you have customers to satisfy. You're not asking visitors only to view your ad and click it; you're also asking them to take the time to find your offer, add an item to their shopping carts, or contact you for more information. You're asking them to go through your website's system, submit their information, and eventually arrive at your receipt, confirmation, or thank-you page, where they can either download their document or receive a ticket number for the item they just purchased. That's an awful lot!

When visitors convert on your site, everyone wins. They get what they've been looking for and you get a lead or a new customer. You can measure performance, because you can calculate the total number of conversions, the cost per conversion, and the conversion rate for any campaign, ad group, ad, or keyword. Clearly, these metrics will become the center of attention, and they routinely are for the majority of advertisers. Some advertisers have specific cost-per-conversion figures already set in stone that the AdWords campaigns must meet. Website owners usually add the costs of doing business to their cost-per-acquisition (CPA) figures. If you have the AdWords conversion tracking script installed, and if your campaigns receive a certain number of conversions within 30 days, you may be eligible to use *CPA bidding*. AdWords will cut down on non-converting clicks and impressions and do the best it can to fall within your limits. Generally, the lower the CPA bid, the lower the chance Google will match, so be reasonable when entering a CPA bid price.

Performance measurement doesn't just happen at the aggregate level — it also happens at the ad and keyword levels. Each ad group should contain a few (three or four) active ads, with the goal being to see which ad performs the best. If you focus on conversions, you can add the conversion rate on top of the click-through rate to measure ad performance. The ad or ads that have higher conversion rates win, and the losers get either eliminated, or edited and put back in the rotation. You should use the optimize option under Ad Rotation within your campaign's settings to ensure that the best-performing ad gets served up more often to your visitors. This way, more impressions and clicks are faced with a well-performing ad, which should raise your conversion rates while lowering your minimum cost-per-click bid prices. Be careful, though — just because an ad or a keyword has a good click-through rate doesn't guarantee that it will have a high conversion rate. These metrics are not dependent on one another, so you'll have to make tough choices from time to time on ads with high click-through rates but low conversion rates. (In that scenario, the ad's landing page usually isn't as good as it could be.)

With respect to keywords, you'll find upon close analysis that your keyword's match type will change its conversion rate. More often than not, exact-matched keywords will have higher conversion rates than broad- or phrase-matched keywords. However, don't switch all your campaign's keywords to exact match just yet. AdWords has a fairly new tool called the Search Funnels report, in which keywords that help in the conversion processes are highlighted and credited with a conversion assist (you can read more about search funnels in Chapter 14). A lot of the keywords in this report will be broad-matched, and some will be phrase-matched, so in order to obtain conversions on your exact-matched keywords, you'll need to have the right broad- and phrase-matched keywords in your ad groups too.

There is a fairly new concept in AdWords called *remarketing*. To briefly recap, remarketing can persuade those visitors who haven't converted yet into making that decision, using some specific advertisements that you designate. These visitors will see ads that the general population won't, which ideally will change their minds and persuade them to convert. In AdWords, when conversion tracking is enabled, a 30-day cookie is dropped on a visitor's computer. If the visitor converts within that 30-day period, AdWords will credit the original keyword, ad, ad group, and campaign with the conversion. Remarketing in AdWords becomes a very powerful tool to help increase conversion rates, because many of your visitors won't convert on their first visits. It may take your visitors 2, 3, 10, or more visits to finally pull the trigger. When you remarket to visitors who have already seen your website, you remind them of your offer, keep your brand fresh in their mind, and can even modify your offer for customers who aren't sure yet. As I discussed in the previous chapter, remarketing does require a bit of setup on your end, but if your focus really is conversions and conversion rate, you'll gladly spend the time to reel lost customers back into the buying cycle.

At the end of the day, regardless of your focus, you must ask yourself if your efforts are worth it financially. Is the return on your investment worth the impressions, clicks, and conversions you receive? Intelligent marketers will never settle for a "yes" answer and will continually optimize, refine, and edit their campaigns to increase their ROI while cutting costs. This means working hard at writing great ad copy, organizing ad groups with tightly themed keywords, geo-targeting appropriately, and working on landing pages to reduce costs and raise keyword Quality Scores. All of this has an effect on ROI, and as you'll learn in later chapters, Google Analytics can show you the ROI for your AdWords campaigns at the campaign, ad-group, ad, and keyword levels. Generally, most advertisers start out wanting an ROI of higher than 300 percent (or a 3:1 ratio of dollars earned to dollars spent). Depending on several factors, one's desired ROI can actually be much higher than 300 percent.

To recap, when you focus on conversions, you should definitely do the following:

- Monitor your **conversion rates** and **cost-per-conversion** metrics, as these are crucial to your campaign's success.

- Use **cost-per-acquisition** bidding for a "hands-off," intelligent approach to managing your AdWords campaigns.

- Optimize your **ad rotation** by displaying the best-performing ads more often to your visitors.

- Convert at higher rates by allocating more money toward your best **exact-match** keywords, while leaving enough for other match-type keywords that appear in the **Search Funnels** report.

- Use the **remarketing** feature in AdWords to reach out to undecided visitors to attempt to reengage them and thereby raise your conversion rates.

- Calculate your **return on investment** and decide if the conversions from your keywords, ads, and campaigns are worth the money spent.

General Actions to Take

Regardless of your focus, there are some general actions that you will probably want to take if you haven't already. These are day-to-day actions, as well as some things we've already discussed in this book to further improve your AdWords campaigns.

First, log in to your campaigns and view the important metrics for your website landing pages at least three times a week, even if you are the most hands-off person in advertising history. Spend some time on your Home tab (Account Snapshot) to get a briefing on recent events, account alerts, and campaign performance across your account. Segment your campaigns within the Campaigns tab to find out more details on their performance, and whether or not they're meeting your goals. Run reports from the Report Center to get a detailed, downloadable file telling you what takes place across campaigns within your account. Don't let your account sit unattended for an extended period; even a few days can be considered *extended* by lots of advertiser standards.

In the same breath, I want to tell you not to make changes to your campaigns simply for the sake of making changes. A lot of advertisers fall into the trap of changing bids, adding keywords, or pausing ads simply because they feel that if they don't do anything, their AdWords will cease being good or a competitor will take their traffic. Online marketing doesn't work well when knee-jerk decision-making takes place. No one should rush through changes. My advice is to make changes reasonably, sensibly, and when you have enough data to justify them. Use the My History tool within the Settings sub-tab within any campaign to keep a running tab of all changes made, so you can replicate the changes that work well and forget about replicating the ones that don't.

Another great action to take is to click the Opportunities tab. Make this a once-a-week habit to discover what insights AdWords has to offer for your campaigns, ads, and keywords, and to take the recommended actions as necessary. Sometimes AdWords will want you to raise your daily budget, which may not be possible. Other times it will suggest relevant keywords and other information, as I mentioned in Chapter 2. You should also use tools like the standard Keyword Discovery tool to find new ways to expand your AdWords campaigns.

Growth in AdWords isn't limited to simply writing more ads and bidding on more keywords. As you learned in Chapters 2, 4, and 5, you can expand your AdWords reach by syncing your account with the Google Local Business Center to allow local information to appear on your ads. You can link your Google Merchant Center account with your AdWords account and allow product images to appear within search results, and use options like Sitelinks to show visitors additional information within your ads.

You'll also want to run the gamut of regular maintenance tasks, like checking your e-mail for important alerts and other information regarding your account. Depending on how large your account is and how active you are in managing your campaign(s), you may receive a lot of e-mails suggesting you take a certain action. Chances are that an ad may be disapproved or your campaign's end date may be approaching, or something to that effect. Use a tool like the Ads Diagnostic tool to ensure your ads are online and, if they aren't, to find out what you can do to get back up and running. And, obviously, keep track of everything that occurs within the My Billing tab to ensure that your campaigns stay online.

Finally, check out what your competitors are doing. In Chapter 17 I'll cover tools like Google Insights for Search and Google Trends that you can use to discover the rising search terms on Google, as well as the sites your visitors are visiting. You'll also want to perform searches on Google once in a while for keywords that you're bidding on (block your IP address with the IP Exclusion tool so that you don't waste impressions; visit `http://www.whatismyip.com` to find out what your IP address is). This way you can view how your competitors are advertising to the same audience as you. Do they have better offers than you? Do they write their ads better than you? Do they send their traffic to more relevant landing pages than you? You'll know the answers to those questions when you perform these searches, and you'll gain insight into how you can better leverage your visitors and persuade them to view, click, and convert on your website instead of a competitor's.

To recap, you'll want to take the following general actions:

- Log in to your AdWords account a bare minimum of three times a week, focusing on your **Account Snapshot** page for a high-level review of account activity.

- Avoid making useless changes just for the sake of making changes in your campaigns; make sound, logical changes when appropriate.

- Use the **Opportunities** tab to view Google's recommendations for next steps to take on your account, from budget to bids to keyword changes.

- Collect new keywords using the standard Keyword Discovery tool.

- Take your AdWords campaigns to the next level by inserting Sitelinks, Local Business information, and Product Extensions.

- Check your e-mail frequently for AdWords updates, and visit the **Ads Diagnostics** tool (covered in Chapter 5) to find out why ads may be offline.

- Search for your competition without accruing impressions by **excluding your IP address** within the AdWords interface.

Answers to Common Questions and Problems

The following few pages highlight common scenarios that play out regularly in offices and meetings, and within advertisers' minds. Knowing what to do and how to do anything in AdWords is great, but as with many things in life, timing is everything. Knowing when to take an action can make the difference between a higher and a lower click-through rate, a better and a worse conversion rate, and more and fewer happy customers.

When Should Ad/Keyword Bids Be Changed?

Let's pretend that the keyword *bunny slippers* consistently does fairly well. Over the last few months the ads within that keyword's ad group have averaged a position of 1.3, its click-through rate has been 9.5 percent and you're paying $0.25 on average per click. (You're bidding $0.50, but you hold the top position and the next-highest bidder isn't bidding anywhere near $0.50, so you pay only one cent above the next highest bid, which in this hypothetical scenario averages out to $0.25 per click.)

Because you're on top of your AdWords game, you routinely check to see what your competition is doing by performing an occasional search for *bunny slippers* on Google. This week, you see that you're no longer holding the top position! Some fly-by-night competitor has overtaken you and is now holding the top position. You refresh your screen and try searching again, only to see the new competitor still holding the top position. Oh, by the way, you're the online marketing manager for the client who pays the bills and sets the budget amounts for Bunny Slippers, Inc. The CEO of Bunny Slippers, Inc. is on the line and wants to talk to you because he performed a search on Google this morning, and his company was no longer number one. Now what?

First, don't panic. Yes, it's the easiest thing to say and not the easiest thing to do when you're put on the spot like that, but panicking is going to get you nowhere fast — and your client will sense it and become even more irritated that the precious ad isn't appearing in the number-one position. Second, calmly explain to the client that you are aware of the situation and would like to follow up with him or her within the hour so that you can collect some information and come up with a strategy. You'll want to look at your ad's click-through rates and average positions before doing anything.

Now, a client who calls you to vent about not being number one anymore probably isn't aware of (or doesn't care about) the full AdWords picture — Quality Scores, conversion rates, and all that. Maybe not right away, but sooner rather than later you will have to teach or re-teach your client that being number one for a particular keyword shouldn't be a goal — it should be the outcome of hard optimization work and tedious efforts on your part. You should then attempt to explain that your *bunny slippers* keyword is consistently earning a Quality Score of 10 out of 10, and that you pay very little for high-quality traffic to the Bunny Slippers website. You should also look to the right-hand side and see the very nice 5.25 percent conversion and $15.75 cost-per-conversion figures that this keyword is boasting. In addition, you have high-click-through-rated ads in rotation. Every other imaginable campaign setting checks out well. Your client, who ideally has relaxed a bit and is rational, will now perhaps hear you out and decide not to order you to raise your *bunny slippers* keyword bid to infinity because of the very nice profit margin and ROI figures that it brings in.

In AdWords, you cannot tell what another competitor is bidding on any given keyword. If this new competitor is bidding $2 per click, you'll have to go to $2.01 to try to reclaim the top position, which you won't know until several bid-change updates take place (remember that your bid price is only one of the many Quality Score factors). Then, the competitor would re-raise your bid and before long, your cost-per-click would skyrocket and so would your cost per conversion. Also, chances are that by avoiding this bidding-war type of scenario you'll eventually reclaim the top spot. In AdWords, the interloper can only temporarily claim the top position before Quality Scores kick in, knocking that competitor back to the lower position that it probably deserves. And, if you want to feel a little sadistic glee, reflect that it may have to pay more than you for a lower position. All this happens because you didn't change your keyword bid out of panic.

Change bids only when they don't damage your profit margins, or if it's early in your campaign's life (to build history and determine a profit margin). Change bids sensibly and avoid bidding wars (trust me, though; this is much easier said than done).

When to Add/Pause/Remove an Ad

Let's pretend that you have an ad group that isn't doing so well in your Search Network campaign, and after you've performed some preliminary analysis, everything points back to the ads as the problem. Your keywords, settings, bid prices, account structure, and landing pages are all good. Your ads, on the other hand, were written by the client herself. You see, she's a hands-on chief marketing officer with a specific message that she's trying to spread to her target audience. However, she's back in the office this week after attending the Search Marketing Extraordinaire conference in New York City, and she now wants you to raise click-through rates from 3.5 percent to 10 percent because conference keynote speaker Jane Doe said that only 10 percent click-through rates are worth it in paid search. Now what?

The worst thing that you can do is dismiss the advice the leader gave your client. This is the equivalent of saying, "You wasted your time at the conference," which is not necessarily true, because conferences are excellent for sharing knowledge with industry peers. However, at the same time, you'd be placing yourself in a most precarious position if you just said, "Okay" and went about the arduous task of nearly tripling your click-through rate within a week's time. (I almost forgot to mention that your client needs this to happen by Friday afternoon or the ad group gets turned off, which cuts into your management fee.)

The first thing you'll want to do is set some level of reasonable expectation. You've historically had a 3.5 percent click-through rate, which isn't the worst rate in the world for a text ad. But there's probably some room for growth. You can't just tell your client, "Excuse me, but I think your ads suck and are bringing down our efforts." What you can do is test different ads within that same ad group. Very quickly — probably by the end of the week — you'll be able to tell that the new ads that you wrote (because you're an excellent marketer who has the pulse of the target audience at your fingertips) are much better and enjoy a 7 percent click-through rate, which is also increasing conversions and slightly decreasing the average cost per click. Armed with this evidence, you can perhaps persuade your client that the new ads are better, and she will figure out that going with your ads equals more clicks and more conversions. The poorly written ads get removed from the ad group, and in their place you'll add one or two new ads to try to top your 7 percent click-through rate by the following week.

Test ads continually. Write new ads, remove underperforming ads, and repeat this process as long as you're advertising online.

When to Change Your Campaign Settings

John Doe is an older man who was extremely successful operating a scrap yard for 30 years. He inherited the family business that had been passed down for four generations. Now he's "gone green" and is investing in a sustainable energy company that recycles scrap metal into usable, Earth-friendly everyday items. He hired you to provide him with suggestions for what to do about his single AdWords campaign — but not before he edited the settings himself. Doe does business worldwide and wants people to fill out a request-for-quote form, which is linked from the landing page. Doe doesn't really know much about how online marketing works, but you do, and you're going to help him.

You could ask him to buy a copy of *Your Google Game Plan for Success* and read it cover to cover. But you surmise correctly that this is unlikely to happen. So your first step is to check out his settings (while wondering why his sole campaign is targeting only Florida and Georgia, when his business is international). He has the resources to write ads in multiple languages, which means your language-targeting options become broader. You'll also notice that the campaign is opted into Google only (not Google's Search Partners), and that there is no ad scheduling in place. You then click Bidding and realize that it's set to cost-per-acquisition pricing, with a seriously low CPA bid, which means that not a lot of clicks will be coming to this campaign. And the daily budget has been set ridiculously low, because the client thought this was the average cost-per-click bid price instead.

Still, after wondering why only one campaign was set up, you see that the internal structure of the campaign isn't half bad (the ad groups and keywords are structured well enough, and the Settings and Networks tabs check out), so you roll with it.

Your campaign settings are a reflection of your business goals or your client's. They should be edited to match.

When to Create New Campaigns

Today is your first day at Moving Faster than the Speed of Light, Inc. The company's owner is a thirtysomething with large ideas, grand plans, and every tech gadget imaginable sprawled across his desk. He's also got specific goals in mind: to reach every pair of eyes possible and gather millions of impressions monthly. Your job as the director of all things online is to pick up where your predecessor left off and see how you can manage the company AdWords account to achieve this monumental goal.

You log in for the first time and notice that Subset, a subdivision of your new firm, has the only active campaign in the account. It's running well but is not focused on the corporate goals and is running only in the Search Network. Your first instinct must be to activate the Content Network and start raking in the impressions, but you can't because you don't want to use these Subset keywords or its highly targeted ads.

The company owner, who is always looking over your shoulder, wants to see what you do because he knows a thing or two about AdWords and online marketing. To impress him, you install AdWords Editor and start creating new search and content campaigns that focus on branding the company. You use Ad Planner and placement-targeting options to choose and refine the sites on which you want your Content Network ads to be displayed, and you use the Search-Based and Keyword Discovery tools to find a way to reach out to your Search Network audience. Next, you blow his socks off by quickly creating ads in the Display Ad Builder tool, while globally targeting the most prominent placements. You then finish the job by uploading all your work from AdWords Editor in one shot while you lean back and sip your cappuccino.

Create new campaigns when jumping into a new network (content or search), or to organize tightly themed ad-group categories.

When to Reorganize Your Account

Because of the tough economic climate, you had no choice but to lay off your online marketing person, who was really a nice guy. You can't afford the time to find a replacement or the salary that a new person will demand, and since you have some free time on your hands, you decide that you'll take on the task. After all, how hard can it be to stare at a computer screen? The AdWords account has been run for so long that it has to be doing well already, right?

Not so fast. After 20 minutes of searching for the log-in and resetting your Google account password, you finally see an account caked with alerts, notifications, and disapproved-ad notices, as well as paused keywords by the pound. You find one (and only one) AdWords campaign with 38 ad groups. Each is exactly the same: one ad with a misspelled title, several hundred keywords each, and Quality Scores that could make you lose your lunch. The campaign is targeted globally, which is a shame because you can ship your products only to the United States and Canada. You also find that ad rotation, ad scheduling, and ad delivery options are the complete opposite of what you had originally asked for a long time ago. Then you notice that the campaign is opted into both the search and Content Networks, which is the reason you see click-through rates of 0.01 percent and cost-per-click bid prices several dollars high. No conversion tracking is enabled, no reports have ever been run, and the daily budget is virtually unlimited.

The only thing you can see that's right about this AdWords account is the fact that you're finally taking a personal look at it. But there's something else that's right about it — you have the ability to make as many changes as you need to in order to right the ship. No matter that you're knee-deep; you can always begin draining the swamp. You can start from scratch or slowly change things around so that they are what you want them to be. In this situation, using AdWords Editor is the best way for you to start fresh and get back on track.

You should reorganize your account when its structure does not match up with the best practices that I've discussed through the first six chapters of this book.

Now that you have a solid understanding of all things related to online marketing and Google AdWords, let's shift gears for Part III of this book and talk about Google Analytics. I'll cover the Google Analytics account and the web analytics industry as a whole, and also show you some advanced functionality available within Google Analytics that you'll find extremely useful. Get ready, because we'll really start cooking now!

Google Analytics

In This Part

Welcome to Google Analytics!

Part III of *Your Google Game Plan for Success* covers Google's web-analytics program, Google Analytics, which is a giant in its industry. The format for this part is one you're already familiar with. Just as in Part II, I'll start by walking you through the interface in this chapter (7), then talk about the industry philosophy and core essentials (8), and dive deep into the advanced features (9). In Part III there is an additional chapter of technical information (10), discussing things like tracking code, goals, Regular Expressions, profiles, and some Google Analytics "hacks."

I'll start by covering how to open a Google Analytics account and then talk about the functionality within the interface — in other words, the things that you can actually do, like segmenting and date-range comparisons. Then I'll cover each report section, starting with the overview dashboard and working my way in. As just mentioned, I'll save things like Advanced Segments and Intelligence for Chapter 9. If you purchased this book, or are standing in a bookstore reading it, because you need technical assistance, you may want to flip to Chapter 10 first before reading this chapter.

NOTE As with Google AdWords, you are required to create a Google account to log in to any of the Google family of products. If you created a Google account in Chapter 2, you can use that same e-mail address and password to open up a Google Analytics account. To avoid repetition of the initial steps, you should revisit Chapter 2 if you still need to open up a Google account.

The Google Analytics Account

Once you have your Google account, you'll want to visit www.google.com/ analytics. Bookmark this page for easier access in the future. From the Google Analytics homepage you can select your language (Google Analytics is currently offered in over 30 languages), search the website, and access your Analytics account (there is a big blue call to action on the upper right-hand side directing you to log in). You can also subscribe to the Google Analytics Blog (I highly recommend it), view product information, and, if you're in the market for it, look up and contact a Google Analytics Authorized Consultant (GAAC) in your area. As you know from reading the introduction, at the time of this writing I work for a GAAC and highly recommend the services of one if you're ready to take your analytics to the next level.

You'll also notice a Sign Up Now text link underneath the main call to action on the right-hand side of the page, as shown in Figure 7-1. If you're not logged in to your Google account, you'll be prompted to log in before continuing. Once logged in you'll be taken to a sign-up screen where you'll click a silver Sign Up button to begin creating your Google Analytics account.

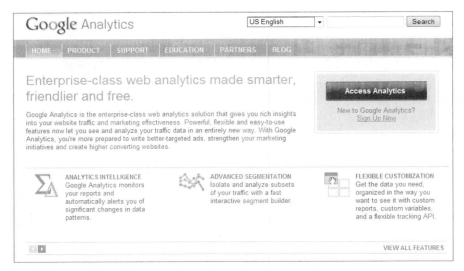

Figure 7-1: The Google Analytics homepage

You'll notice on this sign-up screen that Google Analytics has a five-million-page view cap per month for non-AdWords advertisers. Unless you are the owner of a very high-volume website, you probably don't have to worry about this limit. If you do think (or know for a fact) that your website generates around five million page views monthly (or more), check out Chapter 14, where I discuss syncing an AdWords account with a Google Analytics account. Remember that you'll need to first sign up for a Google account before opening an Analytics account, as I outlined at the beginning of Chapter 2. You can't have access to or create an Analytics account without first having a Google account (any e-mail address can be a Google account — it's not limited to Gmail accounts).

After the sign-up page, you'll be asked to provide general information about your new account, such as the URL of the website you wish to track, an account name, and your country or time zone. (If you don't have an account name, Google Analytics will use the URL that you inserted as the account name.) Figure 7-2 shows this general information screen. Click Continue after filling out this information.

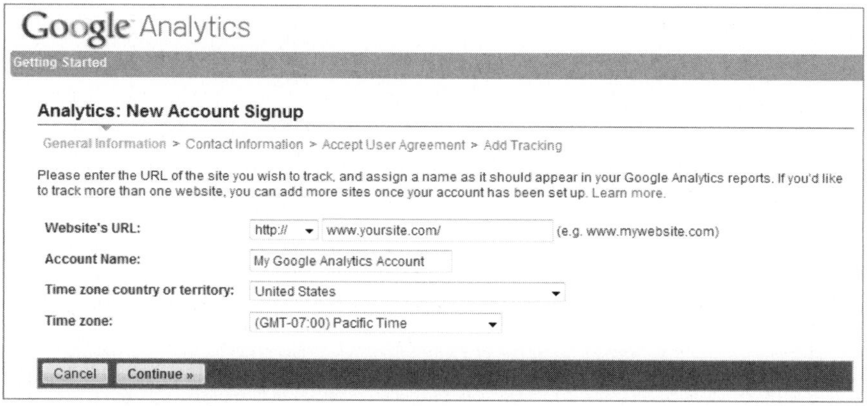

Figure 7-2: Entering general account information

On the next screen that appears, you can enter your first and last names if you want, but it's not required. Then, select the country/territory where you're located. The next screen displays the user agreement, which you should read carefully and understand fully.

There are two parts to this user-agreement screen. First, you'll be able to read the Google Analytics Terms of Service, which are available after the account-creation process toward the bottom of any screen within Google Analytics. You'll need to click Yes . . . Accept before being allowed to create a Google Analytics account. The second part contains your Data Sharing settings. Google Analytics can anonymously aggregate your website's data and share it with other Google products only, such as Google's Conversion Optimizer; you can also choose to anonymously share data with Google products and others, including the Industry Benchmarking section that we'll cover later in this chapter. You may also choose not to share your data with Google Analytics at all by clicking the appropriate radio button, shown in Figure 7-3.

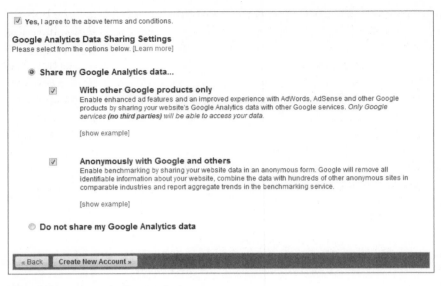

Figure 7-3: Data-sharing settings

To give you a high-level overview of what this all means, sharing your data anonymously with Google products and others allows you access to top-level, aggregated, and anonymous data, like visits, page views, and bounce rate. Think of such sharing as a form of reverse poker — you can see everyone else's cards on the table, but you can't see how the dealer shuffles the cards or deals them. Only here, the players (websites) are also anonymous. You can't look at the Industry Benchmarking section and view your competitors' data by name, and they can't look at yours.

It's good to check with your legal adviser or department before deciding to share your data. If you don't have such a department, check with your superior or major stakeholder. In certain circumstances data sharing may not be allowed. Keep in mind that you can change your data-sharing settings at any time after you open your Google Analytics account.

Once you have reviewed everything, it's time to create your new account. Click the appropriate button, shown on the bottom of Figure 7-3. You'll find some analytics-tracking instructions for your website on the next screen. Google Analytics works by collecting visitor data via a JavaScript snippet of code that will need to be installed on every page of your website.

If you're the person installing the code, take a moment to review the options that you see in Figure 7-4. This Tracking Code Wizard will help you gather the pieces of JavaScript code that you'll need for your specific situation. Or, if someone else will be installing the tracking code, you have the option toward the bottom of this screen of e-mailing the instructions to that person. You may also have the opportunity to learn more details on the bottom right of the page. Don't be overly concerned at this point — you don't have to install the Google Analytics tracking code right now. You can always retrieve your code within any profile's settings page. We'll cover the technical inner workings of Google Analytics in later chapters.

Figure 7-4: The Google Analytics Tracking Code Wizard

Finally, click Save and Finish to complete the Google Analytics account-creation process! Keep in mind that data for your website won't begin to be collected until you install the tracking code on your site's pages. When your account-creation duties are complete, you'll see a screen like the one in Figure 7-5, with your newly created account and profile and (for now) zeroes going across the board.

For now, we're done setting things up and we'll talk about technical matters in Chapter 10. I'll ask you to pretend to jump about a month or so into the future, at which point your tracking code has been installed on your website and your Google Analytics account is successfully collecting data. This is where we'll begin the next section of this chapter.

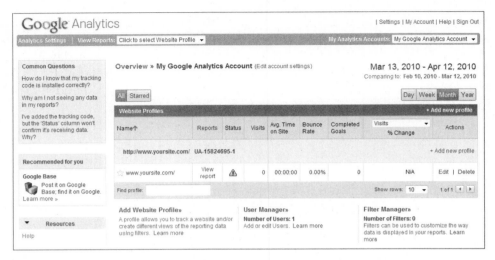

Figure 7-5: Your Google Analytics account immediately after being opened

Basic Functions within Google Analytics

Before you start exploring the interface, you'll need to know the essential functions within Google Analytics, just as we reviewed the essential functions within AdWords in Chapter 2. You'll use such functions as trending graph customizations and segmenting virtually every time you log in to Google Analytics. The first thing that you may notice when you log in is the date-range selection area, located toward the upper right-hand side of any report. We'll start there.

Date-Range Tool and Comparing Date Ranges

By default, Google Analytics displays data to you from the previous 30 days. It does not include the current day, and Google Analytics will not save your date-range selection if you log out and log back in. Anytime I introduce a new person, client, or group to Google Analytics, one of the first things I start talking about is the date-range tool. You should make it a habit to check this each time you log in to Google Analytics, and periodically as you're doing things within the interface. Believe me, this will save you lots of head-scratching.

Figure 7-6 shows what happens when you click that rectangular date-range tool on the upper right-hand side of your screen. You'll notice a standard Roman calendar as the default view, but you can click the Timeline mini-tab to view your calendar in a trending graph view (like the ones on Google Finance). From here, you can also select an individual day to view data for just that one day.

You can also select a full week by clicking the vertical tab next to it, or you can view monthly Google Analytics data by clicking the name of the desired month. You can also select a custom date range by selecting the first day in the date range (click your desired individual day) and then the last day. If you'd just rather type it in manually, you can do that toward the right-hand side of the date-range tool.

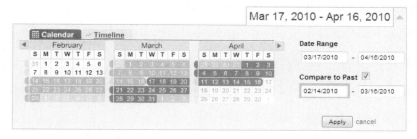

Figure 7-6: The date-range tool in Google Analytics

Comparing two date ranges, as in Figure 7-6, will become very important to you. Choose your starting date range and then click the Compare to Past checkbox. The immediately previous date range of the same size will be selected and highlighted in green. You may also perform a date-range comparison manually by typing in the date ranges on the right-hand side — as long as both ranges are the same size (that is, the same number of days).

The date-range tool is available in all Google Analytics reports. As you'll learn in the next few chapters, performing date-range comparisons is the cornerstone of comparative web analytics.

Trending Graph Customization

Most Google Analytics reports offer a visual aid that accompanies the data, called a *trending graph*. It plots the data on an (x/y) axis, with the individual hour, day, week, or month on the x-axis (going horizontally) and the selected metric on the y-axis (going vertically).

When you move your mouse over any data point, you will be able to see the volume for the selected metric for the selected hour, day, week, or month. If, for example, you're on the dashboard, rolling your mouse over any data point will show you all visits to your site for that particular day. But with the trending graph, you have two types of customizable areas for your convenience.

The first type of customization possibility with the trending graph is changing the metric you wish to view, and changing the *graph mode*. By default, Google Analytics will plot one metric on the trending graph, but you can click the small drop-down menu arrow on the top left of the trending graph to view your options. You will have more, fewer, or different options depending on where you are in the interface. If desired, you can compare two metrics on the same graph, or compare your metrics to the site averages (which options don't add a lot of value on the dashboard but may in other sections). As I've done on Figure 7-7, you can do such things as compare the visits metric to the bounce-rate metric. Rolling over any data point will now show both metric values.

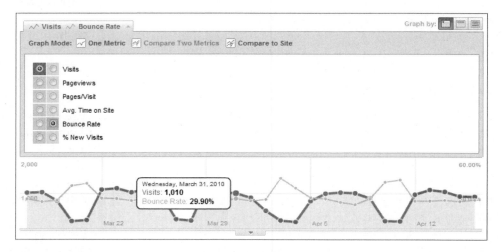

Figure 7-7: Comparing two metrics on the trending graph

The other type of customization possibility is the Graph By options that you see at the top right of Figure 7-7. By default, you'll see data plotted by day, but by clicking the other icons on the top right, you can view data by week or by month. Some reports, like the individual metric reports in the Visitors section, allow you to plot your data by the hour.

The trending graph is available in almost every report in Google Analytics. Some reports do not come equipped with a trending graph, and I'll explain why as we move along in this chapter. I'm saving another feature of the trending graph, called Annotations, for Chapter 9.

Adding Reports to the Dashboard

The dashboard is like your Analytics account "homepage." When you log in to Google Analytics and select a profile from the Overview screen, you'll always see this report first. You're provided with five default dashboard reports to start with, and if you enable e-commerce tracking (which I'll show you how to do), you'll start with six reports.

As we move along here in Chapter 7, you'll see that you can get very specific with your individual report views. You can click tabs, show more or fewer rows, view different table displays, sort by column headings, drill down into individual line items, and segment and even pivot your data by other metrics. Google Analytics provides a way to save your favorite or most useful reports, along with the viewing options that you've created on the fly, with a silver Add to Dashboard button toward the top of almost every report. You'll see it next to the Export and E-mail buttons. Once your report is saved, you can safely log out and then log back in, accessing your report exactly as you saved it.

You can add as many reports to the dashboard as you wish. In Chapter 8 we'll talk about dashboards and how to make a useful one.

Exporting Reports

Google strongly believes that you (the website owner) are in charge of your data. It's up to you, not a vendor, to decide what you want to do with your data. Therefore, each report is equipped with an export feature that allows you to download a file of your selected report. When you do this on the dashboard, you'll be downloading the dashboard summary as well as each individual report that's been saved to the dashboard. For every other report within Google Analytics, you'll simply get that report.

Reports are available in PDF, XML, CSV, CSV for Excel, and TSV file formats. The PDF format is the only format that represents your data with images — it's virtually a screenshot. The other four file formats download your data so that you can perform operations, create formulas, or integrate the data with your own database or data storage. Reports take virtually no time at all to download and there is no limit to the number of reports that you can download.

E-mailing Reports

If you're following along on your own Google Analytics account while you're reading, you may have noticed an E-mail button right next to the Export feature that I was just talking about. At any time, you can e-mail a report to a colleague, friend, or team member by simply clicking on this button. When you do, you'll be taken to a Set Up E-mail screen like the one in Figure 7-8.

From here, you'll notice three tabs: Send Now, which allows you to send your report immediately (it will be in your recipient's inbox literally a second after you hit Send); Schedule, where you can schedule your report for delivery daily, weekly, monthly, or quarterly; and Add to Existing, which enables you to add multiple reports, one at a time, to a scheduled e-mail.

On the Send Now screen, enter the e-mail addresses of the recipients you'd like your report sent to. Separate each e-mail address from the next with a comma and a space after the comma. You can have a copy of the report sent to you via the checkbox that you'll see under the entered e-mails. Below that, enter a subject line and a brief description of your report. Next choose your format (from the five file-download options that are available); when you're finished, enter the word that appears on the screen for verification. Hit Send, and instantaneously your report will appear in your inbox (you'll need to hit Send/Receive if you're using the standard version of Outlook, for example).

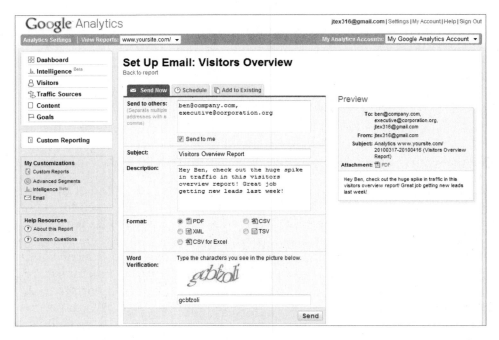

Figure 7-8: The Set Up E-mail screen

The Schedule e-mail screen is almost identical to the Send Now screen, with the only difference being that you're given the option to schedule your report delivery. The options are daily, weekly (sent each Monday), monthly (sent the first of each month), and quarterly (sent the first day of each quarter).

The Add to Existing screen simply shows you any reports that you've already scheduled for delivery. You can add reports to existing reports, rolling them up into one scheduled e-mail.

Any report within Google Analytics is available to be e-mailed, or scheduled for delivery with one of the four scheduling options. Figure 7-9 shows how an e-mail will look in your inbox (if you have Gmail).

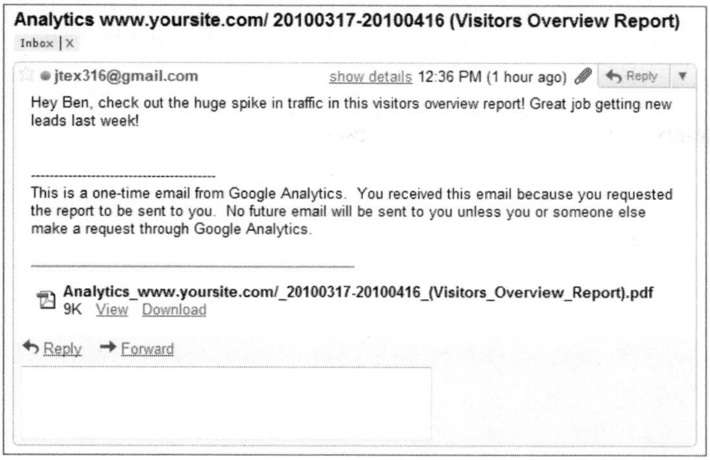

Analytics www.yoursite.com/ 20100317-20100416 (Visitors Overview Report)

Inbox | X

● jtex316@gmail.com   show details 12:36 PM (1 hour ago) 📎 ↩ Reply ▼

Hey Ben, check out the huge spike in traffic in this visitors overview report! Great job getting new leads last week!

This is a one-time email from Google Analytics. You received this email because you requested the report to be sent to you. No future email will be sent to you unless you or someone else make a request through Google Analytics.

📄 Analytics_www.yoursite.com/_20100317-20100416_(Visitors_Overview_Report).pdf
     9K View Download

↩ Reply   → Forward

Figure 7-9: An e-mailed report in your Gmail inbox

Dimensions (Segmenting)

Along with making date-range comparisons, segmenting is one of the most important techniques in all of web analytics. Each web-analytics vendor makes sure that its customers can perform segmentation to learn about their visitors at a deeper, more refined level. Within each table report in Google Analytics you'll find a drop-down menu directly beneath the scorecard (the row of metrics in a bigger font underneath the table's tabs). This drop-down menu lets you change the original segment that the report shows, and in most reports there are 23 different segments to select from (some reports, like the AdWords section, have more). You will need to get to know these segment names, as you'll see them throughout Google Analytics. They are:

- **Source:** The name of the source of traffic (Google, Yahoo! etc.)
- **Medium:** The means by which a user accessed your site (cost-per-click, cost-per-thousand-impressions, e-mail, etc.)
- **Campaign:** The name of the campaign (usually for cost-per-click advertising campaigns)
- **Keyword:** The keyword that a user searched for in a search engine, or the keyword being bid on in a cost-per-click campaign
- **Ad content:** The headline of the ad used in a cost-per-click campaign
- **Visitor type:** The visitor's type (either new or returning)
- **Landing page:** The entry (first) page in a visitor's visit

- **Language:** The language preference on a visitor's browser
- **Continent:** The visitor's continent
- **Sub-continent region:** The visitor's sub-continent (e.g., Central America, Western Europe, etc.)
- **Country/territory:** The country or territory of a visitor
- **Region:** The region or state of a visitor
- **City:** The visitor's city
- **Browser:** The visitor's browser (Internet Explorer, Firefox, etc.)
- **Operating system:** The visitor's computer's operating system (Windows 7, Windows XP, Mac OS X, etc.)
- **Screen colors:** The visitor's screen colors (16-bit, 32-bit, etc.)
- **Screen resolution:** The visitor's screen resolution (1024×768, 800×600, etc.)
- **Flash version:** The visitor's version of Adobe Flash (10.x, 9.x, etc.)
- **Java support:** Whether or not the visitor's browser supports Java (meaning not JavaScript, but Java from Sun Microsystems)
- **Service provider:** The visitor's Internet service provider (ISP)
- **Hostname:** The hostname from which a user originated (what top-level domains a visitor saw)
- **Connection speed:** The visitor's connection speed (T1, T3, OCS, etc.)
- **User-defined value:** The visitor's user-defined cookie value (user-defined segmenting)

For example, if you're looking at the Keywords report, you can click into an individual keyword, find the segmenting drop-down menu, and select the Landing Page segment to view what page of your site visitors saw first after entering that keyword in a search engine (or clicking a paid ad after searching for that keyword). Or you can look at your Traffic Sources report and change the drop-down to Visitor Type to get a breakdown of new vs. returning visitors.

Segmenting is available in most reports in Google Analytics. Not only is it extremely important; it is extremely powerful as well.

Table Filtering

Another useful feature found within each standard report table is the table filter, located toward the bottom of the table. Let's say that you're in the Keywords report and you see that there are more than 2,000 keywords listed within your specified date range. You don't have a lot of time to download the full report in an Excel file, and you need to get all keywords that contain the word *brown*. Instead of sifting through several rows of data and collecting your desired data in some way, type in the word *brown* on the table filter tool and make sure that the drop-down menu to its left says Containing, as in the example shown in Figure 7-10.

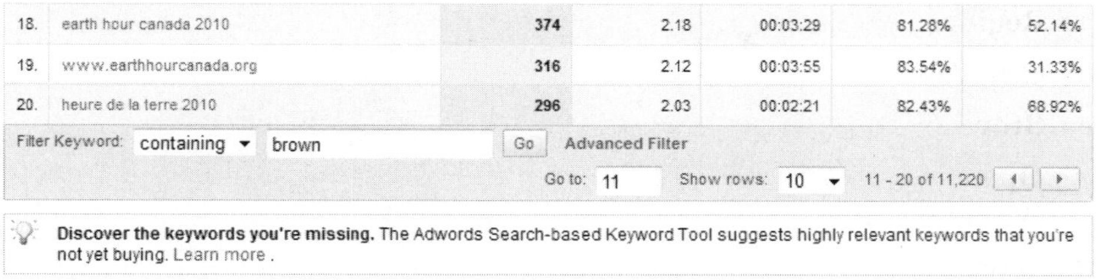

18.	earth hour canada 2010		374	2.18	00:03:29	81.28%	52.14%
19.	www.earthhourcanada.org		316	2.12	00:03:55	83.54%	31.33%
20.	heure de la terre 2010		296	2.03	00:02:21	82.43%	68.92%

Filter Keyword: containing ▼ brown   Go   Advanced Filter

Go to: 11   Show rows: 10 ▼   11 - 20 of 11,220 ◄   ►

🔆 **Discover the keywords you're missing.** The Adwords Search-based Keyword Tool suggests highly relevant keywords that you're not yet buying. Learn more .

Figure 7-10: The table filter tool in action

You can filter something out by selecting the Excluding drop-down menu option. You can also use Regular Expressions in these table filters; you'll learn all about Regular Expressions in Chapter 10 when I talk about creating goals and filters. One particular character in Regular Expression language will be extremely helpful for the table filter tool and is also easy to learn and use. It's the "pipe" symbol, |, which is "either/or" in Regular Expression language. It is located directly above the Enter key on your keyboard (it looks like two vertical dashes). Hit the Shift key and that button on your keyboard and use it to filter multiple keywords together.

There's also an advanced filter option, which lets you use deeper segmenting and filtering possibilities within the report table. I've saved this for Chapter 9.

Other Table Options

If you look at the top right of any report table in Google Analytics, you'll notice a Views row with five or sometimes six different mini-icons laid out in a row. The standard "table" view is the Google Analytics default, but you can view your data in other ways by simply clicking any of the listed icons.

The first one is the *percentage or pie-chart view*, which is highlighted in Figure 7-11. This type of view is the default report view in the New vs. Returning Visitors report. When you change views in Google Analytics, you're provided with two drop-down menus that are not available in the standard report table. The first, on the left-hand side of the percentage view, allows you to change the metric that's being displayed. The second, on the right-hand side, allows you to change the "contribution to total" metric that the pie chart is showing.

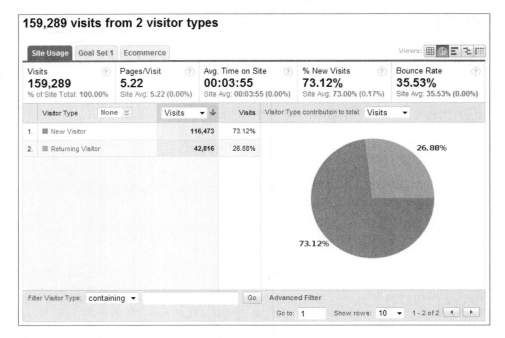

Figure 7-11: The percentage report view

The second view is the *performance view,* which presents a horizontal histogram listing the line items in the report you're looking at. Figure 7-12 shows the performance view in the search engine's report. Here you can change the metric in the drop-down menu on the left-hand side, but on the right-hand side the drop-down menu now changes the individual source performance, instead of contribution to total as in the percentage view. In the example in Figure 7-12 I have changed the individual source performance drop-down menu to the average-time-on-site metric, so I can evaluate each search engine by that metric.

The third view, probably my favorite, is the *comparison view.* This allows you to compare line items in the table data against the site averages, which can be useful for your analysis efforts. When you look at Figure 7-13, you'll see that on the left-hand side the table data is the same as in Figure 7-12; however, on Figure 7-13 I applied the comparison view and changed the individual source drop-down to the bounce-rate metric. Now, I can tell which search engines have a better or worse bounce rate when compared to the site average bounce rate. This view is extremely helpful in reports that I'll show you later in this chapter, like the Top Landing Pages report and the Keywords report.

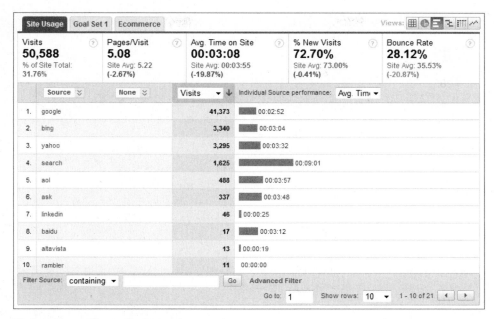

Figure 7-12: The performance report view

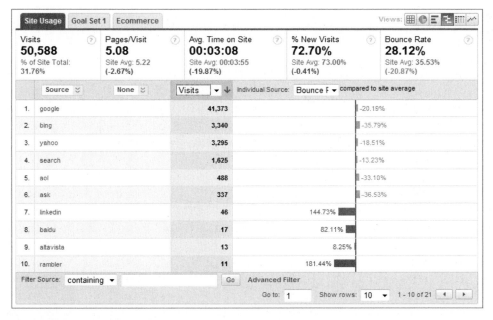

Figure 7-13: The comparison report view

There's also a *pivot view,* but since it's an advanced feature, I'll save it for Chapter 9.

Help, FAQs, and Common Questions

At the bottom of every report you'll find some links that when clicked will send you to some of Google's help resources. There is a lot of great information online that, along with *Your Google Game Plan for Success,* will help you learn and become better at using Google Analytics.

You'll see three links on the bottom left of any report page, underneath the main navigation area. There is an About This Report link, which, when clicked, provides an explanation of the report, as shown in Figure 7-14. Under that link is a link to Google's Conversion University, which is a website set up with articles and more information about how Google Analytics works. This may give you hints for the particular report you're looking at. The last link at bottom left is for common questions that Google Analytics users like you have asked. Perhaps your question has already been asked, and the answer may be available from this link.

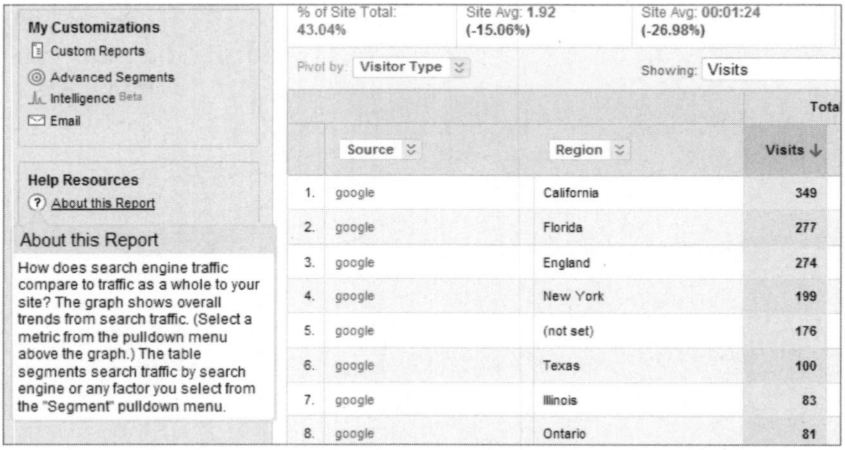

My Customizations	% of Site Total: 43.04%	Site Avg: 1.92 (-15.06%)	Site Avg: 00:01:24 (-26.98%)	
Custom Reports	Pivot by: Visitor Type		Showing: Visits	
Advanced Segments				Tota
Intelligence Beta				
Email	Source	Region	Visits ↓	
	1. google	California	349	
Help Resources	2. google	Florida	277	
About this Report	3. google	England	274	
About this Report	4. google	New York	199	
How does search engine traffic compare to traffic as a whole to your site? The graph shows overall trends from search traffic. (Select a metric from the pulldown menu above the graph.) The table segments search traffic by search engine or any factor you select from the "Segment" pulldown menu.	5. google	(not set)	176	
	6. google	Texas	100	
	7. google	Illinois	83	
	8. google	Ontario	81	

Figure 7-14: The help links on the bottom left-hand side of Google Analytics

There are also little question mark symbols scattered throughout Google Analytics, specifically on the scorecard metrics and within the individual reports themselves. Clicking these will provide a definition of the metric or dimension being displayed.

You may also view the Google Analytics terms of service, read up on the privacy policy, or contact Google Analytics via text links that are at the very bottom of any page within the interface.

The Overview and the Dashboard

Now that you have had a tiny taste of what Google Analytics can do, let's start with a tour of the available sections and reports within this powerful interface. The best place to start is naturally the Overview page, which is the first screen that you'll see upon successfully logging in to Google Analytics.

NOTE If you have access to multiple Google Analytics accounts (if you work for a company that handles multiple client accounts or just have been given multiple access), you'll see a higher-level Overview screen that lists all accounts for which you have access. Simply click the desired account to access it.

On this Overview screen, which you can see in Figure 7-15, you'll notice a lot of different things that you can do if you have administrative access. If you don't, you'll see only your profiles listed, without all the editable regions around them. Starting from the top of the screen, you can edit your account's settings, which include your account name and your data-sharing settings, which I talked about at the beginning of the chapter. On the top right, you'll notice the date range and see that a previous date range has been applied automatically. Directly below the date range, you can toggle the timeframe that appears in the report table by day, week, month, or year. The comparison date range that appears below the main date range will also change to reflect your choice.

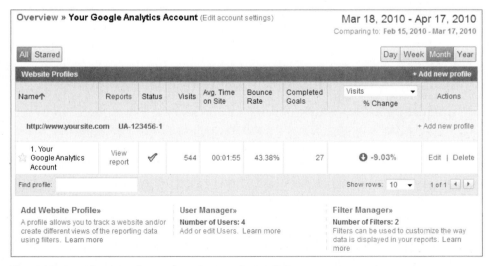

Figure 7-15: The Overview screen in Google Analytics

Moving to the left, you'll notice an All and a Starred button. If you have multiple profiles, you can mark any profile as a favorite and click the Starred button to view only your favorites. This can be convenient if you have access to multiple profiles. Folks who work for agencies or companies serving several clients with Google Analytics will make great use of this feature.

Finally, each profile's data is shown in its own row. Starting on the far left, you can change the name of the profile by simply hovering over it with your mouse and clicking the small pencil icon that appears. Next to that, the View Report link takes you to the profile's dashboard. The Status column tells you whether or not the profile is successfully receiving data (it will show a yellow warning sign if it's not). High-level metrics are shown up until the last column, where you can click to either edit or delete a profile (don't ever delete a profile unless you are 100 percent sure). The only column that you can edit here in the overview is the % Change column. By default, you'll see the percentage change from one date range to the previous one, but you can also view average time on site, bounce rate, and completed goals.

Below the overview table you can create a new website profile, manage the users that have access to your Google Analytics account, and manage your filters. All of these administrative options will be covered in Chapter 10.

The great thing about the Overview screen is that you can get high-level comparative data without even truly entering the Google Analytics interface. This screen makes for a great printout, and I don't say that very often. Make use of this Overview screen, especially if you have access to multiple profiles.

When you click View Report on any profile listed on the Overview screen, you'll be taken to the dashboard. As I mentioned earlier in this chapter, the dashboard can be thought of as the homepage of your website. It's where you'll be able to find high-level information about your website, such as the number of visits, the number of page views, and what your site's bounce rate is. Tools like the date-range tool, the trending graph, and e-mail options are available here. Also, this page is where you'll find any saved reports after clicking the silver Add to Dashboard button that you'll find at the top of each report within Google Analytics.

As you can see on the left-hand side of Figure 7-16, Google Analytics has its own unique organizational structure. As you start to use Google Analytics, you'll quickly become familiar with where data is stored and where to access the reports you need. Starting from the top left and working our way down, we find these navigation items:

- **Dashboard:** The "homepage" of your Google Analytics account. Saved reports appear here.

- **Intelligence:** An advanced feature of Google Analytics that can show you significant events that take place on your website (we'll cover Intelligence in Chapter 9).

- **Visitors:** Statistics and data about the visitors who come to your website are found in this section. This includes reports like the popular Map

Overlay, Benchmarking, and New vs. Returning, and technical data about your website's visitors' browsers, operating systems, and more.

- **Traffic Sources:** The places where visitors come from can be discovered in this section. Reports here include Referring Sites, All Traffic Sources, Search Engines, Keywords, and AdWords, all of which I'll cover later in this chapter.

- **Content:** Information about the pages of your website is found here. The Content section is home to reports like Top Content, Top Landing Pages, and the Site Overlay report. It's also home to features like the navigation summary and entrance paths, and subsections like Site Search and Event Tracking.

- **Goals:** The goals that you set up to measure the very important actions that visitors take on your site are available for analysis here. Reports include Goal Conversions, Goal Verification, and an especially important one called Funnel Visualization.

- **E-commerce:** If enabled and if installed properly on your site, this section can provide you with all sorts of details about the orders that take place on your site. It includes reports on transactions and products, and a neat visits/days-to-purchase histogram.

Figure 7-16: The dashboard in Google Analytics

Each section also contains its own overview page, providing general information about that section.

The Custom Reports, Advanced Segments, and Intelligence links found beneath the main navigation will be covered in Chapter 9. This navigation menu follows you throughout your journey within the Google Analytics interface.

The windows (or the mini-report tables) that appear on the dashboard can be moved to your liking. Simply drag and drop the reports to positions that suit you better. The only element that cannot be moved on the dashboard is anything above the Site Usage table. If you don't want to have a particular report window on your dashboard any longer, you can purge it by clicking the X at the upper right of any window. Click View Report at the bottom of any window to go to that report. Remember, you'll be taken to the report exactly as you left it.

Let's start moving beyond the dashboard and into the first section of reports, the Visitors section.

The Visitors Section

The first report in this section — as in any main section — is the Overview report, where you'll be taken by default when you click the Visitors link in the left-hand navigation. This section is all about the visitors who come to your website. Please note that personal information, such as phone numbers, names, and Social Security numbers, won't appear here. This report section shows only things like regions, cities, browser versions, operating systems, screen resolutions, and custom segments. (As you'll read in Chapter 8, collecting personally identifiable information is a bad practice.)

As you'll see in Figure 7-17, the overview data is neatly displayed on half of the middle of the page. Notice also that the trending graph's default metric is now Visitors, not Visits, as was the case on the dashboard. On the other half of the middle of the page, you're given some links to different reports within that section, like Map Overlay and Custom Segmentation, so you can access these individual reports without fishing through the navigation menu. At the bottom of the Visitors Overview you'll also find some brief technical data, including the browsers and connection speeds that brought visitors to your site. In the Visitors section you'll find the following reports:

- **Benchmarking:** Baseline and anonymous competitive information
- **Map Overlay:** An interactive visualization of visitors' physical locations
- **New vs. Returning:** A report showing the difference between new (first-time) visitors and returning (repeat) visitors
- **Languages:** The language settings used by your visitors
- **Visitor Trending:** Subsection of reports containing basic histograms for the six cornerstone metrics of Google Analytics
- **Visitor Loyalty:** Four interesting histograms showing customer retention and intent

- **Browser Capabilities:** Seven technical reports detailing your visitors' technical browser and operating system data

- **Network Properties:** Three reports identifying your visitors' Internet service providers and the URLs of your sites that they visit

- **Mobile:** A breakdown of the mobile carriers and devices used

- **User Defined:** A report on a subset of visitors that you manually tag

- **Custom Variables:** A newer feature that expands upon the user-defined variables

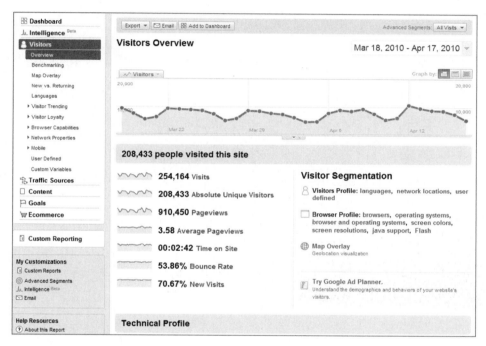

Figure 7-17: The Visitors Overview report

If you're an astute reader (which I know you are), you will have noticed that this report contains the Add to Dashboard button mentioned earlier. If you're following along on your own Google Analytics account as you read this chapter, you may have also noticed that there are now all five report-exporting options to choose from. Both the Add to Dashboard button and the five report-exporting options are now available on the dashboard.

NOTE   It's very likely that you are looking at these screenshots of Google Analytics for the very first time and are wondering what terms like *bounce rate* and *absolute unique visitors* mean. Feel free to flip over to Chapter 8's "Web Metrics and Dimension Definitions" section for a complete list of all terms used in web analytics. We'll save such definitions and deep analysis until after this chapter.

Benchmarking

After enabling data sharing when you open your Google Analytics account (or when you do it from the Account Settings link on the Overview screen), you'll see after a couple of weeks that there's data in the Benchmarking section. At this time you'll be able to compare the six cornerstone metrics (visits, page views, pages per visit, average time on site, percent of new visits, and bounce rate) to those of anonymous websites of a similar size.

Check out Figure 7-18. Here, you'll see the six cornerstone metrics compared to the benchmarks of sites similar in size to yours. Google Analytics automatically determines the size of your site by analyzing the traffic volume you receive monthly. Currently there is no way to know what your website's size is or how to modify the way Google classifies your site. Mouse over any data point within the six metrics to view how your data compared to the benchmark on that particular day. Below each data window you'll see the number corresponding to the metric, the benchmark's number, and the percentage difference.

Figure 7-18: The Benchmarking report

However, you can segment this report by industry so that you can measure your site's metrics against sites classified in your industry. Click Open Category List to view all available categories and subcategories, and select the category that's closest to yours. You can also view your website statistics against the benchmark of any other industry if you desire.

The Benchmarking section is one of the few reports in Google Analytics that cannot be exported, e-mailed, or added to your dashboard. It's also one of the reports in Google Analytics in which Advanced Segments are disabled — you'll learn why in Chapter 9.

Map Overlay

The Map Overlay report may be my favorite report in all of Google Analytics. I simply gush over this report. Not only is it visually appealing, but it's also extremely useful for any advertiser who needs specific geographic information. It's also the first report that introduces you to the standard report table that you've read so much about in this chapter.

When you first arrive at this report you'll see a map of the world. Some countries will be colored light green; others will be dark green. The darker the color, the more visits originated from that country or territory. Mousing over any country, as I've done in Figure 7-19, will show that country's visits. You can edit the default metric shown in the Map Overlay report by clicking the word Visits at the top left of the map. This will bring up a list of all available metrics you can view on your Map Overlay report.

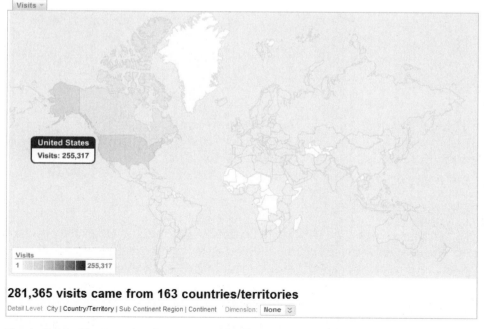

Figure 7-19: The Map Overlay report, with all countries and territories

Below the map you can see the total number of visits (or your desired metric) and the number of countries/territories that were responsible for those visits. When you click a country or territory, you will drill down into that area and view the state/region overlay. Clicking any state or region will show you something like Figure 7-20, which is a "chicken pox" view of each city that generated your selected metric. Mousing over any dot on the city-level view will show the metric total for that city. The bigger the dot is, the more visits (or selected metric) the city generated.

Figure 7-20: The Map Overlay report, city-level detail

The Map Overlay report is one of the few reports that do not contain a trending graph. However, you can e-mail, export, and advance-segment this report, unlike the Benchmarking section. When you scroll down the page you'll see the regular table view that is found in almost every report in Google Analytics.

New vs. Returning

As I mentioned earlier, the New vs. Returning Visitors report shows the pie-chart percentage view by default. Now that you know how to change the views, you can switch back to the table view, or any other view for that matter.

Google Analytics can determine by analysis of a visitor's cookies whether he or she is a new (first-time) visitor to your website or a returning (repeat) visitor. This distinction is referred to as *visitor type*, which you'll see in the segmenting drop-down and in the pivot view.

There are no functionality limitations on this report. You can perform Advanced Segments, table filters, and exporting/e-mailing options. You can also add this report to your dashboard.

Languages

The Languages report tells you what language options your visitors have enabled on their browsers of choice. The browser languages will be listed with their two-letter codes, so you'll have to know that "en" means English and "es" means Spanish. (Some of these codes are self-explanatory, and you'll most likely get the highest percentage of your traffic from the language that's native to you.) The Languages report also provides the first good example of a full-table view to show you how the standard reporting table is structured in Google Analytics, as shown in Figure 7-21.

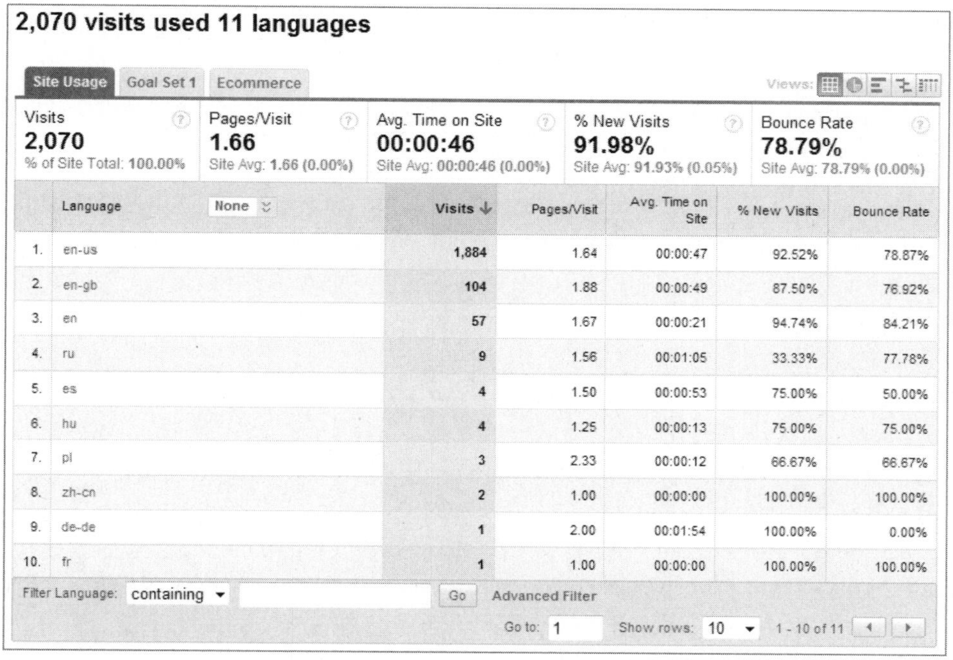

2,070 visits used 11 languages

Site Usage	Goal Set 1	Ecommerce			Views:

Visits	Pages/Visit	Avg. Time on Site	% New Visits	Bounce Rate
2,070	**1.66**	**00:00:46**	**91.98%**	**78.79%**
% of Site Total: 100.00%	Site Avg: 1.66 (0.00%)	Site Avg: 00:00:46 (0.00%)	Site Avg: 91.93% (0.05%)	Site Avg: 78.79% (0.00%)

	Language	None ≈	Visits ↓	Pages/Visit	Avg. Time on Site	% New Visits	Bounce Rate
1.	en-us		1,884	1.64	00:00:47	92.52%	78.87%
2.	en-gb		104	1.88	00:00:49	87.50%	76.92%
3.	en		57	1.67	00:00:21	94.74%	84.21%
4.	ru		9	1.56	00:01:05	33.33%	77.78%
5.	es		4	1.50	00:00:53	75.00%	50.00%
6.	hu		4	1.25	00:00:13	75.00%	75.00%
7.	pl		3	2.33	00:00:12	66.67%	66.67%
8.	zh-cn		2	1.00	00:00:00	100.00%	100.00%
9.	de-de		1	2.00	00:01:54	100.00%	0.00%
10.	fr		1	1.00	00:00:00	100.00%	100.00%

Filter Language: containing ▼ [   ] Go Advanced Filter

Go to: 1   Show rows: 10 ▼ 1 - 10 of 11 ◄ ►

Figure 7-21: The Languages report, showing the standard report table in Google Analytics

The very top of the report table will contain the Site Usage tab, showing you baseline data like visits and pages per visit; up to four Goal Set tabs, showing you conversion rates and goal values for your goal conversions; and an E-commerce tab, which (if enabled) shows you revenue and transaction data.

In a way, clicking these tabs is a form of segmenting your data — you're just using tabs instead of drop-down menus.

Directly across from the tabs are the report views that you are familiar with from earlier in the chapter. Below the tabs and the view toggle buttons is what's known as the *scorecard*. The scorecard shows you data for all line items within the report you're looking at. If you look again at Figure 7-21, you'll see data for all language sets in the scorecard. You'll see the metric name, the value for the metric, and either a comparison to the site average or contribution to total.

Below the scorecard are the column headings for the report data that you see. The first column heading contains a second drop-down menu called *secondary dimension*, which I'll demo in Chapter 9. These column headings are sortable, and default sorting is by the first metric from the left.

Clicking any line item will single it out in most reports and show you that line item's data isolated from the rest of the group. In a few reports you'll actually drill down one level deeper (for example, clicking a search engine name in the Traffic Sources section may show you the keywords searched for from that search engine).

At the bottom of the report table, as you know, is the filter tool, as well as yet another advanced feature for Chapter 9 called advanced table filtering. At the bottom right of the table you can expand to show more rows, go to a line-item number directly, or view the next page of line items. You can view a maximum of 500 rows at one time.

Visitor Trending

The Visitor Trending subsection of reports has six reports that are identical, the only difference being the metric that is displayed. Figure 7-22 shows the most basic of reports that you'll be able to find here in Google Analytics, but with one neat addition that's not available in any other type of report.

Each of the reports for the six visitor trending metrics (the "cornerstone" metrics from the Site Usage window on the dashboard) shows a histogram broken down by your selected date range. In Figure 7-22 I'm showing the visits per day, but I've selected the Graph by Hour trending graph view that's available only in these basic reports. Below the trending graph the breakdown by hour is shown.

The distribution of visits that you see in the trending graph is pretty consistent with that of most websites on the Internet. Most web activity happens during business hours and into the early evening, before midnight. Usually there is a steady drop-off in traffic after seven o'clock at night, and sometimes the drop-off is later. In this example there's a significant drop-off after midnight.

The Visitor Trending reports can be exported, downloaded, e-mailed, and segmented. They cannot be filtered because there is no standard table filter available here.

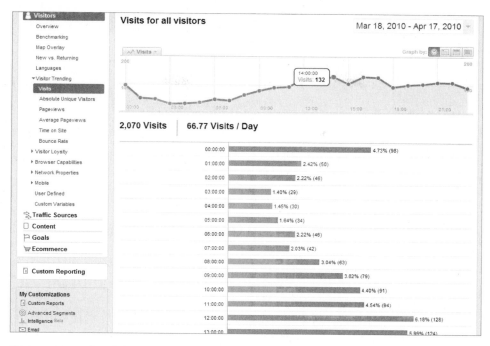

Figure 7-22: The Visitor Trending report for visits, graphed by hour

Visitor Loyalty

The Visitor Loyalty reports are an interesting group of reports in that they allow you to measure visitor retention and to some extent the awareness of your brand by your website visitors. Four reports in this subsection allow you to measure loyalty (how many times visitors visit your site in a given period), recency (how long ago visitors visited your site in a given period), length of visit (how long a visit lasted, on average), and depth of visit (how deep, in terms of page views, each visit went, on average).

Even though these reports are histograms like the Visitor Trending reports, they're an important group for several reasons. For one, this information is available only here, in this section. (The data from this report isn't available in the segmented format you see in Figure 7-23 unless you perform some Advanced Segments, which I'll talk about in Chapter 9.) Another reason is the sheer value of this information.

For most websites, Figure 7-23 will be a familiar representation of the site's data. It tells you the following:

- Most visitors visit a site one time.
- Most visitors are making their first visit to your site.
- Most visitors spend between zero and 10 seconds on your site.
- Most visitors make one page view per visit.

Count of visits from this visitor including current	Visits that were the visitor's nth visit	Percentage of all visits
	Visitor Loyalty	Mar 19, 2010 - Apr 18, 2010 ▾
	Most visits repeated: 1 times	
1 times	25,397.00	▓▓▓▓▓▓▓▓▓▓▓▓▓▓ 86.34%
2 times	2,207.00	▓▓ 7.50%
3 times	690.00	▌ 2.35%
4 times	309.00	│ 1.05%
5 times	183.00	│ 0.62%
6 times	125.00	│ 0.42%
7 times	70.00	0.24%
8 times	57.00	0.19%
9-14 times	159.00	│ 0.54%
15-25 times	81.00	│ 0.28%
26-50 times	65.00	0.22%
51-100 times	38.00	0.13%
101-200 times	31.00	0.11%
201+ times	3.00	0.01%

Figure 7-23: The Visitor Loyalty report

Over time, depending on your marketing, site optimization, and branding work, you'll notice certain trends beginning to develop, such as fewer visitors visiting your site only once in their lifetimes. You can follow these trends over time by using the date-range comparison tool. As you build your audience and customer base, you'll want to get an idea of how often customers come back to your site and how deep they go. A good initial gauge of overall website success comes when you start cutting into that overwhelming group of visitors who interact very little with your site — it's like you're winning them over.

Because this report doesn't have a standard report table, it cannot be filtered. However, it can be e-mailed, added to the dashboard, and exported, and have Advanced Segments applied.

Browser Capabilities

In the Browser Capabilities subsection are seven reports to slice and dice your visitor's technical details, as in Figure 7-24. Google Analytics collects this information for each visitor and stores it in this report section. This section may not seem useful for most folks, but if you're a web designer, it's vital to ensure that your websites are designed optimally for the majority of your visitors.

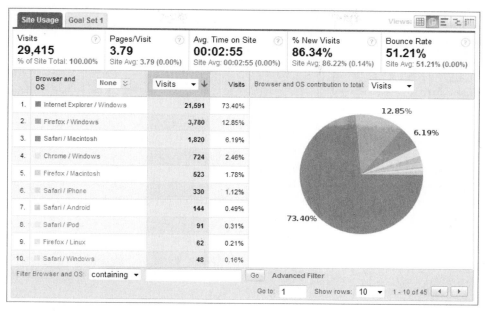

Figure 7-24: The Browser and OS report

Within Browser Capabilities, the seven available reports are:

- **Browsers:** What browsers your site's visitors used (Internet Explorer, Firefox, etc.)

- **Operating Systems:** The operating systems used by your site's visitors (Windows Vista, OS X, iPhone, etc.)

- **Browser and OS:** A report showing you the most popular combinations of browser and operating system (see Figure 7-24)

- **Screen Colors:** How many colors the video cards on your visitors' computers can see (32-bit, 16-bit, etc.)

- **Screen Resolutions:** The screen-resolution sizes for your visitors' computers (1024×768, 800×600, etc.)

- **Flash Versions:** The version of Flash installed on your visitors' browsers (10.0 rx, 9.0 rx, etc.)

- **Java Support:** Whether your visitors have Java installed on their computers

Network Properties

The Network Properties subsection includes a few more technical reports. Two of the reports are mostly for your enjoyment, as they don't provide any real insight. The third report is actually a very valuable technical report that allows you to see what URLs your Google Analytics Tracking Code is installed on.

- **Service Providers:** The Internet service providers for your visitors (Comcast Cable, Verizon, AT&T, etc.)

- **Hostnames:** The domains that your visitors visit (`www.yoursite.com`, `blog.yoursite.com`, `news.yoursite.com`, etc.)

- **Connection Speeds:** The connection speeds for your visitors (cable, DSL, T1, etc.)

Mobile

The Mobile report section includes two reports to help you analyze the visitors who come to your site via a web-enabled mobile phone or a mobile device like the iPad. If you have a mobile site or are just interested in the mobile traffic that your site receives, this report is for you.

The two reports in this section are:

- **Mobile Devices:** This report shows the actual mobile devices that your website visitors use. Be prepared to see a lot of iPhone, Android, and iPad traffic listed here.

- **Mobile Carriers:** The service providers for your visitors' mobile devices are listed here, such as AT&T, T-Mobile, Sprint, and others.

Keep this in mind when looking at this report: Google Analytics can report only on mobile traffic that accepts JavaScript, cookies, and images. If the mobile device being used is not "Web 2.0-enabled," or is configured to block JavaScript, cookies, or images, then Google Analytics cannot report on that visitor, and he or she will not be listed in this (or any) report. Check out Figure 7-25 for an example of the Mobile Devices report.

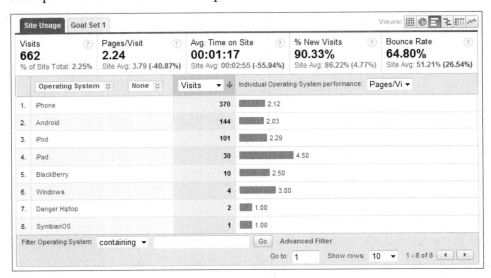

Figure 7-25: The Mobile Devices report

The Traffic Sources Section

The second major reporting section within Google Analytics is the Traffic Sources section. Here you'll find data on how your visitors accessed your site, and just like the Visitors reporting section, this report starts off with its own overview section providing high-level traffic source information.

Excluding the overview, the reports in this section are:

- **Direct Traffic:** Shows the volume of direct traffic to your website
- **Referring Sites:** The traffic that is referred to you from another website
- **Search Engines:** Organic and paid search engine traffic that your site receives
- **All Traffic Sources:** A roll-up report combining all the different sources of traffic in one view
- **AdWords:** A subsection within the Traffic Sources section providing you with data on your AdWords campaigns (more on this in Chapter 14)
- **Keywords:** The keywords visitors searched for to access your site
- **Campaigns:** The campaigns visitors came to your site from
- **Ad Versions:** The ad version that a user clicked to reach your site

As you can see in Figure 7-26, Google Analytics organizes the traffic sources into three different categories: Direct Traffic, Referring Sites, and Search Engines. Direct traffic is traffic that comes to your site directly when visitors type the URL of your site into their browser address bars (or reach it via a bookmark). Referring sites contain traffic from visitors who clicked links to your site from other sites. Search engines are self-explanatory; there are organic search engines and paid search engines (labeled "cpc").

Direct Traffic

The Direct Traffic report shows you the traffic that came to your site directly. Direct traffic can happen when a user types or copies the URL of your website into his or her browser address bar. It can also happen if a user bookmarks your site after visiting your site directly, and accesses your site later via that bookmark. You can also get direct traffic if users have a page on your site as their browsers' starting page.

The Direct Traffic report is quite bland, but since I haven't shown this "individual" report view yet, this is a good opportunity to do just that. Figure 7-27 shows an example of the Direct Traffic report.

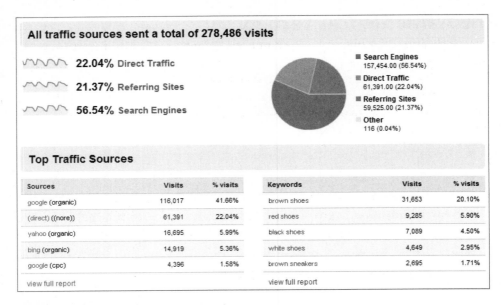

Figure 7-26: The Traffic Sources overview report

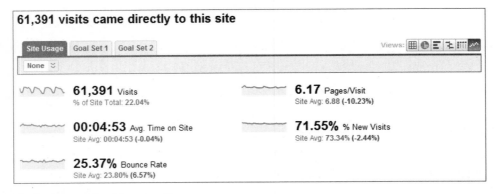

Figure 7-27: The Direct Traffic report

Referring Sites

A referring site in Google Analytics is any website (other than a search engine) that's responsible for sending you traffic. If a site has a text or image link pointing to your site, and a user clicks it, the user will be counted as a referral. The visitor's referring site URL will be listed in this valuable report.

All referring sites are listed that are responsible for at least one visit to your site within your specified date range. This makes life interesting — sites that you may never have heard of will appear on this list, piquing your curiosity and leaving you wondering where your link actually resides on the referring site, and what it looks like. But with Google Analytics, you're very rarely left just wondering. Clicking any individual referring site listed in the report table will show you the page(s) on that site that contain your link (and have sent at least one visit to your site). The great part about this report is the little icon that appears next to the page name, which you can make out in Figure 7-28. Clicking that icon will open up a new window and take you directly to the page where your link is located on the referring site! In the example shown in Figure 7-28 I'm taking a look at the pages from www.yellowpages.com, which is a referring site sending my website traffic.

Figure 7-28: The Referring Sites report

Search Engines

The Search Engines report within the Traffic Sources section offers a neat toggle feature that is not available in any other report in Google Analytics. You'll notice three text links at the very top of Figure 7-29 that enable you to show the total volume for both paid and organic search engines, paid search engines only, or non-paid (organic) search engines only. This can be very helpful, since you don't have to switch among reports on the navigation menu — you can simply use the text links above the report.

In this report, when you click a name of a search engine you will view a list of keywords that drove traffic from that selected search engine. This is the easiest possible way to perform segmenting in Google Analytics, and if you advertise with Google AdWords or do SEO on your site, you're definitely going to want to dive into Google, Yahoo!, and Bing at least.

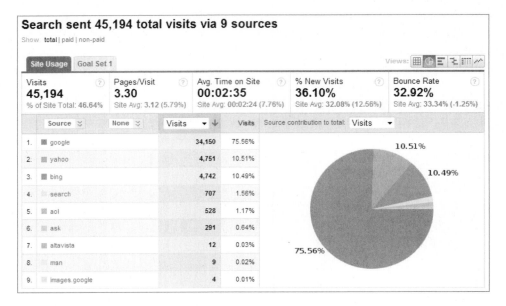

Figure 7-29: The Search Engines report

Notice two interesting things in Figure 7-29: the eighth row says MSN, which is also considered a search engine (remember that before the Bing days, MSN.com was Microsoft's search engine), and the ninth row says images.google, which is considered a search engine as well. (Seeing traffic from images.google reminds me to advise you to optimize your images, if you don't already, by using the ALT image tag and descriptive text near the image itself on your web page for higher presence in this engine.)

All Traffic Sources

This is possibly the most accessed report in all of Google Analytics, and one you should become very familiar with. The All Traffic Sources report combines the traffic you receive from direct, referring, and search engines (paid and organic), and rolls them all up in this awesome report.

Look at Figure 7-30. First the report lists the traffic sources paired with their corresponding media. Remember that a medium is the means by which a visitor accesses your site. So, the second line item in Figure 7-30 reads google/organic, which is the source/medium combination. The tenth line item at the bottom reads charter.net/referral, which you now know is a referring site. If there were any traffic from Google AdWords, it would be listed as google/cpc. Finally, the first line item is direct/(none) because direct traffic doesn't have a medium (so Google Analytics labels it as "none"). Here, as in the Search Engines report, you can click an organic or paid search engine to drill down and view its keywords, but when you click either a referring site or the direct line item, you'll be taken to the individual report (which looks exactly like the one I showed earlier in Figure 7-27).

Figure 7-30: The All Traffic Sources report

This is a great report on which to use the filter tool at the bottom of the report table. For example, you could type the word **google** into the filter tool and view all data for any source containing the word Google (paid, organic, or referral site, such as `images.google.com`). Or, you can exclude the word *google* to see what traffic you get that does not come from a Google property.

NOTE   Looking for the AdWords report subsection of the Traffic Sources section in Google Analytics? Flip over to Chapter 14.

Keywords

Another of the most popular reports in Google Analytics (and the web-analytics industry, for that matter) is the Keywords report. All website owners want to know what keywords drove traffic to their websites, and with good reason. You can view more information about your organic keywords here, and you can see which pages visitors land on and lots of other information by segmenting. If you're a paid advertiser, this report is pure gold because it provides the missing information that you've been yearning for ever since Part II of this book, when I covered Google AdWords.

To really get an idea of how valuable your keywords are, you can click the Goal Set or E-commerce tab in this report, as you can in any standard report view. Click an individual keyword to isolate it from the other keywords, and use segmenting to backtrack and discover which search engine(s) drove traffic via this keyword, among many other segmenting possibilities.

This report, like the Search Engine report shown in Figure 7-29, also contains the Total, Paid, and Non-Paid toggle links for your convenience. The report itself looks like the Search Engines report, so I'll spare you a repetitive image.

Campaigns

Mainly for pay-per-click advertising efforts, this report lists all campaigns that have generated traffic to your site. Organic, referral, and direct traffic does not have to carry a campaign name, but cost-per-click initiatives like AdWords and manually tagged URLs (which I'll talk about in Chapter 17) do.

Ad Versions

Ad Versions is the final report of the Traffic Sources section, and it lists all headlines of all ads in any cost-per-click campaign you're running. If you're using the Keyword Insertion function that you learned about from the AdWords chapters, those will appear in this report as well. You'll have to perform some basic segmenting here to discover what search engines, keywords, campaigns, and other data are associated with any entry in this report. If you manually tag links in the way I explain in Chapter 17, the ad content variables (like banner ad sizes and ad names) will show up in this report as well.

The Content Section

Up next in the Google Analytics interface is the Content section of reports (see Figure 7-31). On the overview report of the Content section, you'll quickly realize that this section is all about the actual pages of your site. You'll learn what pages were popular ones, and which were the most entered and exited. This section has a unique set of features unavailable in any other report.

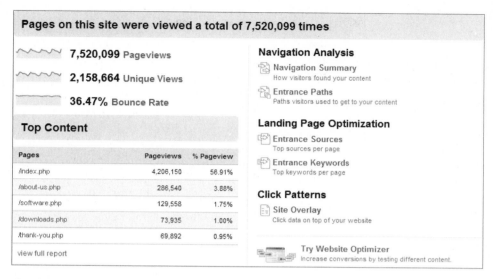

Figure 7-31: The Content overview report

The Content section of reports in Google Analytics offers you the following reports:

- **Top Content:** A full listing of every page of your website
- **Content by Title:** A list of your site's pages by each page's title tag
- **Content Drilldown:** Your pages grouped together by subdirectory
- **Top Landing Pages:** The pages that served as entry points into your site
- **Top Exit Pages:** The pages that served as jumping-off points for your site visitors
- **Site Overlay:** Click data shown graphically on top of your site
- **Site Search:** Data on your site's internal search function (more on this in Chapter 9)
- **Event Tracking:** Reporting on your Flash- and AJAX-based website events
- **AdSense:** Reports on your Google AdSense account

By looking at the earlier Figure 7-31, you'll notice on the right-hand side of the overview screen that you're provided with links to perform a navigation summary or look at your site's entrance paths. We'll save those for the very end of this section of the chapter.

Top Content

Along with the All Traffic Sources report, the Top Content report is one of the most popular and most accessed in Google Analytics. It is a full listing of all of your website's pages that have received at least one page view. In the Content section you are shown a modified report table with different metrics. For example, in Figure 7-32, you'll see that the sole tab of the Top Content report is called Content Performance. The columns of metrics now include the page views metric, the unique page views metric, the percentage of exits metric and the $index metric. Gone from this report table are the visits, pages per visit, and percentage of new visits metrics that you've been accustomed to until now.

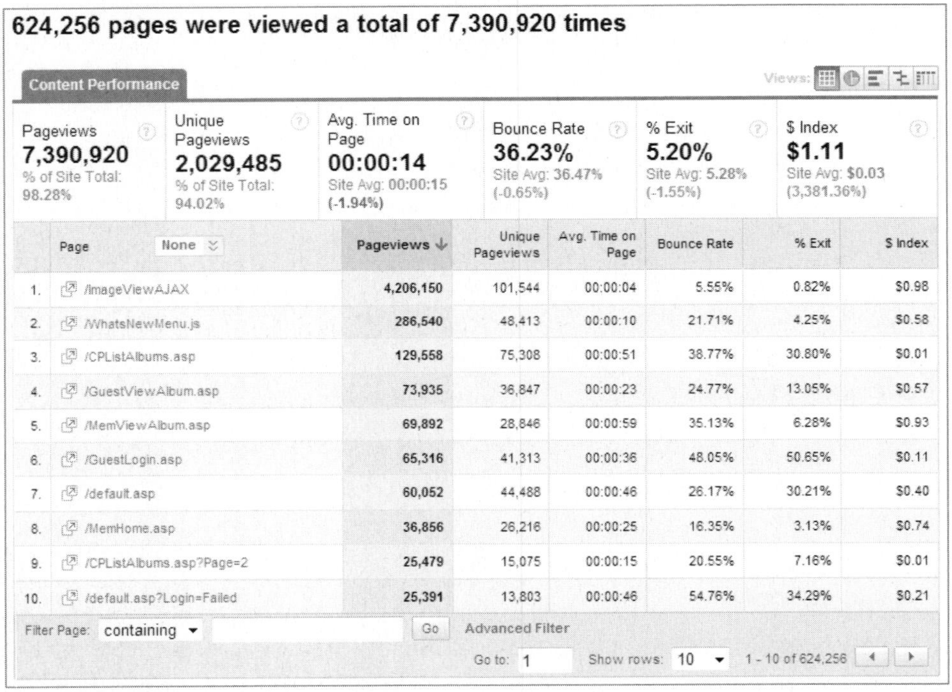

624,256 pages were viewed a total of 7,390,920 times

		Content Performance					Views: ⊞ ◑ ≡ ⅄ ⅏
	Pageviews ⑦	Unique Pageviews ⑦	Avg. Time on Page ⑦	Bounce Rate ⑦	% Exit ⑦	$ Index ⑦	
	7,390,920	**2,029,485**	**00:00:14**	**36.23%**	**5.20%**	**$1.11**	
	% of Site Total: 98.28%	% of Site Total: 94.02%	Site Avg: 00:00:15 (-1.94%)	Site Avg: 36.47% (-0.65%)	Site Avg: 5.28% (-1.55%)	Site Avg: $0.03 (3,381.36%)	

	Page	None ≽	Pageviews ↓	Unique Pageviews	Avg. Time on Page	Bounce Rate	% Exit	$ Index
1.	/ImageViewAJAX		4,206,150	101,544	00:00:04	5.55%	0.82%	$0.98
2.	/WhatsNewMenu.js		286,540	48,413	00:00:10	21.71%	4.25%	$0.58
3.	/CPListAlbums.asp		129,558	75,308	00:00:51	38.77%	30.80%	$0.01
4.	/GuestViewAlbum.asp		73,935	36,847	00:00:23	24.77%	13.05%	$0.57
5.	/MemViewAlbum.asp		69,892	28,846	00:00:59	35.13%	6.28%	$0.93
6.	/GuestLogin.asp		65,316	41,313	00:00:36	48.05%	50.65%	$0.11
7.	/default.asp		60,052	44,488	00:00:46	26.17%	30.21%	$0.40
8.	/MemHome.asp		36,856	26,216	00:00:25	16.35%	3.13%	$0.74
9.	/CPListAlbums.asp?Page=2		25,479	15,075	00:00:15	20.55%	7.16%	$0.01
10.	/default.asp?Login=Failed		25,391	13,803	00:00:46	54.76%	34.29%	$0.21

Filter Page: containing ▼ [   ] Go   Advanced Filter

Go to: 1   Show rows: 10 ▼   1 - 10 of 624,256 ◀ ▶

Figure 7-32: The Top Content report

Just as with the Referring Sites report, you can click the small icon next to a page name to pop open a new browser window that will show you the web page on your site. When you click a page name you'll see that page singled out and separated from the rest of the pages listed, allowing you to perform some deeper analysis on that page by itself.

The reports in the Content section do not come equipped with Goal Set or E-commerce tabs. Instead, Google Analytics provides the $index metric, which gives you insight into the value of each page (the higher the $index metric, the more valuable the page is, essentially).

Content by Title

The Content by Title report looks exactly like the Top Content report, except for the fact that the line items in the report are page titles, not page file names. The number of pages listed in the Content by Title report could very easily not be identical to the number of pages in the Top Content report for the simple reason that if you have multiple pages using the same title meta-tag, those pages will be grouped together under the same line item. If all your pages use the same title meta-tag, then this report will show you one line item. I hope this isn't the case, and that each of your pages has a unique title meta-tag.

Content Drilldown

This report is almost exactly like both the Top Content and the Content by Title reports. They look, smell, and taste the same. What makes the Content Drilldown report different is the fact that this report groups subdirectories together, and lists all pages without a standalone subdirectory structure. If you use subdirectories for organizing your pages, you can make use of this report. Many people reading this book will never have need of this report.

Top Landing Pages

Unlike the previous report, this report should *always* be used! The Top Landing Pages report is one of my all-time favorites in Google Analytics. It shows you all the pages that were used as entry points into your website. It's not the Top Content report, which lists all pages that have had at least one page view in the selected date range. Here, you get only pages that have been used as entrances, so not all website pages will be seen here.

Figure 7-33 shows the Top Landing Pages report in action. It features a very simple layout, focusing on entrances, bounces, and the bounce rate metric that you've been hearing about throughout this book and especially in this chapter. When combined with the comparison view, with the individual drop-down menu focused on bounce rate, this makes for one of the most useful and best reports Google Analytics has to offer. I find that the simplicity of this report is also a nice change of pace from the mountains of data that other reports throw your way.

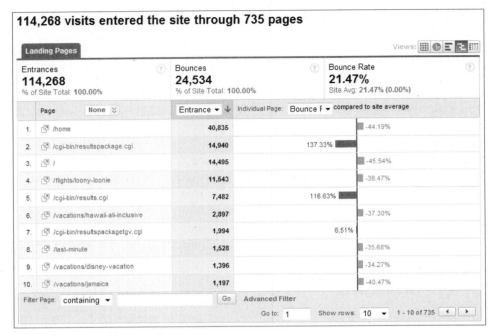

Figure 7-33: The Top Landing Pages report

Top Exit Pages

The Top Exit Pages report is the complete opposite of the Top Landing Pages report, since it shows you the pages that directly led to exits from your website. For reasons that I'll save for Chapter 8, this report is not to be used for any type of analysis, and is for informational purposes only (see the "Unfortunate and Common Misconceptions" section of the next chapter).

Site Overlay

The Site Overlay report is among the most unusual reports in Google Analytics. There are no report table, no segmenting possibilities, and no trending graph to see. Instead, when you click the Site Overlay report link, a new window will automatically pop up and your website's homepage will be displayed. After a few seconds the screen will refresh and you'll see click data on top of your website. You'll see the percentage of clicks that each link on your site received, and when you mouse over any of the click data points, you'll see how many goal conversions and e-commerce transactions each link received.

Figure 7-34 is an image of the Site Overlay report that I found on images.google.com from the http://blog.sageinternet.com/ website. It shows the website bWEST Interactive and the site overlay data on top of that website.

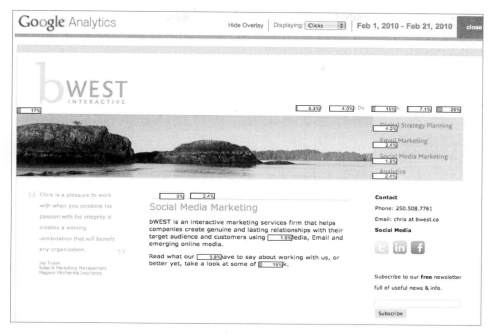

Figure 7-34: The Site Overlay report

I feel obligated to point out that the Site Overlay report isn't perfect. In fact, there are lots of ways in which this report can break or not work properly. Normally, heavy amounts of Flash or AJAX objects will break the report, causing a wide variety of problems. When the report works, it is a great one, as you can actually see where people are clicking on your website. However, it has been plagued by functionality issues for years. It's my hope that one day this report section will be fixed and made to work with the Web 2.0 elements that are a part of so many websites today.

Navigation Summary

One of the two tools I want to highlight from the Content section is the Navigation Summary. When you click any page individually, you are provided with the option to perform this navigation summary on the right-hand side of the page. Figure 7-35 shows an example of the navigation summary for the default. aspx page of this particular website (which is the homepage). The Navigation Summary report gives you a three-page scenario for all visitors who encountered the selected page.

On the left of Figure 7-35 you'll see the top 10 pages that people viewed before the default.aspx page , sorted by the percentage of clicks that each page received (the total contribution). In this example, 68.85 percent of all traffic consisted of entrances directly to the default.aspx page, and 31.15 percent of the traffic originated from a previous page. The small page icon in the very middle of the screenshot represents the selected page, which in this case is the default.aspx page.

This page was viewed 1,732 times

⫟ Visit this page Analyze: **Navigation Summary** ⯆ Content /default.aspx ⯆

68.85% Entrances		**0.00%** Exits	
31.15% Previous Pages		**100.00%** Next Pages	

Content	% Clicks
/Default.aspx	5.90%
/Outdoor-Displays.aspx	1.65%
/Restaurant-Menu-Displays--	1.52%
/Shadow-Boxes-|-Empty-Wa	1.14%
/Bulletin-Board-And-Cork-Bo	0.95%
/Poster-Displays-|-Sign-Fram	0.89%
/Poster-Snap-Frame-Display!	0.63%
/SwingSnaps-Front-Loading-	0.63%
/Lightboxes-|-Backlit-|-Edge-l	0.63%
/Multi-Panel-Displays-|-Poster	0.63%

Content	% Clicks
/Default.aspx	23.12%
/Outdoor-Displays.aspx	8.11%
/Bulletin-Board-And-Cork-B(	6.90%
/Poster-Snap-Frame-Display	6.29%
/Poster-Displays-|-Sign-Frar	5.68%
/Restaurant-Menu-Displays-	5.38%
/Shadow-Boxes-|-Empty-W(	4.87%
/Display-Stands-And-Floor-!	3.85%
/Multi-Panel-Displays-|-Poste	2.94%
/Lightboxes-|-Backlit-|-Edge-	2.84%
/Changeable-Letter-Boards-	2.43%

Figure 7-35: The Navigation Summary view

On the right-hand side of Figure 7-35, the page visited immediately after the default.aspx page is shown. In this example there were no site exits after the default.aspx page was viewed (which is very good), and 100 percent of the traffic coming through this page visited another page of the site. Here the top 11 pages are listed.

One question usually asked about the Navigation Summary is why the same page sometimes appears as both the previous and next page in the report. The answer is actually somewhat complex — the simplest explanation is that there are lots of user reasons this happens (page refreshes, back/forward browser button usage, clicking the link for the same page a user is on, and others). This confusion of activity results in some confusion in the report.

Entrance Paths

The other scenario-analysis tool that may be of use to you in the Content report section is the Entrance Paths report. The Navigation Summary report shows a three-page scenario of traffic that flows in and out of the selected page. Here, in the Entrance Paths reports, you select a starting page, view the pages that were seen by your visitors immediately afterward, and then manually select a page to view where visitors who chose that page ultimately wound up.

An example of the Entrance Paths report is shown in Figure 7-36. I once again selected the default.aspx page as my starting point. Directly to the right of the This Page symbol, I saw the top 10 pages to which visitors went after viewing the default.aspx page. I then clicked Outdoor-Displays.aspx, which is the fourth line item in that column, in order to view where visitors wound up who came from the homepage and then immediately visited the Outdoor-Displays.aspx page. As you'll notice, some returned to the homepage, while others went back to the Outdoor-Displays.aspx page or some other website page.

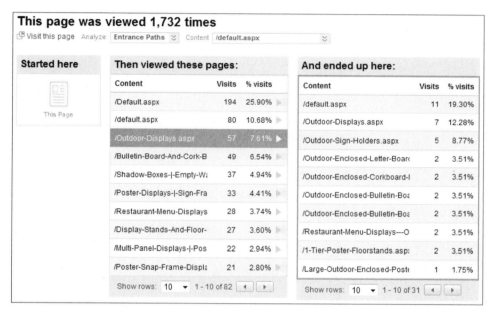

Figure 7-36: The Entrance Paths view

To be completely honest with you, I seldom use either the Navigation Summary or the Entrance Paths report in Google Analytics. I find that they are lacking in the simplicity department, and while I understand what can cause the same page name to appear as both the previous and next page, the general population doesn't.

The Goals Section

The next-to-last section in Google Analytics (and in this chapter) is the Goals section. This section focuses entirely on the outcomes that you can set up within the Google Analytics profile settings. Goals are important actions that visitors take on your website, such as viewing a key page, filling out a contact form, or purchasing something from your online store. In Google Analytics, a goal is counted when a unique page view is made. This is on purpose so that multiple page views by the same user on the same page aren't replicated, which can heavily inflate your goal counts.

Aside from the Overview report, the Goals section includes the following reports:

- **Total Conversions:** A histogram showing the conversions that occur each day
- **Conversion Rate:** Another histogram displaying the total and daily conversion rate for your site
- **Goal Verification:** The page URLs that match your goals
- **Reverse Goal Path:** The last four pages that users visited to reach a goal page
- **Goal Value:** A histogram showing the goal value by day
- **Goal Abandoned Funnels:** A report that displays the abandonment rate
- **Funnel Visualization:** A highly important report showing how visitors travel through a predefined funnel

If visitors encounter a message to "Set up goals and funnel before continuing," it means this task has not been done yet, and they may have to contact an administrator to help them set up the goals.

When you click Goals from the left-hand navigation menu, you'll see a simple overview page showing you the number of completed goals for each goal that you set up, as well as the total goal-conversion rate and total goal value for all active goals. In Figure 7-37 there are only two goals set up for this profile, but remember that you can set up as many as 20 goals per profile.

Figure 7-37: The Goals overview report

Total Conversions

As I just mentioned, this report is a simple histogram showing your conversions for each day listed vertically. With the provided drop-down menu you can view each goal individually, or the total conversions for all goals. For good measure, I'll throw in Figure 7-38 to show an example of this report.

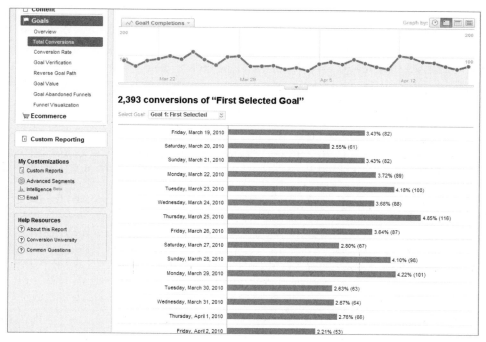

Figure 7-38: The Total Conversions report

Conversion Rate

The Conversion Rate report is exactly the same as the Total Conversions report, except that — you guessed it — it shows conversion rate instead of the total number of conversions. So in essence Google Analytics is giving you two options for viewing a daily breakdown of your goals: either by the count of conversions or by the rate of conversions.

Goal Verification

When we start talking about Regular Expressions in Chapter 10, I'll show an example of this Goal Verification report, which can come in handy if you're matching a single goal to multiple URLs. This report can show you all matches within your date range for a specific goal. For example, if you're tracking any view of your /partners/ subdirectory as a goal, and have set up /partners/ as a goal, you'll see all the pages within that subdirectory that resulted in a goal match. Remember that goals equal unique page views, so repeated page views within a subdirectory won't be counted as goals.

Reverse Goal Path

The Reverse Goal Path report shows you the last four steps taken by visitors to reach any selected goal. This report can provide a little bit of insight for you, as you'll quickly notice that several different combinations are shown as paths users take to reach your goal page(s).

Figure 7-39 shows an example of the Reverse Goal Path report for Goal 2, which shows that there were 127 conversions for a Thank You Page in this date range. On the left-hand side in the middle of the page, the last four page-path combinations are shown, and on the right, percentage bars are displayed with the percentage of goals and the goal count for each combination. For this goal, the top reverse goal path had three conversions. All the other reverse goal paths had only one apiece. This suggests that there are as many ways to reach this goal as there are interested visitors to this site (another reason to optimize *every* page of your site, not just your homepage or what you perceive to be the important pages).

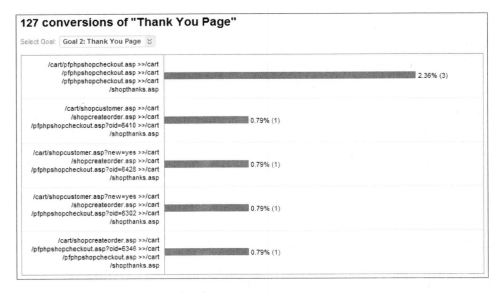

Figure 7-39: The Reverse Goal Path report

Goal Value

As you've read up to this point, you can insert a goal value for each and every goal that you create. I always encourage people to use numerical values for goals (aside from the actual total counts of goals) because it's a vital part of analysis intelligence (which I'll discuss in more depth in Chapter 8). This report is another one of the basic reports, like Total Conversions and Conversion Rate, for which the sums of daily goal values are listed vertically.

Goal Abandoned Funnels

Even though this is yet another basic type of histogram report, it introduces a very important metric — abandonment rate. Abandonment rate is the percentage of visitors who leave your goal funnel before completing it. As you'll read much more about, especially when I start talking about Google Website Optimizer, goal funnel optimization is one of the hidden treasures for increasing one's conversion rate. Not a lot of folks bother optimizing the pages that they define as goal funnels, leading to a lot of folks being unable to increase their conversion rates no matter what they try. As you continue reading, you'll find out ways to do just that.

Funnel Visualization

The last report in the Goals section is quite possibly the most vital, and is arguably the single most important report in terms of conversion rate optimization. The Funnel Visualization report provides a neat visualization showing you your defined funnel, where visitors enter the funnel, and where visitors exit the funnel, detailing the information through each individual funnel step.

Figure 7-40 shows an example funnel that starts at a faux First Funnel Page, as you can see from the top of the figure. To the left of that area are the top five pages from which visitors enter this first funnel step. To the right of that area are the top five pages to which visitors go when they exit the funnel without continuing to the second step. Notice the (exit) line item — these are the visitors who exit the website entirely. In the middle portion below First Funnel Step, where the green arrow points down, is the number of visitors who have continued to the second step of the funnel, and the percentage of visitors who do so is represented in parentheses.

The process repeats itself for each of the individual funnel steps until you reach the goal page. For each individual goal, you can create up to 10 goal funnel steps. The Funnel Visualization report is awesome for e-commerce websites (with shopping carts and long checkout processes), but it also works great for anyone who simply wants to measure how each page in the conversion process behaves.

You'll want to look at this report to see if any step along the way is preventing visitors from successfully completing the goal, such as pages for which (exit) is listed as a "page" to which visitors often go instead of the next funnel step.

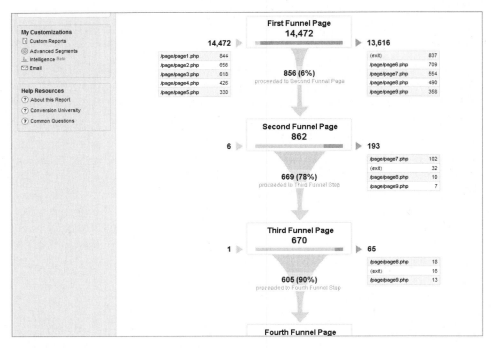

Figure 7-40: The Funnel Visualization report

The E-Commerce Section

The final section of reports in Google Analytics is the E-commerce section. If you sell a product or service online, this section will help you view transaction, product, and revenue data right within this last reporting section. As you'll learn in Chapter 10, you'll need to install additional JavaScript programming to your shopping cart's receipt or the thank-you page a user sees after successfully making a purchase on your site.

The E-commerce report section includes the following reports:

- **Total Revenue:** Revenue in a daily histogram

- **Conversion Rate:** Similar to the report in the Goals section, but calculating the e-commerce conversion rate vs. the goal conversion rate

- **Average Order Value:** A histogram charting the average order value for all transactions within the specified date range

- **Product Performance:** A subsection of reports detailing all product-oriented data

- **Transactions:** Another vertical histogram charting daily transactions

- **Visits to Purchase:** A Visitor Loyalty–style report showing how many visits visitors perform before making a transaction

- **Days to Purchase:** How many days it takes visitors to perform a transaction

Figure 7-41 shows the overview of the E-commerce report section. The conversion rate, transactions, average order value, and number of purchased products are immediately shown, along with some revenue analysis links on the right-hand side. On the bottom part of the overview page you can see the top products and traffic sources in terms of revenue.

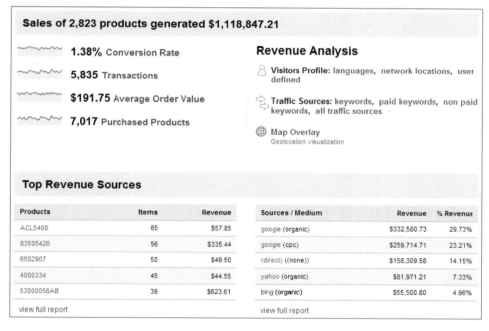

Figure 7-41: The E-commerce overview report

The interesting thing about the E-commerce section — and to some extent the Goals section — is that you won't find yourself spending too much time here. Instead, you'll find yourself using the Goal Set and E-commerce tabs available in almost every report within Google Analytics, obtaining your e-commerce data that way. The in-report tabs are super-convenient and come pre-segmented for the individual report you're in (keywords, traffic sources, visitor type, etc.).

Total Revenue

One of four histogram-style reports in this section, Total Revenue plots your overall revenue (including shipping and tax) per day. Remember that this information is also available in the E-commerce tabs throughout Google Analytics.

Conversion Rate

This Conversion Rate report is *not* the same as the Conversion Rate report in the Goals section. This conversion rate is for e-commerce only — the report in the Goals section counts conversions from all goals. One of your goals could be the receipt or "Thank You" page from your e-commerce shopping system — check with your Google Analytics account administrator, who should be able to tell you for sure. The conversion rate from your goal that may be the "Thank You" page of your shopping cart system should be very close to the figures that appear in this report.

Average Order Value

This metric is very important for any business owner, accountant, or C-level executive (that's "C" as in CEO or CPO). It's vital for the life of your business to know how much money on average you're bringing in from online sales. You may want to check this histogram report from time to time, since your average order value can fluctuate depending on what you do in terms of marketing, site optimization, or SEO work.

Product Performance

This mini subsection of reports highlights the information about the individual products ordered from your site.

- **Product Overview:** Each product ordered from all transactions in the specified date range is listed. You'll notice that in the report table, some new metrics appear in the scorecard, all of which are very easy to understand. Quantity, Unique Purchases, Product Revenue, Average Price, and Average Quantity are the five scorecard metrics that appear, instead of the standard visits and page views you see in most every other report.

- **Product SKUs:** Google Analytics collects the SKU or the code of each one of your products, and provides you with a report categorized by SKU.

- **Categories:** As you'll learn in Chapter 10, one optional piece of information that you can add to any product within any order is the product's category. Some online stores aren't organized by category, which is why this field is optional.

Transactions

The Transactions report is a standard report table with data about the individual transactions performed on your site. Each transaction is denoted by a transaction ID that is pulled in from your system. In the scorecard, you'll see Revenue, Tax, Shipping, and Quantity metrics.

The neat part about this report table is evident when you click an individual transaction ID. Let's say that you see the first transaction ID listed with a very large purchase price next to it. You can click to view the details of that transaction, including the purchased products as well as the quantity and price of each individual product. The trending graph above the report table will refresh and show one spike on one day, showing you the day on which the transaction occurred.

Visits to Purchase

Figure 7-42 shows an example of what the final two reports of this section look like. The Visits to Purchase report essentially displays your sales cycle in the style of the Visitor Loyalty report from the Visitors section. The Days to Purchase report is very similar.

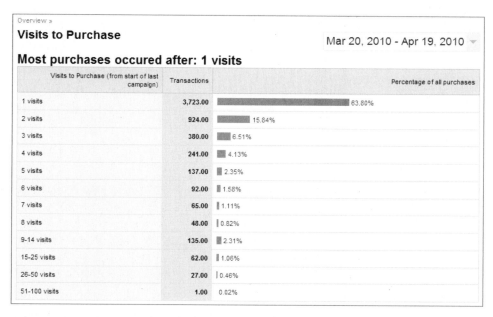

Figure 7-42: The Visits to Purchase report

You don't need me to tell you how important it is to know your online sales cycle. However, I will tell you that for most online stores, most purchases happen within one visit. For the largest percentage of merchants, this is optimal. You want visitors to buy in as few visits as possible, to reduce the chance that they will go somewhere else (remember, you probably have lots of competitors hungry to take your business away from you).

As you refine your marketing efforts and optimize your website over time, do visitors start purchasing within fewer visits? Do 70 percent of visitors purchase an item this month within one visit, against 65 percent within one visit last month? Pay close attention and even go as far as adding this report to your dashboard to stay on top of your online sales cycle.

Days to Purchase

The Days to Purchase report looks and feels exactly like the Visits to Purchase report, except that it shows you how many days it takes visitors to purchase something from your website.

As you may have guessed, the highest percentage of visitors make a transaction within the same day that they visit your site (represented in this report by "0 days"). Keep in mind that while most visitors purchase on the same day, some visitors may make a few visits in the same day before purchasing. A solid idea of how many days it takes for your visitors to purchase, combined with the Visits to Purchase report, can help you gauge your e-commerce efforts.

The Web-Analytics Industry

Now that you've been given the grand tour of Google Analytics, let's take a step back before we take a giant step forward to understand the industry that is web analytics.

There are a lot of moving parts, definitions, explanations, and rationales in this chapter. I'll talk about how web analytics works, define some metrics, and debunk some common misconceptions. I'll talk about the tools that you'll need to understand to become a great web analyst. It's not the most exciting and entertaining subject matter you've ever read, but if you're into being successful online, you don't want to skip this chapter.

As an industry, web analytics is young. It's extremely young. It's so young that only now are online business owners coming to the realization that they need to be able to measure what's happening with their initiatives. I strongly believe that web analytics is the next big thing. And as in the mid-'90s, everybody will be jumping on board.

How Google (Web) Analytics Works

When you launch a browser and visit a website of your choice, a lot of things happen behind the scenes within a few seconds. After you connect with the Internet (using Internet Explorer, Firefox, Google Chrome, Safari, Opera, or some other browser), your home screen or homepage will load, along with browser preferences, plug-ins, settings, and privacy options. Then you can type the URL of a website into the browser's address bar or access it from a bookmark. Sometimes you'll use a search engine to find a site, or you'll click a link from another site to go to your site of choice. Once you choose to visit a site and click the link (or click Enter or Go), the magic happens behind the scenes.

NOTE I spoke of both home screen and homepage earlier, and there is a slight difference in this case. With Internet Explorer you set your default page (homepage). With Google Chrome you have a "home screen" with the eight favorite websites that you visit.

Before the website loads, or even as it's loading, a piece of JavaScript tracking code that the website's owner installed on every page of the site instructs it to look for browser cookies. Browser cookies are very small text files that are set by almost every website on the Internet today — some websites won't even work properly if you don't have cookies enabled on your browser. These very small text files can contain sensitive data about the websites you visit, like the time of entry, time of departure, referring website, and saved login information.

If the site cannot find the appropriate cookies, then because of the JavaScript tracking code it will install at least four of these cookies on your machine (keep reading for what information Google Analytics collects). If the site does find cookies, meaning you've visited before, then it will simply update the cookies to indicate that you've visited the site one more time, and to note whether or not you've used different referral information to access the site this time.

After this happens and as the site either is still loading or has just finished, data about your visit is sent to Google Analytics servers for processing. The same raw data that's stored in your browser's cookies is sent over the Internet in a neat, tiny package called a *utm.gif hit*, sometimes also referred to as a *1x1 pixel request*, which is a small file that is sent to Google Analytics. This tiny image is captured by Google Analytics and its data is processed and recorded. As the visitor moves about the site, additional data is sent with each page view, which will be associated with the visitor's current visit.

When Google Analytics detects that there hasn't been any more activity by the user after roughly 30 minutes, the session will close. After a few hours (if that), Google begins the process of converting this raw utm.gif session data into the reports that I showcased in Chapter 7. The data is cleaned up, calculated, and run through any settings and filters that may be applied to your Google Analytics profile. It then is reported in your profile and is guaranteed by Google to remain there for two years. This data can then be segmented, exported, e-mailed, and everything else we just covered in the previous chapter.

All this happens for each visitor, every single time. Multiply that by the thousands upon thousands of visitors your site receives daily, and the tens of thousands of websites large and small that have Google Analytics tracking codes installed, in 30-plus different languages, with an unimaginable number of settings and filters and profiles. It's amazing how smoothly and rather unnoticeably to the everyday visitor this all happens.

Figure 8-1 shows a set of cookies that were installed on my Firefox browser from the website `www.metallica.com`. You can see the four __utm cookies, which are the Google Analytics cookies. The __utma cookie stores the time stamps and counts of visits that each visitor performs on a website. The __utmb and __utmc cookies are temporary and are used to calculate session lengths. The __utmz cookie stores the referral information, such as the keyword, search engine, referring site, and medium.

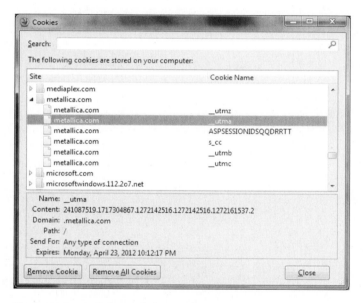

Figure 8-1: Google Analytics cookies

Tag-based web-analytics solutions like Omniture SiteCatalyst (`http://www.omniture.com/`) and VisiStat (`http://www.visistat.com/`) collect data and use cookies in a similar way, each using its own language and data-collection methods. Server-based web-analytics platforms like Urchin Software (`http://www.google.com/urchin/`) from Google and CoreMetrics (`http://www.core-metrics.com/`) parse log files and clean up the data before showing it to their customers.

What Information Does Google Analytics Collect?

Google Analytics collects information about your website visitors that pertains to their experiences on the website. This information includes:

- Where a visitor came from (Google, Yahoo!, etc.)
- The means by which the visitor accessed the site (CPC, CPM, etc.)
- The website(s) visited
- The entry page (landing page)
- The exit page
- The pages viewed
- The time stamps of each page view
- The number of visits to the site
- Any search queries performed on the site
- Any events performed on Flash- or AJAX-based applications (event tracking)
- Geo-location information (continent, country, state, city)
- Browser language options
- The browser (Internet Explorer, Firefox, etc.)
- The operating system (Windows, Macintosh, etc.)
- Screen colors
- Screen resolution
- The version of Flash
- Java (from Sun Microsystems)
- Service provider (ISP)
- Internet connection speeds
- Mobile carrier and device (if applicable)
- Custom variables (if applicable)
- The visitor's IP address (not displayed in reports)
- Activity pertaining to Google AdWords (if applicable)
- Activity pertaining to Google AdSense (if applicable)
- E-commerce transaction and product information (if applicable)

None of this information, with the glaring exception of the visitor's IP address, can be directly tied back to an individual user. Even the custom variables are collected and displayed anonymously and aggregately, so that any individual user's information cannot be found in Google Analytics. The IP address that's collected is merely used for processing and used against any filters that a profile owner may have set up — you won't find any IP addresses in Google Analytics.

Depending on the web-analytics platform, you may see slightly different information in the reports. For example, in Yahoo! Web Analytics you can see demographic data such as the visitor's age range and household income. Other platforms do show you the visitor's IP address, but have clear statements in their terms of service that prohibit users from taking those IP addresses and using them for their own efforts.

> **NOTE** Actually, you will find non-individual IP addresses listed in Google Analytics, within the Hostnames report found within the Network Properties subsection in the Visitors report section. These IP addresses are servers and in some cases will be the IP addresses of websites where your tracking code is installed. But they are not individual visitor IP addresses.

Personally Identifiable Information (PII)

Google Analytics *does not* collect any personally identifiable information, and *does not* display any personally identifiable information in reports. Google Analytics also does not allow anyone to rig the Google Analytics data collection process in any way to collect information that may be submitted on a website via a form or another method. Since this is such a sensitive topic in web analytics, I encourage you to at least be aware of the terms and conditions, and even the privacy policy, of your web-analytics vendor. If that vendor is Google Analytics, you can visit http://www.google.com/intl/en/analytics/tos.html and be completely caught up.

Google Analytics does not collect or display in reports any of the following information:

- Visitor IP address (except for the purpose of processing data; it is not displayed)
- Personal first and last names
- Street addresses or post office box numbers
- ZIP codes
- Salary information
- E-mail addresses
- Phone numbers
- Credit card information

Most if not all web-analytics vendors follow the same guidelines. When integration with a customer relationship management (CRM) software like SalesForce is present, this type of data is still not available from Google Analytics — only in SalesForce or your CRM tool of choice.

When you read `http://www.google.com/intl/en/analytics/tos.html`, you'll come across point number 7, which deals with privacy. This single paragraph outlines everything I just talked about under this subheading, but it also includes an interesting final sentence: "You must post a privacy policy and that policy must provide notice of your use of a cookie that collected anonymous traffic data."

Some websites do this already, but most don't inform visitors about what web-analytics programs they're using or what tracking methodologies they employ. I recommend finding a way to inform your users that you are collecting their usage statistics (but not their personally identifiable information).

First-Party vs. Third-Party Cookies

I mentioned in the beginning of this chapter that Google Analytics sets first-party cookies on a visitor's computer. It uses only first-party cookies, and no third-party cookies.

A *first-party cookie* is a cookie that can be read only by the website that sets it. If you visit `metallica.com` as I did back in Figure 8-1, and Google Analytics is installed there, then only `metallica.com` can open up those cookies, read them, and update them when necessary. First-party cookies are safe and secure, and cannot be sold or referred to other websites for any purpose. Most web-analytics vendors use them.

A *third-party cookie* is a cookie set by a website other than the one you're visiting. Let's say that you visit `aol.com` and there is an image ad running on that site for `brownshoes.com`. Let's also say that `aol.com` allows third-party cookies to be set. The `brownshoes.com` site is therefore able to set and read cookies on your site, even though you didn't visit `brownshoes.com`. This means that `aol.com` is allowing your sensitive web information to be read and accessed by another website. For security reasons alone, this is a dangerous practice that can open visitors up to all sorts of privacy problems. Sites can use third-party cookies to do things like use behavioral advertising (targeting), which allows sites to advertise to you based upon the history of your online activities. Some programs still allow third-party cookies. So be aware of all the facts before you decide to allow third-party cookies to be set on your computer.

Today there are also *Flash cookies* that can be set to track users, and in some cases to reset deleted cookies. A lot of Flash applications use cookies to remember your audio preferences, video preferences, and other settings. However, some also use them for nefarious reasons. You can manage your Flash player settings by visiting `http://www.macromedia.com/support/documentation/en/` `flashplayer/help/settings_manager.html`, clicking Global Privacy Settings, and then clicking the Website Privacy Settings Panel link at the very bottom of that section. Figure 8-2 shows what a settings panel looks like, and you can manage your Flash cookie settings from here.

Google Analytics does not use Flash cookies either, *only* first-party cookies.

Figure 8-2: Adobe Flash cookie/privacy settings

Limitations of Google Analytics

As great as Google Analytics is and as much as I'm a fan of it, it's not perfect. In its defense, it's not designed to be perfect. In some respects it's only as good as the data that it can collect from its users, which is something that every user is in full control over.

Some of Google Analytics' limitations are:

▪ **Robots/search engine spiders:** Google Analytics is a tag-based web-analytics solution using JavaScript and cookies. Search engine spiders do not have the ability to execute JavaScript; therefore, Google Analytics doesn't have the ability to collect and display that type of information. Only log-file parsing web-analytics solutions like WebTrends can report on search engine spider activity (for now).

▪ **Non-"Web 2.0" mobile phones:** A lot of standard mobile phones, like some BlackBerrys, the T-Mobile Sidekick, and the formerly popular Motorola Razr flip phone, do not have a web browser that can execute JavaScript. Therefore, Google Analytics cannot track individuals accessing a site from one of these types of non-"Web 2.0" mobile phones.

▪ **Cookies/JavaScript/images:** If a user has any one of these three disabled, Google Analytics cannot collect its data and cannot display the data in reports. The natural follow-up question to this is almost always, "How many users block cookies/JavaScript/images?" The answer is not simple. Even though many different reports and studies have been performed, there isn't anywhere near a consensus on the percentage of online visitors with any one of these three disabled. I've read one report that fewer than 2 percent of all online users have disabled JavaScript, cookies, or images, but I've read another saying that the figure is close to 25 percent! As you'll read about later in this chapter, it's unwise and a waste of energy to concentrate on what's not being collected. By no means am I making excuses for web analytics, but in today's world, it's just not possible to be 100 percent accurate.

- **500 rows of data at a time:** The maximum number of rows that you can view at any one time in Google Analytics is 500. If you need to view the rows of data between 501 and 1,000, you'll have to hit the right arrow on the very bottom right of reports.

- **Five million page views for non-AdWords advertisers:** Each month you're allowed to collect up to 5 million page views if you're not synced with a Google AdWords account in good standing. If you are synced, then there is no page-view limit.

- **Data sampling:** Data sampling occurs when you segment a large volume of data. It sometimes happens if your date range is very large. Basically, data sampling means that only partial data can be shown to you when you have your segment applied. Plus-minus figures will appear next to each data point, informing you of the margin of error that Google Analytics is currently showing on your data. This is done in an effort to reduce the load that Google Analytics servers are placed under when large segments, sometimes paired with large date ranges, are requested. When you see your report with yellow-colored boxes labeled with plus-minus signs, as in Figure 8-3, try shortening the date range or removing the segment to undo data sampling.

- **Fifty profiles per Google Analytics account:** Within each Google Analytics account, you're allowed a maximum of 50 profiles. If you need to create more than that, you will have to create a new Google Analytics account (I'll discuss this more in Chapter 10).

- **Profiles cannot be moved from one account to another:** Because the profile is tied to the UA account number, and for workload reasons, profiles cannot be moved around.

- **Historical data:** Historical data cannot be filtered or modified in any way after data processing occurs. What you see is what you'll always get.

- **Account recovery:** Once an account or a profile is deleted, it cannot be brought back to life. You really should use extreme caution with your profiles and Google Analytics account to prevent an accidental account or profile deletion from occurring.

- **Cost data from non-AdWords sources:** Cost-data cannot be imported from Yahoo! Search Marketing, MSN AdCenter, or any other pay-per-click advertising platforms at this time.

Show: **total** | paid | non-paid

Site Usage	Goal Set 1	Ecommerce				Views:
Visits (?)	**Pages/Visit** (?)	**Avg. Time on Site** (?)	**% New Visits** (?)	**Bounce Rate** (?)		
3,670,922	**4.26**	**00:02:50**	**0.00%**	**43.49%**		
% of Site Total: 27.43%	Site Avg: 4.44 (-3.99%)	Site Avg: 00:03:00 (-5.72%)	Site Avg: 0.00% (0.00%)	Site Avg: 38.50% (12.96%)		

	Source ⌄	None ⌄	Visits ↓	Pages/Visit	Avg. Time on Site	% New Visits	Bounce Rate
1.	google		3,048.740 ±1%	4.21	00:02:48	0.00%	44.36%
2.	yahoo		256,032 ±3%	4.23	00:02:50	0.00%	41.01%
3.	bing		229,715 ±3%	4.89	00:03:11	0.00%	36.03%
4.	aol		57,428 ±7%	4.40	00:02:51	0.00%	41.18%
5.	search		52,143 ±7%	4.49	00:03:01	0.00%	43.47%
6.	ask		22,230 ±11%	4.66	00:02:57	0.00%	38.24%
7.	msn		2,397 ±32%	3.68	00:02:22	0.00%	34.09%
8.	alltheweb		980 ±46%	2.78	00:01:16	0.00%	22.22%
9.	images.google		272 *	3.00	00:06:46	0.00%	40.00%
10.	naver		272 ±88%	5.40	00:04:57	0.00%	0.00%

Figure 8-3: Data sampling in Google Analytics

The limitations of other web-analytics solutions are as varied as you can imagine. Some limitations of Google Analytics are duplicated in Omniture SiteCatalyst, and some WebTrends limitations are default features of Google Analytics. For example, consider the "bounce rate" metric. This is not a supported metric in the latest version of WebTrends. But it's standard in Google Analytics. Lyris HQ (formerly ClickTracks; http://www.lyris.com/solutions/lyris-hq/web-analytics/) and TeaLeaf (http://www.tealeaf.com/) have features that no other platform offers. Only Google Analytics has native Facebook Markup Language (FBML) integration, while platforms like Klout and Twitalyzer are the only ones that measure your Twitter influence. As you can see, different platforms report and behave differently (which is a lead-in to one of the most common web-analytics misconceptions, discussed later in this chapter).

Web-Analytics Metrics

It's about time that I defined which metrics are used in web analytics. You've seen them throughout this book and you've also seen plenty of images of them in Chapter 7. Each metric has a purpose and a definition, and there's one organization out there that is helping every web-analytics vendor come up with consistent definitions and calculations for the wide variety of metrics they all report on.

The Web-Analytics Association

This not-for-profit organization is the de facto governing body of the web-analytics industry. It has published research documents and metric standards with the ultimate goal of influencing every web-analytics vendor to adopt consistent, standard naming conventions and metrics definitions across the board.

The group's *2008 Standards Definitions Volume I* can be downloaded via this URL:

```
http://www.webanalyticsassociation.org/resource/resmgr/pdf_standards/
webanalyticsdefinitionsvol1.pdf
```

When you have some time, read up on how this body classifies metrics into four categories and how it defines every one of the standard metrics.

Web Metrics and Dimension Definitions

Everything that Google Analytics collects is bucketed into one of two categories. It's either a metric or a dimension. A metric is a count of something, like a page view or a goal completion. A dimension is an informational text string, like a search engine, page title, or keyword.

Let's define the metrics first and then the dimensions.

Metrics

- **Visit:** A visit to your website
- **Page view:** A single page view of any page on your website in a visit
- **Unique page view:** A unique, unduplicated page view of a single page within a visit
- **Pages/visit:** The average pages viewed in each visit
- **Visitor:** An actual website visitor (person)
- **Unique visitor:** A unique, unduplicated individual who visits your website
- **New visits:** The count of first-time visitors to your website
- **% new visits:** The percentage of new visits in comparison to all site visits
- **Time on page:** The amount of time spent on a page by a visitor

- **Time on site:** The amount of time spent on the entire site by a visitor
- **Entrances:** The number of entries into a particular page of your site
- **Exits:** The number of exits from a particular page of your site
- **Bounces:** The number of single-page visits by your visitors
- **Bounce rate:** The percentage of single-page visits by all visitors to your site
- **Goal starts:** The number of times a goal is started but not necessarily completed
- **Goal completions:** The number of unduplicated times a visitor reaches a goal page (converts)
- **Goal value:** The value of an individual goal, based upon goal completions
- **Per-visit goal value:** The average value of each visit to your website, based upon goal completions
- **$ index:** The average value of each page on your site, based upon goal completions and e-commerce revenue

Dimensions

- **Visitor type:** The type of visitor (new or returning)
- **Hour of the day:** The hours of each day (12:00, 1:00, etc.) at which a visitor visits your site
- **Page depth:** The number of pages viewed in a single visit
- **Days since last visit:** The number of days since a visitor's last visit to the site
- **Visit duration:** The length of each visitor's visit
- **Language:** The visitor's language browser preference
- **City:** The visitor's originating city
- **Region:** The visitor's originating region or state
- **Country/territory:** The visitor's originating country
- **Sub-continent region:** The visitor's sub-continent region (Western Europe, Central America, etc.)
- **Continent:** The visitor's originating continent
- **Custom variable:** The custom variable set on a visitor's computer
- **Mobile:** The mobile device information for a visitor
- **Campaign:** The advertising campaign that led a visitor to your site
- **Ad group:** The advertising ad group that led a visitor to your site
- **Keyword:** The advertising keyword that led a visitor to your site

- **Ad content:** The advertising ad that led a visitor to your site

- **Ad slot position:** The actual location of the ad on the search engine results page that led a visitor to your site

- **Source:** The name of the website or marketing initiative that led a visitor to your site

- **Medium:** The means by which a visitor accessed your site

- **Referring site:** The site on which a link to your site appears that led a visitor to your site

- **Referral path:** The specific page on the referring site that led a visitor to your site

- **Page:** The page viewed on your site

- **Page title:** The page's title meta-tag that was viewed on your site

- **Hostname:** The URL(s) of the site(s) visited by your visitors

- **Landing page:** The page used as the entry point into your site by a visitor

- **Exit page:** The page used as the exiting point from your site by a visitor

These are a lot of definitions, but even by eyeballing this list you should have seen the word *visits* and the word *visitors* quite often. It's important throughout your web-analytics adventures that you make a clear distinction between the two. A visitor can have multiple visits, and multiple visits can be made by one visitor. The visitor is the actual person on the other end of the keyboard and mouse; the visit is the act of visiting a website.

Unfortunate and Common Misconceptions

Any industry has its disagreements and misconceptions, its myths to be debunked, and its arguments, ranging from tussles about minutiae to deep philosophical debates. In web analytics, it's no different. There are a host of misconceptions and misunderstandings about our industry and especially Google Analytics. No one is to blame for this — it's simply the nature of the beast. Many misconceptions stem from a lack of understanding of the basics of how things work and what things were designed to do. In this section I hope to cover the important misconceptions about web analytics and also about Google Analytics to put to rest any fears you may have.

Misconception: Web Analytics Is Accounting Software

Remember that Google Analytics isn't QuickBooks. Many, many folks feel that Google Analytics was created to collect 100 percent of all web visitors and match up to the exact decimal point the number of seconds spent by all users on the site. They feel that keyword searches, goal completions, and e-commerce transaction and revenue data should be exactly what they see in their server logs, in their version of QuickBooks, and in their CRM database. Even the slightest deviation is often unacceptable and is used as a basis for reasoning that Google Analytics or any other web-analytics platform is broken.

The thing these folks should realize is that web-analytics programs aren't designed to function as hit counters or as accounting software that requires absolutely precise totals and tabulations. Web analytics has its limitations, and therefore it will never be able to provide such a level of completeness that you can compare it side by side with more precise tools. If a user has cookies or JavaScript or images or anything else blocked, the chances that Google Analytics or any other tool will be able to collect that user's info become zero. If a user has an extremely slow Internet connection and is making moves on the website before it fully loads (and before the JavaScript tracking codes load), you can kiss accuracy goodbye. If tags are not installed correctly, if URLs aren't tagged properly, or if other factors intrude, it's so long data.

These sound like simple hurdles to get over, right? Not necessarily. Many of you readers will have bosses to answer to, or key stakeholders to present to. Bringing up the topic of total accuracy (or its lack) may ruffle feathers and poke giant holes in conventional wisdom, and could cause you to commit unintentional career suicide. Totally perfect data is fool's gold: Even if you get there one day, what are you going to do with it? Is having 5,423 goal conversions in a perfect data-collection world going to change your rationale and make you do things differently than if you had 5,419 goal conversions instead?

Web analytics is designed to analyze trends, provide insights, and highlight key data that you can use on your site and in your marketing initiatives. The sooner your boss or your colleagues understand this concept, the easier everyone's jobs and lives will be, and the sooner you can make progress and improvements online.

Misconception: Google Analytics Publicly Shares and Sells My Information

In high school I gave a senior-class presentation on the JFK assassination. I remember talking about how it was impossible for Lee Harvey Oswald to have been the lone assassin. Yes, I'll believe a lot of things, but even I can't buy the theory that Google publicly shares and sells your information.

In the data-sharing section within your Google Analytics account, you have the option to anonymously share your data with Google services and other products. The data is used to create tools like those in the benchmarking section. Other than that, there's no evidence other than accusatory blog posts that

Google is just waiting for the right time to sell everyone out and rake in huge profits. If there were evidence, it would probably trigger lawsuits and congressional investigation. There isn't any such evidence. Google isn't selling your data, period.

Misconception: A $125,000 Tool Will Solve All My Problems

I think Omniture SiteCatalyst, WebTrends, and CoreMetrics are excellent web-analytics platforms. They have features beyond anything Google Analytics can currently do, and in my opinion they provide the type of competition required for Google to continue to improve its own product. However, these tools come with a pretty hefty price tag, going all the way up to the six-figure range, depending on your package and service selections.

What's at work here is the idea that you get what you pay for. Google Analytics is free; therefore, it can't be all that good, right? However, big expensive programs should be able to answer all questions, solve all problems, and even iron your pants for you. Unfortunately, while they may be good, they aren't that good either, no matter how much money you paid.

The truth is that it still takes a human being to use the tool and to extract insights and data from that tool. The web-analytics platform is only as good as the person using it. Think about a first-time driver getting behind the wheel of a Formula One racing car — he'd crash it within seconds! But take Michael Schumacher and put him behind the wheel of a Fiat, and I'm sure he'll get the most out of that Italian compact.

Just because you pay a lot of money for a web-analytics tool doesn't mean that it will raise your conversion rates and bring you more revenue. You're still going to need a great web analyst and a great marketing team to help you along the way.

Misconception: One Tool Should Be Enough for Me

People who buy a big-dollar web-analytics platform also feel sometimes that it should be the only tool they'll need. That same feeling can extend to Google Analytics — those who use it can begin to see it as the only thing around, and be unaware of what other tools are out there.

Over time you'll want to develop a repertoire, a bag of tricks that includes diverse tools and services. Just as you'd want to diversify your 401(k) stock portfolio, you'll want to diversify your web-analytics strategy to cover the most possible ground.

You have Google Analytics/Yahoo! Web Analytics/Unica NetInsight? That's great. You also need a customer-feedback service like Kampyle or

4Q by iPerceptions. If you use social media — and who doesn't these days? — you'll need to make use of Facebook and YouTube Insights, Twitalyzer (http://www .twitalyzer.com/), Klout (http://www.klout.com/), or paid services like SAS (http://www.sas.com/) or Radian6 (http://www.radian6.com/).

Your arsenal won't be complete until you dive into tools like HitWise (http:// www.hitwise.com/), comScore (http://www.comscore.com/), Google Insights for Search (http://www.google.com/insights/search/), or Google Trends for Websites (http://www.google.com/trends/).

That is, until you want to start doing mobile analytics with tools like PercentMobile (http://www.percentmobile.com/) or Bango Analytics (http:// www.bango.com/), or you need to measure blog statistics and performance with FeedBurner (http://www.feedburner.com/) or Sentiment Metrics (http:// www.sentimentmetrics.com/). Oh, and don't forget about tools like CrazyEgg (http://www.crazyegg.com/) and clickdensity (http://www.clickdensity .co.uk/), which allow you to view click data on top of your website's pages.

As you mature in web analytics, your current lone tool will not be able to answer every question or measure every statistic that you ask it to. It's not the tool's fault; it's just not designed for it. So you'll have to expand your horizons and get out of your comfort zone to find new data sources with interesting and useful information. I'll highlight some of these in Chapter 17, but for now, check out any of the tools that I named in the previous paragraph for a good head start in what will be discussed toward the end of the book.

Misconception: Web-Analytics Tool X Should be Exactly the Same as Web-Analytics Tool Y

I often come across a website with more than one web-analytics package. More often than you may think, a website may be using Google Analytics, Yahoo! Web Analytics, WebTrends, and Omniture SiteCatalyst all at the same time. (Okay, maybe not exactly that scenario, but it's quite common to find more than one web-analytics tool installed on a site — simply view the source code or install a tool like the Web-Analytics Solution Profiler (WASP) tool for Firefox, to view what web-analytics tools are setting cookies on your machine.)

People also tend to compare the statistics from one platform with those from another, and wonder why the two systems don't match. A common conversation can start out like this: "So I'm looking at WebTrends and I see 4,350 page views for the month of March. But then we installed Google Analytics and we see 3,780 page views for the same month. Why is this happening and which one is right?"

From reading up to this point you know why this happens — tools collect, process, and calculate differently from one another. Some tools (like WebTrends) count search engine spider activity, while other tools (like Google Analytics) do not. Also, some settings, like filters, are applied on one tool and are not applied (or aren't possible) on another. But you knew that already. The next question may be the tricky one to answer: "Which one is right?"

The answer is that both of them are right. This is a tough pill to swallow, especially if it's a client you're talking to. But assuming that both platforms are installed and configured correctly, the logical conclusion is that there are two correct answers, even though the answers themselves are different. The key is to not "use the bigger number" all the time (which is easy to do with things like e-commerce transactions or goal conversions). Remember that web-analytics platforms are designed to analyze trends and are focused on cultivating insights — they're not a replacement for server logs or accounting software. Train yourself and your clients to think this way and to stop comparing statistics from one tool against those from another.

Misconception: Google Analytics Can't Handle Large Volumes (Because It's Free)

To the contrary, Google Analytics can handle large volumes of data just fine. The root of this misconception is the five-million-page-view limit per month for non-AdWords advertisers. This is simply a limit for those web analytics accounts that are not synced to an active AdWords account in good standing. If you wished, you could open up an AdWords account, sync it to your Google Analytics account, and have as many page views as your website can handle.

At the time of this writing, both Facebook and Twitter — two of the Internet's largest-volume websites — use Google Analytics on their sites. They wouldn't be using it if it couldn't handle volume.

Misconception: The More Data My Dashboard Has, the Better!

In Google Analytics you can add as many reports to your dashboard as you like, which you already know from Chapter 7. When you make an executive dashboard in Excel, there are also no limits to what you can do with it. Sometimes the dashboard is dictated by your CEO or VP, and you basically just have to follow orders.

But it's high time that folks started creating dashboards that made sense. Far too many executive dashboards, high-level overviews, or top-tier presentations include pages upon pages of stuff with charts, graphs, metrics, columns, rows, and data, until the view gets dizzy. The entire purpose of a dashboard is to have a high-level review of what's going on — not to provide every single detail. If detail is requested, then that can be provided in a separate tab, worksheet, or file, but don't pollute your dashboard with too much data. Save the good stuff for later. Unfortunately, far too often I see dashboards that remind me of an episode of *Hoarders*, with so much data piled in one small place that I wonder what I'm supposed to do first.

When I create a dashboard I try to think like a salesperson, whose objective is to make that sale or renew that contract. When the salesperson is putting together a presentation or sales pitch, it usually has at most a summary of bullet points, some high-level information, and possibly one or two paragraphs of explanation. In essence the salesperson is creating a dashboard that will be reviewed and looked at by potential clients. Try this approach the next time you're creating or working on your dashboard — remove the clutter, cut the fat, and don't become a dashboard hoarder.

Misconception: Too Many Visitors Are Listed on the Top Exit Pages Report

Another one of the most common web-analytics misconceptions concerns the Top Exit Pages report, found within the content section in Google Analytics.

Take a look at Figure 8-4, where I show the top half of the Top Exit Pages report, purposely without listing the page names. What insights, actions, or intelligence can you derive from this information?

Figure 8-4: The top half of the Top Exit Pages report in Google Analytics

As I discussed earlier, visitors have to leave a site eventually. They can't stay on your site forever. Looking at this report and trying to get anything out of it other than some fun facts will drive you insane. You will think your homepage is "leaking traffic," and will make some radical change that won't work and will wind up breaking your CMS System, while simultaneously taking your website offline. If that's going to happen to you, at least do it after looking at the Top Landing Pages report, which is far more useful than this report could ever be even on its best day.

If you have colleagues, customers, or clients who use this report, please attempt to discourage them from doing so. Offer metrics like bounce rate and reports like Top Landing Pages as alternatives.

Misconception: You Should Use Year-over-Year and Decade-over-Decade Comparisons

When a year-over-year comparison is performed, I bite my tongue really hard so as not to say anything. It's even harder when I see comparisons ranging back a couple of years, or (as has happened) a comparison between log-file web stat online data from 2000 and 2010. I added this final piece of this section to cover just this topic.

Online data is like a jar of mayonnaise — it's perishable and it has a shelf life. Your data, after a certain period, is just not usable anymore. It could very well be rotten and ready to be thrown down the garbage disposal. On the Internet, things change really fast. In 2006 Twitter had just been born, and the topic of social media was new. Our offline and online worlds have completely changed in a relatively short time. Comparing web data from 2005 to web data from 2010 is like comparing Nielsen television ratings from 1950 and 2010.

There are a few reasons why you might compare year-over-year data, but only a few. If you know people who habitually compare visits from 2005 to visits from 2010 or page views from 2003 to page views from 2010, you might try to educate them.

Becoming a Great Web Analyst

So you now know how Google Analytics works, you know the definitions of a lot of metrics and dimensions, and you have read through a lecture on the common misconceptions, all while obtaining some insight into this new and exciting industry that we know as web analytics. Now, it's time to learn the tools of the trade for becoming a great web analyst for yourself or your organization.

Part of achieving greatness is knowing the common misconceptions that I just discussed. You know what they are, you know how to spot one when you see one, and you know what to do about it. You're already more ahead of the game than most. Now, what else is there to learn about?

Failing

If you haven't failed yet at doing online marketing or web analytics, then you probably haven't been doing it very long. If you *have* been doing it a long time without a failure, consider yourself one of the very few extremely fortunate ones. It's virtually inevitable that you'll fail sometime at measuring, implementing, or doing web analytics (or online marketing). You'll make a mistake, and it may even cost you time, resources, money, or, worse, your data.

Just as in sports, you learn more from your failures than from your successes. What I've learned from my failures is that I don't know everything, and I don't like to consider myself an "expert" or a "guru" (I actually don't like either term). But early on I thought I knew everything, until I made that inevitable screw-up that cost a client some important data. I learned the hard way that I don't walk on water, and it humbled me. This knowledge was reinforced soon afterward when I struggled to answer a client's web-analytics business questions, despite my very nice summary of web data and stats, which were of no help to the client.

You will fail in web analytics. Don't fear it — simply be prepared when it happens. Try not to get mad or frustrated — learn from the experience, store it away in your bag of tricks, and move on to the next assignment. And don't call yourself an "expert" or a "wizard" or any other self-promoting noun — there is always someone out there who knows more than you, or is going to know more than you someday.

Segmentation

The key to success in web analytics is segmenting your data. Data at an aggregate level can take you only so far and can answer only a few questions. You need to know which keywords came from Google, and which visitor types landed on your homepage. You need to be able to customize your data segments, as I'll show in Chapter 9. Without the ability to slice and dice your data, you won't be able to obtain the deep insights that are required in order to truly understand your website. Figure 8-5 shows you an example of a segmented report in Google Analytics.

Let's say that you start at the very top with all visits, and see that there were 50,000 visits to your site during August. This is the highest-level, most unsegmented data possible, and it doesn't tell you anything at all other than how many visits you received. What action can you take on your website, AdWords campaign, or e-mail marketing blasts from knowing that number? You can't take any action, and that's the whole point of segmentation with web analytics.

So you start drilling into the Traffic Sources Overview report and find that 60 percent of your site's traffic was from search engines, 20 percent was direct traffic, and the other 20 percent was from referring sites. Your large and costly e-mail campaign isn't even a blip on the radar, but you see as you segment one level deeper that almost all your search engine traffic came from your Google AdWords campaign. Now, because you segmented, you know that your website's traffic is highly dependent upon AdWords, which means that you have no organic visibility and not very many people are typing in your website's URL directly. You have SEO and branding work to do.

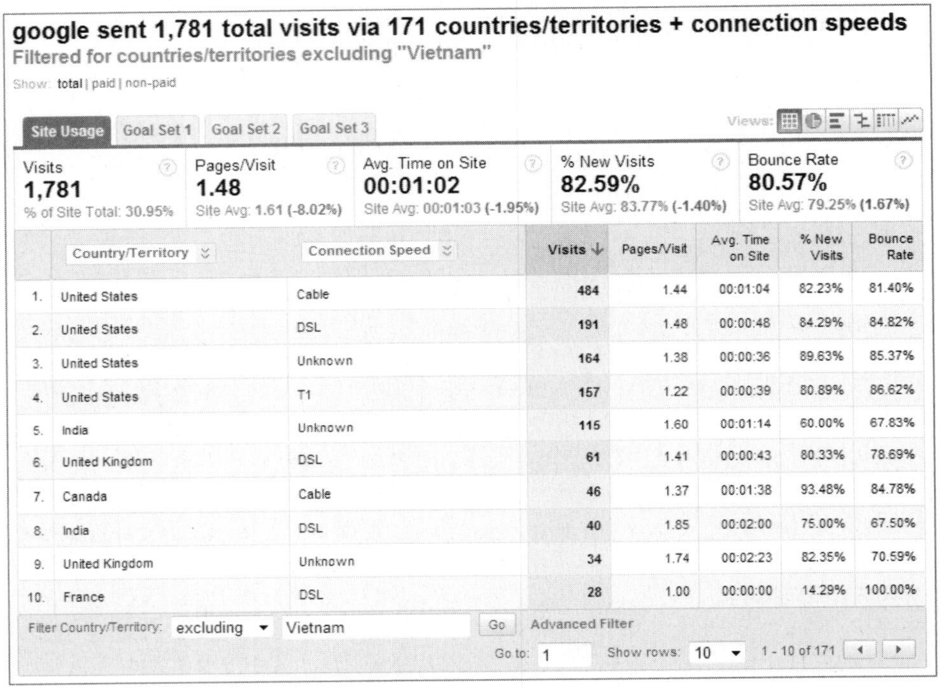

google sent 1,781 total visits via 171 countries/territories + connection speeds					
Filtered for countries/territories excluding "Vietnam"					
Show: total | paid | non-paid					

Site Usage Goal Set 1 Goal Set 2 Goal Set 3					Views:
Visits **1,781** % of Site Total: 30.95%	Pages/Visit **1.48** Site Avg: 1.61 (-8.02%)	Avg. Time on Site **00:01:02** Site Avg: 00:01:03 (-1.95%)	% New Visits **82.59%** Site Avg: 83.77% (-1.40%)	Bounce Rate **80.57%** Site Avg: 79.25% (1.67%)	

	Country/Territory	Connection Speed	Visits ↓	Pages/Visit	Avg. Time on Site	% New Visits	Bounce Rate
1.	United States	Cable	484	1.44	00:01:04	82.23%	81.40%
2.	United States	DSL	191	1.48	00:00:48	84.29%	84.82%
3.	United States	Unknown	164	1.38	00:00:36	89.63%	85.37%
4.	United States	T1	157	1.22	00:00:39	80.89%	86.62%
5.	India	Unknown	115	1.60	00:01:14	60.00%	67.83%
6.	United Kingdom	DSL	61	1.41	00:00:43	80.33%	78.69%
7.	Canada	Cable	46	1.37	00:01:38	93.48%	84.78%
8.	India	DSL	40	1.85	00:02:00	75.00%	67.50%
9.	United Kingdom	Unknown	34	1.74	00:02:23	82.35%	70.59%
10.	France	DSL	28	1.00	00:00:00	14.29%	100.00%

Filter Country/Territory: excluding ▼ Vietnam   Go   Advanced Filter

Go to: 1   Show rows: 10 ▼   1 - 10 of 171 ◄ ►

Figure 8-5: Segmenting in Google Analytics

But then you go even deeper and see that there are only two campaigns that are converting out of the nine campaigns you have running in AdWords. You drill down into those two campaigns to find the ad groups containing the three converting keywords in each that are the sole contributors of business for your online initiatives. You then segment those keywords by geo-location to find that the conversion rates are the best in New York City, Chicago, and Los Angeles, and segment again to discover that almost all purchases happen in the afternoon Monday through Friday. These purchases from those very lucrative keywords are only by returning visitors with fast connection speeds using Firefox. They take six visits and three days to purchase on average.

You then backtrack to find out that the non-converting keywords are money-guzzlers in need of strong optimization efforts, because they are bouncing from your pay-per-click landing page. The keywords that do make it but don't convert are leaving on Step 3 of the goal conversion funnel, and visitors are spending less than four minutes on the site on average. They're also searching for product catalog IDs on your site's internal search function, which is not working properly. This could very well be another reason they're not converting.

Yes, I love segmenting. And so should you. Or you can continue to use aggregate metrics like 50,000 visits to make your decisions. I'll be seeing you at next year's holiday party with all your clients in my portfolio.

Comparisons

I don't like doing year-over-year comparisons, but to become a great web analyst you're going to have to perform at least some month-over-month ones. You need to have some frame of reference, like the most recent month, to be able to tell you how your efforts are progressing (or regressing) over a reasonable period.

With Google Analytics you can click the Compare to Past checkbox within the date-range tool to perform a comparison of data between one date range and a previous one. Figure 8-6 shows a 30-day date-range comparison by search engine, to see if my conversion rates have increased or decreased over time. In Figure 8-6, at least for Google, I am showing a very strong increase in the conversion rates across the board in this particular set of goals, which reaffirms to me that whatever my optimization efforts were, they are paying off big-time. The interesting thing to note is the very first column on the left-hand side. You can't see the column heading in Figure 8-6, but it's the number of visits within my specified date range. Notice that I'm getting many fewer visits in the most current time period than in the previous time period, yet my rates of conversion are much higher. This is another great indicator of success — I've refined my site and my efforts in such a way that the traffic I am now receiving is much more ready to convert. In essence I've been able to weed out the irrelevant traffic, which wasn't doing anything of value anyway, so it's not that important.

1.	google							
	March 25, 2010 - April 24, 2010	1,823	2.91%	2.19%	1.10%	1.26%	0.33%	10.86%	$0.01
	February 22, 2010 - March 24, 2010	3,391	0.44%	0.80%	0.09%	0.06%	0.03%	1.74%	$0.00
	% Change	-46.24%	557.24%	175.57%	1,140.08%	2,039.14%	1,016.07%	524.24%	524.24%
2.	bing							
	March 25, 2010 - April 24, 2010	199	3.52%	1.01%	1.01%	1.01%	0.00%	8.04%	$0.01
	February 22, 2010 - March 24, 2010	200	0.50%	1.00%	1.50%	0.50%	0.00%	4.50%	$0.00
	% Change	-0.50%	603.52%	0.50%	-33.00%	101.01%	0.00%	78.67%	78.67%
3.	yahoo							
	March 25, 2010 - April 24, 2010	165	3.64%	0.61%	1.82%	0.00%	0.61%	7.88%	$0.01
	February 22, 2010 - March 24, 2010	142	0.70%	0.70%	0.00%	0.70%	0.00%	2.11%	$0.00
	% Change	16.20%	416.36%	-13.94%	100.00%	-100.00%	100.00%	272.93%	272.93%

Figure 8-6: Comparisons in Google Analytics

Executive Dashboards/Reports

Yes, your dashboard should never be a candidate to appear on the show *Hoarders*. It needs to be clean, crystal-clear, free of clutter, and easy to read, not just by your client or colleagues, but by you as well. After all, you are the keeper of the flame, the web-analytics practitioner who will give advice to your client, boss, or yourself if you own your own website.

Try to find a way to show what's really important on one page. If you absolutely need to have more data for a weekly meeting or client report, attach it in subpages, leaving you with one executive summary page. Use a font size that's easy to read and big enough that no one has to squint. Use simple, plain color schemes and don't get too creative with your background logos or Flash pieces. Organize your columns and rows neatly and with common sense. Of course, double-check the validity and accuracy of your data — nothing ruins a dashboard like data that's incorrect.

If you're planning on using the Google Analytics dashboard, make sure you add only the reports that you need. Feel free to reposition or remove the default dashboard reports. Limit the reports you add to your dashboard to six (any more than six will generate another page when downloaded). Remember that there's nothing you can do about the Site Usage window or the trending graph — those two will always be there on your dashboard and cannot be removed.

Take the feedback that you receive about your dashboard or executive summary constructively, not as a personal attack. Remember that the data you're presenting has to satisfy your clients or stakeholders, so ultimately they're in charge. Temper their requests to fit the framework of what you know works best in a dashboard, and try your very best not to let it get out of control.

Competitive Intelligence

I mentioned this earlier in this chapter as well as in Chapters 3 and 6. You are not the only fish in the sea. There are competitors doing what you do and thinking of ways to do it better than you. So you're going to have to incorporate some competitive-intelligence insights into your framework to stay on top of your rivals, and keep your clients or customers right at home with you.

If you have the budget for it, try using HitWise's wide range of competitive-intelligence services (www.hitwise.com). Figure 8-7 shows HitWise's weekly retail intelligence report, which is freely available on its website. You can view industry rankings arranged by the percentage of visits, the fast-rising search terms, and the industry search terms. This is great data that you can have for your site if you can afford the paid version of HitWise.

If you don't have the budget for it, try Google Insights for Search and Google Trends for Websites, which I'll talk about in Chapter 17. You can view hot trends and fast-rising search terms, but unlike in HitWise's freely available report, you can modify date ranges and segment by country, state, or city without even logging in to your Google Account.

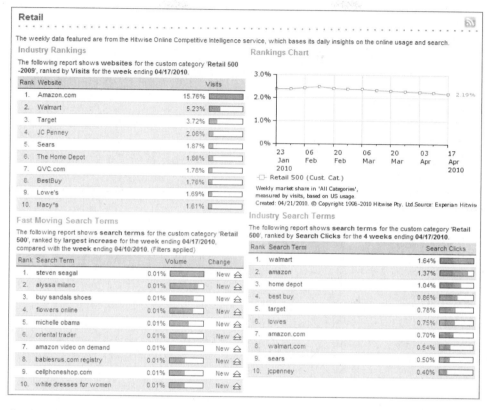

Figure 8-7: HitWise weekly retail report

Understanding Your Website

In Chapter 1, I talked about asking yourself the question "What is the purpose of my website?" To be a great web analyst, you're going to have to understand your website like no other person on the planet. You're going to need not only to answer the "purpose" question, but also to know what the secondary purposes of your website are, what functionality the site provides, and where all the nooks and crannies are. You need to understand your website's target audience, the site's content, and what actual visitors are viewing your website. This is aside from knowing how to perform analytics and calculate metrics. You're going to have to become that word that I hate — an expert — on your own website in order to truly be a great analyst.

Now, I understand that those reading this book may include consultants, marketers, and analysts in charge of looking at multiple websites. If you don't build in some time to learn as much as you can about the business, the website, and anything else you can get your hands on, you will eventually fail at doing web analytics. Take as much time as you possibly can to test-drive the site you're analyzing. Ask questions. Fill out test form submissions. Download files and play with the Flash applets. Make test purchases on the shopping cart and go through the order process. These experiences will help you become intimate with the website, which is what you'll need to do to effectively speak the language that your client or website owner is speaking, and to provide the insight and recommendations necessary to succeed and be a great web analyst.

Flip over to the next chapter to learn about some advanced tools that Google Analytics has to offer to make you even better at web analytics than you already are.

Sophisticated Google Analytics Features

You didn't think that I was finished talking about Google Analytics after Chapter 7, did you? Good, because there's a lot more where that came from!

Google Analytics really earns its stripes by providing users with a roster of advanced features, like Intelligence, advanced filters, and event tracking. Some of the advanced features you'll see in this chapter are available in other web-analytics platforms, but you'll have to pay for them. These are usually add-on features that require a higher premium, or are packaged with the enterprise-level suite of reports that may not be competitively priced. With Google Analytics, they're all free of charge.

The first feature I want to talk about is a relatively new one, added toward the end of 2009 and the beginning of 2010, called simply "Intelligence."

Intelligence and Custom Alerts

When you log in to the Google Analytics interface, you'll see an item on the left navigation menu labeled Intelligence, underneath the Dashboard button. Clicking it opens up a whole new world of analysis, insight, and perspective that you don't currently have anywhere else in Google Analytics.

Intelligence provides insight into metrics and dimensions that perform above or below expectations in a given date range. These Intelligence notifications are automatic from Google and cannot be edited; however, you can create your own custom alerts that meet your own criteria.

Understanding "Intelligence"

As you know from reading Chapter 7 or from your own experience, Google Analytics collects a lot of data. Visitor data, traffic-source data, pages, goals, e-commerce, on-site searches, and much more are collected, processed, and displayed to you as needed, 24 hours a day, seven days a week. With that much information at your disposal, how do you know what information is mission-critical? What data do you need to know right away, and what data can be pushed off to the side? With the Intelligence section, Google hopes to be able to sift through this massive amount of data that your website collects and provide you with the information that you need to know, so that you can make intelligent decisions on your website or marketing initiatives.

Let's analyze Figure 9-1 for a moment. I've clicked the Intelligence section for my website. On the left-hand navigation you'll notice that you'll be able to view daily, weekly, and monthly alerts. I've selected Weekly Alerts, which changes the trending graph and the alerts graph below it. As you can also see, the week that I've selected is April 18 to April 24, when 1,231 visits were made to my website, and nine alerts were reported. If I wanted to, I could scroll to the next week or the previous week by clicking the arrow immediately below the trending graph on either side. I could also uncheck Automatic Alerts, removing these alerts from this view and showing only custom alerts, which I'll talk about next.

Finally, toward the bottom of Figure 9-1, you can see the first two of my nine Intelligence alerts for the week of April 18 to April 24. Let's start with the first one that you see, Bounce Rate. The bounce rate for this week was 79.95 percent, which is staggeringly high. To the right of that, an arrow pointing up indicates that the bounce rate is 23 percent higher. "Higher than what?" you may ask. The bounce rate for this week is higher than what Google Analytics expected it to be. The expected range is listed directly underneath, which shows that Google Analytics expected your bounce rate to be between 64.81 percent and 65.95 percent. As you know by now, a higher bounce rate than expected is not good news, so the arrow and percentage to the right of the bounce rate metric is shown in red.

However, this bounce rate metric that's increased by 23 percent in this week isn't the bounce rate for my entire site. As with most things in Google Analytics, each metric is paired with a dimension. To the right of the bounce rate metric information you can see the phrase Landing Page, followed by a slash (which represents the homepage of the site — the slash always represents the homepage of your site, which could also be a landing page). Below the Landing Page dimension you can see that there were 803 visits, which made up 46 percent of the total visits to the site.

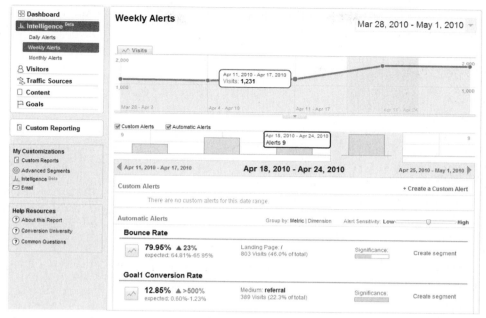

Figure 9-1: Intelligence, plotted weekly and pivoted by metric

What this is telling you so far is that the bounce rate for the homepage rose 23 percent this week beyond Google's expectations of a bounce rate between 64.81 percent and 65.95 percent for the homepage. This is very important information for any site owner: A near-80 percent bounce rate for your homepage in a week means either that the marketing to drive visitors to the homepage is not working at all, or that there is something broken on the homepage that's causing visitors to leave the site without visiting another page. Hypothetically, the homepage could contain enough information for visitors to leave the page and still get all the information they were looking for, but for this example I'm assuming this is not the case.

The metric below Bounce Rate is Goal1 Conversion Rate, which, as you can see, increased by more than 500 percent for this week from the medium of referral. Google expected a conversion rate between 0.6 percent and 1.23 percent, but instead the Goal1 Conversion Rate for referring traffic was 12.85 percent. This is a highly significant increase in conversion rate from any medium of traffic, and it's a great sign for this website. Why this occurred is information that only a website owner would know. Perhaps a new website added a link to mine (which is what referring traffic is), and the link was very popular and heavily clicked. Because it was such a highly positive increase, I want to do whatever I can to replicate this performance every week from here on out.

Significance and Sensitivity

You may have noticed in Figure 9-1 a horizontal Significance bar to the right of both the metric and the dimension. This is Google's way of telling you how significant any alert may be.

When we talk about basic statistics in Chapter 12 you'll learn about standard deviation, which is what these Significance bars visually represent. A full Significance bar represents an increase or decrease beyond Google's expectations by about seven standard deviations from the mean. An alert will usually be reported in this interface when a metric rises or falls below two standard deviations from the mean. To give you some basic perspective, in statistics, something two or more standard deviations above or below mean usually represents a statistically significant event (in other words, an important event).

There's also a sliding bar toward the bottom right of Figure 9-1 that allows you to adjust your alert sensitivity. By default the sliding bar will be right in the middle, which means that you'll see a moderate number of Intelligence alerts for any given time period. Sliding the bar all the way to the right to High will allow you to see all possible Intelligence alerts for any given time period. This maximum setting may be too much for some folks, as you can easily get 50 or more alerts at any one time. Sliding the bar all the way to the left to Low will show you only extremely important alerts with nearly full Significance bars, like my last alert in Figure 9-1, where my Significance bar is completely full. However, this sensitivity setting may be too restrictive.

My advice: Slide the bar back and forth a few times to see the types of alerts that you're left with, and go with the option that makes you most comfortable.

Group by Dimension

In the Intelligence section, the default views for all your alerts are automatically grouped by metric, like visits, bounce rate, or goal conversion rate. You can group your Intelligence alerts by dimension, to see all the alerts corresponding to one dimension.

Figure 9-2 shows an example of what this looks like. To toggle the grouping, click either the metric or the dimension directly to the left of the sensitivity slider. In the figure you'll see dimensions (like Total Traffic, Country/Territory, and Visitor Type) on the left, and metrics (like Page Views, Visitors, and Visits) to the right of dimensions.

Also notice how the third metric within Total Visits has the button next to it highlighted. When you click any button to the left of a metric, you'll see that metric plotted on the trending graph at the top of the page. When you're not looking at Total Visits alerts (as in the Country/Territory dimension in Figure 9-2), you can find a Create Segment link that, when clicked, will take you to the Advanced Segments creation screen.

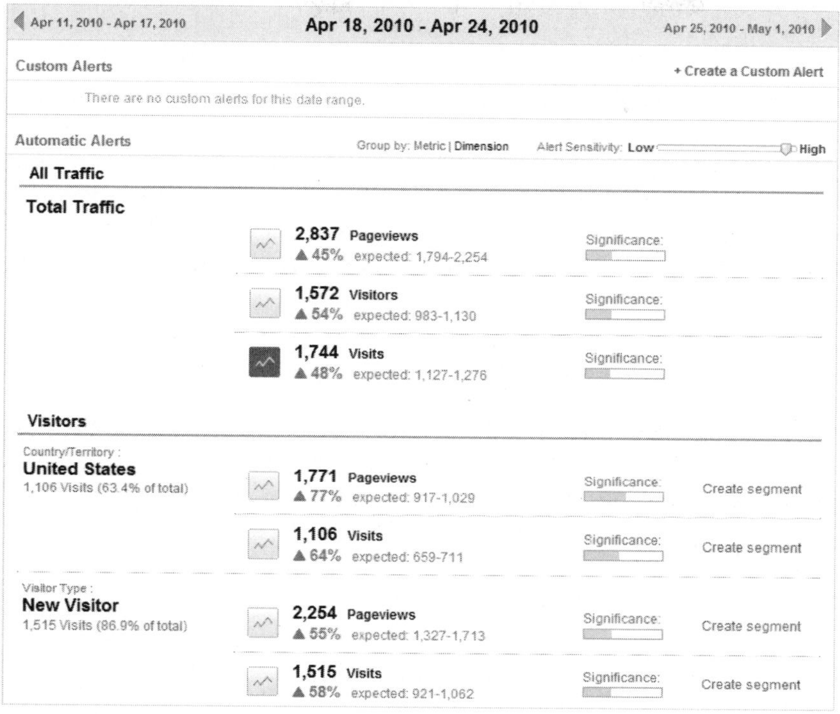

◄ Apr 11, 2010 - Apr 17, 2010   **Apr 18, 2010 - Apr 24, 2010**   Apr 25, 2010 - May 1, 2010 ►

Custom Alerts   + Create a Custom Alert

There are no custom alerts for this date range.

Automatic Alerts   Group by: Metric | Dimension   Alert Sensitivity: **Low** ═══════◯ High

All Traffic

Total Traffic

2,837 Pageviews   Significance:
▲ 45% expected: 1,794-2,254

1,572 Visitors   Significance:
▲ 54% expected: 983-1,130

1,744 Visits   Significance:
▲ 48% expected: 1,127-1,276

Visitors

Country/Territory :
United States   **1,771** Pageviews   Significance: Create segment
1,106 Visits (63.4% of total)   ▲ 77% expected: 917-1,029

1,106 Visits   Significance: Create segment
▲ 64% expected: 659-711

Visitor Type :
New Visitor   **2,254** Pageviews   Significance: Create segment
1,515 Visits (86.9% of total)   ▲ 55% expected: 1,327-1,713

1,515 Visits   Significance: Create segment
▲ 58% expected: 921-1,062

Figure 9-2: Intelligence grouped by dimension

Creating a Custom Alert

Google Analytics provides several automatic alerts that will appear by default on your Intelligence dashboard. But what if you want to create your own alerts that meet your own criteria? You can do it by clicking the Intelligence link on the bottom of the left-hand navigation menu (under the My Customizations section), which will bring you to the screen that appears in Figure 9-3.

Starting at the top of Figure 9-3, you can select whether or not you'd like the automatic alerts in the Intelligence section from Google to continue being displayed to you. If not, you can uncheck the Enable Automatic Alerts box. Below that you can set the default sensitivity scale so that you don't have to do it each time you view the Intelligence section.

In the area below this you'll be able to see any custom alerts that you've created, and at the bottom of the screen you'll be able to select an alert template with which to begin creating your alert by clicking the Copy link to the far right of each alert's name.

For our example I'll create a custom alert from scratch. Click Create New Alert, shown in the middle section of Figure 9-3, to view the creation screen.

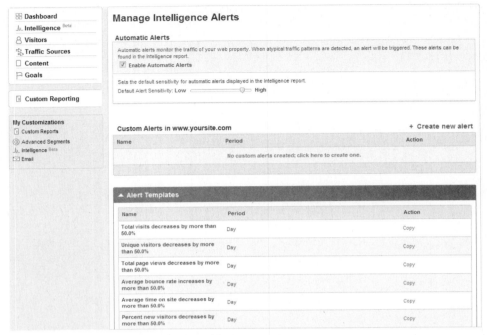

Figure 9-3: The Manage Intelligence Alerts screen

When you begin creating your alert, you'll need to provide Google with some information about the alert, such as how it's supposed to work and to what profile it's applicable. Figure 9-4 shows the Create an Alert screen, and I'll start from the top and work my way down the screenshot.

First give your alert a name so that you can identify it when it appears in your Intelligence dashboard. Next you can apply your custom alert to multiple profiles if you wish. The number of profiles to which you can apply your custom alerts is unlimited, so go through the drop-down menu on the right of this option and pick out the profiles on which you'd like this alert to appear.

After that, select your time period. Just as with the navigation menu, you have the option to create a daily, weekly, or monthly alert. Below this drop-down menu, check the box if you want the alert e-mailed to you. You can receive alerts and not even log in to Google Analytics if you wish!

Now it's time to create your alert and set its conditions. First, select the dimension from the green drop-down menu under the This Applies To heading. At the time of writing there were 12 different available dimensions, including source, medium, campaign, and landing page. To the right of that you'll need to set the dimension's condition, including matching exactly, containing, starting with, and ending with (I'll talk much more about these choices in the next section of this chapter). Then select a value based on your condition. In the example of Figure 9-4 my custom alert is going to be applied to the source dimension, with the condition that it contain a value of `Google`. Below the condition I also have the option to make my condition case-sensitive, which I've chosen not to select.

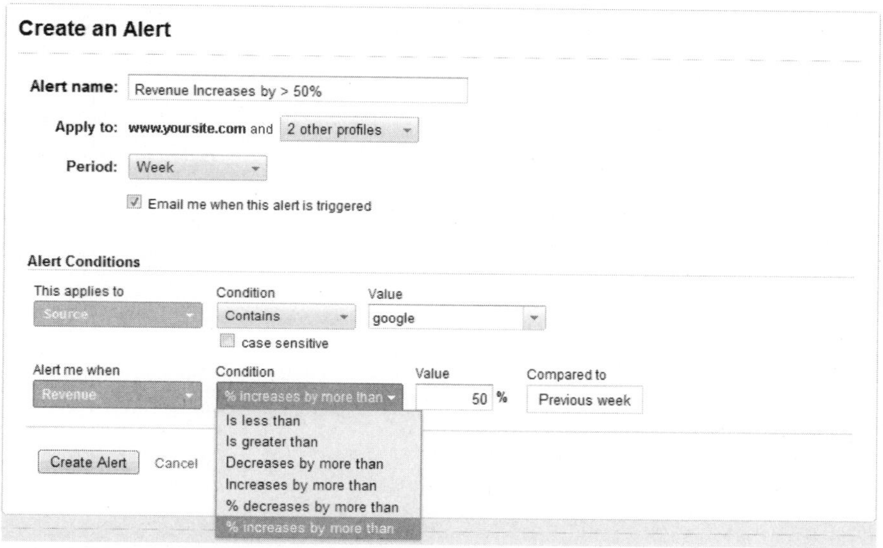

Figure 9-4: Creating a custom alert

Finally, you'll need to choose a metric so that Google knows when to apply this alert. There are almost 20 metrics to choose from at the time of writing. Here you'll also select a condition, such as greater-than or less-than. Enter a value, like **50%**, and your custom alert is finished. In the Figure 9-4 example, I am setting up this alert to fire when the revenue metric increases by more than 50 percent compared to the previous week. Click Create Alert at the bottom left, and you're done.

At this time custom alerts cannot be e-mailed to multiple addresses. Only the user who is logged in and creates the alert will receive it by e-mail. A good workaround for this limitation would be to create a rule in your e-mail client that automatically forwards a copy of the incoming e-mail from Google to your desired e-mail address.

When an alert occurs it will appear alongside your automatic alerts in the Intelligence dashboard, unless you've disabled the automatic alerts from Figure 9-3.

You now know how to interpret the alerts that you see in the Intelligence dashboard, and how to create your own custom alert. But I'm not going to stop the chapter here — Google Analytics has some more sophisticated features, including Advanced Segments, which is the subject of our next section.

Advanced Segments

By default, when you log in to Google Analytics you're automatically viewing all the data your Google Analytics account has collected from your website. But what if you want to view segmented data — for example, only returning visitors? What if you want to see only paid traffic? Better yet, what if you *need* to view only paid traffic, excluding everything else? With an Advanced Segment, this is possible.

At the top right of most reports in Google Analytics you'll see a silver drop-down menu reading Advanced Segments: All Visits. Clicking this menu will open up the layer and allow you to view what you see in Figure 9-5. You can create a new Advanced Segment, manage your current Advanced Segments, or select a default segment, which you can enable on the fly within your report.

Figure 9-5: The Advanced Segments menu

Before you create a custom segment, let's talk about what default segments currently exist in Google Analytics.

Default Advanced Segments

The team at Google Analytics has created some default Advanced Segments for your convenience. These default segments are:

- **All Visits:** The default segment when you log in to Google Analytics.
- **New Visitors:** When applied, this segment will show you only data on new visitors. Returning visitors are excluded.
- **Returning Visitors:** This is the opposite of the New Visitors segment. When it is applied, only returning visitors are shown.
- **Paid Search Traffic:** This segment will show you only traffic whose medium is CPC.
- **Non-Paid Search Traffic:** This segment shows all traffic whose medium is organic.

- **Search Traffic:** This segment shows both CPC and organic traffic. It's very important to know this because most folks are surprised to find non-organic traffic in this segment.

- **Direct Traffic:** Any visitors who came to your site directly without using a search engine or clicking a referring link will be counted in this segment.

- **Referral Traffic:** Traffic from visitors who have clicked links from other websites makes up this segment.

- **Visits with Conversions:** Any visit that included a goal conversion is counted in this segment.

- **Visits with Transactions:** Visits that include an e-commerce transaction are counted here (you must have e-commerce enabled in order to see this default segment).

- **Mobile Traffic:** Traffic from a mobile device is counted in this segment.

- **Non-Bounce Visits:** Visits that do not bounce (that view more than one page) make up this last default segment.

You can apply up to four segments — default or custom — at any time. When you apply more than one segment, the All Visits segment will automatically be applied to your reports. On certain reports, like the funnel visualization report, Advanced Segments are disabled and cannot be applied.

Figure 9-6 shows an example of what the Google Analytics dashboard will look like when an Advanced Segment is applied to it. In this screenshot I have the All Visits, Non-Paid Search Traffic, and Direct Traffic segments applied. On the top right you'll see that the drop-down menu now reads "3 segments." The segments can be disabled and you can go back to the default All Visits view from this drop-down menu.

Figure 9-6: Advanced Segments applied to the dashboard

The trending graph now charts three lines, and mousing over any data point as I have done will show you the visits per segment. The site-usage window is also updated to show data for each segment applied to the report. Individual reports within each section will also be updated to show you data for each segment until you disable the segment from the top-right drop-down menu.

When you log in to Google Analytics, try using Visits with Conversions or Visits with Transactions, which are my favorites among the default segments. You can really learn a lot from your website visitors who convert, and when you compare that segment to all visits, you'll see some stark differences that will enlighten you.

Creating a Custom Advanced Segment

The default Advanced Segments are great, but more often than not you're going to need to create your own custom Advanced Segment. Some slice of data, some group, or some bucket of information will be pertinent to you and your business, and this will require you to create your own set of rules for how you want your data to look in Google Analytics.

When you're on the Advanced Segments menu that I showed in Figure 9-5, click the Create a New Advanced Segment link to get started. You'll be directed to a page that will look like a shell of a Google Analytics report. This is all AJAX-based technology, and it will allow you to drag and drop dimensions and metrics from the left-hand side to the area on the right-hand side. The page that you should receive for starters should look like Figure 9-7.

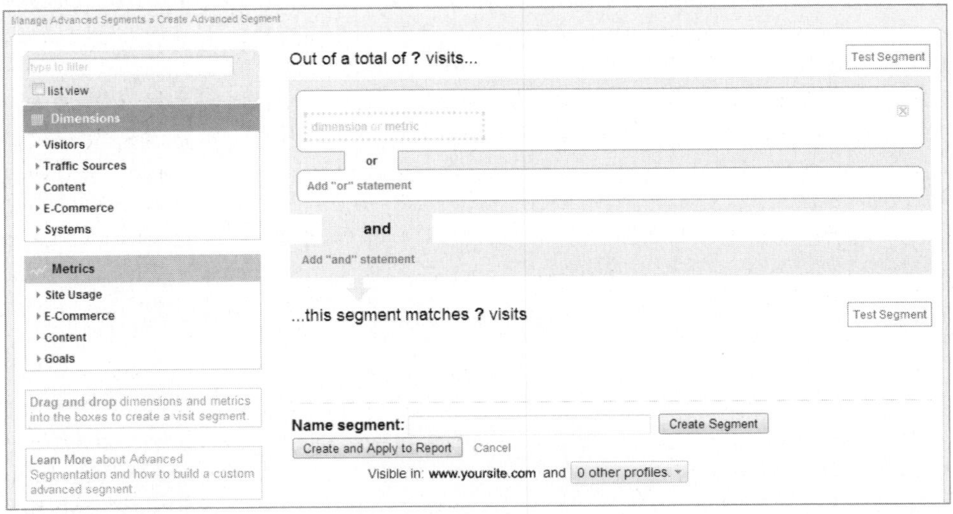

Figure 9-7: The Advanced Segments creation screen

The first thing you'll notice here is the left-hand navigation menu. As you know by now, Google Analytics breaks everything into two categories: dimensions and metrics. Click any of the dimension or metric category groups to view the available options. If it's easier, you can click the List View checkbox above the Dimensions pane to view an alphabetized list of all dimensions and metrics.

When you've chosen a metric from the left-hand side, simply drag and drop it into the dotted area on the right-hand side. Let's say you select the Keywords dimension, and have dragged and dropped it into the dotted area on the right. When you release it you'll be prompted to enter in a condition and a value, as you are when you create your own custom alerts in the Intelligence section.

The conditions that are available for a custom segment are as follows: matches exactly, does not match exactly, matches Regular Expression, does not match Regular Expression, contains, does not contain, starts with, does not start with, ends with, does not end with, less than, less than or equal to, greater than, and greater than or equal to. Choose the condition that best suits what your Advanced Segment is meant to do, and enter a value for it. Once you start typing your keyword (your value), you'll see a menu appear listing all possible matches for your value. You can either finish typing or select it from the menu.

What I recommend you do next is name your segment at the very bottom of the creation screen, and click the Test Segment button at the top right of the screen. This will show you how many visits your segment has received out of the total number of visits that will appear on the top of the page.

Before you create the segment and apply it to your report, you have the option to add to it, and you'll need to decide whether you want to add an "or" or an "and" statement.

An "or" statement will match your segment if either A or B happens. For example, let's say the first part of your segment is the dimension of source that matches exactly the value of Google. Then you add an "or" statement and add a second part of your segment, which is the dimension source that matches exactly the value of Yahoo. When you apply this segment to your report, Google Analytics will return data to you that either matches Google *or* matches Yahoo. So you'll see both Google and Yahoo data appear in your report when this custom Advanced Segment is applied.

An "and" statement will match your segment if both A and B happen. For example, the first part of your segment is the dimension of source that matches exactly the value of Google. Then you add an "and" statement and add a second part of your segment, which is the dimension medium that matches exactly the value of cpc. When you apply this segment to your report, Google Analytics will return data to you only if it is from the source Google and the medium CPC (that is, AdWords data). No other data will be shown when this custom segment is applied to your report.

There is no limit to the number of "or" or "and" statements that you can pile onto your Advanced Segment. Keep clicking the Test Segment button as you move along to keep yourself updated about how many visits your segment gets as you build it.

Toward the bottom of the screen you'll see how many visits your full segment leads to. Click the silver Create and Apply to Report button to save the segment and automatically apply it to your report. By default, your segment will be the only one applied to your report; click the Advanced Segments drop-down menu on the top right to compare your newly created segment to All Visits or another default Advanced Segment. You'll also be taken by default to your dashboard.

The one quirk that you'll encounter when creating an Advanced Segment is the lack of the date-range tool on the editing screen. You won't be able to edit your date range within the Advanced Segments screen, so you'll actually need to go back or cancel the report to modify the date range.

Figure 9-8 shows an example of an Advanced Segment being created. Notice the visits within each part of the Advanced Segment — this is what a segment looks like after you click the Test Segment button.

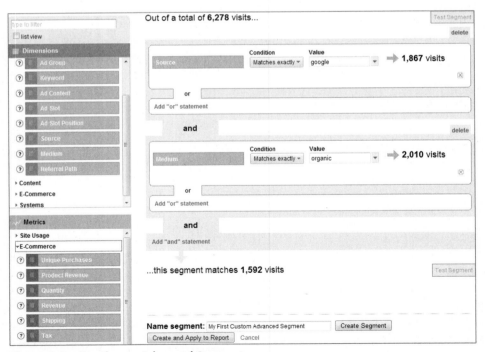

Figure 9-8: Creating an Advanced Segment

Sharing and Editing Your Custom Segment

Your custom Advanced Segment isn't set in stone. You can edit and revisit it as many times as you like. Click the Advanced Segments drop-down menu that appears on the upper right-hand side of every report, and click the Manage Your Advanced Segments link to open up the menu shown in Figure 9-9.

From this screen you can click the Advanced Segments that you've created and edit them. Or click the Edit link on the right-hand side. You can also copy an Advanced Segment (which brings you to the Advanced Segments editing screen), delete it (remember that you can't recover a deleted segment), or share it. To share an Advanced Segment, click the Share link, and a URL will pop up in a dialog box. You'll be provided with a long URL that you can e-mail or instant-message to a colleague. The colleague will need to log in to Google Analytics and then will be able to copy and paste the URL in the address bar of a browser.

If desired, you can hide the Advanced Segment from the profile by clicking the button to the left of the Edit, Copy, Share, and Delete text links.

Figure 9-9: Sharing an Advanced Segment

Custom Reports

Another high-level feature that Google Analytics offers for free is Custom Reports. In Google Analytics (and several times in Chapter 7) you've seen the standard report table and the report views like the percentage and comparison views. These reports can be sorted and filtered, but the metrics or dimensions that appear cannot themselves be edited. You also cannot add any tabs to any standard report in Google Analytics. But what if you want to create a report displaying metrics from different sections, showing a dimension that allows you to drill down to other dimensions? What if you also want a specific report with metrics and dimensions that are important to you and your boss — what do you do? By creating a custom report, you are in control of how Google Analytics serves up your data to you.

Clicking Custom Reports under the My Customizations area of the navigation menu will bring you to the Manage Custom Reports screen, where you can click Create New Custom Report to get started.

Creating a Custom Report

You should now be very familiar with the screen shown in Figure 9-10, which you see when you begin to create your report. The navigation here is just as it is in the Advanced Segments screen: you drag and drop dimensions and metrics from the left-hand side into the right-hand side. The only difference is that here the metrics are listed on top and the dimensions are listed on the bottom. The right-hand side is a shell of a report table that you'll find virtually everywhere in Google Analytics.

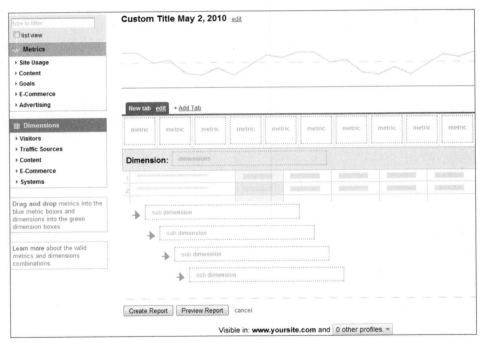

Figure 9-10: The custom report creation template

First name your report by clicking the Edit link next to Custom Title. Next it's a good idea to name your first tab by clicking its Edit link. You can create additional tabs if you like that will house other metrics going across the scorecard, but keep in mind that each tab will need to share the dimensions going down the report.

Next you can begin adding up to 10 metrics across the scorecard. The metric that you place in the first position (the position on the far left) will be the metric that the report will highlight: for example, if you place the Visits metric in the first position, the actual custom report will read "X number of Visits happened across X dimension." If you wish to create additional tabs, you can add other metrics, or share metrics between tabs, depending on what you decide to create.

After selecting your metrics, choose at least one dimension that the custom report will highlight. You can have up to four sub-dimensions, which you can access by clicking each line item to drill down into the report. For example, if you select Campaign as your first dimension and then Keyword as your sub-dimension, clicking a campaign name in the report will show you all the keywords within that campaign.

The custom report creation screen will sometimes "gray out" metrics or dimensions based upon your current selections. Google Analytics does this on purpose to ensure that you're not duplicating similar metrics in a custom report, for maximum report effectiveness.

Once you're finished, click the silver Create Report button at the bottom to see your report in action. Figure 9-11 shows what a built custom report looks like.

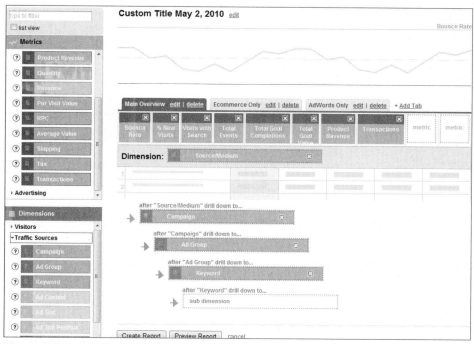

Figure 9-11: A built custom report

Figure 9-12 shows what the report created in Figure 9-11 looks like in the Google Analytics interface.

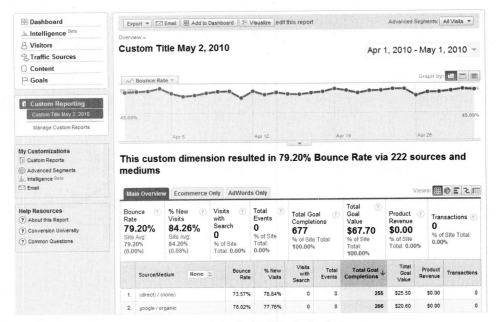

Figure 9-12: Your custom report as it looks in Google Analytics

Sharing and Editing Your Custom Report

Sharing and editing a custom report is simple to do. Click Custom Reporting in the left-hand navigation menu, and then click Manage Custom Reports, which is a blue link that will appear underneath your created custom reports.

The screen that follows is almost identical to the one in Figure 9-9, in which you manage your Advanced Segments. You can click a custom report name to edit it, and you can share it via the URL that pops out when you click the blue Share link. You can also delete a custom report from this same screen if desired.

Advanced Segments and Custom Reports Together

One of the great things about custom reports in Google Analytics is that you can apply Advanced Segments to them. Just as you would in any other report, click the Advanced Segments drop-down menu and select the Advanced Segment to apply to your report. In Figure 9-13 I've applied my first custom Advanced Segment from earlier in the chapter, where I set the segment criteria to the source Google and the medium Organic. I've applied this segment to my newly created custom report. Now I have a custom set of metrics displaying against my selected dimensions as I want it to look, with an Advanced Segment weeding out the traffic that I don't want to see. What a great combination!

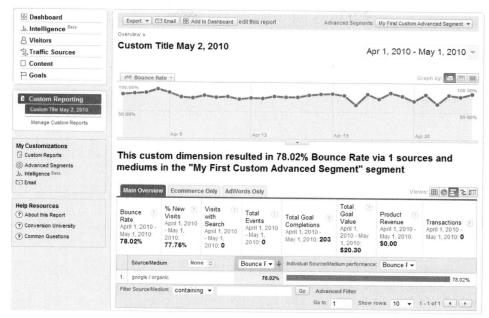

Figure 9-13: A custom report with an Advanced Segment applied to it

Motion Charts

In my opinion, custom reports, Advanced Segments, and the Intelligence section are the three most important sophisticated features that Google Analytics has to offer; hence the amount of space that I've devoted to them in this chapter. But there are other features that are important to cover as well, so we'll run through them in the next few pages.

Motion charts are neat visualizations that appear in every individual report in Google Analytics. Find the silver Visualize button on the very top of any individual report (excluding the dashboard, overview reports, or non-standard table reports like Funnel Visualization). Clicking this button will show you the report's data in a bubble chart. In Figure 9-14 I've clicked the Visualize button from within the Languages report. Visits are plotted vertically on the y-axis, and pages per visit are plotted horizontally on the x-axis. Each language has a unique color represented by the bubbles in the middle of the chart, and the size of a bubble represents the average time on site (the bigger the bubble, the higher the average time on site).

You can select any item and make it stand out in a bolder color, as I have for the en-us language and the nl language. When you select the Trails checkbox near the bottom right of the graph, your graph will be put in motion (hence the name), and you'll be able to follow your data's progression throughout the date range.

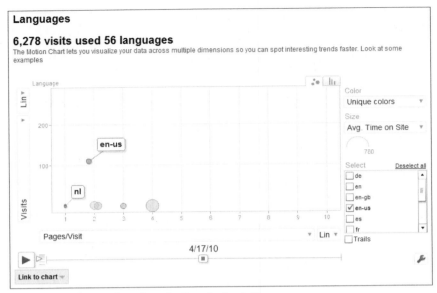

Figure 9-14: A motion chart in Google Analytics

Site Search Reports

The next feature is really a section of reports within Google Analytics. You may remember from Chapter 7 that I purposely left the Site Search section of reports for the current chapter.

The Site Search section allows you to track the activity within your website's search function. You can track where visitors make searches (which pages), where they go next, when they leave your site after making a search, and, of course, what search terms they use.

This information — the searches that your visitors perform on your site — is a great listening device for you. By analyzing the search queries performed on your site, you can place your ear to the ground and learn what people are searching for, what people are having trouble with, and what people can't find on your site. How great would it be to be able to know what catalog numbers people need to find? How insightful is it to discover what part numbers your customers can't locate? And how useful is it to know what literature your students need to find on your site? With site search, not only is all this possible, but you can also use this information to improve how your site's search function operates. In the next chapter I'll talk about how you can enable Site Search to track data in your profile.

When you click into the Content section of reports in Google Analytics, you'll find a large Site Search button, which, when clicked, will take you to the Site Search overview screen. Figure 9-15 shows an example of the overview screen within the Site Search subsection.

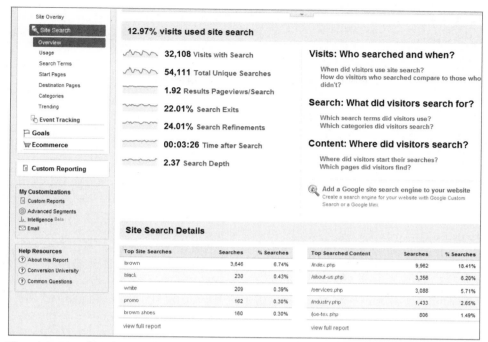

Figure 9-15: The Site Search overview report

The overview report card that you see in the middle of the overview page highlights the usage of your site's internal search function. From this example you can see that 12.97 percent of all visits to this particular website used Site Search, which is a robust amount of visits interacting with a feature on a website. Exactly 32,108 visits (12.97 percent) of all visits used Site Search, and there were 54,111 total unique searches performed by the 32,108 visits, which resulted in 1.92 results page views per site search (or 1.92 search result pages on average per each individual search).

This site in this time period received a 22.01 percent search-exits figure. This is your site search bounce rate — 22.01 percent of all searchers left the website after performing a search (which is usually not good, but there are situations in which this is acceptable). When optimizing your website's search function, you'll want to ensure that it's easy to use, that it produces relevant results, and that the page clearly demonstrates to a user what the user needs to do next (e.g., click on a desired search result). This will help lower the search-exit percentage figure, which increases your chances that your site-searching web visitor will convert.

In Figure 9-15, 24.01 percent of searchers performed a search refinement — they entered in a new search after originally searching on your site. If this percentage is higher than, say, 33 percent, then you may have a search result issue on your hands. It's inevitable that some percentage of searchers will refine their searches, but if most of your site search constituency has to do this, they are not finding what they're looking for right away. This should be a cause for concern, as it will eventually lead to a high search-exit percentage ratio.

The last two metrics are self-explanatory: on average, visitors who searched spent three minutes and twenty-six seconds after searching and viewed 2.37 additional pages (not necessarily site-search result pages).

What I'd really like for you to focus on is the bottom area, where the Site Search Details section is found. If this is your first foray into Site Search analysis, you may be taken aback by the search terms you see listed. Clicking View Full Report will take you to the search-terms report from the left-hand navigation menu; this is shown in Figure 9-16. Single-word terms like *brown*, *black*, and *promo* are the top searches on this site. If you don't know your business or your site very well (you'd be surprised how many don't), these search terms are going to rock your entire world and flip it upside down. Why would a group of people enter the single word *brown* in your site's search function, after being so deliberate in Google and using a refined search query of two, three, or more words? Are people expecting the website to read their minds and serve up relevant search results to them based on a single word? What if you sell multiple items (like shoes, hats, and gloves) that all come in brown — how is your website supposed to know which product to serve to the visitor?

When I co-authored *Google Analytics, 3rd Edition* last year, this was quite possibly my favorite subject to discuss. It should be interesting and fascinating to you as well, because, after all, it's your website. You must find a way to serve up some relevant and easy-to-digest search results to your visitors if their search terms are even in the ballpark. (You can't keep some people from typing in garbage search terms because they don't know what they're doing or are trying to be funny.) If you don't find a way to serve up relevant items, and if you don't give enough attention to your site's search function, you're going to put yourself in danger of losing visitors and frustrating them to the point at which they may not come back to your site. In the very beginning of the book, I expressed hope that each reader of *Your Google Game Plan for Success* would be able to take away and learn three unique things. How to optimize your internal site search and the Site Search section in general is the second of three things I hope you can take back to your company, your organization, or your own website if you are the owner.

NOTE In *Google Analytics, 3rd Edition*, a book I co-authored in 2009, I talk extensively about site search. You might want to pick up this book and flip to Chapter 18 to get a complete, in-depth look at this section.

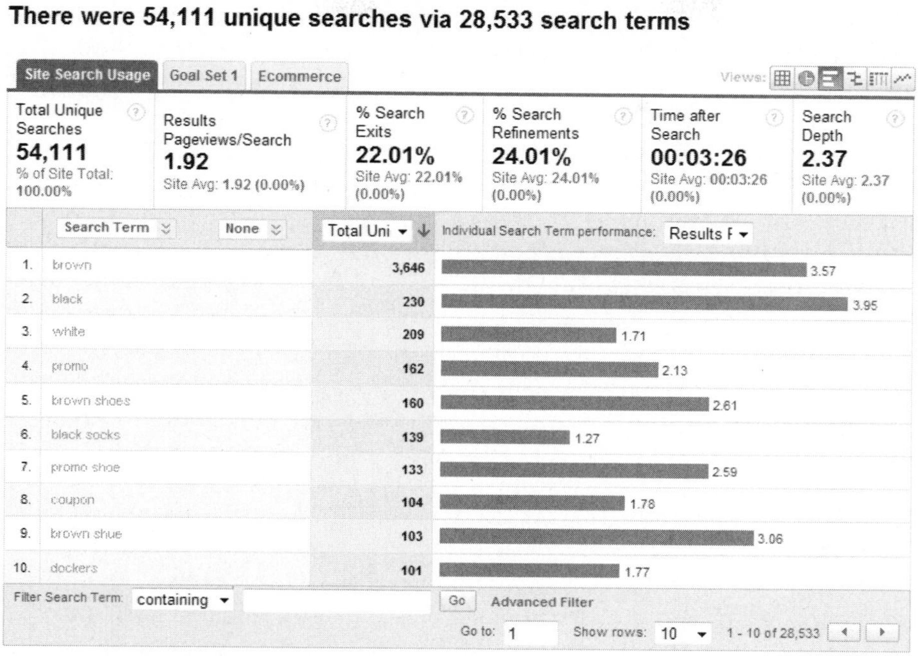

There were 54,111 unique searches via 28,533 search terms

Site Search Usage	Goal Set 1	Ecommerce				Views:

Total Unique Searches	Results Pageviews/Search	% Search Exits	% Search Refinements	Time after Search	Search Depth
54,111	**1.92**	**22.01%**	**24.01%**	**00:03:26**	**2.37**
% of Site Total: 100.00%	Site Avg: 1.92 (0.00%)	Site Avg: 22.01% (0.00%)	Site Avg: 24.01% (0.00%)	Site Avg: 00:03:26 (0.00%)	Site Avg: 2.37 (0.00%)

	Search Term	None	Total Uni	Individual Search Term performance: Results F
1.	brown	3,646	3.57
2.	black	230	3.95
3.	white	209	1.71
4.	promo	162	2.13
5.	brown shoes	160	2.61
6.	black socks	139	1.27
7.	promo shoe	133	2.59
8.	coupon	104	1.78
9.	brown shue	103	3.06
10.	dockers	101	1.77

Filter Search Term: containing ▼ [   ] Go   Advanced Filter

Go to: 1   Show rows: 10 ▼   1 - 10 of 28,533

Figure 9-16: Search terms report, performance view

Secondary Dimensions and Pivoting

Within each standard table report in Google Analytics you can apply a second dimension to enhance your reporting. If you're looking at the Keywords report, which is the first dimension, you could view each keyword's landing page by using the second-dimension drop-down menu within the report table, without having to leave the report or toggle between reports. This feature is very cool, and it's very widely used.

You can further enhance your reporting view with the pivoting view, which is the very last view option, available on the top right of each report table. With pivoting you can add a couple of additional dimensions to view your metrics by, and when you couple pivoting with secondary dimensions you'll get a total of five different data points to look at simultaneously. Spreadsheet junkies everywhere just love to pivot their data by other data, and this feature is great for those of you who need multiple data points in a single view.

In Figure 9-17 I've arrived at my search engine report and clicked the non-paid search engine text link (my first data point). Then I applied a secondary dimension in the drop-down menu to the right of Source, and chose the

Region dimension, which breaks down my search engine dimension by state (my second data point). Then I decided to click the pivot icon on the top right of the report table, and also to pivot my data by Visitor Type (third data point). When you pivot your data you can show it by two additional metrics, and, as you can see above the columns in the report, the two additional metrics that I've chosen for my pivot are Visits (fourth data point) and Average Time on Site (fifth data point). I can now — in one screenshot — see a breakdown of new vs. returning visitors by organic search engine and region, viewed against the visits and the average time on site for each.

If longer spreadsheets are your thing, select virtually any other dimension to pivot by on the left-hand side, and you'll see the first five stretched across your screen. You can click the left and right arrows that appear on the bottom of the report table to move through additional columns. You can always re-pivot by another dimension and change your metric drop-downs at any time.

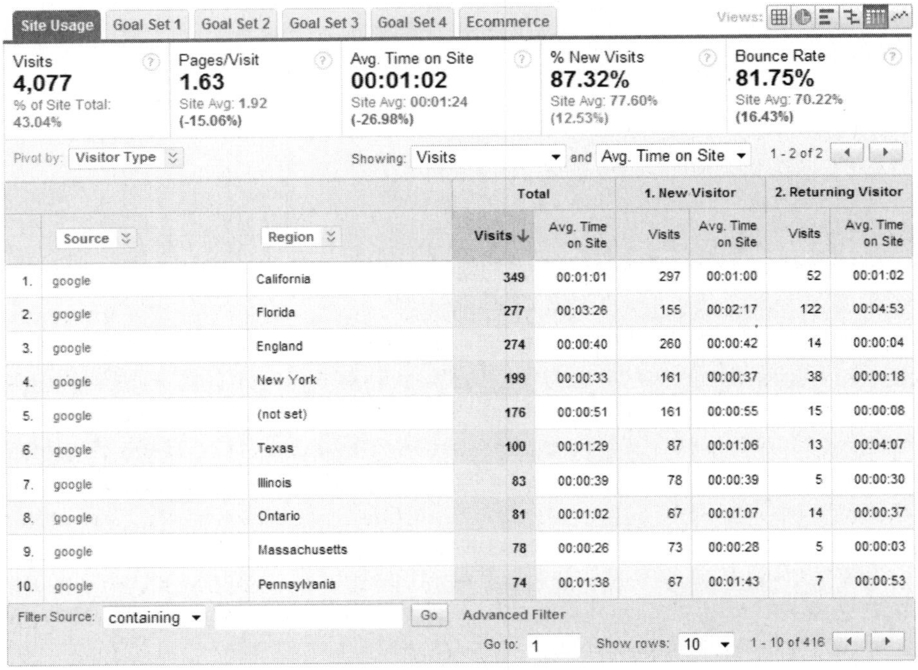

Figure 9-17: Secondary dimensions and pivoting

Advanced Table Filters

In Figure 9-17 you can see an Advanced Filter link toward the bottom of the screenshot. Clicking this link provides you with a more robust version of the filter tool directly to its left, with options resembling the Advanced Segments creation screen.

When you click this link you'll see the layer expand: it will look like Figure 9-18. In that figure I am performing an advanced table filter in which my source contains `Yahoo` (so only Yahoo! traffic will appear), and the bounce rate for the Yahoo! traffic that I want to have appear must be greater than 30 percent (this is an "and" statement from the Advanced Segments creation screen). When I apply the filter, the current report will show me all Yahoo! traffic that has bounced at a rate of 30 percent or higher.

Please note that an advanced table filter is not the same thing as a profile filter; I'll talk about filters in the next chapter. Advanced table filters expire the moment you leave a report.

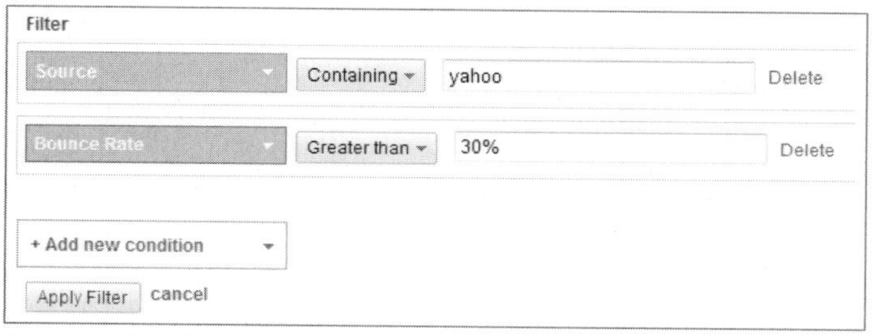

Figure 9-18: Advanced table filtering

Annotations

The final advanced feature for this chapter is *annotations*. For the first time ever, Google Analytics is allowing its user base to insert data into Google Analytics. Since its inception you've been able to collect and retrieve data from Google Analytics. Now, in addition to creating custom reports and Advanced Segments to manipulate the way your data looks, annotations allow you to insert 160-character bytes of data that you can view on top of your Google Analytics data.

Within any trending graph you can insert data for a day, week, or month (or hour if you're in a report with hourly graphing). Click the point in the graph and then click the Create New Annotation text that will appear underneath the pop-out showing you the number of visits in that particular time. Once you do, a layer will appear underneath the trending graph, as I've shown in Figure 9-19. Starting on the left, you'll be able to make any annotation a favorite (great for multiple annotations) and edit its date manually. Then, enter your annotation text, which can have a maximum of 160 characters (imagine you're posting a tweet on Twitter, but you get 20 extra characters). You can then decide which users see your annotation: you can share it with everyone by leaving the Shared radio button selected, or make it private so that only you can see it by switching to the Private button. Then you save your annotation, and it will appear within every trending graph in Google Analytics (not just the dashboard).

You can expand or collapse this viewing pane by clicking the up arrow shown on the very bottom of Figure 9-19.

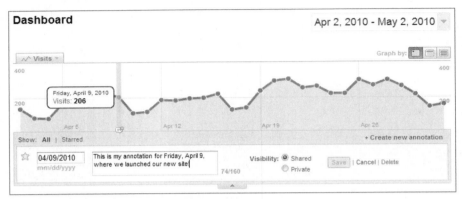

Figure 9-19: Creating an annotation in a trending graph

> **NOTE** Looking for Event Tracking and Custom Variables? These report sections are discussed in the very next chapter, as they require some technical expertise on your behalf.

Annotations are a truly one-of-a-kind feature. You don't need to be technically savvy in order to enter data into Google Analytics. The same cannot be said for many CRM and analytics packages out there today.

Speaking of being technically savvy, that's what I have next for you. In Chapter 10 I'll cover lots of technical specifications, customizations, filters, Regular Expressions, and hacks, and I won't be shy about any of it. If that sounds like your cup of tea, please keep reading. However, if you're not a technical person and you're more on the marketing/executive side, you can probably flip through the next 35 or so pages (but remember the section headings and do try to get the jist of it — you may need to refer to this section sometime).

CHAPTER 10

The Technical Side of Google Analytics

This chapter takes an in-depth approach to the technical aspects of Google Analytics. If you're working in IT, are a webmaster, or are in charge of making sure your Google Analytics account is running smoothly and tracking properly, this chapter is tailor-made for you. However, if you're more of a marketer, an analyst (who doesn't manage profiles or tracking codes and just analyzes data and provides insights), or a director/vice-president of marketing, this is the only chapter in the book that you may want to skim. Fair warning: This chapter contains highly geeky material. Its pages should be handled with caution, as their contents may become volatile.

Let's start by talking about the data-collection process, which — obviously — happens with the Google Analytics Tracking Code.

The Google Analytics Tracking Code (GATC)

The Google Analytics Tracking Code (normally abbreviated GATC) is a piece of JavaScript code that is placed on every page of a website. When a visitor reaches a web page that has the GATC installed on it, the visitor will have a set of Google Analytics cookies added on his or her computer, or the visitor's existing Google Analytics cookies will be updated. As I mentioned in Chapter 8, visitor data is also sent to Google's servers for processing via an image named utm.gif that is one pixel square.

The interesting thing about the GATC is that there are three active generations being used online. There's the *urchin* tracking code, which is the first generation of the GATC. About two years after the first-generation tracking code was released, Google developed the *ga.js* tracking code, which was more robust, faster, and better capable of handling the Web 2.0 Internet world. In the first half of 2010 Google released a third-generation tracking code called the *async* code, which is lighter, faster, and more accurate than the previous codes. The async code also loads into the browser before the web page loads, which is something that neither urchin nor ga.js can do.

Since all three tracking codes are prominent on the Web, and since all three tracking codes still allow you to collect data, let's take a look at each one separately, so you can see the progression and development of the GATC over time.

NOTE For the "Common Customizations" section of this chapter I will be showing only examples that use the async tracking code. If you are using urchin or ga.js, this would be a good opportunity to upgrade your site to async.

The urchin Tracking Code

Urchin is the first-ever tracking code released by Google Analytics to collect visitor data. It's currently not available within the Google Analytics interface; you can find it only within Google's help articles online or on a website that has not updated its tracking code for quite a few years. The name "urchin" is a derivative of the name of the company that Google acquired in 2005 that became Google Analytics.

There are some reasons that the urchin tracking code may still be on a website. A site's owner may have a contract with its web developer or content-management system whereby he or she is allotted a certain number of updates per month. Since the urchin tracking code still works, site owners don't see the value in upgrading. They are going to miss out on things like event tracking and custom variables, which cannot be used with urchin.

The base urchin tracking code looks like this:

```
<script src="http://www.google-analytics.com/urchin.js"
type="text/javascript"></script>
<script type="text/javascript">
_uacct = "UA-1234567-1";
urchinTracker();
</script>
```

The `urchinTracker` function that you see in the second-to-last line of code is the modern-day equivalent of the `trackPageview` function, which is what makes the data-collection process happen. Since urchin does not have auto-detection for secure and non-secure servers, site owners have to update the first line of the tracking code to call the urchin.js file from the secure Google server, as in this example:

```
<script src="https://ssl.google-analytics.com/urchin.js"
type="text/javascript">
</script>
<script type="text/javascript">
_uacct = "UA-1234567-1";
urchinTracker();
</script>
```

The urchin tracking code should be found toward the bottom of the source code, somewhere in the vicinity of the closing `</body>` tag. However, I have seen Google tracking codes in virtually every imaginable place.

NOTE There is often a mix-up between urchin (the first-generation tracking code) and Urchin Software from Google (which is a server-based web analytics platform sold exclusively by Google Analytics Certified Partners). If someone claims to "use urchin," make sure you know which urchin that person is referring to.

The ga.js Tracking Code

The ga.js tracking code was released a few years after Google's acquisition of Urchin in late 2005. This tracking code is a vast improvement over urchin, as it has automatic secure/non-secure detection, is more Web 2.0–ready, and uses an object-oriented JavaScript file, which is more dynamic and fluid than the static urchin.js JavaScript file. Basically, it's a big improvement.

At the time of this writing, ga.js is the most prominent GATC on the Internet, because async has been out for only a few months. Again, people often take their time upgrading. It costs time and resources, and ga.js still works fine.

Following is the base ga.js tracking code that you'll find in your Google Analytics account or on many websites using Google Analytics:

```
<script type="text/javascript">
var gaJsHost = (("https:" == document.location.protocol)
? "https://ssl." : "http://www.");
document.write(unescape("%3Cscript src='" + gaJsHost +
"google-analytics.com/ga.js' type='text/javascript'%3E%3C/script%3E"));
</script>
<script type="text/javascript">
try {
var pageTracker = _gat._getTracker("UA-1234567-1");
pageTracker._trackPageview();
} catch(err) {}</script>
```

Instead of using `urchinTracker` for collecting page view data, as the urchin tracking code does, ga.js uses the `trackPageview` function to do the same thing. The ga.js tracking code, like the urchin.js tracking code, should be placed somewhere near the bottom of the source code, preferably immediately before the closing `</body>` tag. This is recommended by Google so that if Google ever experiences downtime, your website won't be affected as it would be if you had placed the tracking code in the `<head>` of the document. However, it's safe to place the code in the `<head>` of the document — I've been working with Google Analytics virtually since its inception, and I can recall only one unscheduled period of downtime, which was repaired within the hour.

The async Tracking Code

Released in early 2010, the async tracking code is the latest innovation by Google to track your website's data. The idea behind async is that it loads asynchronously with the web page — it does not wait for the web page to load in order to start executing. It's also faster, lighter, and more accurate in terms of data collection than previous Google tracking codes.

Google recommends (as do I) that you use this generation of the tracking code on all your site's pages. This chapter will show only examples using the async code, and over time this will become the default tracking code that you'll find in your profile's tracking wizard.

This is what the base async tracking code looks like:

```
<script type="text/javascript">
   var _gaq = _gaq || [];
  _gaq.push(['_setAccount', 'UA-1234567-1']);
  _gaq.push(['_trackPageview']);
  (function() {
var ga = document.createElement('script');
ga.type = 'text/javascript'; ga.async = true;
ga.src = ('https:' == document.location.protocol ? 'https://ssl' :
'http://www') + '.google-analytics.com/ga.js';
var s = document.getElementsByTagName('script')[0];
s.parentNode.insertBefore(ga, s);
  })();
</script>
```

Unlike urchin and ga.js, the async code isn't split into two separate `<script>` tags — everything is nested within one `<script>` tag. It is also different in that you are asked to place the tracking code within the `<head>` of the document, not toward the closing `<body>` tag. This is so that async can load into the web browser as the web page is loading. However, as you may have seen in the middle of the async JavaScript snippet, the async code also calls the ga.js file from Google's servers.

The JavaScript File

It may be confusing to see me refer to the ga.js tracking code and a ga.js file that is called from Google's servers. These are two separate things: the ga.js tracking code refers to the second-generation GATC, while the ga.js file is a JavaScript file hosted on Google's servers that makes the data collection and cookie creation possible.

For some website owners and IT managers, it may be helpful to host this ga.js JavaScript file locally instead of having the tracking code call it each time a visitor visits your site. To do this you'll need to modify the tracking code (in the async code, you'll modify the ga.src command line and update it with the domain and placement that you choose), and you'll need to download the ga.js JavaScript file and upload it to your own web server. You may download the latest version of the ga.js JavaScript file from `http://www.google-analytics.com/ga.js`, but be sure to re-download it about once each month, as Google is constantly tweaking it and making minor improvements. You always want to have the latest version of the JavaScript file if you are hosting it locally.

The Tracking Code Wizard

One of the biggest questions on site owners' and Google Analytics account owners' minds is always, "Where can I find the Google Analytics Tracking Code?" It's not immediately visible when you log in to Google Analytics.

If you are the administrator of the Google Analytics account, find the Edit link in the same row as your profile information. It will be located toward the far right of the screen. Click that link and then find the Check Status link, which will be directly above the Main Website Profile Information table in your profile's settings. Once you click that second link, you'll see your tracking code toward the bottom of the page, and the status of your tracking code on your site toward the top. Figure 10-1 illustrates. At the time of this writing, the default code shown in the tracking wizard is the ga.js tracking code — you can see a link to try the new asynchronous (async) tracking code.

This Tracking Code Wizard is quite neat if you're more of a hands-off person (which is kind of an oxymoron, to be a hands-off technical person). It's a good instructional tool that can show you what you'll need to do to your tracking code if you select any of the options within the three mini-tabs shown to the left in Figure 10-1. In the Tracking Code Wizard you'll see three steps. The first asks you what you are tracking, the second shows you your tracking code, and the third (not pictured, below the second step) will show any additional action items that need to be completed.

Figure 10-1: The Tracking Code Wizard

By default, Google Analytics is set up to track a single domain, for example `www.yoursite.com`. You can add to or configure the tracking code for other situations, which I will cover toward the end of this chapter. The Tracking Code Wizard can help you configure your tracking code if you need to do any of the following:

- Track one domain with multiple sub-domains (Standard tab)
- Track multiple top-level domains (Standard tab)
- Track AdWords campaigns (Standard tab)
- Track online ad campaigns from other providers (Advanced tab)
- Track online campaigns from other providers that use different marketing tags from the ones used by Google Analytics (Advanced tab)
- Use Google Analytics and Urchin Software from Google together (Advanced tab)
- Track dynamic content (Advanced tab)
- Track PHP pages (Advanced tab)
- Edit your tracking code in a custom editing area (Custom tab)

The wizard also gives you the option to e-mail instructions for adding the tracking code to the person who will actually do the work of installing the tracking code on your site's pages. Click to copy the text shown at the very top of Figure 10-2, and then paste it into the body of an e-mail.

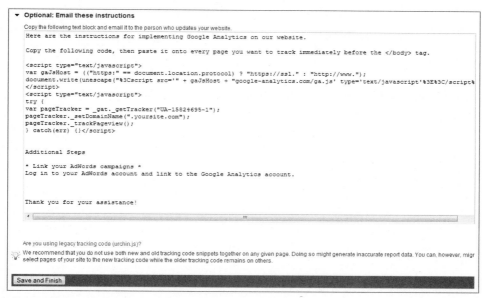

Figure 10-2: Optional e-mail instructions screen

For now, use the Tracking Code Wizard simply to see what code would look like if you selected any of the options that are available. Later in this chapter I'm going to dive much deeper and explain how to customize your tracking code by hand.

What the GATC Can't Track

You may have been able to reach the following conclusion by now, but if a user is blocking JavaScript, he or she cannot be tracked by Google Analytics.

Users who block JavaScript, cookies, and even images cannot be tracked by Google Analytics. This includes most search engine spiders that you'll see pop up in server log files and log-based web-analytics packages like WebTrends. Users using mobile phones without browsers that can execute JavaScript or load images also cannot be tracked, even though you may again see them in log files. Any user who intentionally blocks cookies, tracking scripts, or Google cannot be tracked. Those same users blocking cookies and JavaScript are also missing out on a lot of functionality on the Internet that requires cookies and JavaScript in order to function, like Flash players, video players, and many other web applications.

This almost always brings up two separate issues. The first is that you want to know how many people block cookies or JavaScript, or otherwise make themselves untrackable. The answer you want to hear is "Eight percent," or some other figure put together by some research company. The real answer is that there is no way to know for sure. There really isn't a consensus in the industry. You should use web analytics to compare your data against historical trends and site average trends, and extract valuable insights.

The tail end of the first issue rolls right into that of comparing data sets — that is, comparing the statistics provided by Google Analytics. It shouldn't matter to you if there's a 5 or 10 or 20 percent difference between your log files and Google Analytics, or any two packages. Again, the purpose of web analytics is to compare trends, segment data, and extract insights — not to keep records or update accounting spreadsheets.

As tough as it sounds, don't fall into the trap of trying to make your web-analytics data perfect. It won't happen, and you'll waste a lot of energy. Trust me, I've been down that road myself, and I realized that web analytics is about much more than collecting exactly perfect data.

Google Analytics Cookies

We talked about the fact that Google Analytics sets up to four, possibly five, first-party cookies on a user's computer when he or she visits a website for the first time. If a visitor has already been to your website and already has existing cookies, the JavaScript will work to update those cookies to reflect additional visits and page views. Just so that everyone is clear, a cookie is a small text file that contains data about a visitor's interaction with a website.

There are four first-party cookies that will be set automatically, assuming a user is accepting cookies. There could be a fifth first-party cookie, depending on whether or not a website is using custom segmentation. Let's look at the Google Analytics cookies, but first check out Figure 10-3, which shows a set of Google Analytics cookies on my Firefox browser for the Google Analytics blog site.

The __utma Cookie

The __utma cookie (that's a double underscore and the letters "utma") is the visitor identification cookie. This cookie is persistent (meaning it remains on your computer after your browsing session ends), and it has a default lifespan of two years.

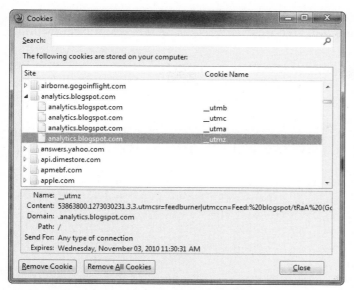

Figure 10-3: Google Analytics cookies

This cookie tells Google Analytics the domain and the time of the current and initial visit, and acts as the session counter to tell Google Analytics if you're a new visitor or a returning visitor (and, if you're a returning visitor, how many visits you have to your credit). When you open up the cookies in your browser, as I did in Figure 10-3, and click to view the __utma cookie, you should see something like this:

```
53863800.397018497.1272945173.1273030231.1273531162.4
```

Each set of numbers is separated by a dot, and each set of numbers means something. The first number that you see in my example — 53863800 — is called a *domain hash*. Google Analytics uses it to keep the domain information (the actual URL of the website you visited) confidential and encrypted so that no one else can read this sensitive data, except for the website that sets the cookie. First-party cookies work this way to safeguard a user's identity. The domain hash is present on all other Google Analytics cookies for security reasons. This domain hash number will be different for each set of cookies that you may have on your computer.

The second number — 397018497 — is a random unique ID that is associated with your __utma cookie. This unique ID, plus the third number, which in my example is 1272945173, is what Google Analytics uses to count unique visitors for any given date range. That third number, 1272945173, is the Unix time stamp of the initial visit to the site. Google Analytics keeps time using Unix time stamps, like most software applications today.

The fourth number — 1273030231 — is the time stamp of the beginning of the previous session, and the fifth number — 1273531162 — is the time stamp of the current session. This data is used to calculate the visitor loyalty and recency reports in the Visitors section.

The sixth and final number, at the very end of my example __utma cookie string — 4 — is the session counter. In this example I've visited the Google Analytics blog four times in my two-year cookie lifetime.

The __utmb and __utmc Cookies

Both the __utmb and __utmc cookies are session identifiers. They serve the purpose of collecting page-view time stamps so that Google Analytics can record and calculate the average-time-on-site metric.

This brings up a new issue that is vital to understanding how Google Analytics works. The __utmb cookie is a persistent cookie, like the __utma cookie. The difference between the two is that the __utma cookie lasts by default for two years, while the __utmb cookie lasts only 30 minutes after the session expires. The __utmc cookie is a temporary cookie and expires as soon as you close your browser, thereby ending your browsing session.

What the __utmb and __utmc cookies do is take the time stamp of your first page view to the site in a given session. They then wait until you make a second page view to record the second time stamp, and subtract the value of the first time stamp from the value of the second time stamp. The remainder is the time you spent on the first page. Google Analytics will keep doing this for each subsequent page view, and at the end of your session all of your page view times will be added up, and the time you spent on the site (and on each individual page) will be recorded and sent to Google, along with your other cookie data.

Now, what if a person views only one page, and does not give an opportunity for the __utmb and __utmc cookies to record a second time stamp? How does Google Analytics know how much time you spent on the first page of the site? The answer is that it doesn't know, leaving you with a result of a single-page visit (a bounce) without an average-time-on-site metric. A visitor may spend 25 minutes on a site, but if he or she never makes a second page view, it won't be possible to record the actual time of the one he or she does make.

You could most likely write some code to modify the way that page views are detected by the __utmb and __utmc cookies so that you can record a second page view after a certain amount of time has elapsed.

The __utmz Cookie

The __utmz cookie is the referral cookie that stores all a visitor's referral information. It's also known as the *campaign* cookie, as campaign information is stored here.

Like the __utma and __utmb cookies, the __utmz cookie is a persistent one, with a default shelf life of six months. This can be edited, and I'll show you how to do that later in this chapter (the "Modifying Cookie Timeout Values" subsection). If you click an AdWords ad that is properly synced to a Google Analytics account, or for which campaign tracking URLs are being used (both of which will be discussed in later chapters), the __utmz cookie will store the source, medium, campaign, term, and content data, which Google Analytics will take and use in the Traffic Sources report section. For reasons that will become very clear toward the end of the chapter, maintaining the integrity of the __utmz cookie should be taken very seriously. The __utmz cookie can be compromised in a few precarious situations, like crossing between sub-domains or top-level domains.

The following is an example of the __utmz cookie for the Google Analytics blog site on my computer:

```
53863800.1273030231.3.3.utmcsr=feedburner|

utmccn=Feed:%20blogspot/tRaA%20(Google%20Analytics%20Bl

og)|utmcmd=feed|utmcct=Google%20Feedfetcher
```

There are two parts to the __utmz cookie: on the left are numbers, and on the right are words. The first number on the left — 53863800 — is the domain hash, which is present in all Google Analytics cookies. The second number — 1273030231 — is the time stamp showing when the campaign data was collected. The next two numbers — 3 and 3 — are the session number and the campaign number, respectively. The session number increases by one for every session in which the campaign cookie is overwritten. The campaign number increases by one for every time you arrive at the site by means of a different campaign. Google needs these counts to know how to best attribute page view, conversion, and e-commerce data in reports.

The first wording after the campaign number — utmcsr=feedburner — shows the source of the referral. In this case I came from FeedBurner, which is an RSS feed-aggregating service used by virtually everyone who owns a blog. The second wording — utmccn=Feed:%20blogspot/tRaA%20(Google%20Analytics%20 Blog) — shows the name of the campaign, which is "Feed blogspot/tRaA (Google Analytics Blog). It's quite lengthy, but this is how Google wants it to look in its reports. Notice the "%20" occurrences in the campaign name — %20 is the encoded value for a space.

The third wording — utmcmd=feed — is the medium, which is the means by which I accessed the site. Here it's feed. Other common media include organic, cpc (for cost-per-click campaigns), and referral. The fourth and final wording in my example — utmcct=Google%20Feedfetcher — is the ad content, which usually identifies the ad or the link that a visitor clicked.

There is a fifth possible string that is not shown in my example, which would look like this:

```
utmctr=google%20analytics%20blog
```

This would be my string, if I had either used an organic search engine or clicked a cost-per-click ad. In this example I used the keyword "google analytics blog" in a search engine and clicked either an organic listing or a pay-per-click advertisement.

Even if you're not in marketing or online advertising, you can quickly see how valuable the data in this cookie is, and how important it is to keep it clean and not compromised.

The __utmv Cookie

The __utmv cookie is a special fifth cookie that can be dropped on a visitor's machine if you are using custom segmentation, which we will talk much more about later in this chapter. The __utmv cookie can hold up to five different labels for a unique visitor that can associate him or her with an important action or an important flag that allows advertisers to segment by these groups in Google Analytics reports.

The __utmv cookie has a shelf life of up to two years, making it a persistent cookie. It holds the domain hash like the other cookies, and holds up to five key/value pair combinations that identify certain unique visitors in a unique way. As we'll discuss later in the chapter, how you plan for custom variables is critical to their use.

E-Commerce Tracking

Quite possibly the most-used code customization is the Google Analytics e-commerce tracking module. This information is displayed as transaction and product data in the e-commerce reports that were highlighted at the end of Chapter 7.

This tracking code is appended to the standard GATC on the shopping cart's receipt, order confirmation, or thank-you page displayed to a visitor after a purchase. It can also be used on any page that comes after a transaction without a shopping cart, like a donation form or one-time payment form. If you're creative enough, you can find useful ways to use the e-commerce tracking code on your non-e-commerce site.

Enabling E-Commerce Tracking

Figure 10-4 shows the Edit Profile Information screen within your profile's Main Website Profile Information settings. Before you install the e-commerce tracking script, you'll need to ensure that your profile is set up to report on the e-commerce data that your site will begin to collect. Simply select Yes under E-Commerce Website, click Save, and your e-commerce reporting section will be displayed as shown in Chapter 7.

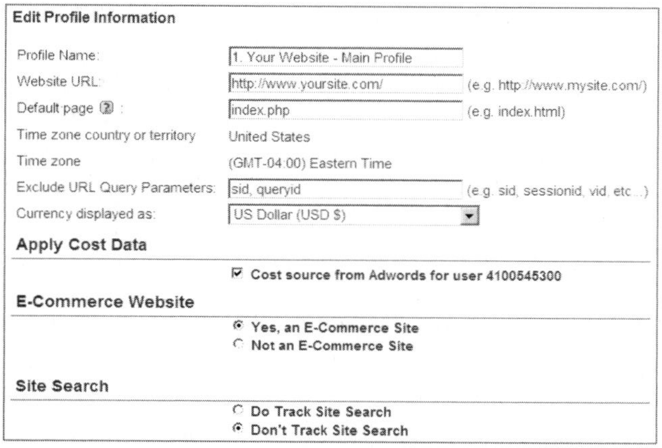

Figure 10-4: Enabling e-commerce in your profile settings

The E-Commerce Tracking Snippet

Let's take a look at the e-commerce code snippet, and its location relative to the critical `trackPageview` function in the GATC:

```
_gaq.push(['_setAccount', 'UA-1234567-1']);
_gaq.push(['_trackPageview']);
_gaq.push(['_addTrans',
   '1234',              // order ID - required
   'Mountain View',     // affiliation or store name
   '11.99',             // total - required
   '1.29',              // tax
   '5',                 // shipping
   'San Jose',          // city
   'California',        // state or province
   'USA'                // country
]);
_gaq.push(['_addItem',
   '1234',              // order ID - required
   'DD44',              // SKU/code
   'T-Shirt',           // product name
   'Green Medium',      // category or variation
   '11.99',             // unit price - required
   '1'                  // quantity - required
]);
_gaq.push(['_trackTrans']);
```

There are three main components of the e-commerce tracking snippet. The first is the `addTrans` function, which is in the third line of my example. The `addTrans` function collects the following transaction information:

- **Order ID:** This is a required field, which means it must be filled out in order for e-commerce tracking to function. This is the order ID that your shopping cart or transaction system generates.
- **Affiliation:** This is a store name, like Mountain View or San Francisco, or any other name you want to use.
- **Total:** The transaction total, which is a required field.
- **Tax:** The tax charged in the transaction.
- **Shipping:** The shipping charged in the transaction.
- **City:** The city in which the transaction originated.
- **State or Province:** The state or province in which the transaction originated.
- **Country:** The country in which the transaction originated.

You're required to fill in only the `order ID` and `total` fields in the `addTrans` function, but to get the most relevant data possible for your Google Analytics account, I recommend filling out all fields.

The second component of the e-commerce tracking code is the `addItem` function, which will be in charge of collecting all product data. The fields collected by the `addItem` function are the following:

- **Order ID:** Just like the `addTrans` function, the `order ID` in the `addItem` field is required, and, additionally, it must match the `order ID` in the `addItem` function exactly.
- **SKU/Code:** This is reserved for a product number or SKU that you may find on the UPC label or on the back of an off-the-shelf product.
- **Product Name:** The name of the product ordered.
- **Category or Variation:** A category or a variation that the item ordered belongs to.
- **Unit Price:** A required field, this is used to indicate the individual item price (not the combined price of multiple quantities of the same item).
- **Quantity:** The quantity of each item purchased (a required field).

Again, while you're required only to fill in `order ID`, `unit price`, and `quantity`, it's a good idea to fill in as much product data as possible (preferably all fields).

For the `addItem` function, Google Analytics requires that for each additional unique item ordered, you create a second, third, or *n*th `addItem` entry in the e-commerce tracking module, so that Google Analytics can accurately collect transactions that contain multiple products. For example, let's say that not only did I purchase a T-shirt from the Google Store, I also purchased two large blue hats. The e-commerce coding would then appear as the following in the source code of the page:

```
_gaq.push(['_addTrans'
    '1234',            // order ID - required
    'Mountain View',   // affiliation or store name
    '11.99',           // total - required
    '1.29',            // tax
    '5',               // shipping
    'San Jose',        // city
    'California',      // state or province
    'USA'              // country
]);
_gaq.push(['_addItem',
    '1234',            // order ID - required
    'DD44',            // SKU/code
    'T-Shirt',         // product name
    'Green Medium',    // category or variation
    '11.99',           // unit price - required
    '1'                // quantity - required
]);
_gaq.push(['_addItem',
    '1234',            // order ID - required
    'HT12',            // SKU/code
    'XLS-Hat',         // product name
    'Blue Hat- LG',    // category or variation
    '11.95',           // unit price - required
    '2'                // quantity - required
]);
_gaq.push(['_trackTrans']);
```

Notice how the order ID field is the same for both products, but each individual product has its own SKU/code. Also notice that this particular transaction contains a quantity of 2, yet the unit price of 11.95 is the individual item price for each hat. Don't automatically multiply the quantity by the unit price — Google Analytics will do this for you on the report-processing end.

The third and final component of the e-commerce tracking code is the trackTrans method, which sends the addTrans and addItem data to Google Analytics servers for processing. Strangely, the trackTrans line is chopped off or simply forgotten about more often than seems logical. Without the trackTrans function, e-commerce data from Google Analytics will not be able to be collected.

You may be wondering how Google's e-commerce tracking script is able to collect this transaction data. This is where you, the developer/programmer, are going to come into the picture. With the e-commerce tracking snippet, you must write some application code or some piece of programming that will copy the values of the transaction and print them into the addTrans and addItem fields.

It's also your responsibility to ensure that each unique product is given its own `addItem` function. This can be done in PHP, .NET, ASP, ColdFusion, and any other non-HTML language that you can think of. It doesn't matter how your programming or application code is written — as long as it does the job of printing the transaction data for the e-commerce coding snippet, you're good to go.

Some off-the-shelf products like Miva Merchant and osCommerce offer Google Analytics plug-ins, where you'll only be required to provide the UA account number for your Google Analytics account. Check with your vendor to find out whether it offers a plug-in — you may be able to bypass having to hard-code everything.

Common E-Commerce Tracking Mistakes

Those of you who own *Google Analytics, 3rd Edition* (a book released in 2009 by Wiley Publishing that I had the pleasure of coauthoring) will recognize this subhead from that book's Chapter 8. There are several different types of mistakes you may make when programming your site for collecting e-commerce data, and these mistakes can affect the way your data ultimately appears in the reports. You need to be aware of all of the following common mistakes and pitfalls in order to collect the cleanest, most accurate data possible for your website. Your marketing department will thank you on bended knee for your diligent efforts.

- **Different Order IDs on** `addTrans` **and any** `addItem`**:** The Order ID for each transaction must be exactly the same in both the `addTrans` function and every `addItem` function. If not, your data will be heavily distorted in Google Analytics.

- **SKU/Code inconsistency:** If a visitor's order contains multiple items, making it necessary for multiple `addItem` functions to be called, each item must have a SKU/Code field filled out. This may sound like a no-brainer, but if for some reason you accidentally (or purposely) do not include a SKU/Code for any `addItem`, that item won't be recorded and you'll see wild inconsistencies in your e-commerce reports. Make sure that each `addItem` line contains a SKU/Code field.

- **Special characters:** Currency symbols, quotations marks, asterisks, commas (especially commas), and any other characters like that in any e-commerce field will cause data distortion. You will probably need to check the source code of an order as it appears online to ensure that special characters aren't appearing in any field. If they are, write some additional code to replace these characters with letters, numbers, or dashes.

- **The number zero:** The standalone number zero has also been known to cause some issues with reporting data in the past. Some accounts do not have any problems using zeroes for either the Tax or Shipping fields, while others do. My best advice is to not use zeroes and simply to skip the field entirely (leave it blank — no white space, no zero, no nothing — just two consecutive quotation marks).

- **Commas:** Commas are just dangerous, and cause problems when used as thousands-place separators. We've all been taught in math classes to use commas to separate places by the thousands for large numbers. For Google Analytics e-commerce transaction data collection, you'll want to forget all about that advice.

- **Pre-multiplying the Unit Price field:** I mentioned this earlier, but it definitely bears repeating, as it's very common. Do not pre-multiply the Unit Price field by the quantity; Google Analytics will do this for you during report processing.

- **Leaving out the** `trackTrans` **function:** This last line of Google Analytics e-commerce coding is surprisingly left off the final product quite often. Don't forget that the actual call to Google Analytics servers happens via the `trackTrans` function, so it's required in order for e-commerce tracking to function.

- **Not using required fields:** Just so that you're clear, the required fields in the `addTrans` function are Order ID and Total. The required fields in the `addItem` function are Order ID, Unit Price, and Quantity. You *must* use at least these five fields to record a successful transaction.

- **Not running** `addItem` **when necessary:** Don't forget to run `addItem` for each unique item in a transaction. If your order contains one T-shirt, two hats, and three watches, there should be three `addItem` functions, as three unique items were ordered.

Event Tracking

In the earlier Google Analytics chapters, I told you that you could track the "Web 2.0" interactions that users have when they are on your website. Event tracking is one of the fancier features and nicer customization possibilities provided by the Google Analytics Tracking Code, as you can track all non-page-view actions that a user may perform while on your website.

The important phrase to note is that event tracking with Google Analytics is designed for anything that is specifically not a standard page view. This could be anything that a user can do on a Flash piece, a web application that uses AJAX, or any other interactive application in any language on your site. You could use a virtual page view to track these interactions, as I'll show you later in the chapter, but it wouldn't be very appropriate to do so, as the user really isn't visiting a page or downloading a file that cannot be tracked with the GATC. Also, the event tracking schema allows for some organizational and numerical value associations to collect some fairly insightful data on the activities of your Web 2.0 elements.

NOTE At the time of this writing, goals cannot be created as events. As you'll learn at the end of this chapter, a goal can be created as a page view, as time on site, or as a number of pages per visit. Keep this in mind as you're developing your event-tracking functions.

Categories, Actions, Labels, and Values

The event-tracking functionality is usually in the form of a standalone JavaScript event, like onClick or onLoad. However, you can use any standard JavaScript command function that will fire off an event tracking hit. As a standalone example, event tracking can be used as an onClick event on a video's play button, like this:

```
onClick="_gaq.push
(['_trackEvent', 'Videos', 'Play', 'Avatar Trailer', 150]);"
```

Event tracking can also be used in line with the GATC, like this:

```
<script type="text/javascript">
  var _gaq = _gaq || [];
  _gaq.push(['_setAccount', 'UA-1234567-1']);
  _gaq.push(['_trackEvent', 'Videos', 'Play', 'Avatar Trailer', 150]);
  _gaq.push(['_trackPageview']);
  (function() {
    var ga = document.createElement('script');
ga.type = 'text/javascript'; ga.async = true;
    ga.src = ('https:' == document.location.protocol ?
'https://ssl' : 'http://www') + '.google-analytics.com/ga.js';
var s = document.getElementsByTagName('script')[0];
s.parentNode.insertBefore(ga, s);
  })();
</script>
```

You'll notice in the onClick event and in the fourth line from the top of the GATC example that there is a call to _trackEvent, followed by four pieces of data: Videos, Play, Avatar Trailer, and the number 150. These correspond to the four event tracking fields: Category, Action, Label, and Value.

The first one from the left, Category, is a required field, which means that if you don't have the first field filled out, you will not be able to record an event tracking hit. Category is designed to be the home of a top-level name from which actions occur. Videos, applets, MP3s, downloads, files, and brochures are all good examples of names for categories.

The second field from the left is the Action field, and it is also required by Google Analytics. The Action field is exactly what it sounds like: the action that a visitor performs. If the visitor clicks the play button, then "play" is the perfect name for that action. Other actions include click, fast-forward, rewind, volume up, mute, drag, drop, enlarge, full screen...you get the idea.

The third field from the left is an optional field for a label. A label is a piece of information that can further describe the category/action pair. Most people find it very helpful to use the page name as the Label field, so that when they're looking in Google Analytics in the Event Tracking section they can see which pages actions were performed on. You can also use the Label field for names of movies or applications that someone interacts with, like Avatar Trailer in my example.

The last field is another optional field that is reserved for a value. You can create any numerical value for an event, and numerical values help assign weight and meaning to category/action pairs in the Google Analytics reports. In my example I used a value of 150, but you can use any value that you'd like. Don't use commas to separate thousands places in your values (if you use figures that are that high). Also, notice in the event tracking example that the value did not have quotation marks encompassing it. Make sure that you leave it this way, as quotation marks around the value number may cause your event to not be recorded.

A limit of 500 GATC requests for each session can be tracked by Google Analytics. GATC requests include both page views and event tracking, as well as e-commerce transaction hits. I would advise caution, especially when configuring event tracking for Flash or web applications using AJAX that have lots of moving parts and lots of things that a visitor can do. Don't track things like mouse movements, and limit what mouse-click events you track. Five hundred may seem like a lot, but if you're tracking something like a "shoot 'em up" game in which each left mouse click counts as an event, 500 requests may be used up in a couple of minutes.

Event Tracking Reports

Once your data begins to collect, log in to Google Analytics and visit the Content section of your reports. You should see a large Event Tracking link in bold letters on the bottom of the Content sub-navigation menu. Clicking that will take you to the Event Tracking Overview report, where a summary of your event tracking data will appear. You'll be able to see the total events, visits with event, and events-per-visit metrics, and below this a summary of your top event categories and the actions that took place from each. On the right-hand side of the Event Tracking Overview are a few links to drill down into the reports, and as always you'll find the standard trending graph above the data. Figure 10-5 shows an example of what all of this looks like.

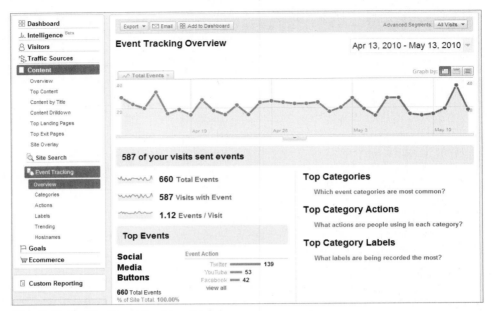

Figure 10-5: The Event Tracking Overview

As you can see in Figure 10-5, the navigation menu contains links to the overview, a report for three of the four event-tracking fields (Categories, Actions, and Labels), and a trending histogram report showing the daily event-tracking activity. Finally, there's a hostnames report showing the domains on which event tracking hits originated. This is useful if you're tracking multiple sites.

In Figure 10-6 I am showing an example of the Actions report. In the Event Tracking section, actual event data is collected in this first Events tab, which you see in Figure 10-6. You can also view site usage and e-commerce data for each event, but remember that at the time of this writing, goal data cannot be tied to an event. Original metrics for events like total events, unique events, event value, and average event value line the top scorecard and are displayed within the report rows themselves. Clicking any action name will show the categories and the optional labels that pertain to the action.

Figure 10-6 is actually a really good example of not using the Event Value field for your event category/action pairs. You will not be able to provide any weight or numerical measurement value to your actions, other than the total count of actions performed.

> **NOTE** Event tracking with Google Analytics is also compatible with Adobe Flash/Flex, as well as Microsoft Silverlight technology. Check the appendix of this book for links to information about implementing Google Analytics event tracking with those technologies.

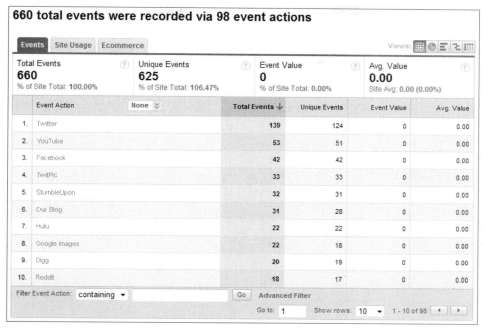

660 total events were recorded via 98 event actions

	Event Action	None ⌄	Total Events ↓	Unique Events	Event Value	Avg. Value
1.	Twitter		139	124	0	0.00
2.	YouTube		53	51	0	0.00
3.	Facebook		42	42	0	0.00
4.	TwitPic		33	33	0	0.00
5.	StumbleUpon		32	31	0	0.00
6.	Our Blog		31	28	0	0.00
7.	Hulu		22	22	0	0.00
8.	Google Images		22	18	0	0.00
9.	Digg		20	19	0	0.00
10.	Reddit		18	17	0	0.00

Figure 10-6: The Actions report within Event Tracking

Custom Variables

One of the newer features of Google Analytics, custom variables allow a website owner to tag a group of visitors that perform a certain action, sign up for a certain event, or register for something on your site. For example, let's say that your site has a members-only section. You can use a custom variable for any visitors who successfully enter the members-only area of your site, and label them so that you can group your members and segment their data separately from that of nonmembers. With custom variables you are given the room to create up to five different variables for any unique visitor.

Like event tracking, custom variables can be implemented on any page or link on your site either via an additional line of JavaScript code in your GATC, or as an `onClick` or similar JavaScript function. More often than not you'll be using custom variables in line within the GATC, but there are definitely some cases in which it is a good idea to use custom variables as onClick or other JavaScript events.

Google Analytics officially released custom variables toward the end of 2009, replacing the longstanding user-defined report section and its `setVar` JavaScript function. `setVar` has been officially deprecated and replaced with the `setCustomVar` function. Using `setCustomVar` will install on a user's machine the __utmv cookie that we discussed earlier in the chapter, which has a default life span of two years.

Schema and Key/Value Pairs for Custom Variables

Custom variables work by labeling unique visitors with a name/value pair, much as events are tracked via a category/action pair. There are four parameters for the custom-variables schema, three of them being required. The format for custom variables looks like this:

```
_setCustomVar(index, name, value, opt_scope)
```

The index is the slot for the custom variable, whose value ranges from 1 to 5 (inclusive). The indexes are the "pockets" that unique visitors have available to carry custom variables around with them in their __utmv cookies. If a slot is reused or accidentally duplicated somewhere on your site, the new data will overwrite the existing data in that slot.

The name will be the piece of data that appears in the Custom Variables report in the Visitors section of Google Analytics. The names and the number of visitors who have been hit with a custom variable will be listed in this report, which can be further segmented (as most reports in Google Analytics can be).

The value parameter is the other piece of data that is paired up with the Name field in the custom-variables string. The maximum length that both the name and the value together can be is 64 bytes (characters).

The last parameter that you can use for custom variables is the scope, which is an optional field. There are three types of scope that you can use for your custom variable: 1, 2, and 3. Scope 1 will set the custom variable at the visitor level, scope 2 will set the custom variable at the session level, and scope 3 will set the custom variable at the page level. If you don't use this optional field, it will default the custom variable to the page level (3).

Generally speaking, you would use scope 1 (visitor level) to differentiate visitors across multiple browser sessions. The member/nonmember example from earlier is an example of a visitor-level custom variable. You could set the visitor-level scope on your membership registration's receipt or thank-you page, and then, for the "life" of that visitor, he or she will always be identified as a member with scope 1. Scope 2 (session-level) custom variables could be used on a site containing a message board to which a user would need to log in to view and comment on threads. The session-level custom variable could be set after the user logs in, and could track the user's statistics for the length of that session. Scope 3 (page-level) custom variables can be used to track interactions with important pages on your site. If you want to know if a visitor encounters a special section of your website or sees your price sheet page, you could set the page-level custom variable on the desired page and view data for it in Google Analytics.

You can also get creative and set multiple custom variables throughout your website, or on the same page. But be extremely careful not to overwrite yourself and use the five index slots with great caution. Using an Excel spreadsheet or making a table on your notepad before implementing these custom variables across your website may not be a bad idea.

Here's a working example of custom variables within the GATC:

```
<script type="text/javascript">
  var _gaq = _gaq || [];
  _gaq.push(['_setAccount', 'UA-1234567-1']);
  _gaq.push(['_setCustomVar', 1, 'Log-In', 'Success', 2]);
  _gaq.push(['_trackPageview']);
  (function() {
var ga = document.createElement('script');
ga.type = 'text/javascript'; ga.async = true;
ga.src = ('https:' == document.location.protocol ?
'https://ssl' : 'http://www') + '.google-analytics.com/ga.js';
var s = document.getElementsByTagName('script')[0];
s.parentNode.insertBefore(ga, s);
  })();
</script>
```

Within this particular GATC I'm using a custom variable in the first (1) slot. It's a session-level custom variable (scope 2), and I'm tracking my log-in function (name). Depending on what happens when a user logs in during a browser session, that user is labeled as success (value) or failure. In this example I am attempting to determine the rate of successful versus failed log-ins in hopes of improving the secure area of my website, which I want only my clients to access.

Custom Variables Reports

Once you've planned and implemented some custom variables for your website visitors, it's time to see what the site looks like in Google Analytics. Log in to your account and go to the Visitors report section. The very last link on the navigation menu should be Custom Variables. Click that to view the standard report table that you're used to seeing throughout all of Google Analytics. The Custom Variables report won't show you a trending graph, but it will list the unique custom-variable names and their statistics. Clicking each name will bring up the values for that name, which will allow you to segment those values by any of the standard dimensions available. The powerful part of the Custom Variables report is that you can attribute values to goal-conversion and e-commerce data by clicking the respective tabs within the report table. Figure 10-7 shows an example of the Custom Variables report.

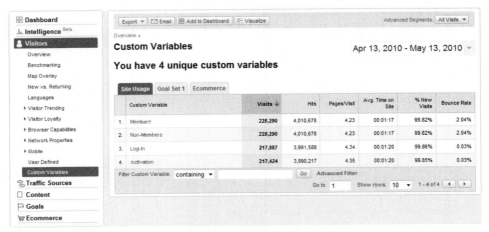

Figure 10-7: The Custom Variables report in the Visitors section

Common Customizations

There are a lot of different ways to customize the Google Analytics Tracking Code. Most of the ones that you see online in websites' source code are supported by Google. Some are not. Many, many others are simply bad implementations badly disguised as customizations. You could write an entire book about customizations and the technical aspects of Google Analytics — Jerri Ledford and I did so in 2009 with *Google Analytics, 3rd Edition*. However, for this book I must limit this subsection to the most common customizations that one would perform with Google Analytics. At the end of the book is an appendix that contains links to resources on the Web, including a few links to some technical customizations that are possible with Google Analytics.

Virtual Page Views

Using virtual page views with Google Analytics Tracking Code is very simple and very convenient. Let's say you have a situation on your website in which the actual page changes when a user clicks Next or More Info, yet the URL in the browser's address bar doesn't change. You can use a virtual page view within the GATC to identify to Google Analytics that this is a unique page view, and to count it as such in the Content Report section.

What you'll want to do is populate the `trackPageview` field as shown in the following example:

```
<script type="text/javascript">
  var _gaq = _gaq || [];
```

```
    _gaq.push(['_setAccount', 'UA-1234567-1']);
    _gaq.push(['_trackPageview', '/page-step-2.html']);
    (function() {
var ga = document.createElement('script');
ga.type = 'text/javascript'; ga.async = true;
ga.src = ('https:' == document.location.protocol ?
'https://ssl' : 'http://www') + '.google-analytics.com/ga.js';
var s = document.getElementsByTagName('script')[0];
s.parentNode.insertBefore(ga, s);
    })();
</script>
```

Visiting this page will result in /page-step-2.html's registering as a page view in the Content report in Google Analytics.

PDF and Other File Downloads

Using the same `trackPageview` technology, you could use a JavaScript `onClick` event on any PDF, MP3, Windows Media file, or any other non–web page type of file and track it as a page view. Using the `trackPageview` function as a JavaScript `onClick` event will increase your page count, as files that cannot contain the GATC will be tracked and displayed in the Top Content report within the Content Report section. Using `trackPageview` on downloadable files or even on outgoing (external) links is the only way to then use them as goals, if desired.

An example of the `trackPageview` function as a JavaScript onClick event is shown here:

```
onClick="_gaq.push(['_trackPageview', '/pdf/name-of-file.pdf']);"
```

In some rare cases, placing this `onClick` event above the GATC in the source code can throw some scripting errors on the page. Even though your async GATC should be in the `<head>` of the document, if you install the `onClick` event and are receiving some type of script error, you may have to move the GATC higher up in the source code (above the `onClick` event).

Sub-Domain and Cross-Domain Tracking

It is very common nowadays to have a website "family" or network in which sites with multiple sub-domains or even sites with multiple top-level domains interact with and link to each other. Because of the standard GATC and the way first-party cookies use the `domain.hash` function, only the website that set the cookie can read and access it. So, by default, if `www.yoursite.com` sets a cookie, and a visitor clicks a link from your site to `blog.yoursite.com`, and both `www.yoursite.com` and `blog.yoursite.com` have the same tracking code, the visitor will have two fresh sets of cookies on his or her browser. You will see self-referrals appear in the Traffic Sources report section, and you will have other referral tracking issues. This is of course assuming that you *want* to track both sites simultaneously within one profile.

Read the rest of this section very carefully. You will need to see which situation applies to you, and ensure that your site is configured appropriately.

Sub-Domain Tracking

Just as in my previous example, if you have www.yoursite.com and blog .yoursite.com, and you wish to track both sites simultaneously, you will need to update your GATC to include the setDomainName function on both sites, while defining your domain name as shown here:

```
<script type="text/javascript">
  var _gaq = _gaq || [];
  _gaq.push(['_setAccount', 'UA-1234567-1']);
  _gaq.push(['_setDomainName', '.yoursite.com']);
  _gaq.push(['_trackPageview']);
  (function() {
var ga = document.createElement('script');
ga.type = 'text/javascript'; ga.async = true;
ga.src = ('https:' == document.location.protocol ?
'https://ssl' : 'http://www') + '.google-analytics.com/ga.js';
var s = document.getElementsByTagName('script')[0];
s.parentNode.insertBefore(ga, s);
  })();
</script>
```

Now every sub-domain of .yoursite.com that has this GATC will be tracked cleanly without your losing the original referring information for any visitor. Remember to update *both sites* with the exact same GATC.

Cross-Domain Tracking

Cross-domain tracking involves two parts. First the GATC must be updated on both (or all) sites to include a call to both setDomainName and setAllowLinker, as shown here:

```
<script type="text/javascript">
  var _gaq = _gaq || [];
  _gaq.push(['_setAccount', 'UA-1234567-1']);
  _gaq.push(['_setDomainName', 'none']);
  _gaq.push(['_setAllowLinker', 'true']);
  _gaq.push(['_trackPageview']);
  (function() {
var ga = document.createElement('script');
ga.type = 'text/javascript'; ga.async = true;
ga.src = ('https:' == document.location.protocol ?
```

```
'https://ssl' : 'http://www') + '.google-analytics.com/ga.js';
var s = document.getElementsByTagName('script')[0];
s.parentNode.insertBefore(ga, s);
  })();
</script>
```

Remember to update both sites with this updated GATC. After you do so, you will need to do at least one of the following. You will positively need to update *each and every link to and from* each domain, with a JavaScript `onClick` `_link` function in order for cross-domain tracking to work. A user needs to be able to have his or her cookie data sent via HTTP (in the browser's address bar) to the destination site in order for cross-domain tracking with Google Analytics to work. If you don't do this part, or you skip some links, it will not work.

The `_link` function should be used like so:

```
onClick="_gaq.push
(['_link', 'http://www.secondsite.com/page.html']); return false;"
```

It bears repeating that this `_link` function should be installed not only on every link on your first website, but also on any link back to that website from the second website. You will also need to make sure that you update the URL shown in the example with the actual URL of the destination page on the second website.

If you send data via a form from one website to another, instead of using the `_link` function you can use the `_linkByPost` function as a JavaScript `onSubmit` function, like this:

```
onSubmit="_gaq.push(['_linkByPost', this]);"
```

Once a user clicks a link using `_link` or submits a form using `_linkByPost` and successfully arrives at the second site (or back at the first site), he or she should see something like this in the browser's URL address bar:

```
http://www.secondsite.com/page.php?id=12345&__utma=1.312038497.127
3891238.1273891238.1273891238.1&__utmb=1.1.10.1273891238&__utmc=1&__
utmx=-&__utmz=1.1273891238.1.1.utmcsr=%28direct%29|utmccn=%28direct
%29|utmcmd=%28none%29&__utmv=-&__utmk=123238411
```

That really long string of characters is the cookie information making its way from one website to the next. When checking for accuracy and validation of implementation, perform some test clicks and see if you get something like this in your browser's address bar.

Modifying Cookie Timeout Values

Possibly one of the most popular features of Google Analytics is the ability to edit cookie settings. While you can't do too much to the cookies themselves, you can make some modifications to when they expire.

The first thing you can do is modify the session timeout. By default Google Analytics uses a 30-minute session timeout. If no activity is detected after 30 minutes, Google will stop the session, and the user will create a new session and visit when he or she resumes activity on the site. Using the setSessionCookieTimeout function within the GATC can allow you to modify the __utmb cookie to delay or speed up the session timeout:

```
_gaq.push(['_setAccount', 'UA-1234567-1']);
_gaq.push(['_setSessionCookieTimeout', 3600000]);
_gaq.push(['_trackPageview']);
```

Next, you can modify the campaign duration timeout. By default Google Analytics will track campaign data (referral data) for a unique visitor for up to six months. To edit this value you can call the setCampaignCookieTimeout function within your GATC and edit the __utmz cookie:

```
_gaq.push(['_setAccount', 'UA-1234567-1']);
_gaq.push(['_setCampaignCookieTimeout', 31536000000]);
_gaq.push(['_trackPageview']);
```

A third cookie-modification option is to edit the visitor cookie timeout. By default this happens after two years, but you can modify it to be sooner or later by calling the setVisitorCookieTimeout function, which edits the __utma cookie:

```
_gaq.push(['_setAccount', 'UA-1234567-1']);
_gaq.push(['_setVisitorCookieTimeout', 63072000000]);
_gaq.push(['_trackPageview']);
```

In case you are wondering, the numerical values that you see for these cookie-modification functions are set in milliseconds. Multiply the number of seconds by a thousand to get the number of milliseconds to use for modifying these cookie values.

Adding an Organic Search Engine

A neat and common customization to have in your back pocket is the ability to add an organic search engine directly to your GATC, without having to wait for Google to update the ga.js tracking file. You never know when someone will invent the next big thing, and you don't want to wait to track it as an organic engine in your reports. Be proactive here and use the addOrganic function on all pages on which you have the GATC installed, defining the domain of the search engine and its search query parameter:

```
_gaq.push(['_setAccount', 'UA-1234567-1']);
_gaq.push(['_addOrganic', 'joeteixeira.com', 'q']);
_gaq.push(['_trackPageview']);
```

Perform a test search on your search engine and view the URL, and pick out the variable or string that immediately precedes your search query. A lot of the time it's going to be the letter q, but it isn't always that simple.

> **NOTE** There's an entire level of "tech" that we didn't even get a chance to cover in this book, such as mobile tracking, SDKs, and the Google Analytics API, as well as some other not-so-common GATC customizations. I felt that these were a bit too technical for the general population, and, quite honestly, we didn't have the room for them in this jam-packed book. There are some links in the Appendix that will point you to the most up-to-date online versions of this information, which will probably be more current than any book.

Creating Profiles, Goals, Filters, and Other Settings

Before I let you go to discover the wonderful world that is Google Website Optimizer, I need to cover some administration options that you will probably be tasked with from time to time. These include options for creating new profiles, editing goals, and possibly writing your own filters. Any of this can be done after you create your Google Analytics account (as described in Chapter 7), or, once you've done that, after you install the Google Analytics Tracking Code on your website.

Creating a Profile

When you're logged in to your Google Analytics account (assuming that you are an administrator), you'll see your profiles listed in rows and you'll also see some links toward the bottom of the overview report table. Clicking Add Website Profile will do just that, but you can also click any of the blue Add New Profile links integrated within the report table rows. This does the same thing.

Next you'll be given the option of adding a profile for a new domain or adding a profile for an existing domain. If you add a profile for a new domain you'll enter your URL, as shown in Figure 10-8. You'll also be able to keep cost data imported from your AdWords account to this new profile, if both AdWords and Analytics are synced. A profile for a new domain will create a new UA number and group it separately from your existing profile(s). Creating a profile for an existing domain will allow you to select the domain for which you want to create your profile. Click Continue when you're finished, and you'll be taken to the Tracking Code Wizard to grab your GATC.

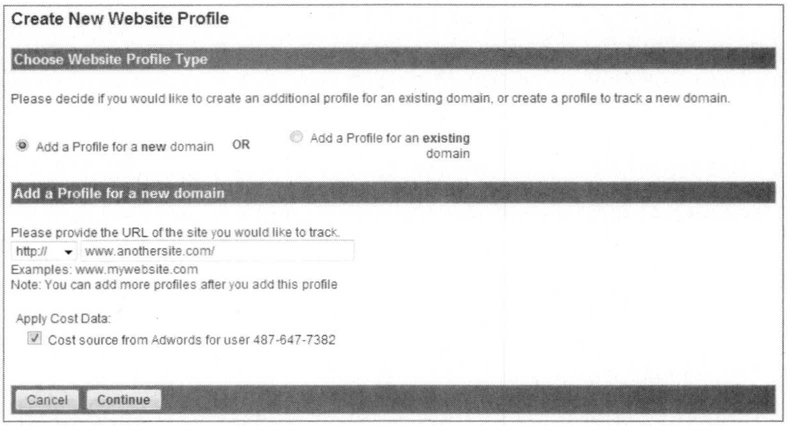

Figure 10-8: Creating a new profile

After completing profile creation you'll be redirected back to the overview screen, where you'll see a yellow triangle next to your new profile. This will go away and be replaced by a green checkmark once you install the GATC on your website's homepage.

Editing Profile Settings

When you click the Edit link directly underneath the Check Status link in any profile's row, you'll be taken to the main website profile information screen, where you'll be able to edit the profile's settings, create goals, add filters, and manage users. Figure 10-9 shows what this screen looks like. This is where you'll be able to assign a default page and enable e-commerce and Site Search reports. You can also exclude query parameters from appearing in your content reports, if your website generates cumbersome, difficult-to-read URL query parameters.

Goals, Values, Funnels, and Engagement

Below the profile settings you will see the Goals table, and if it's a new profile there should be four blank rows without any goals inside them. You can create up to 20 goals within four goal sets, each goal set having a maximum of five goals. Click Add Goal to create your first goal in any goal set (start with Goal Set 1 for simplicity's sake). Once you arrive at the goal-information page, enter a name for your goal and ensure that the goal is set to on (if you wish to turn a goal off in the future, this is the place to do it). Then define your goal position (which goal set you want your goal to be located in) and select your goal type. You may remember from earlier in this chapter that there are three goal types: URL destination, time on site, and pages per visit. Figure 10-10 shows an example of what your screen will look like when you select URL destination as the goal type.

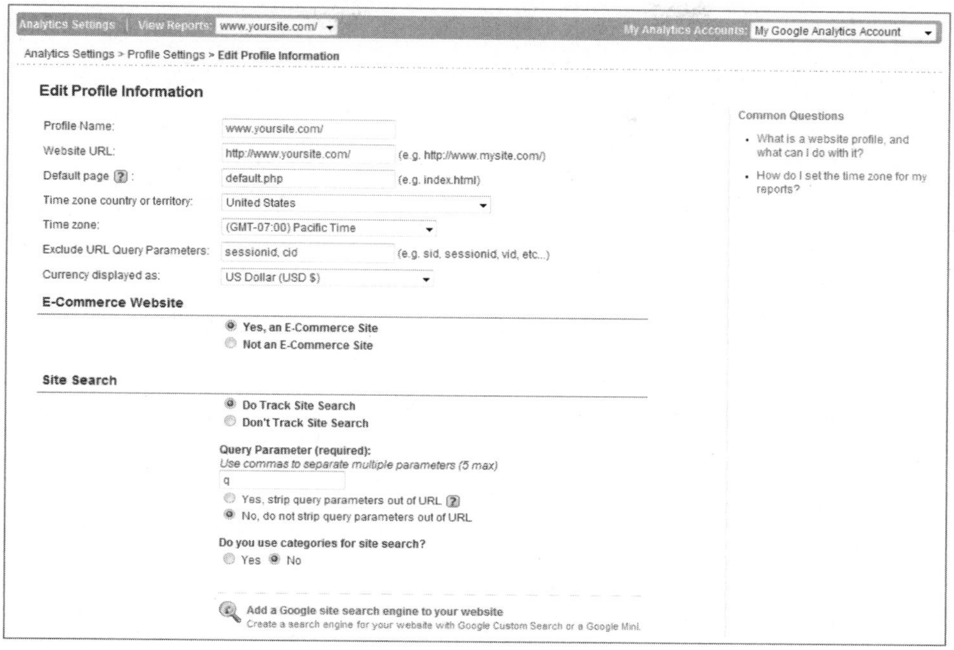

Figure 10-9: Editing profile settings

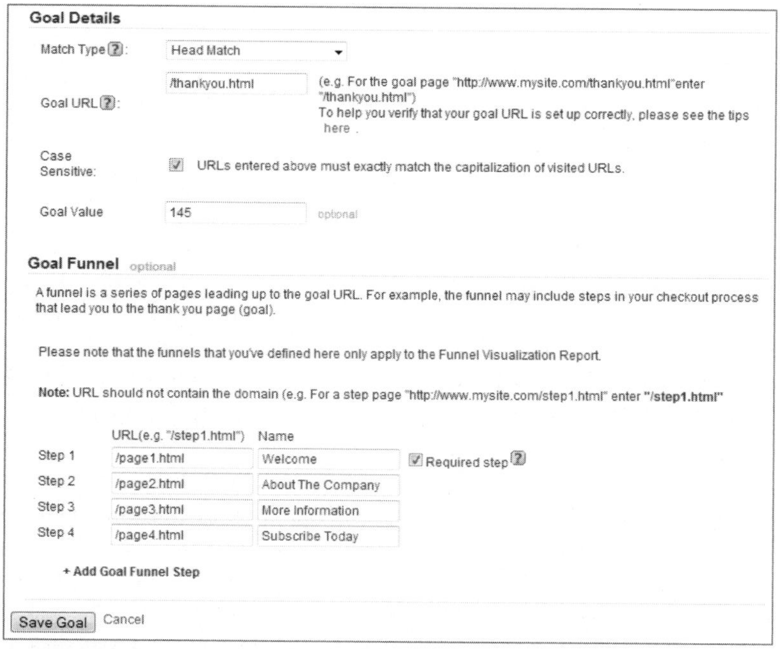

Figure 10-10: Creating a URL destination goal

For the URL destination goal type, you will need to define the match type, enter a goal URL, and create a numerical value for your goal, as shown in Figure 10-10. You will also have the option to enter a funnel, which is the defined path from start to finish reviewed in Chapter 7.

Figure 10-11 shows an example of one of the two engagement goal types (time on site). Here you have a much simpler set of controls to work with — you basically enter the desired time and a value for the goal.

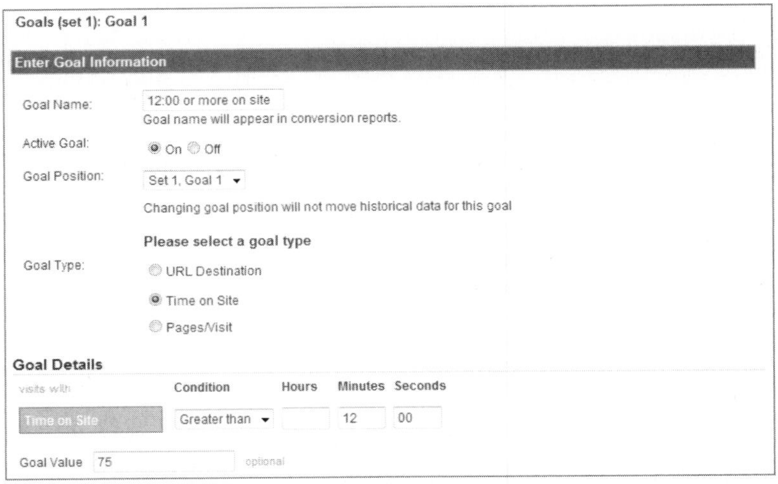

Figure 10-11: Creating a time-on-site engagement goal

Filters and Regular Expressions

Below your goals in your profile settings will be the location in which you'll find your filters for your profile. Filters define how you want your data to appear in Google Analytics, and before processing happens you can manipulate that data. You can create filters to exclude your own traffic or to include only traffic to a specific subdirectory, or you can create an advanced filter array to combine data from two different reports. Filters in Google Analytics must be written in POSIX Regular Expression format, and are extremely sensitive. I don't have the space to cover Regular Expressions here, but check the appendix for more details and links to learn more about it.

There are quite a few filter options available, and you may be asked to do anything in the following list. Once a filter is created, it will take about 24 hours for it to be activated on your profile. You can edit, add, or remove a filter at any time via the filter settings area within each profile or the Filter Manager link on the overview screen of your Google Analytics account.

- **Predefined Exclude or Include filter:** This filter can either exclude or include traffic from a domain, from an IP address, or to a subdirectory. If this is your first time using filters, try creating one of these predefined filters first.

- **Custom Exclude filter:** This filter excludes traffic by any of the 40+ filter fields available. You can exclude traffic by visitor type, e-commerce transaction ID, or country. You're most likely going to be using this type of filter to exclude an IP address, a source, a medium, or a hostname (URL). Figure 10-12 shows an example of a Custom Exclude filter.

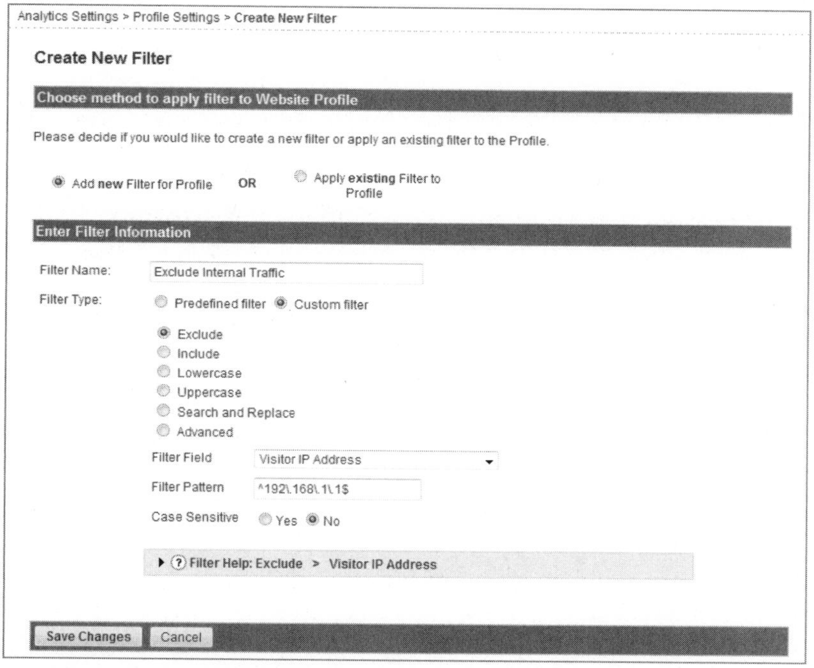

```
Analytics Settings > Profile Settings > Create New Filter

Create New Filter

Choose method to apply filter to Website Profile

Please decide if you would like to create a new filter or apply an existing filter to the Profile.

   ◉ Add new Filter for Profile    OR    ○ Apply existing Filter to
                                              Profile

Enter Filter Information

Filter Name:      Exclude Internal Traffic

Filter Type:      ○ Predefined filter  ◉ Custom filter

                  ◉ Exclude
                  ○ Include
                  ○ Lowercase
                  ○ Uppercase
                  ○ Search and Replace
                  ○ Advanced

     Filter Field     Visitor IP Address          ▼

     Filter Pattern   ^192\.168\.1\.1$

     Case Sensitive   ○ Yes  ◉ No

        ▶ ⑦ Filter Help: Exclude  >  Visitor IP Address


 Save Changes    Cancel
```

Figure 10-12: An Exclude filter, excluding an IP address

- **Custom Include filter:** Including data excludes everything *except* what you enter in the Filter Pattern field. For example, if you include Google, and select Campaign Source from the Filter Field drop-down menu, you will be excluding everything *except* Google.

- **Lowercase and Uppercase filters:** These are very self-explanatory. You may use them for lowercasing source, campaign, or medium names to clean up data in your reports.

- **Search and Replace filter:** If you have a long, ugly-looking URL you can replace it and clean it up with a nicer-looking one, so that you can distinguish it better in your reports. You can also search for and replace campaign names, request URI names, and re-write any other items that you wish.

▪ **Advanced filter:** An Advanced filter lets you take data from two different fields and combine them. A popular Advanced filter is one in which the hostname (URL) and request URI (page/file path name) are combined together so that you can see the URL of the website in reports. This filter is used in situations in which multiple websites are tracked simultaneously, because page file names may be the same on multiple sites.

User Management

Finally, you'll definitely be asked to add users so that they can have access to Google Analytics reports.

You can add a user from your overview screen (look for the User Manager link) or from within each individual profile. Scroll all the way down to the bottom of the profile settings to find a table listing the users who have access to the profile. Click Add User to enter the user's e-mail address and to specify whether he or she will be granted "view reports only" access or account administrator access. "View reports only"-access users cannot create profiles, edit settings, or manage users. Administrators can do everything within a Google Analytics account, including removing you from having access. Needless to say, use caution when determining who gets administrative access. Figure 10-13 shows the user manager screen.

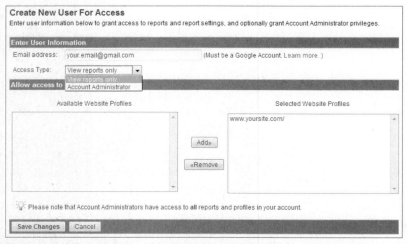

Figure 10-13: Assigning an e-mail address access to Google Analytics

Remember, each e-mail address must also be a Google account in order for the user to be able to access Google Analytics (or any other Google product, for that matter). You may want to flip all the way back to Chapter 2, where I show step-by-step examples of making an e-mail address a Google account.

Part

IV

Google Website Optimizer

In This Part

Welcome to Google Website Optimizer

The fourth part of *Your Google Game Plan for Success* talks about Google Website Optimizer. You've read Chapter 1 and thought about what the purpose of your website is. You've learned about Google AdWords and cost-per-click advertising to drive traffic to your site, and you've digested the concept of Google Analytics and how to analyze your website traffic. Now, how do you optimize your site for conversions in an intelligent, statistically confident way? You do this with Google Website Optimizer, of course!

In this chapter you'll learn all about Google Website Optimizer, creating an experiment, and interpreting the results. You'll also see two terms quite frequently in this chapter: *conversions* and *landing pages*. These are what Google Website Optimizer is all about.

What Is Google Website Optimizer?

Let's take a step back for a minute so that everyone is on the same page as to exactly what Google Website Optimizer is. As I mentioned in Chapter 1, there's a sort of "ego" present in some organizations and how they approach their online business. In the offline world, a powerful, name-brand product or service that's been around since your grandparents' early years is very tough to go up against from a competitive standpoint. Joe, the local businessman, cannot compete with a big organization because it has millions of dollars allocated to its advertising budget, and Joe does not. Because it's such a dominant player, the big company isn't pressed to make changes and optimize its business services; if it loses customers, it will simply gain others down the road, and everyone sleeps well at night. Joe doesn't have this luxury and must provide fantastic service and price, and must optimize his business and earn the trust, respect, and confidence of each and every customer, because his livelihood depends on it. One customer lost could mean the difference between making payroll and having to lay off a hard-working employee.

Now let's move to the online world, where there is an even playing field. Yes, you read that correctly, an even playing field. The millions of dollars in advertising that the big conglomerate has offline won't make up for the fact that its website is horribly optimized for SEO, has a clunky navigation menu, and does not offer compelling calls to action, price points, or value propositions. Its site search function doesn't work and neither does its live chat function, and buying something through its online shopping cart is as tough as having a root canal. Yes, the big company can dump thousands of dollars daily into an AdWords campaign, but as you know from the first few chapters of this book, there are so many factors that make up things like Quality Score and bid prices that while that company may get a lot of impressions and even clicks on its site, any user with sense will see that everyone on Twitter hates its service, its packages are way overpriced, and there's even a Facebook fan page for people who have had bad experiences with it. A user will have one interaction with the broken search function and almost unusable shopping cart, and that will be the end of it for that visitor.

Joe has a plan. He's purchased my book, he's purchased Avinash Kaushik's two phenomenal web-analytics books, he has been doing his due diligence, and he knows what it takes to build and maintain a successful website. With a fraction of the resources of the big company, Joe is able to convert visitors, engage with customers on social media, and rank/perform better. Joe knows that the changes he has made over time on his site have been successful in converting more visitors, and he knows that he must continually experiment and try new things to continue that level of success. Joe uses an online-experimenting tool called Google Website Optimizer, and within a few weeks he can get the results of an experiment and use the page or variation on a page that performs best in terms of conversions. The big company still thinks the Internet is a fad that will go away in a couple of years.

That is the essence of Google Website Optimizer. It is an A/B or multivariate experiment tool that allows you to optimize pages or sections of pages to increase your conversion rates. You tell Google what page is your original page and what pages are your variation pages, and after you install a few snippets of JavaScript tracking code on your site, Google will take care of the rest for you. You can come back in two or three weeks, and Google will tell you which variation led to more conversions.

Then, after you've seen the results, the idea is to continue testing on your site to continue increasing your conversion rate and customer satisfaction. You won't want to run just one experiment in your website's lifetime — you'll want to run experiments every few weeks so that you're always improving.

Google Website Optimizer, like Google Analytics, is completely free of charge. You can run as many experiments as you can think of without Google's ever sending you an invoice or a bill, which is a good segue into the next point I want to make.

Why do website owners fear Google Website Optimizer? Well, let's see. Google Website Optimizer is free, and you can create as many experiments as you want. You can set up experiments quickly and easily. The results of running a Google Website Optimizer experiment are a higher conversion rate, increased website performance, and greater customer satisfaction. So why would Google Website Optimizer be a tough sell to website owners?

From my experience, it comes down to the situations described in Chapter 1 and in the previous section of this chapter. When you're a website owner and you've had complete creative control of your website since inception, it's tough to admit that website isn't doing as well as it could be. It's not easy to tell a person who owns a website that its conversion rate isn't that great, or that its shopping cart is poor, or even that its homepage is badly flawed. Basically, it's very difficult for people to believe that their baby is ugly.

Before you go running to your boss or your client and start bombarding him or her with suggestions and advice, make sure that you'll have a receptive audience. Use an approach that your boss or client is going to be comfortable with. As well-intentioned as your desire may be to use Google Website Optimizer on someone else's site, do remember that it is someone else's site. You're going to have to earn that person's trust and tread lightly, or you won't be able to sell Google Website Optimizer.

Are you the website owner? Do you trust me enough to allow Google Website Optimizer to improve your conversion rate? Are you comfortable with changing items on your website, even your favorite applet or widget, if it means more business? Try to get comfortable with that idea. Those who don't experiment and test on their websites are the ones who get left in the dust, while their competitors soar past them and take their business.

How Google Website Optimizer Works

Chapter 13 provides all the technical schematics that you'll need to know about when and where to install Google Website Optimizer. For this chapter I'll talk about the different experiment types, as well as show you some visual examples of experiments that you can conduct on your own website.

As you're going to learn in this chapter, two types of experiments are offered by Google Website Optimizer: *A/B experiments* and *multivariate (MVT)* experiments. With a few snippets of JavaScript tracking code on select pages of your site, a visitor will see one of the variations of your testing page, determined at random by the JavaScript snippets. Your website, using the Google Website Optimizer JavaScript tracking code, will create a cookie for that visitor and follow that visitor during that session. If the visitor converts and reaches the page containing the conversion JavaScript snippet, Google will assign credit for the conversion to the page or section variation that the visitor encountered. Over time, Google Website Optimizer will provide statistics comparing all the page or section variations that you have running, and after enough time has passed Google will inform you via the online interface of which page or combination has the highest chance of increased conversions, based on the experiment's data. The experiment will continue to run until you decide to turn it off, and when that time comes Google will suggest that you make the winning combination or page variation permanent on your website, as it has the best chance for conversions. You can then run a follow-up experiment that may increase your conversion rate even more.

Google Website Optimizer counts unique visitor data when compiling reports for you. A unique person can't convert more than once in any particular experiment — so someone can't disrupt the natural flow of the experiment and artificially inflate the statistics. This keeps the experiment data pure and more statistically meaningful.

A common misconception about Google Website Optimizer is that experiments work only on pay-per-click traffic from Google AdWords. While you can create an experiment with Google Website Optimizer and send AdWords traffic to the landing page, any traffic to a live experiment page will be subject to that experiment, regardless of where the visitor comes from. Organic traffic and referral traffic can find your experiment page, and their conversion rates will be figured into the totals that you see within the interface.

A/B Experiments

The first type of Google Website Optimizer experiment is called an A/B experiment. This allows website owners to create one or more alternate versions of a page, and to run an experiment in which either the original page or a variation page is shown to visitors. The page that winds up with the highest conversion rate will be the winning page, and it will be the page that Google suggests you use permanently. This could be the original page or any of the variation pages.

Take a look at Figure 11-1, which is the homepage of the National Basketball Association (www.nba.com), and let's run through a hypothetical scenario. As you're looking at Figure 11-1, pretend that you're in charge of improving this website's conversion rate. The conversion that you're focusing on this week is having visitors click the series matchup link for either the Western Conference Finals or the Eastern Conference Finals.

Figure 11-1: The original NBA homepage

The URL of the homepage during the NBA playoffs this year was www.nba .com/playoffs2010/index.html. Your job is to see if you can improve the rate for the aforementioned conversion, so you crack open a Google Website Optimizer experiment and get your web-design team to provide you with a variation of this page that may help. You work with your team and come up with a variation of the page and upload it live at the (fictitious) www.nba.com/playoffs2010/ index2.html URL. On this page you have removed the schedule of games under the series matchup link, and added a link under the Amazing Is the Journey banner toward the top of the page. You run the experiment, and after a week or so you notice that your website's visitors have visited the series matchup page at a much higher rate from the variation page than from the original page. The result is the page that you'll use, in Figure 11-2.

This simple yet effective A/B type of experiment can yield great results that don't require a lot of time or resources.

When should you run an A/B experiment? I could say "all the time," but it's more efficient to run it specifically when you have an easy and quick experiment that you'd like to try out. If you have one major element to test, or one significant change that you're thinking of making, an A/B experiment may be your best bet.

Figure 11-2: The faux variation of the NBA homepage

Sites like NBA get lots of traffic, but your website may receive only a fraction of what the NBA website gets. If you have a low- to medium-volume site (anywhere from a few thousand to 10,000 visitors a month), an A/B experiment is the experiment type you should go with. Multivariate experiments (which I'll talk about next) require a much higher volume of traffic because of the multiple combinations involved.

If you're just starting out with Google Website Optimizer, I recommend performing one A/B experiment, just to get your feet wet. After the experiment concludes, and if your site receives enough volume per month, you can run other A/B experiments or a multivariate experiment.

Multivariate (MVT) Experiments

The second type of experiment with Google Website Optimizer is called a multivariate (MVT) experiment. Unlike an A/B experiment, in which you're testing two or more separate pages, an MVT experiment is conducted with different sections of one page.

With an MVT experiment, you and your web designer come up with alternatives for a few different sections on the same page. Instead of going to either Page A or Page B, all visitors will see the same page, but with different combinations of page sections, including the original page sections. For example, let's say that in a multivariate experiment you test three new headlines plus the original (a total of four), two new call-to-action buttons plus the original (a total of three), and two new bottom-footer images plus the original (also a total of three). That adds up to a total of 36 separate combinations (four headlines, multiplied by three call-to-action buttons, multiplied by three bottom-footer images). In essence, you're running 36 separate pages, but without actually creating the pages and uploading them live on your web server. Google will start to serve up combinations and, just as with an A/B experiment, your winning combination(s) will be highlighted within the Google Website Optimizer interface.

Check out Figure 11-3, which is Twitter's homepage as of this writing. Running a multivariate experiment on this site would be fun because of the sheer volume of traffic that it receives! Let's pretend we can do just that, and that our conversion goal is to get new people signed up. The call to action on this page is located on the right-hand side and is the Get Started Now button.

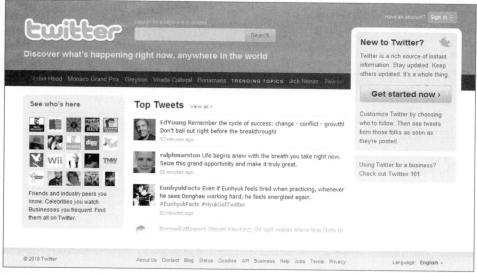

Figure 11-3: Twitter's homepage

You have some ideas for other areas of this page as well, so you get with your web designer to come up with some variations on the call-to-action button, as well as a heading other than "New to Twitter?" Your hypothesis is that you can obtain a higher sign-up rate by simply changing the text that appears to a user who is looking to join Twitter for the first time. Figures 11-4 and 11-5 show the variations that you have come up with and the variations that Google Website Optimizer will rotate for you during the multivariate experiment. Please excuse the crudity of the image variations themselves — I'm not the best graphic artist around, but you get the idea.

Get started now ›	Sign-up Now!!	Join Twitter Today >
Stay Updated >	Enter Twitter Now!	Just Do It.
Create an Account >	Try Twitter Today >	Start Tweeting!!

Figure 11-4: Possible button variations for Twitter for a multivariate experiment

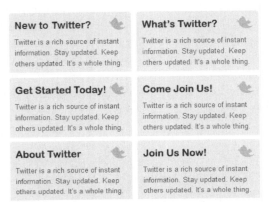

Figure 11-5: Possible heading variations for Twitter for a multivariate experiment

In the examples of the previous two images, Google Website Optimizer would take the nine buttons (including the original) and the six heading variations (including the original). Multiplied together, you have a total of 54 combinations for a very nice multivariate experiment! You wouldn't think something that might appear to be insignificant, like the text of a button or the text of a heading, would have any impact whatsoever on performance, but it surely does. If someone from Twitter is reading this and wondering if it would have an impact, go ahead and run this experiment with these variations, and I'll guarantee that one of the 54 combinations will outperform the original.

Do keep in mind that your website should receive a lot of traffic (high volume) in order to successfully run a multivariate experiment. If you decide to run a multivariate experiment on your site and it doesn't receive a lot of traffic, the experiment will run for an indefinitely long period of time.

But who am I? I'm just an author, and while I may like a certain combination the best, and while the person in charge of the Twitter website may like another combination better, it's ultimately up to the visitors. Whichever combination the visitors to the Twitter homepage like the best is the one that Twitter (or your own website) should go with. Personally, I like the Create an Account button and the Get Started Today headline. What's your favorite combination?

When should your run a multivariate experiment? When you have grand ideas for testing portions of a popular page on your site, as in my Twitter homepage example — that's when you'll want to run a multivariate experiment. Instead of testing two or three separate pages, the experiment runs on one page, and things like buttons, headlines, images, or other elements get rotated at random to all your visitors until you stop the experiment.

Multivariate experiments on low-volume and even sometimes medium-volume sites tend to move really slowly, because of all of the combinations involved. Even a multivariate experiment with only six combinations can take a great deal of time to complete, let alone a multivariate experiment like the one in my Twitter example with 54 combinations. If you have a high-volume site or a lot of patience, you can use a multivariate experiment. Everyone else should use an A/B experiment, simply because it's much easier to run and faster to complete.

As you'll see in a little while, setting up a multivariate experiment requires more technical expertise than setting up an A/B experiment: you'll need to know basic HTML to be able to edit the individual experiment sections.

Reports and Data Available in Google Website Optimizer

After you complete your experiment setup and during the life of your experiment, you'll be able to log in to Google Website Optimizer and view a progress report. If your experiment is completed, or if Google Website Optimizer has found a winning combination, you can view those statistics by logging in to your Google Website Optimizer account and selecting your experiment from your account's overview page (shown in the next section of this chapter).

A/B Experiment Data

Figure 11-6 shows a good example of a report from a completed A/B experiment. At the top you're given links to uninstall the experiment tracking code, copy the experiment, and make a new experiment; run a follow-up experiment; and view your experiment settings. You can also see below these links what the experiment launch date was and when it was originally created. Remember that your web developer or IT person will need to install and verify the JavaScript tracking codes before the experiment launches and data begins to be collected by Google Website Optimizer.

Below this you'll see a trending graph plotted by estimated conversion rate. In the example shown in Figure 11-6 there are two lines, representing the A and B versions of this experiment. Variation 1 is the line with a better conversion rate than the original, and this visualization is reflected in the data found on the table below the trending graph.

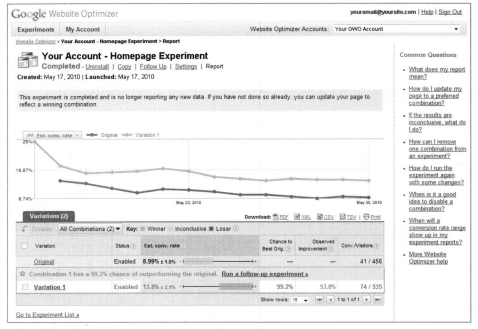

Figure 11-6: The report view in Google Website Optimizer

From left to right on the data table shown on the bottom of Figure 11-6, your variations are listed and are hyperlinked so that you can view the variation in a web browser. The Status column indicates whether the variation is enabled or disabled, something that you have the option to change as the experiment progresses.

The next item is that sliding bar that you see under the heading of Estimated Conversion Rate. The number 8.99 percent is the estimated conversion rate for the original variation in the first row. The number next to that — plus or minus 1.9 percent — is the margin of error of Google's estimated conversion rate. So the conversion rate for the original variation could be anywhere between 7.09 percent and 10.89 percent. This is represented graphically on the sliding bar and in comparison to the other conversion rates of the other variations. In this example Variation 1 had a 13.8 percent conversion rate, with a margin of error of plus or minus 2.1 percent. Again, this means that the conversion rate for Variation 1 could be anywhere between 11.7 percent and 15.9 percent. The sliding bar is all the way to the right and highlighted in green, making it easier to see that it crushed the original page. The stats to the right of the sliding bar for Variation 1 help show why the website owner should go with Variation 1 in this particular case. The odds of beating the original are 99.2 percent, which is remarkable. Variation 1 beats the original combination almost all the time. Observed Improvement is the improvement of Variation 1 during the course of this experiment, and it improved by 53.8 percent (it gained traction). Finally, the very last column of data on this report shows the number of conversions per the number of visitors for each combination.

Clearly Variation 1 dominated this experiment and should be the one that is permanently used on this site. You can download this report in a PDF or a file of any of the other formats available in Google Analytics by clicking the respective icon toward the top right of the data table. You can also print the experiment by clicking the very last icon on the top right of the experiment table.

Multivariate Experiment Data

The example in Figure 11-6 is from an A/B experiment. When you run a multivariate experiment you're provided with a Page Sections tab, as shown in Figure 11-7. The first column on the left-hand side is labeled Relevance Rating, and it rates each section's importance to the performance of the experiment, on a scale from 1 to 5, with 5 being the greatest relevance. Next to that you'll see each variation that you've created for this experiment, and to the right the estimated conversion-rate statistics and sliding scales. The rest of the statistics are the same as the ones shown in an A/B experiment. The idea behind relevance rating is to give you an idea of how important each portion of your website is as it relates to conversion rate. This may give you some great insights as to what your website visitors are looking at and what they're not looking at.

Relevance Rating	Variation	Est. conv. rate	Chance to Beat Orig.	Observed Improvement	Conv./Visitors
Heading 2 / 5	Original	11.7% ± 2.8%	—	—	40 / 343
	Buy Today	11.5% ± 2.8%	47.3%	-1.64%	39 / 340
	Save Lots of Money!	9.47% ± 2.6%	21.0%	-18.8%	32 / 338
Top Paragraph 2 / 5	Original	12.8% ± 3.6%	—	—	33 / 257
	Paragraph 3	10.7% ± 3.4%	27.8%	-16.3%	26 / 242
	Paragraph 1	10.1% ± 3.2%	21.6%	-21.2%	26 / 257
	Paragraph 2	9.81% ± 3.1%	18.8%	-23.6%	26 / 265
Bottom Par... 2 / 5	Original	10.4% ± 2.6%	—	—	36 / 347
	Take it to the Bank!	12.1% ± 2.8%	74.0%	17.1%	43 / 354
	Recycle Your Money!	10.0% ± 2.7%	44.5%	-3.61%	32 / 320

Combinations (36) | Page Sections (3) Download: PDF XML CSV TSV | Print

Figure 11-7: The Page Sections report in Google Website Optimizer

As I'll talk about in Chapter 16, you can extract other meaningful and insightful data from Google Analytics as it pertains to your Google Website Optimizer experiment page(s). And in Chapter 13 I'll talk about some interesting experiment ideas for you to try out on your own website.

Creating an A/B Experiment with Google Website Optimizer

Now that you have a good grasp of Google Website Optimizer, let's walk through creating an A/B experiment first, and a multivariate experiment right after. The next portion of this chapter is organized by the steps that you need to take from start to finish in order to successfully set up an A/B experiment.

Let's get started!

Step 1: Website Owner Buy-In

Don't forget about the words that you read earlier in this chapter. Earn your website owner's trust, respect, and confidence before starting a Google Website Optimizer experiment. You may also need that person's permission first, so inform him or her of everything he or she needs to know about what visitors might see and what page they might see it on.

If you're the website owner, then you obviously don't need to perform this step.

Step 2: Create a Google Account

As with Google AdWords and Google Analytics, you'll need to create a Google account in order to use Google Website Optimizer. If you already created one for either AdWords or Google Analytics, you should probably use the same account for Google Website Optimizer. If you haven't yet created a Google account, go back to Chapter 2 where I detail the steps involved. Remember, you don't necessarily need a Gmail account — you can make a Google account with any e-mail account.

Step 3: Logging in to Google Website Optimizer

Once you have your Google account, visit www.google.com/websiteoptimizer and log in on the right-hand side of the page. Once you log in, you'll see a page like the one shown in Figure 11-8.

In the future this is where the experiments for your account will be listed. For now you'll want to click either Create a New Experiment, located above the table on the bottom, or the Create Experiment link within the table.

Step 4: Choosing the Experiment Type

Figure 11-9 shows you the options that you already know about from reading this chapter. You can choose either an A/B experiment or a multivariate experiment. For this section we're going to choose an A/B experiment.

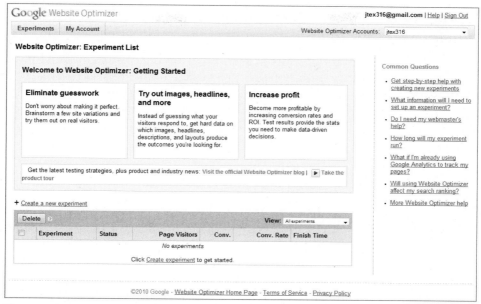

Figure 11-8: Your Google Website Optimizer welcome screen

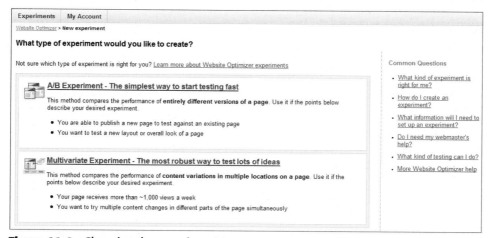

Figure 11-9: Choosing the experiment type

Step 5: Review Experiment Checklist

The next step in setting up your experiment is reviewing a checklist of items before starting the experiment, as shown in Figure 11-10. This is usually the page where people who create Google Website Optimizer experiments jump ship and log out of the system. Don't worry if you don't have any of the items listed — Google Website Optimizer auto-saves your work as you go along.

If you log out at any point during the experiment setup process, you can log back in and pick up where you left off. For an A/B experiment you'll need to choose your test page (original page) and your variation page(s), and identify your conversion page. When you're finished reviewing this page, click the I've Completed . . . checkbox at the bottom to continue to the next step.

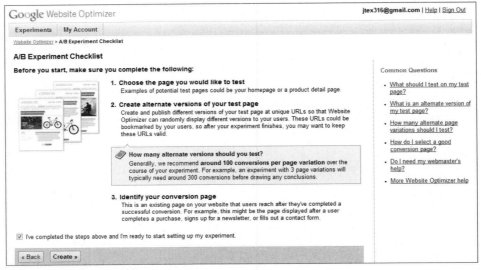

Figure 11-10: A/B Experiment Checklist

Step 6: Identify Experiment Pages

Now it's time to name your experiment and identify your experiment pages. Figure 11-11 shows what the page for this step looks like. On the very top, give your experiment a unique name.

Then identify the pages of your experiment by pasting the full URL of the page as it appears online. This means that you'll have to upload your variation pages online so that Google Website Optimizer can go and check that they exist and are ready to go. (Notice in my example in Figure 11-11 that Google Website Optimizer can't find the index2.html page, and that it gives me an error message under the URL.) Lastly, identify your conversion URL. When all pages of your A/B experiment have been found, click Continue to get the necessary JavaScript tracking codes.

Step 7: Tag Your Experiment Pages

Now comes the tricky part of setting up an experiment. Check out Figure 11-12, which is the page you see after identifying your experiment pages. First you'll need to select the party that is going to be responsible for setting up the Google

Website Optimizer tracking codes. If it's your webmaster, as in Figure 11-12, you'll be provided with a link that you can forward to your webmaster. He or she will then need to follow the on-screen instructions and install the JavaScript snippets on the original, variation, and conversion pages that you identified in Step 6.

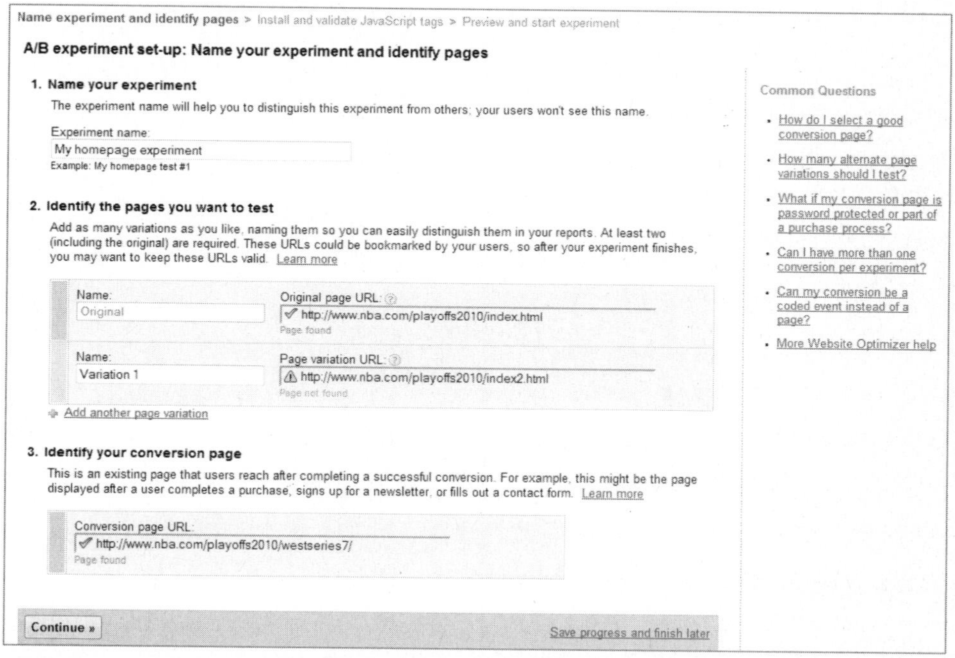

Figure 11-11: Naming your experiment and identifying pages

If you're the person who is going to install the tracking codes, you'll receive an additional page that will provide you with the necessary JavaScript snippets.

Before you're allowed to continue to the next step, you'll need to click the Check Status button toward the bottom of the page. As you can see in Figure 11-12, the status shows as not completed. Until the JavaScript tags are installed entirely correctly, you will not be allowed to continue to the next step.

I'll get more technical and show you JavaScript snippet examples in Chapter 13.

Step 8: Review Settings and Launch

Once your tracking codes are finally installed properly, you'll be allowed to review your experiment settings and launch your experiment. Figure 11-13 shows you an example of what your review page may look like (it's always changing, so it may look slightly different from Figure 11-13). You'll see your experiment pages (which you can click to preview), the total number of combinations (in an A/B experiment it will be two), the total traffic sent through the experiment, and some other settings, including experiment notes. Once you've finished reviewing your experiment settings, it's finally time to launch the experiment. Click Launch Experiment (which is cut-off from Figure 11-13 — but when you reach this page online, it will be at the bottom of the screen). Your experiment will now be live on the Internet! Check back often to see the progress of your experiment and to see which variation Google Website Optimizer determines is the winning one for your site.

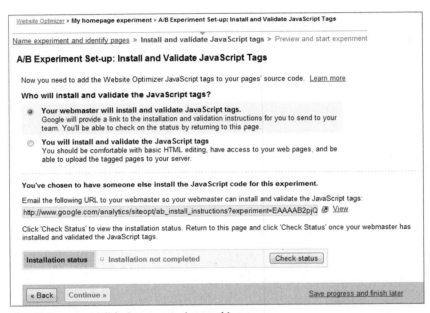

Figure 11-12: Validating JavaScript tracking tags

Step 9: Follow-up Experiments

After your experiment concludes at the end of a few weeks or a month, you'll want to run follow-up experiments, as I mentioned earlier in this chapter. Don't just run one experiment and forget about Google Website Optimizer — get into the habit of running experiments to continually improve your website little by little.

Creating a Multivariate Experiment with Google Website Optimizer

The steps for creating a multivariate experiment with Google Website Optimizer are very similar to the steps for an A/B experiment. However, there is an extra editing step after you validate your JavaScript tracking code, which requires you to create your variations as shown in Figure 11-14.

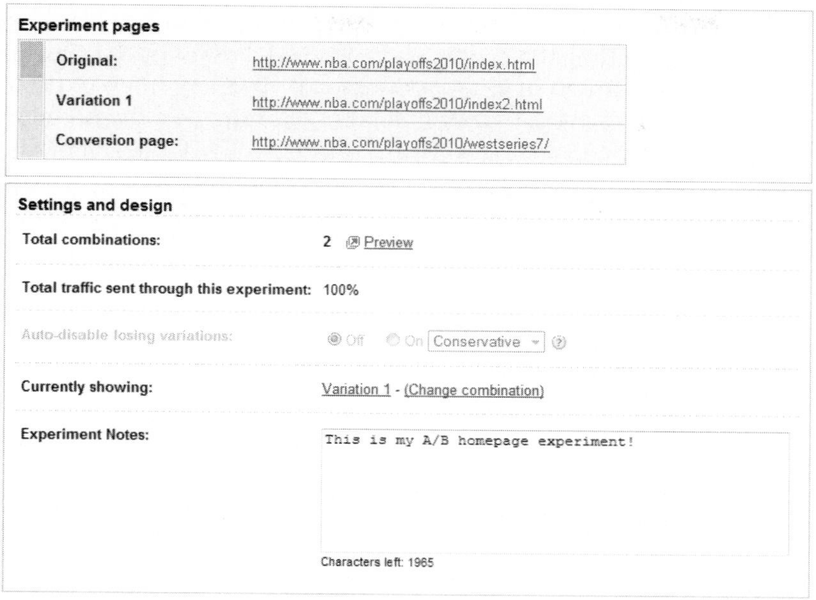

Experiment pages

Original:	http://www.nba.com/playoffs2010/index.html	
Variation 1	http://www.nba.com/playoffs2010/index2.html	
Conversion page:	http://www.nba.com/playoffs2010/westseries7/	

Settings and design

Total combinations: 2   🗗 Preview

Total traffic sent through this experiment: 100%

Auto-disable losing variations: ◉ Off   ○ On [Conservative ▾] ⑦

Currently showing: Variation 1 - (Change combination)

Experiment Notes: This is my A/B homepage experiment!

Characters left: 1965

Figure 11-13: Reviewing your experiment

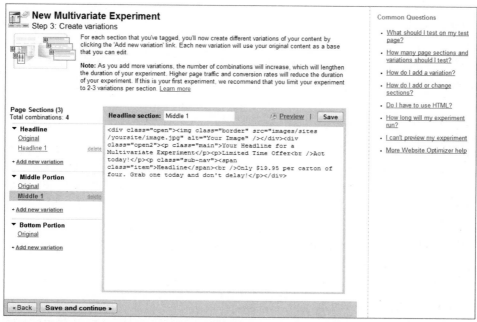

Figure 11-14: Creating multivariate variations

Figure 11-14 shows an example of the pages of a multivariate experiment being edited. In this example three page sections have been tagged on the actual experiment page. Your job is to create the variations right here within the interface. You can preview your variations before you upload them, and I highly recommend doing so to make sure your variation HTML doesn't break the page or cause any errors. You'll need to be somewhat familiar with HTML to be able to do this, because there is code that you may need to negotiate. We'll dive much deeper into this in Chapter 13.

CHAPTER 12

Elementary Statistical Concepts

Using Google Website Optimizer opens the door for us to talk about the sub-industry within web analytics that deals with testing, experimentation, and multivariate analysis — a sub-industry, mind you, that is growing exponentially and rapidly making its way into department meetings and boardrooms across the globe. A few website owners today are starting to understand that if they do not run experiments on their websites, landing pages, and marketing initiatives, they are setting themselves up for failure. No longer can you get away with a website that is not touched for years and ads that run unattended on Google for months at a time. (Could you ever have gotten away with it in the first place?)

This small subset of website owners who "get it" know that testing in general, and using tools like Google Website Optimizer in particular, are the keys to victory over their competition. They're also getting that the statistics you saw in the previous chapter use elements from beginning statistics courses taught at colleges and universities all over the world. To take it a step further, the entire package of data in Google Analytics is a statistics package, and so are most of the metrics you see in Google AdWords. Needless to say, having some knowledge of elementary statistics will help you greatly in your quest for success.

In this chapter I'll discuss some of the basic statistical concepts that are covered in an elementary statistics class, and show you how they apply to your daily website advertising and measurement life. You'll learn about things like measures of center, standard deviation, and Z-scores, and throughout the chapter you'll see some examples of how they apply to web analytics and online testing.

Elementary Statistics

Statistics are used everywhere online. Clicks, impressions, conversion rate, bounce rate, visits to purchase, and just about everything else you've read about so far in *Your Google Game Plan for Success* has something to do with statistics. As I mentioned in the introduction to this chapter, it's vital to have at least an elementary understanding of statistics so you have the deepest possible understanding of how the Web works. Statistics are used daily online, on the radio, on television, in sports, by your friends, and by your boss to justify statements or corroborate information being presented.

Why Is Elementary Statistics Important?

Elementary statistics is important to enrich your knowledge and open new doors for you. Not only will you become a better analyst and experiment designer, you'll also be able to apply your new knowledge in the real world. You don't have to complete a bachelor's in math or a master's in statistics to at least understand some fundamental concepts.

Performing a search on Google for *statistics* brings up about 500 million search results. Performing the same search on Google Images brings up a little over 200 million images of book covers, pie charts, graphs, and formulas, and even some screenshots of web-analytics programs. Statistics is seemingly everywhere you look.

There's also a dark side to statistics. There's a side that produces misinformation, and that you also need to be aware of. We've all heard the unsubstantiated claims in radio ads, in TV commercials, and online. Sometimes the claims are even made in person by friends and colleagues. Claims such as "Four out of five people hate their jobs" or "Eighty-five percent of teenage boys play video games" could very well be true, but are most likely regurgitations of what someone read or heard somewhere. So, as important as having an elementary knowledge of statistics is, it's equally as important to know which statistics have to be taken with a grain of salt.

Types of Statistical Data

Naturally, when we talk about statistics, we must talk about some of the definitions within elementary statistics. As I've written in some previous chapters, programs like Google Analytics are not server log files or accounting software like QuickBooks. Programs like Google Analytics are web-analytics programs that a website owner can use to observe statistical trends and extract valuable insights in order to take meaningful and intelligent action. At its very core, that's exactly what statistics is all about, too!

Let's start by defining two different types of data: *qualitative* and *quantitative*.

- **Qualitative data:** Data that describes a non-numerical characteristic
- **Quantitative data:** Data that consists of numbers that represent counts or measurements

The following sentence has both qualitative and quantitative data. Can you spot both types?

"I have 12 chocolate-chip cookies."

The qualitative data here is *chocolate chip*, which is a quality of the data set (here the data set is *cookies*). And, clearly, the quantitative data in the example sentence is *12*, which is the count of chocolate-chip cookies that I have.

Basically, qualitative data describes something (chocolate chip, vanilla, keyword, source, medium) and quantitative data counts something (one, two, five hundred, a million, a bazillion). In Google Analytics, for example, and speaking in general terms, qualitative data includes the dimensions and quantitative data the metrics. Look at Figure 12-1 and you'll see the metrics (quantitative data) going across the top of the page and dimensions (qualitative data) going down the page in the custom report that I am building.

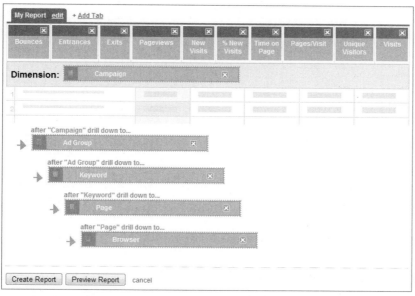

Figure 12-1: Dimensions and metrics as qualitative and quantitative data sets

In Figure 12-1 the quantitative data points are the metrics going across the scorecard on the top. Bounces, Entrances, Exits, Page Views, and the other metrics are all numerical counts. The qualitative data points are the five dimensions going down the custom report. Campaign, Ad Group, Keyword, Page, and Browser are all descriptions of a data point that complement a quantitative measure.

It's very important to note that some qualitative data can be represented numerically, but are not counts of anything, so they are not metrics. The Transactions report within the E-commerce section in Google Analytics is a perfect example of this. Notice in Figure 12-2 how the transaction IDs that were generated in this particular date range are all numbers. However, you can't add all these numbers up into something that is meaningful, and each transaction ID itself isn't a sum or a count of anything in particular. It is simply a *qualitative* attribute of a transaction, much as a ZIP code is a qualitative attribute of where you live.

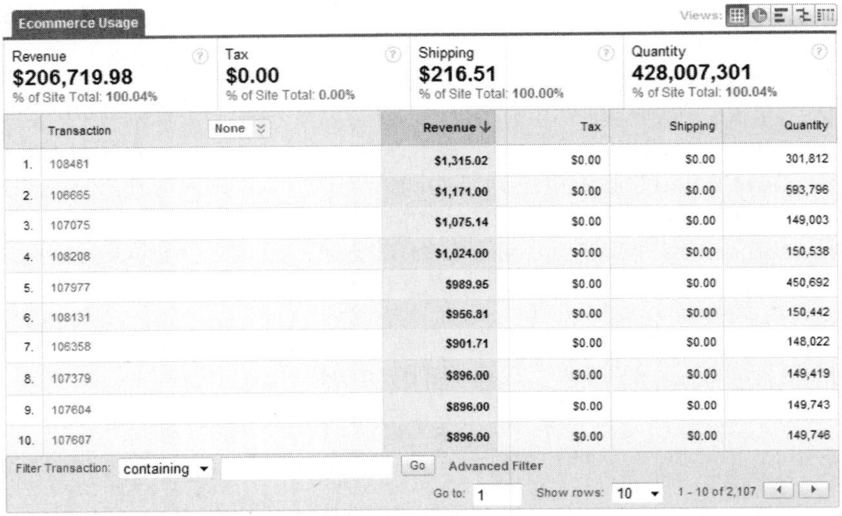

Ecommerce Usage							Views:
Revenue **$206,719.98** % of Site Total: 100.04%		**Tax** **$0.00** % of Site Total: 0.00%		**Shipping** **$216.51** % of Site Total: 100.00%		**Quantity** **428,007,301** % of Site Total: 100.04%	

	Transaction	None	Revenue ↓	Tax	Shipping	Quantity
1.	108481		$1,315.02	$0.00	$0.00	301,812
2.	106665		$1,171.00	$0.00	$0.00	593,796
3.	107075		$1,075.14	$0.00	$0.00	149,003
4.	108208		$1,024.00	$0.00	$0.00	150,538
5.	107977		$989.95	$0.00	$0.00	450,692
6.	108131		$956.81	$0.00	$0.00	150,442
7.	106358		$901.71	$0.00	$0.00	148,022
8.	107379		$896.00	$0.00	$0.00	149,419
9.	107604		$896.00	$0.00	$0.00	149,743
10.	107607		$896.00	$0.00	$0.00	149,746

Filter Transaction: containing ▾ [   ] Go Advanced Filter

Go to: 1   Show rows: 10 ▾   1 - 10 of 2,107 ◀ ▶

Figure 12-2: The Transactions report showing qualitative data represented numerically

The two other types of data that you should know of are called *population* and *sample*.

- A **population** is the complete collection of all data (to be analyzed).
- A **sample** is a portion of data from a population (to be analyzed).

When statisticians perform numerical measurements on a population, they are analyzing the full collection of data at their disposal. Suppose a statistician is able to determine the shirt color of each individual person at a basketball game. The population here would be everyone in the arena. Then the statistician can group the members of the population by shirt color.

When a statistician performs a numerical measurement on a sample, he or she is analyzing only a percentage of the population. Let's suppose that the same statistician at the basketball arena is going to determine the shirt color of every adult male in a particular seating section. These adult males would be considered a sample of the population of all adult male ticket holders in the entire arena.

A numerical representation of a large population (for example, all the males in the world, or everyone in the arena, who could be surveyed only at halftime) is called a *parameter*. A numerical measurement of a sample (for example, the adult males in the particular arena section) is called a *statistic*. All online programs like Google AdWords, Google Analytics, and Google Website Optimizer use statistics, not parameters. As you know from earlier chapters, there is no possible way to collect data from the entire population of visitors with a tag-based web-analytics solution like Google Analytics. Google Analytics uses data from a sample of that population, and generates statistics for you to analyze.

Types of Surveys and Samples

One interesting topic that I've saved for later is on-site survey tools, like 4Q by iPerceptions (www.4qsurvey.com/) and Kampyle (www.kampyle.com/), which record user input — feedback — about your website and your visitors' browsing experiences. You can use this data to make modifications and improvements on your site, and such tools are used by the savviest of website owners. Usually a small piece of JavaScript tracking code is installed on the pages of your website, and either during a visit or immediately after, the visitor will be prompted with questions and possibly a survey.

In the world of statistics, these types of on-site surveys are known as *voluntary response surveys*. In traditional statistics, voluntary response surveys are considered fundamentally flawed, and conclusions about a larger population should not be made from them. This is because the subjects (the sample) have made the decision to respond to the survey, which in itself taints the survey results. For a survey to be considered good in the traditional world, the survey subjects must not have decided whether or not to participate. In the traditional world, a good survey is made up of subjects in what's called a *random sample*, in which each subject of a population has an equal chance of being selected.

In the online world, voluntary response surveys actually work well, and website owners can collect valuable and insightful information from their visitors. There's no way to know whether a person will register a compliment or criticism, so the testing process itself seems to work out because of the variety of the replies of the respondents.

There are four sampling types other than random that you should know about. They are:

- **Systematic sampling:** With systematic sampling, a starting point is determined, and then every *n*th subject is selected. A great example that you can use to visualize systematic sampling is a police officer who plans to pull over every tenth driver who passes by. The police officer selects a starting point (when he or she arrives) and then starts his or her systematic sampling technique by pulling over every tenth driver. Systematic sampling is usually not conducted by professional statisticians because it takes a long time to accumulate a large-enough sample, and a systematic sample is not a random sample (which is desired). Not every member of the population (every driver on the road) has the same odds of being selected (pulled over).

- **Convenience sampling:** This sampling technique involves collecting data via the most convenient method available. An example of convenience sampling would be conducting a survey by selecting people who happen to be standing near you. Convenience sampling is a bad idea because it can lead to heavy pollution in the quality of the data itself, making for unreliable insights. For example, taking a sample at the Democratic National Convention and asking people nearby what they think of the opposing Republican candidate will heavily distort the results in a one-sided way.

- **Stratified sampling:** Here a population is divided into groups (such as "all female students of this university"), and a sample is taken from that group (such as "all female chemistry students of this university"). Stratified sampling is usually performed when the survey taker wants a specific target.

- **Cluster sampling:** Finally, cluster sampling occurs when a population is divided into groups (as in stratified sampling), and all members of a portion of those groups are used for a survey. Think of a state that is divided by county, with a survey taker polling a particular county. In stratified sampling, a sample (not everyone) from the county would be surveyed. In cluster sampling, everyone in that particular county would be surveyed, although residents of other counties might not be. In Google Analytics you could say that cluster sampling occurs when you create a duplicate profile with an include filter. For example, an "organic traffic only" profile would count only the cluster of organic traffic to the site.

Histograms and Normal Distributions

With programs like Google Analytics and Microsoft Excel, you can build charts, graphs, and histograms by entering data into a set of rows and columns, or by logging in and accessing the desired report. When you take an elementary statistics class you'll most likely be required to build a histogram to show your instructor that you know how to organize a set of data and build a report on your own.

Simply speaking, a histogram is a bar graph, usually using vertical bars. In web analytics, bar graphs are usually represented as trending graphs that you see toward the top of most reports. Another reason statistics professors ask you to build a histogram is so you can evaluate whether or not the histogram is a *normal distribution*. When a histogram is normally distributed, it resembles the shape of a bell, where the extreme ends of the histogram are flat and the line rises until it reaches a high point in the middle. Normally distributed graphs are very important for the development of statistical methods and programs, but you won't find many histograms that look normally distributed. Figure 12-3 shows the trending graph by hour in the Visits report in the Visitors section of Google Analytics. This is probably as close to a normal distribution as you're going to get.

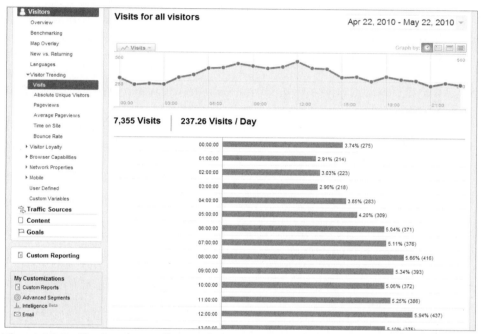

Figure 12-3: The hourly trending graph in Google Analytics, close to a normal distribution

There are many types of charts, and each has its own name in statistics, but the normally distributed histogram is the most important of all. Google Website Optimizer uses a modified form of a time-series graph and a bar graph, while Google Analytics uses histograms, pie charts, and clusters (motion charts).

Mean, Median, Mode, and Midrange

You've most likely heard of all four of these terms, and you've most likely heard them used interchangeably by peers, colleagues, and even your own college professors. They are used interchangeably by the general population, but each means something entirely different. They do have one thing in common: they are all *measures of center*.

- **Mean:** You find the mean (or the arithmetic mean) of a set of values by adding all the values and dividing by the total number of values. The mean corresponds to the term *average* used in web-analytics programs like Google Analytics. Figure 12-4 shows the Average Time on Site report, which is the mean of the time spent on a particular website.

- **Median:** The median measures the value that falls directly in the middle of a set of data, when that set of data is organized from the lowest value to the highest (or vice versa). For example, let's say you have five numbers: 3, 5, 9, 14, and 75. The mean (average) of these five numbers is 21.2, but the median (the value in the center) is 9. Median and mean get mixed up all of the time in the real world, but as you can see, they are two different measures of center.

- **Mode:** The mode is the number in a group of data that occurs most frequently. In the data set of 3, 4, 4, 5, 5, 5, 5, 6, and 7, the mode is 5, as it's the number that is repeated most often. The mode measure of center is seldom used.

- **Midrange:** You calculate the midrange by taking the highest number in a set, adding it to the lowest number in the set, and dividing the result by two. In the 3, 5, 9, 14, 75 data set, the midrange is 39 (75 plus 3, divided by 2). The midrange is also seldom used as a measure of center.

Figure 12-4: The mean of all visitors to a site

Averages and Outliers

Let's discuss the four measures of center in greater depth for a moment. The mean (average) takes all the values and divides their sum by the number of values. Take the data set that we used for the median example: 3, 5, 9, 14, and 75. The value 75 is the one that really doesn't fit in with this group. It's more than five times greater than the next-highest value. Is it an error? Possibly, but let's assume for the moment that it's not. That value is called an *outlier*, a value that is much higher or much lower than the others.

What I'm leading up to here is that while the mean is used most often in statistics to measure the center of a data set, it is sensitive to outliers, like 75 in the previous data set (but it is also very sensitive to small outliers in a set of data with large values). In a set with a few extremely large or small outliers, it may be more beneficial to use the median measurement of center, as it will be much closer to the "true" average of the data set. The median can actually be calculated very easily using Microsoft Excel and one of the predefined formulas.

But really, who's going to have the time to download an experiment or web-analytics data into Excel and determine outliers and discover the median of a data set? Not many businesspeople that I know of, that's for certain. To determine outliers, you would have to sort your data from low to high (or high to low) and pick out the extreme values on the low and high ends. To determine the median, you take the lowest value, add it to the highest value, and divide the sum by 2. Perhaps there's a better way — a best way — to obtain a measure of center?

The answer is that there really is none. You should use averages with caution and know that average calculations can be heavily affected by outliers. The Average Time on Site metric from Google Analytics is a perfect example of a metric that doesn't provide much insight, even though on the surface it sounds wonderful. But there are other metrics, like Average Order Value and Per-Visit Value, in which the presence of only a few extreme outliers can heavily distort the figures without your knowing it.

There's a popular saying these days in web analytics: "Averages lie!" You should know that there's a lot of truth in that saying. Don't rush to decisions based on an average — you can do better than that!

Standard Deviation and the Range Rule of Thumb

One of the most important concepts in elementary statistics is known as the *standard deviation*, a measure of variability from the mean (average). It's a compound statistic in that you must first calculate the mean (among a few other algebraic operations) in order to figure out the standard deviation.

Because the center of a data set only has a limited meaning and at times only a limited amount of value can be derived from it, statisticians developed the standard-deviation statistic to help place more context behind an average. For example, if I were to tell you that the average football player's career length has a mean of three years and a standard deviation of one year, this would indicate to you that if a particular football player's career lasted four years (the mean of three years plus the standard deviation of one), it would not be an unusual event. Likewise, if a particular football player's career lasted two years (the mean of three years minus the standard deviation of one), it would also not be unusual. The standard deviation is the allowance, plus or minus, that any piece of data can fall within and still be considered normal. In fact, most statistics texts and statisticians will allow values to range two standard deviations above or below the mean before considering them unusual. In our example, that would mean that a particular football player's career could last anywhere between one and five years (two standard deviations above or below the mean of three) and still be considered normal (or expected).

The *range rule of thumb* states that about 95 percent of all data in a set will fall within two standard deviations of the mean. Five percent of data in a set will fall outside this range. This isn't an exact figure, but it's close enough to be used as a rule of thumb.

What happens when a set of data ranges further than two standard deviations from the mean? What if some piece of data is 3, 4, or 10 standard deviations from the mean? If you said, "It's an outlier," you were correct. The question is what to do about it. Figure 12-5 is the Intelligence section from Google Analytics, which displays alerts to you when some metric or dimension falls or rises beyond two standard deviations from the mean. Take a close look at Figure 12-5. The first alert is the source containing Google for the % New Visits metric. The expected value (the mean with a few standard deviations built in) is 78.88 percent to 88.66 percent. However, for this particular day in comparison to the previous day (and in comparison to the expected value), the % New Visits metric hit 93.55 percent, which is equivalent to an increase of 16 percent. This increase was significant enough for this particular website owner to be alerted to it, because it was more than two standard deviations above the mean.

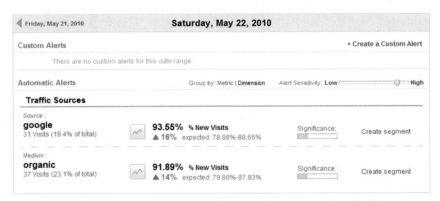

Figure 12-5: Deviations shown as percentage increases in the Intelligence section of Google Analytics

When the expected values fall more than two standard deviations below the mean, you'll see the percentage of decrease and its significance, as in the examples in Chapter 9. Standard deviations and the range rule of thumb play a critical role in how the Intelligence section works to provide you with important insights about what's happening on your website.

Z-Scores

Z-scores are an interesting concept in statistics that allows you to compare values from different populations. Personally, I like using Z-scores to compare metrics between two different types of traffic, like paid and organic. You can use Z-scores as a great comparison tool for any two or more populations.

Z-scores take the value to be compared, the mean, and the standard deviation algebraically and produce a score that is usually between –2 and +2. For example, let's say there was the following question: "Which is relatively more chocolaty: a chocolate-chip cookie with 14 chocolate chips or a chocolate-chip ice cream cake with 350 chocolate chips?" Since the number of chocolate chips used in a cookie is so much smaller than the number of chocolate chips used in a chocolate-chip ice cream cake, and their sizes are also so different, it is impossible to compare the two populations without using a standard scoring system. By converting both population scores into Z-scores, you can compare the two Z-scores to be able to determine which dessert is the most chocolaty. When you compare your paid traffic to your organic traffic, it's easy to say that one is better than the other based upon a raw side-by-side comparison. As it turns out, they are two separate populations, and without a standard score like a Z-score, comparing them becomes iffy at best. You can find Z-score calculations online, but not within any web-analytics package that I'm currently aware of. I usually calculate my Z-scores on an Excel spreadsheet after downloading the raw data.

In essence, a Z-score is a number that you can use to compare two different data sets with different population sizes.

Confidence Intervals and Margin of Error

The final two statistics that I want you to learn about are *confidence intervals* and *margin of error*. Both play a critical role in traditional statistics, and both should be understood to have a critical role in experiment data and web analytics.

A confidence interval is normally expressed as a range of plus or minus a percentage. It is designed to show the person analyzing the data that the statistic can be plus or minus the percentage represented in the confidence interval and still be considered accurate. For example, take a look at Figure 12-6, which is an experiment from Google Website Optimizer that's still in progress.

For the original variation, you will see the estimated conversion rate metric listed as 3.82 percent. Next to that number you'll see plus or minus 0.9 percent. This is the conversion rate range for this variation that Google Website Optimizer predicts your variation will fall within. For the original variation, the conversion rate can be as high as 4.72 percent or as low as 2.92 percent and still be considered as accurate for this sample. For Variation 1, the confidence interval is a full plus or minus 1.0 percent.

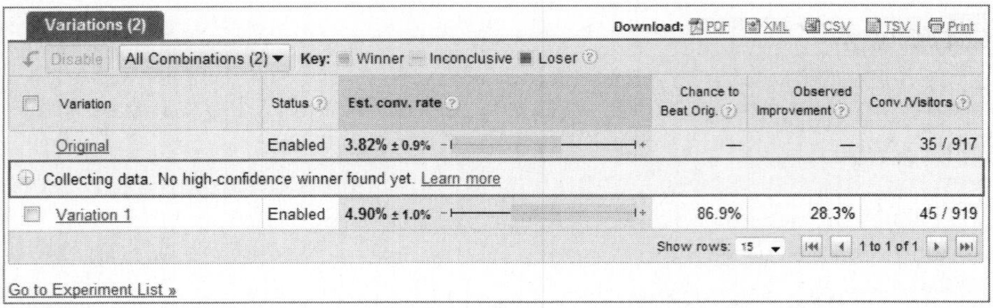

Figure 12-6: Confidence intervals expressed as percentages in Google Website Optimizer

A confidence interval is not necessarily the same thing as the margin of error. The margin of error in statistics is essentially the amount of the error in sampling. In one way, confidence intervals and margins of error are very similar, but technically they are not the same thing. Also, statistics is not an exact science — it's intended to be used to observe trends and extract valuable insights (where have you heard that before?).

You'll see confidence intervals appear when you encounter data sampling in Google Analytics. Data sampling usually occurs as in Figure 12-7, when you attempt to segment by a very large number of visits, usually over a lengthy date range. Google Analytics enables data sampling as a means of conserving processing speed for all the other users. Data sampling (as performed in Google Analytics) means that Google can only show a portion of your data, albeit a very large portion. Without data sampling, one could theoretically crash a Google Analytics server, and that would not be desirable.

In Figure 12-7, the yellow highlighted boxes under the Visits column indicate Google's assessment of the accuracy of the metrics it is displaying. It's tough to make out from Figure 12-7, but for the first row (google/organic), Google shows a plus or minus 1 percent confidence interval in the Visits metric for this particular date range.

How to Approach Your Data After Reading This Chapter

Now that you've gotten a very good sense of elementary statistical concepts, you'll be able to approach your experiment data and your web-analytics data in a whole new way. You'll have obtained a greater insight into how tools like Google Website Optimizer and Google Analytics work to display the data that you use in your daily business life. You're also very well aware of the pitfalls and dangers of the statistics on a random sample that tag-based web-analytics programs produce.

Figure 12-7: Sampled data showing confidence intervals in Google Analytics

You'll definitely encounter bosses or clients who will not be able to get past the fact that these tools are not "100 percent accurate." To them, the accuracy of their web data (such as the number of banner clicks from a partner website that equal dollars for them) seems like their lifeline, but most of the time they simply need to be taught about how these systems work and what they can and can't do. Depending on your boss or coworker or client, he or she may be either very receptive to learning about statistics and the inner workings of Google Website Optimizer or Google Analytics, or he or she may be completely turned off by such concepts. You'll have to play it by ear and use your best judgment with each individual. For those who are hard to deal with, you will simply need to explain yourself clearly (as with anything in life). They may not like the answer because it doesn't provide them with their unachievable "100 percent accuracy," but explaining how it all works to your boss or co-worker is for their own good at the end of the day.

The Technical Side of Google Website Optimizer and Experiment Ideas

Before I turn to combining Google Analytics, Google AdWords, and Google Website Optimizer to achieve online measurement success, I have one more chapter that focuses exclusively on Website Optimizer. This chapter includes technical requirements for Google Website Optimizer, including all the coding and HTML editing that you'll need to know to successfully launch either an A/B or a multivariate experiment.

If you are not the person who will be performing coding changes (and if you felt that Chapter 10 was kind of dry and boring), you may want to skip ahead to the next chapter, where I'll talk about the AdWords section of reports in Google Analytics and using those two programs together. If you like things like JavaScript code and HTML (who doesn't, right?), then you'll want to carefully comb through this short chapter to view how Google Website Optimizer works from a programming standpoint for both an A/B and a multivariate experiment.

NOTE You will find quite a few JavaScript code snippet examples in this chapter. Be sure to copy and paste the actual code that you will use on your own website pages from within your own Google Website Optimizer account. Copying them straight from this book will not be successful, as your account and test numbers will not be included in these example JavaScript snippets.

The Google Website Optimizer Tracking Code

You'll need to install code on your experiment's pages in order for Google Website Optimizer to function, and this code will vary according to the type of experiment you're running. The tracking codes are in JavaScript, which means that the visitors to your experiment page(s) must have JavaScript and cookies enabled in order to be exposed to your experiment. As with Google Analytics, if visitors to your experiment page do not have JavaScript or cookies enabled, they will not be able to be a part of the experiment.

Google Website Optimizer calls the siteopt.js file that is hosted on the Google Analytics domain to process data and run the experiment. You'll notice in either the A/B experiment code or the multivariate experiment code that there are a lot of similarities to the Google Analytics Tracking Code (read Chapter 16 to learn what to do when running both Google Analytics and Google Website Optimizer together).

When visitors who have both cookies and JavaScript enabled land on your experiment page, they will have two cookies set on their computers: a __utmx cookie and a __utmxx cookie. Both cookies contain data such as the domain hash of the website, a unique identification string that's shared between both cookies, and the experiment combination that was viewed. These cookies are necessary in order to count not only the number of visits to the experiment, but also the number of conversions that were successfully achieved. Both these cookies are persistent and have a shelf life of two years from inception.

Tracking Code for an A/B Experiment

When you log in to Google Website Optimizer using your Google account and start setting up your experiment, you'll eventually encounter the page that asks you whether you want your webmaster to install the tracking code or you will do it yourself. Unlike in Chapter 11, for the purposes of this chapter you'll want to choose the option that shows you the tracking code, which is the option that suggests you'll be implementing the tracking codes yourself. Once you choose this option you'll see a page that looks like Figure 13-1.

In an A/B experiment with Google Website Optimizer, you'll be required to add JavaScript code to at least three separate pages. You'll have to add two pieces of tracking code to the original page, a piece of tracking code at the bottom of each variation page (remember you can have more than one variation page if desired), and a piece of tracking code at the bottom of the conversion page.

Original Page Coding

On the original A/B experiment page, you'll need to install two pieces of JavaScript tracking code. First you'll need to install the control script at the very beginning of your page's source code. This control script should be installed as high as possible, even above any `<html>` declarations (definitely above the `<head>` section, at least).

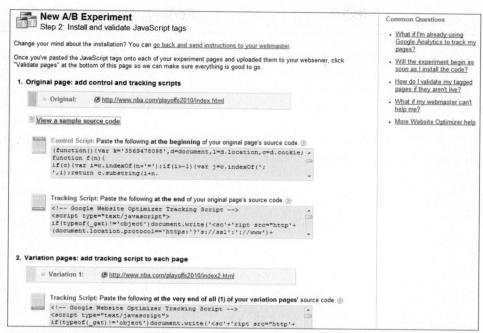

Figure 13-1: The Google Website Optimizer tracking-code page

The original page control script looks like this:

```
<!-- Google Website Optimizer Control Script -->
<script>
function utmx_section(){}function utmx(){}
(function(){var k='123456123456',d=document,l=d.location,c=d.
cookie;function f(n){if(c){var i=c.indexOf(n+'=');if(i>-1){var
j=c.indexOf(';',i);return c.substring(i+n.
length+1,j<0?c.length:j)}}}var x=f('__utmx'),xx=f('__utmxx'),
h=l.hash;d.write('<sc'+'ript src="'+
'http'+(l.protocol=='https:'?'s://ssl':'://www')+
'.google-analytics.com'
+'/siteopt.js?v=1&utmxkey='+k+'&utmx='+(x?x:'')+'&utmxx='+
(xx?xx:'')+'&utmxtime='+new Date().valueOf()+(h?'&utmxhash='+
escape(h.substr(1)):'')+'" type="text/javascript"
charset="utf-8"></sc'+'ript>')})();
</script>
<script>utmx("url",'A/B');</script>
<!-- End of Google Website Optimizer Control Script -->
```

The original A/B experiment page also receives a tracking script, which should be installed toward the bottom of the page's source code, before the closing `</body>` tag. Sometimes experiments do not function properly if the original page tracking code is placed outside (after) the closing `</body>` tag.

The original page tracking script for your experiment will look very similar to this:

```
<!-- Google Website Optimizer Tracking Script -->
<script type="text/javascript">
if(typeof(_gat)!='object')document.write('<sc'+'ript src="http'+
(document.location.protocol=='https:'?'s://ssl':'://www')+
'.google-analytics.com/ga.js"></sc'+'ript>')</script>
<script type="text/javascript">
try {
var gwoTracker=_gat._getTracker("UA-1234567-2");
gwoTracker._trackPageview("/123456123456/test");
}catch(err){}</script>
<!-- End of Google Website Optimizer Tracking Script -->
```

Notice that while the Google Website Optimizer tracking script uses the `trackPageview` function that the Google Analytics tracking code uses, the `gwoTracker` declaration is used in front of `trackPageview`. Google Analytics uses the `pageTracker` declaration, and this is done on purpose so that the two tracking codes are less likely to interfere with each other. Another interesting note is the UA number, which for Google Analytics denotes the account and the profile number. Notice that you'll see an account number that ends with at least a dash two (-2), if not a greater number. The creation of a Google Website Optimizer experiment unlocks the ability to create a new profile for a new domain within Google Analytics.

Figure 13-2 shows an example of where to install the original page's JavaScript tags within the page's source code.

Variation(s) Page Coding

You need to install only a tracking script at the bottom of all variation pages. You need not (and should not) install a control script at the very top of the page — the control script is specifically reserved for the original page.

The variation page tracking script that you'll copy and paste into your variation pages is identical to the original page's tracking script. I recommend editing the comment tag in the source code so that you can differentiate between codes. I've edited the comment tags in the following tracking code to show you an example of doing this:

```
<!-- Google Website Optimizer Tracking Script - Variation 1-->
<script type="text/javascript">
if(typeof(_gat)!='object')document.write('<sc'+'ript src="http'+
(document.location.protocol=='https:'?'s://ssl':'://www')+
'.google-analytics.com/ga.js"></sc'+'ript>')</script>
<script type="text/javascript">
try {
var gwoTracker=_gat._getTracker("UA-1234567-2");
```

```
gwoTracker._trackPageview("/123456123456/test");
}catch(err){}</script>
<!-- End of Google Website Optimizer Tracking Script - Variation 1-->
```

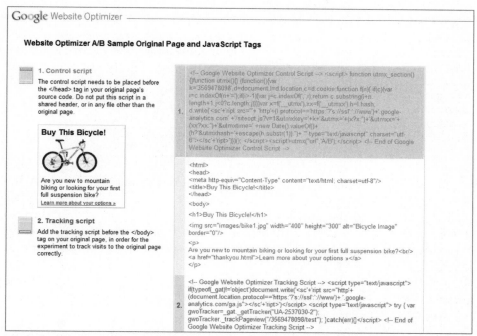

Figure 13-2: The sample A/B page coding example from Google Website Optimizer

Conversion Page Coding

Finally, the conversion page receives a tracking code that is also placed at the very bottom of the page's source code. This code is almost identical to the other tracking codes, except that the final piece of the `trackPageview` function is set to `/goal` instead of `/test`. Do not edit that — or any piece of any Google Website Optimizer code for that matter. Install the codes on your site "as is."

```
<!-- Google Website Optimizer Conversion Script -->
<script type="text/javascript">
if(typeof(_gat)!='object')document.write('<sc'+'ript src="http'+
(document.location.protocol=='https:'?'s://ssl':'://www')+
'.google-analytics.com/ga.js"></sc'+'ript>')</script>
<script type="text/javascript">
try {
var gwoTracker=_gat._getTracker("UA-1234567-2");
gwoTracker._trackPageview("/123456123456/goal");
}catch(err){}</script>
<!-- End of Google Website Optimizer Conversion Script -->
```

After you've installed the tracking codes and uploaded your newly edited pages live, you must validate that your tracking codes are installed correctly. If Google cannot validate your tracking codes, you won't be able to launch your experiment. To validate your page coding click the Validate Pages button that you'll find toward the bottom of the page shown back in Figure 13-1.

If your pages do not validate, you'll see something like Figure 13-3. You should not see the pop-up shown in the figure, and ideally you'll see green checkmarks instead of red Xs.

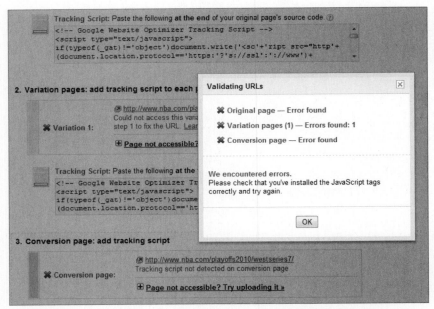

Figure 13-3: An unsuccessful validation of an A/B experiment tracking code

Tracking Code for a Multivariate Experiment

Tagging your multivariate experiment is a bit different from tagging your A/B experiment. In a multivariate experiment you'll tag a test page with a minimum of three different sections, and install tracking code on a conversion page. There's also more work to do within the Google Website Optimizer interface, as I showed in Chapter 11: you'll have to actually create the HTML combinations online after you've tagged the appropriate sections on your page's source code.

Test-Page Coding

There are three different types of JavaScript code that you'll need to install on your test page. The first of these is a control script:

```
<!-- Google Website Optimizer Control Script -->
<script>
function utmx_section(){}function utmx(){}
(function(){var k='123456123456',d=document,l=d.location,c=d.
cookie;function f(n){if(c){var i=c.indexOf(n+'=');if(i>-1){var
j=c.indexOf(';',i);return c.substring(i+n.
length+1,j<0?c.length:j)}}}var x=f('__utmx'),xx=f('__utmxx'),
h=l.hash;d.write('<sc'+'ript src="'+
'http'+(l.protocol=='https:'?'s://ssl':'://www')+
'.google-analytics.com'
+'/siteopt.js?v=1&utmxkey='+k+'&utmx='+(x?x:'')+'&utmxx='+
(xx?xx:'')+'&utmxtime='+new Date().valueOf()+(h?'&utmxhash='+
escape(h.substr(1)):'')+'" type="text/javascript" charset="utf-8">
</sc'+'ript>')})();
</script>
<!-- End of Google Website Optimizer Control Script -->
```

The control script in a multivariate experiment, as for an A/B experiment, is placed toward the very top of the test page. If you just read the previous section, there shouldn't be any surprises here.

There is also a tracking script that goes toward the bottom of the source code, before the closing </body> tag. Again, as in an A/B experiment, your page could produce errors if this code is inserted outside (after the closing </body> tag), so try to place it before the closing </body> tag. As you can see in the following snippet of JavaScript code, the multivariate experiment tracking code is identical to the A/B experiment tracking code.

```
<!-- Google Website Optimizer Tracking Script -->
<script type="text/javascript">
if(typeof(_gat)!='object')document.write('<sc'+'ript src="http'+
(document.location.protocol=='https:'?'s://ssl':'://www')+
'.google-analytics.com/ga.js"></sc'+'ript>')</script>
<script type="text/javascript">
try {
var gwoTracker=_gat._getTracker("UA-1234567-2");
gwoTracker._trackPageview("/123456123456/test");
}catch(err){}</script>
<!-- End of Google Website Optimizer Tracking Script -->
```

Now here's the kicker, and here's what differentiates a multivariate experiment from an A/B experiment. For each page section that you'll want to experiment on, you'll need to install page-section tags immediately before and immediately after the content that you'd like to experiment with.

For each section that you want to experiment with, first insert this line of code immediately before (above) it in the page's source code:

```
<script>utmx_section("Insert your section name here")</script>
```

You'll want to replace `"Insert your section name here"` with a name that makes sense and is easy for you to identify. This name will be shown in the multivariate reports and in the HTML section-editing interface that comes up after you validate this code.

Then insert this closing tag immediately after (below) your experiment section in your page's source code:

```
</noscript>
```

Don't worry about the unbalanced `</noscript>` tag. This won't cause any script errors on your test page.

The following is an example of what the section code would look like wrapped around a part of my page's source code. In this example I am testing the call to action on the right-hand side of my test page. After I validate this code I will create some additional variations in the HTML editor on the next page in Google Website Optimizer.

```
<script>utmx_section("Right-Banner")</script>
<a href="/playoffs.html"><img src="images/button-2.gif"
width="122" height="76" alt="click to buy" /></a>
</noscript>
```

There is no limit to the number of section scripts that you can install on your test page, but do keep in mind that the more section variations you create, the longer your experiment will take to complete.

Conversion-Page Coding

The conversion-page code is the same code as in an A/B experiment. Install it at the very bottom of the conversion page, before the closing `</body>` tag.

```
<!-- Google Website Optimizer Conversion Script -->
<script type="text/javascript">
if(typeof(_gat)!='object')document.write('<sc'+'ript src="http'+
(document.location.protocol=='https:'?'s://ssl':'://www')+
'.google-analytics.com/ga.js"></sc'+'ript>')</script>
<script type="text/javascript">
try {
var gwoTracker=_gat._getTracker("UA-1234567-2");
gwoTracker._trackPageview("/123456123456/goal");
}catch(err){}</script>
<!-- End of Google Website Optimizer Conversion Script -->
```

After you install your tracking codes and upload your pages live, you will need to validate your code within Google Website Optimizer. Once your code has been cleared and is good to go, you'll be able to create section variations within the Google Website Optimizer interface.

Creating MVT Combinations and Editing HTML

When you reach the page shown in Figure 13-4, you'll see the names you assigned to your page sections on the left-hand side. The "original" section is the one taken directly from the website. On the right-hand side you'll see the HTML code for the page section. To create a new variation, simply click the small Add New Variation link. You'll need to provide a name for your section (this name cannot exceed 25 characters). Once you do, you'll see the page refresh, and the original variation's HTML code will appear in the editing panel in the middle of the page.

From this point, simply edit your HTML and click the silver Save button on the upper right of the editing panel when you're finished. At this point I strongly advise you to work closely with your web developer, if you are not that person, to make sure you don't "break" the HTML code. You'll need to edit the HTML cautiously and leave any tags that aren't a part of the additional variation alone. For example, let's suppose this is your original code:

```
<h1Try the new Crystal Light energy drink!</h1>
```

Don't remove the `<h1>` tags when entering in a variation for this heading, as you'll be removing the style that is associated with it. The lack of a closing angle bracket after the first <h1 indicates a bad HTML copy/paste job, but since the Google Website Optimizer HTML editor doesn't have HTML validation, you can actually upload broken code. You can also remove both the opening `<h1>` and the closing `</h1>` tags and it won't break your HTML, but do not do something like this (i.e., add the closing bracket):

```
<h1>Try the new Crystal Light energy drink!</h1>
```

As you are editing and saving your multivariate variations, make frequent use of the Preview link next to the Save button on the upper right. You'll want to make sure, even if your HTML looks good in source-code format, that it also looks good in a browser. Clicking Preview does not affect experiment counts and does not inflate visits to your site. Once you are finished previewing all your experiment variations and are finished creating them, click Save and Continue to review your experiment and launch it.

Whether you run a multivariate experiment or an A/B experiment (or both simultaneously) is up to you. As long as you're setting up and running experiments, you're already improving matters for yourself. This chapter may have been dry and tedious for some of you, but it will have been worth it when you begin to see how valuable setting up and running these experiments can be.

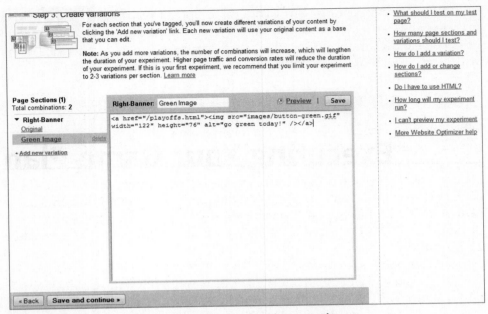

Figure 13-4: Editing HTML sections for a multivariate experiment

OK, so now you've been through 13 chapters covering three different Google programs. It's finally time to start combining them and using the combined power of three programs for maximum success. Start by reading the next chapter, which covers Google AdWords and Google Analytics together.

Executing Your Game Plan

In This Part

Google AdWords and Google Analytics

The payoff for learning three of Google's most popular and successful programs is finally here! You've read through 13 chapters covering everything you need to know (and then some) about Google AdWords, Google Analytics, and Google Website Optimizer. For the next few chapters I'll write about using the combined power of these products for your continued success in all things online.

The first of the three chapters in this part of *Your Google Game Plan for Success* talks about using Google AdWords and Google Analytics together. Luckily, Google makes this easy for advertisers by allowing you to use them in tandem — you can log in to Google Analytics and find your AdWords data, which you can analyze and extract insights from. This functionality is unique in the advertising industry, and it's the fulcrum of this particular chapter. I'll also talk about Search Funnels, a Google Analytics style report available in Google AdWords, and about how to import your goals from Google Analytics into Google AdWords.

Let's start by making sure that your AdWords data is being imported into your Google Analytics account.

Syncing Google AdWords and Google Analytics

As I mentioned in the opening of this chapter, the ability to directly import your online marketing statistics into a web-analytics program is something unique in the industry. Some web-analytics vendors allow you to upload a tab-separated file or a spreadsheet that you first download from Yahoo! Search Marketing or another pay-per-click platform. This is a manual process that you must do on your own to ensure that your platform's cost data can appear in your web-analytics program. Sometimes this imported data is not segmentable — it can be viewed in the interface only as it was uploaded from your downloaded spreadsheet.

Because syncing between Google AdWords and Google Analytics is possible, none of that business is necessary. Within three simple steps your AdWords data, such as clicks, impressions, and click-through rates, will be imported into a subsection of the Traffic Sources section specifically reserved for Google AdWords. To much jubilation within the industry, this section was recently redesigned and is now more powerful than ever before. There are new segmentation options, views, and reports, which I'll walk you through in this chapter.

First let's get you synced up. Follow the next three steps, and you'll be on your way to combining the power of Google AdWords and the power of Google Analytics.

Step 1: Administrative Rights

The only prerequisite for syncing your AdWords data and your Analytics data is that your log-in e-mail address *must* be an administrator on both your Google Analytics account and your Google AdWords account.

If you are an administrator on both accounts, great! You are in a very small minority, and you can move on to Step 2. For most of you, keep on reading.

For Google Analytics the process of becoming an administrator is very easy. If you are not one already, please alert the person who gave you access to your Google Analytics account. Ask this person to log in and click User Manager from the account overview screen, and then point him or her to Figure 14-1. Make sure your access is changed from View Reports Only to Account Administrator, as shown in Figure 14-1.

Remember that account administrators are able to do everything that can be done within a Google Analytics account. This includes creating and deleting profiles, editing settings, and adding or removing users.

For Google AdWords the process is a little bit stickier, because there are a few extra steps involved. First of all, please note that any e-mail address can have access to only one AdWords account at a time. If for whatever reason your e-mail address has access to another Google AdWords account that you're not going to sync, please ask another AdWords administrator to terminate your access. The administrator can do so by logging in to AdWords, clicking the My Account tab, and clicking within the Account Access link. From there the other administrator will need to find your e-mail address and select Terminate Access from the Actions drop-down menu.

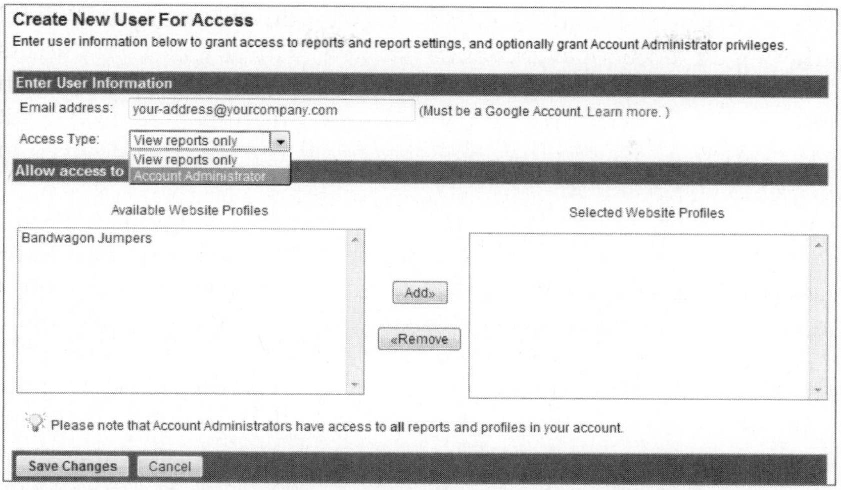

Figure 14-1: Assigning administrative rights to a Google Analytics account

If you are the only person who has access to the Google AdWords account (if you created the account), you will actually need to cancel it using the Preferences link in the My Account tab. You may need to contact an AdWords representative if you're one of those rare individuals who have created an accidental AdWords account, or who still have access to an older (inactive) AdWords account.

Let's assume for the moment that you don't have issues with AdWords. Chances are actually pretty good that you'll have administrative access to your AdWords account. If you don't have any access or you have a different access level, please contact your AdWords account administrator — the only person who can help you switch your access level to Administrator, or assign you any access at all (see Figure 14-2). If you need access (i.e., you don't have access currently), you will need to be invited to the AdWords account by your account's administrator. Then you'll exchange a few e-mails, generated by Google, with your account's administrator, who will help you receive access to your account.

Remember, the e-mail address through which you have administrative access to a Google Analytics account must be the same one that gives you access to a Google AdWords account. If you're having issues with your account administrator, and for whatever reason this person cannot give you administrative access to either account, there's always the option of using a different e-mail account (controlled by your administrator) to get the AdWords and Analytics accounts synced. Your personal e-mail address doesn't have to be the one that has administrator standing in both accounts — as long as there is one e-mail address that is in both accounts, you can begin the process of syncing the accounts.

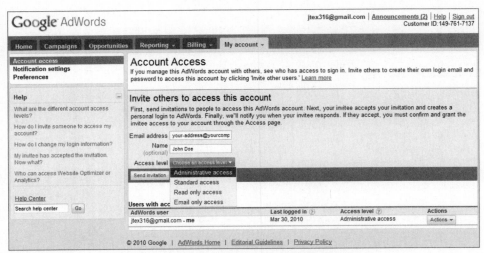

Figure 14-2: Assigning administrative rights to a Google AdWords account

Step 2: Destination URL Auto-Tagging

Assuming the worst is over and you have administrative access to both accounts, you can now actually start syncing them. The first thing you'll need to do is enable destination URL auto-tagging on your AdWords account. You can do this via the My Account tab by clicking the Preferences link. A checkbox will enable you to turn on auto-tagging, as shown at the bottom of Figure 14-3. You'll want to ensure that this option is checked.

Destination URL auto-tagging appends a `gclid` query string parameter at the end of the destination URLs used on your AdWords ads and keywords. Once you apply this function, perform a test click on one of your ads, and you'll see something like the following example:

```
http://www.zwee.com/apple/cheap-ipod-nano-4th-gen/?gclid=CIH1-
bOv_KECFQ0hnAodsgInDg
```

That string of encoded characters at the end of the destination URL sends the referral information, such as the keyword, ad group, campaign, and landing page, to Google Analytics.

Step 3: Syncing and Applying Cost Data

Once your destination URL auto-tagging is applied, you can now sync the accounts together. Click the Reporting tab and then the Google Analytics link. Doing so will bring you to a screen that looks like Figure 14-4. Since I'm working under the assumption that you already have a Google Analytics account, you'll want to click the second radio button and then click Continue. But if you wanted to, you could create a Google Analytics account from right here.

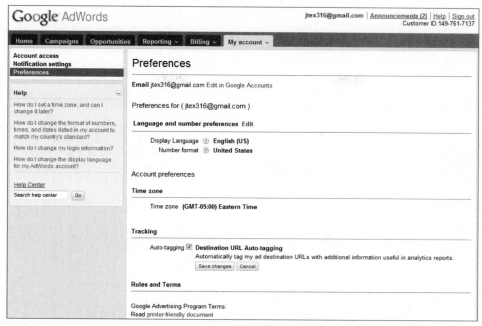

Figure 14-3: Enabling destination URL auto-tagging within your AdWords Preferences section

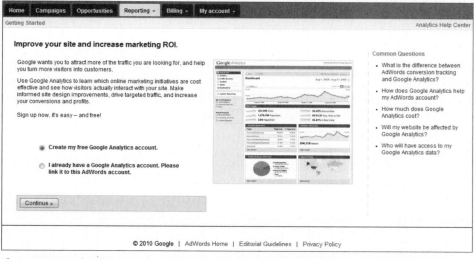

Figure 14-4: The first step in syncing your AdWords account to your Analytics account

The next screen that you'll see will look like Figure 14-5. Here you should see your Google Analytics account in the drop-down menu (if you have administrative access to multiple Google Analytics accounts, they should all be listed here). Ensure that the desired Google Analytics account is selected. In case you missed Step 2 (destination URL auto-tagging), you're again reminded of it here with a checkbox.

When you're finished, click Link My Account, and the sync is completed!

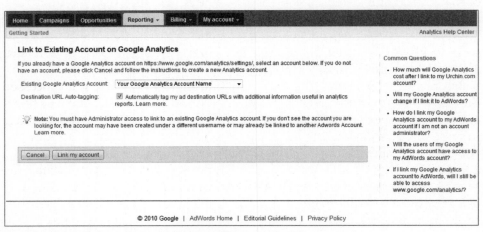

Figure 14-5: Selecting your Google Analytics account

You can verify that this sync has been properly created, and that AdWords data is being received by your Google Analytics account, by clicking within the main website profile information of your Google Analytics profile. Now you'll see a new checkbox, under the new subheading Apply Cost Data, which will show your AdWords account ID as in Figure 14-6.

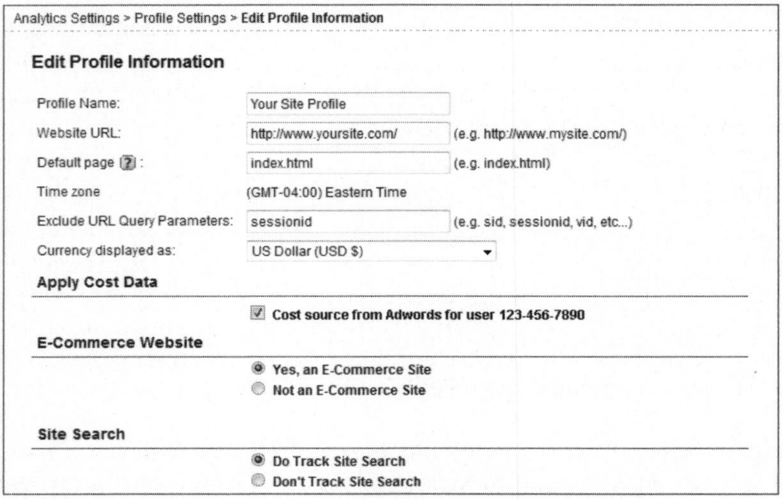

Figure 14-6: Cost data applied to a Google Analytics profile

The Google AdWords Report Subsection

Now that you're synced you'll start to see your AdWords data appear in Google Analytics within a new AdWords report subsection, found at the very bottom of the Traffic Sources report section in Google Analytics. I've been saving this report section from all the way back in Chapter 7 until this point in the book. This newer section of reports in Google Analytics features eight reports, a unique set of tabs, metrics, and dimensions, and a dozen new segmenting options that are available only in this subsection.

Before you start diving in, please note that AdWords data is not processed the same way as Google Analytics data. Every day, sometime in the wee hours of the morning, Google Analytics will pull in the previous day's AdWords data in one lump and process the data into the AdWords subsection of reports. If you synced your accounts on May 25, for example, you most likely won't see any AdWords data until May 27, and at that point you'll see only the data from May 26 (the previous day). Google Analytics cannot import AdWords data from before you synced the accounts. You also can't edit AdWords bid prices or ad copy from Google Analytics (sorry!). You'll still have to use Google AdWords for that. But now that you're all synced up, you can access either program at any time by first logging in to AdWords and then using the Reports tab to access Google Analytics. No longer will you have to switch tabs or browser windows to access either program.

New AdWords Segmentation Options

Within the new AdWords report subsection you'll be able to segment your data using some new segmentation options that were previously available only in AdWords. These are available from any of the standard first- or second-dimension drop-down menus within the standard report tables. You'll see them in the first group of segments in either of the two drop-down menus.

Within any report in the new AdWords subsection, look at the reporting table in the middle of the page. Below the scorecard (the row of metrics in a bigger font, directly underneath the report tabs), you should see two drop-down menus. These drop-down menus are where you'll be able to utilize the new AdWords segmentation options. The first four new segments — Campaign, Ad Group, Keyword, and Ad Content — are already familiar to you, as they are available throughout Google Analytics. The other segmentation options currently available are:

- **Ad Distribution Network:** These are the networks where your ads are being shown. You know them as Google Search, Google Search Partners, and the Content Network. Now you get the evidence that you've desperately needed to evaluate which networks are doing the best job of matching your advertising goals.

■ **Match Type:** One of my favorite new options, this segments keywords, ad groups, and campaigns (or any report) by keyword match types, which are *broad*, *phrase*, and *exact match*. Google Analytics makes it very easy to discover which match type performs best in terms of conversion rate or e-commerce.

■ **Matched Search Query:** An interesting and insightful segment, the Matched Search Query allows you to see what a searcher actually typed into Google to bring up your ad. Remember that while you may be bidding for certain keywords of the broad or even phrase-match type, a user may actually type in something different to bring up your ad. This segment can put the spotlight on new keyword-bidding opportunities.

■ **Placement Domain:** Are you advertising in the Google Content Network? Would you like to see which website domains are actually showing your ads and how each individual domain performs? Find your desired Content Network campaign and use this segment to view not only how much traffic each domain is bringing to you, but also how many conversions or how much revenue it is responsible for.

■ **Placement URL:** Much like the Placement Domain segment, the Placement URL segment shows you the full destination URL path of the page on which your Content Network ads are appearing. Use these URLs to view the specific pages on which your ads appear. As a good practice with AdWords (also discussed earlier in the book), you should go as far as copying the placement URL and visiting it for yourself, so that you can see where your ad is appearing and how it looks.

■ **Ad Format:** Google AdWords allows advertisers to run text, image, video, and rich media ads. In the new AdWords subsection of reports you can segment by ad format and compare performance across campaigns, ad groups, and even ad formats.

■ **Targeting Type:** This segment allows you to see the targeting type for your campaigns. You'll usually see either keyword or site targeting, as these are the options that advertisers use in AdWords.

■ **Display URL:** Your display URL is an important part of your AdWords ad, and it now can be segmented within Google Analytics. Using multiple display URLs across your ad groups? Compare their performances by segmenting by display URL, and make appropriate changes to your campaigns afterward.

■ **Destination URL:** One of the big factors determining keyword Quality Score and campaign performance is the destination URL (landing page) of your ads. With this final segment, view the full destination URLs as you typed them into your AdWords campaigns, and view traffic and performance data for each individual one. This is one way of analyzing the performance between two landing pages in a poor man's A/B experiment, without using Google Website Optimizer.

As I walk you through the reports in this section I'll make use of some screenshots that will show some of these new segments in action.

The Overview Screen

When you access the AdWords subsection from within the Traffic Sources section of reports, the default report that you will see is AdWords Overview. This screen provides you with an overview of what your AdWords campaigns are doing and how they're performing.

Let's examine Figure 14-7 to get a sense of the type of data you'll see in this section. First, the trending graph at the very top of the report defaults to comparing two very important metrics: click-through rate (abbreviated CTR, as you know) and bounce rate. As you can see just by looking at the trending graph, when the click-through rate peaked at the end of April, the bounce rate decreased, and after that surge in click-through rate, in early May, the bounce rate increased again. You haven't even really seen anything in this section, and already you are receiving valuable information about your AdWords account.

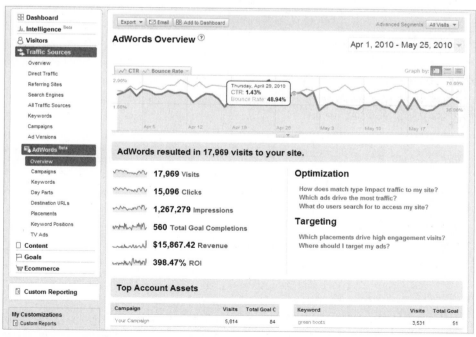

Figure 14-7: The AdWords Overview screen

Below the trending graph you'll see a potpourri of metrics from AdWords and Analytics combined. You can see the number of visits, clicks, and impressions that AdWords generated, as well as the number of goal completions, the revenue (for e-commerce sites or goals with goal values enabled), and an ROI (return-on-investment) metric that is available only in this subsection (you can't even get it in AdWords). Toward the very bottom of the overview screen you'll see your top five AdWords account assets (campaigns and keywords) sorted by visits but displaying goal completions for each one.

This overview section represents a shift in philosophy from what you're accustomed to seeing throughout Google Analytics. The focus is clearly on providing insights and showing you performance-oriented metrics, and not so much on displaying raw visits and statistics in aggregate.

As with any report in Google Analytics, the AdWords Overview screen can be added to your dashboard, e-mailed to a colleague, or viewed under an Advanced Segment.

Campaigns Report

The second report in the AdWords subsection is the Campaigns report. Here you'll find a Site Usage tab, but with slightly different metrics on the scorecard. An example of the Campaigns report is shown in Figure 14-8.

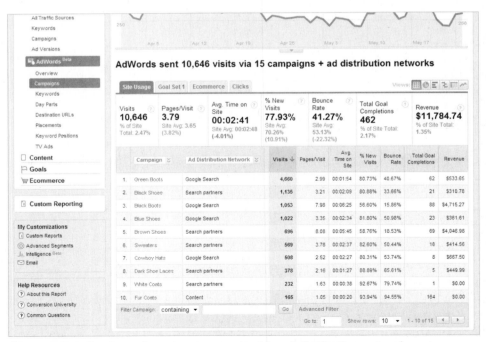

Figure 14-8: The Campaigns report segmented by ad distribution network

Here I'm using the secondary dimension of Ad Distribution Network so that I can see which campaigns correspond to which distribution networks. My job as an analyst and an online marketer would be to see which networks are providing me with the best ROI and conversion-rate figures (or are matching up to my advertising goals the best).

But the Site Usage tab isn't the best feature of this report. There is a fourth tab on the top of this report, called Clicks, which holds all your AdWords data. This can be seen in Figure 14-9. This tab shows AdWords metrics, but also includes metrics like ROI and RPC (revenue per click) that are not available in AdWords.

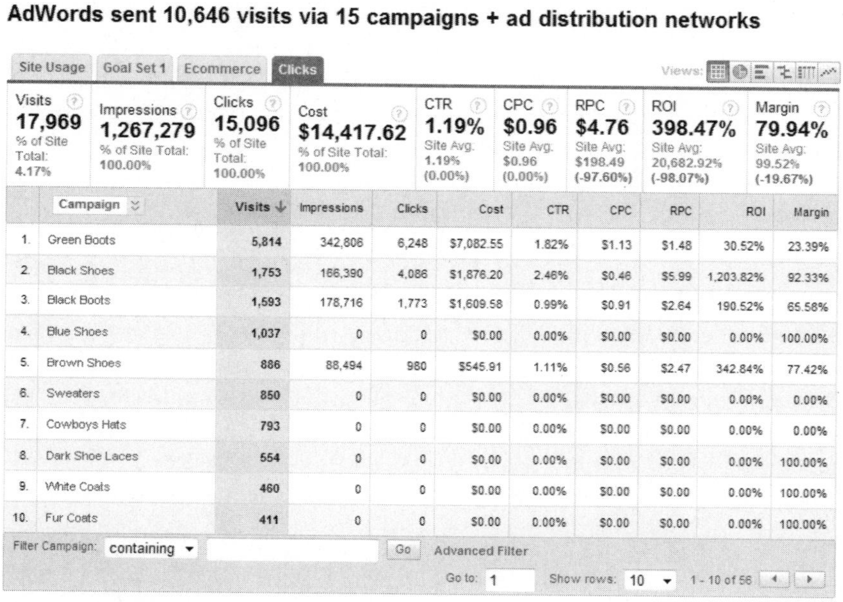

AdWords sent 10,646 visits via 15 campaigns + ad distribution networks

Site Usage | Goal Set 1 | Ecommerce | Clicks   Views:

Visits	Impressions	Clicks	Cost	CTR	CPC	RPC	ROI	Margin
17,969	1,267,279	15,096	$14,417.62	1.19%	$0.96	$4.76	398.47%	79.94%
% of Site Total: 4.17%	% of Site Total: 100.00%	% of Site Total: 100.00%	% of Site Total: 100.00%	Site Avg: 1.19% (0.00%)	Site Avg: $0.96 (0.00%)	Site Avg: $198.49 (-97.60%)	Site Avg: 20,682.92% (-98.07%)	Site Avg: 99.52% (-19.67%)

	Campaign	Visits ↓	Impressions	Clicks	Cost	CTR	CPC	RPC	ROI	Margin
1.	Green Boots	5,814	342,806	6,248	$7,082.55	1.82%	$1.13	$1.48	30.52%	23.39%
2.	Black Shoes	1,753	166,390	4,086	$1,876.20	2.46%	$0.46	$5.99	1,203.82%	92.33%
3.	Black Boots	1,593	178,716	1,773	$1,609.58	0.99%	$0.91	$2.64	190.52%	65.58%
4.	Blue Shoes	1,037	0	0	$0.00	0.00%	$0.00	$0.00	0.00%	100.00%
5.	Brown Shoes	886	88,494	980	$545.91	1.11%	$0.56	$2.47	342.84%	77.42%
6.	Sweaters	850	0	0	$0.00	0.00%	$0.00	$0.00	0.00%	0.00%
7.	Cowboys Hats	793	0	0	$0.00	0.00%	$0.00	$0.00	0.00%	0.00%
8.	Dark Shoe Laces	554	0	0	$0.00	0.00%	$0.00	$0.00	0.00%	100.00%
9.	White Coats	460	0	0	$0.00	0.00%	$0.00	$0.00	0.00%	100.00%
10.	Fur Coats	411	0	0	$0.00	0.00%	$0.00	$0.00	0.00%	100.00%

Filter Campaign: containing Go Advanced Filter

Go to: 1 Show rows: 10 1 - 10 of 56

Figure 14-9: The Clicks tab in the Campaigns report

The Clicks tab is also available in the next report section, which is the Keywords report.

Keywords Report

The next report in this subsection is the Keywords report, which is a virtual carbon copy of the Campaigns report. Each of the keywords that you're bidding for is listed here, and all the tabs available in the Campaigns report are also here.

Figure 14-10 shows the Keywords report, and shows another good example of using secondary dimensions to view the new segmentation options from the AdWords section. In Figure 14-10, I am using the Match Type segment to view performance-based metrics for the keywords in my campaigns.

Because I'm bidding on different match types for the same keyword in AdWords, I can break the keywords down in this report with the Match Type segment.

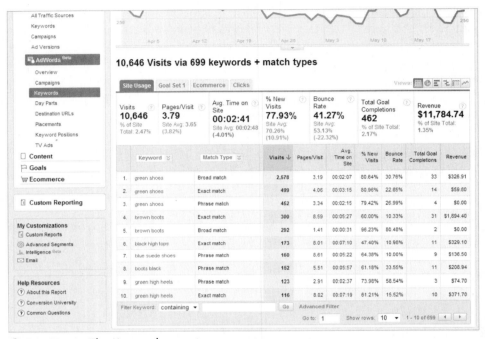

Figure 14-10: The Keywords report

Day Parts

The Day Parts report shows you two interesting pieces of information from your AdWords account. In Figure 14-11 you can see toward the top of the screen that the trending graph shows you data plotted by the day of the week. I've enabled two metrics to show the correlation between the visits that each day of the week receives and the e-commerce conversion rate.

The other piece of data, the hour of the day, appears as dimensions going down the report table. Because I'm looking at the E-commerce tab and I'm sorting my data by revenue, the highest-revenue hours are shown (by default, this report is listed starting with 00:00 and ending with 23:00). I've also decided to compare this report's e-commerce conversion rate to the site average. Interestingly, only three of the top 10 revenue-generating hours yield an e-commerce conversion rate higher than the site average.

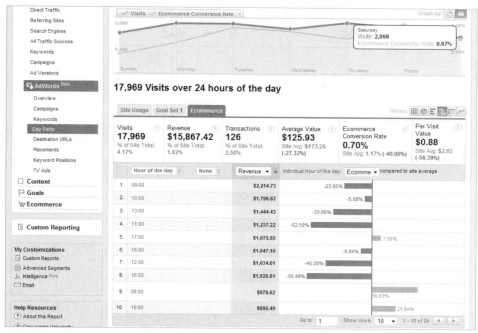

Figure 14-11: The Day Parts report

Destination URLs

The Destination URLs report shown in Figure 14-12 shows you the actual destination URLs (landing pages) that you are using in your AdWords account. This is very similar to the Landing Pages report in the Content section, only you're looking at the URLs that you use in AdWords.

Figure 14-12 shows the Destination URLs report segmented by the targeting type, which is either keyword targeting or site targeting. Since I'm using both in different campaigns in my AdWords account, I can see listings for both when I perform a segment.

Placements

The Placements report shows you the difference in performance between your managed Content Network placements and your automatic Content Network placements. This is a good way to analyze your content campaigns, but when you click either Managed or Automatic (depending upon which placement types you're running in AdWords), you'll be able to drill down to view the actual placement domains that are being advertised on. Clicking a placement domain will show you the placement URL (the URL of the page your ad is actually appearing on).

AdWords sent 10,646 Visits via 383 destination URLs + targeting types

	Destination URL	Targeting Type	Visits ↓	Pages/Visit	Avg. Time on Site	% New Visits	Bounce Rate	Total Goal Completions	Revenue
1.	http://www.site.com/page.h	Keyword	3,529	3.34	00:02:17	80.53%	29.16%	51	$386.71
2.	http://www.site.com/defaul	Keyword	460	8.59	00:05:25	61.52%	10.22%	40	$2,030.90
3.	http://www.site.com/index.	Keyword	372	6.74	00:06:31	56.18%	21.77%	26	$538.04
4.	http://www.site.com/page.h	Site	295	1.41	00:00:31	95.93%	80.68%	2	$0.00
5.	http://www.site.com/lp/hom	Keyword	176	2.51	00:02:15	78.41%	64.77%	3	$74.70
6.	http://www.site.com/produ	Keyword	171	2.84	00:03:45	74.85%	48.54%	4	$157.70
7.	http://www.site.com/lp/02.h	Site	165	1.05	00:00:20	93.94%	94.55%	164	$0.00
8.	http://www.site.com/www	Keyword	133	9.19	00:07:22	60.15%	13.53%	12	$371.70
9.	http://www.site.com/p90x	Keyword	133	2.10	00:01:09	82.71%	63.16%	1	$0.00
10.	http://www.site.com/abcde	Keyword	130	3.21	00:02:25	74.62%	34.62%	0	$0.00

Figure 14-12: The Destination URLs report

Of course, if you are not advertising in the Content Network, nothing will appear in this report.

Keyword Positions

This is one of the more interesting reports of the entire AdWords section. Here you can view keyword performance per ad position on www.google.com. When you click a keyword, as I've done in Figure 14-13, you can view how many visits you've received from each of the standard positions in which your ads appear on a search engine results page. You can change the Position Breakdown drop-down menu to view other metrics, such as revenue, bounce rate, and goal-conversion rate.

TV Ads

The final report in the AdWords subsection imports your TV ads data from your Google AdWords account. If you are one of the few advertisers running TV ads through AdWords, you'll be able to view metrics such as TV impressions, ad plays, initial audience reach, and the total cost of your campaigns.

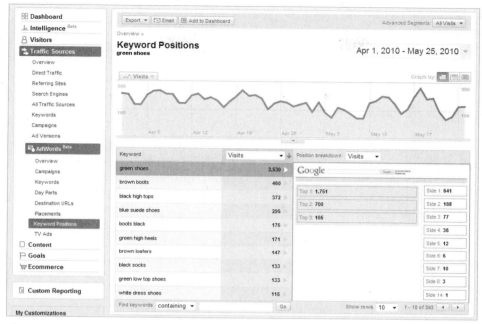

Figure 14-13: The Keyword Positions report

You can use this report to compare your site metrics to your TV ad campaigns and to determine the effectiveness of your TV ads.

Other Ways to Combine AdWords and Analytics

There are some other ways that you can use the power of both programs outside the AdWords subsection of reports. There are a few reports within Google AdWords that will be interesting to you, such as the Search Funnels report, which is not available in Google Analytics at the time of this writing. I'll close out this chapter with some of the other things that you can do to harness the power of both Google AdWords and Google Analytics.

Importing Your Google Analytics Goals into Google AdWords

One of the things that you can do when synced is to import your goals into your AdWords account. Instead of having to create conversion tracking actions as shown in earlier chapters of this book, you can simply import the goals that you create in your Google Analytics profile directly to AdWords.

When you click the Reporting tab within your AdWords account you'll see a Conversions link, which is where you'll be able to find the conversion actions and code associated with conversion tracking. But this time you'll also notice a silver Import from Google Analytics button toward the top of the Conversions sub-tab table. Click this button, and you'll see all the goals that you've set up. If any of the goals have received any conversions within the last 30 days, you'll be able to import them into this report section. You can then return to the Conversions report and see Google Analytics goals listed within your Google AdWords account.

Please note a few things before importing your goals. First, you must have benchmarking (data sharing) enabled in your Google Analytics account to be allowed to import your goals into AdWords. Then you'll need to have "active" goals (goals that have received conversions sometime within the last 30 days). Finally, you should know that importing your goals from Google Analytics does not replace, deactivate, or change any actions that you have taken with the Google AdWords conversion tracking tool. That piece of JavaScript code will always operate independently from your Google Analytics goals. In the Campaigns report within AdWords you won't see your Google Analytics goal data (it won't be duplicated within AdWords if one of your imported goals happens to be a page where you also have AdWords conversion tracking installed).

AdWords Search Funnels Report

Within the Conversions section of your AdWords account you should notice a link on the left-hand side of the screen pointing you to a new report section, available only in AdWords, called the Search Funnels report. This report highlights the keywords and keyword paths that assist other keywords to get conversions.

What this means is that AdWords is able to determine which search terms help the keywords that get credited with the conversion in AdWords and Analytics reports. This allows advertisers to shift their focus from paying attention to and spending money on only those keywords that get credited for conversions, and to focus also on other keywords that assisted in the conversion process. Figure 14-14 shows the Search Funnels Overview screen, which looks a lot like a Google Analytics report.

In the overview shown in Figure 14-14, the total number of conversions is shown, as well as some averages, such as days, clicks, and impressions to conversion. Below these data are the top conversion actions (these can be both AdWords and Google Analytics goals), and to the right are some helpful links to reports within the Search Funnels section.

This report section features a report showing top conversions and a report highlighting the campaigns, ad groups, or keywords that received assisted clicks and impressions, as well as reports showing first- and last-click analyses, time lag, and path length. There is also a Top Paths report, showing you the keywords that assisted the converting keyword.

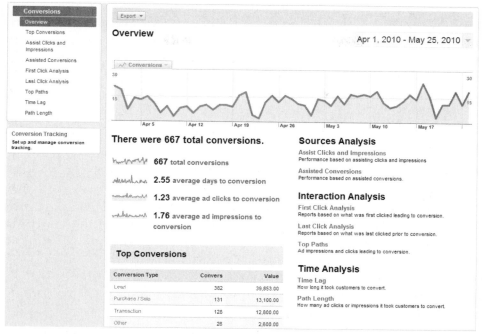

Figure 14-14: The AdWords Search Funnels report

The only unfortunate thing about the Search Funnels section is that space doesn't permit a thorough explanation of this very interesting and insightful new section of reports in AdWords. Make sure your account is synced and make sure that you use this report section to uncover nuggets of information that can help you allocate more of your marketing dollars to the keywords that help your conversion process.

Running Multiple AdWords Accounts at the Same Time

You may be working with another individual or organization that is running AdWords ads for the same client as you. This means that two active AdWords accounts are running simultaneously for the same client, and only one of these accounts is synced and sending data to your Google Analytics account.

You have two options at this point — it's critical that your AdWords account data is being imported into your Google Analytics account. First, you can contact a Google representative, if you have one. There are some links within your AdWords account that allow you to contact Google via e-mail or a form that's provided. Your second option is to reach out to a Google Analytics Certified Partner, like the company that I work for at the time of this writing. It may be able to assist you in getting your multiple AdWords accounts synced and sending cost data to your Google Analytics account.

CHAPTER 15

Google AdWords and Google Website Optimizer

For a Google Website Optimizer experiment to provide you with insightful data on your A/B or multivariate tests, you'll definitely need a good amount of traffic volume exposed to your experiment. Google can't even determine a winner for your experiment until it has collected a certain number of visits and conversions. (Google uses the terms "winner" and "winning combination.") Waiting for search engine spiders to crawl your new page can take weeks, if not months, and doing an offline or direct campaign can be extremely costly. An e-mail campaign requires additional setup, creatives, and tracking beacons, not to mention the price. So how do you send traffic to your experiment pages to receive results, without needing to take out a second mortgage? Enter Google AdWords, of course, which leads into this chapter.

By now you know how great and cost-effective Google AdWords is, and from Chapter 11 you also know that you can create as many Google Website Optimizer experiments as your heart desires. For your next experiment, you should seriously consider using AdWords to drive traffic, especially if you're using a brand-new page or pages for that experiment.

I'm also going to talk about some ideas for new landing pages that you can implement either on your next landing page or on an existing landing page on your site, as well as some other important things to know and think about concerning AdWords and Website Optimizer.

Using AdWords for Your Website Optimizer Experiments

How I think about using these two programs together usually depends on the situation I find myself in. I have come up with the following four subsections to help organize this portion of the chapter; what actions you should take is dependent upon the status of your AdWords campaign and your experiment/landing-page situation. Is your AdWords campaign a brand-new one that you're starting from scratch, or has it been running for a while? Are you uploading brand-new landing pages to use for Google Website Optimizer, or are you using an existing page off your website to run an experiment?

The following is a review of four possible combinations and the steps you should take to ensure a smooth experiment with the help of Google AdWords.

Experiment: New AdWords, New Landing Pages

When launching a new AdWords campaign, you have only a limited idea of how it's going to perform. Sure, you may have an established AdWords account with some good history behind it, but it will take you some time to tweak settings, bids, ads, keywords, and other things before it's running just right. Now, throw in a new set of landing pages that have not been indexed by the search engines and for which you have no history (e.g., bounce rate, conversion rate, etc.). It may take several weeks, if not months, for the search engines to index your new pages, which means that without AdWords you'll have to wait a while for traffic to come to the pages so your Website Optimizer experiment can show you anything significant.

To pull off an experiment with Google Website Optimizer and a new AdWords campaign successfully, you'll need to start off very lightly and not spend a lot of money right away. You're going to need to evaluate how your campaign grows over the first couple of weeks and make the necessary adjustments to improve its performance, just as I said in the AdWords chapters of this book. Why ramp up your daily budget right away without knowing how that money is going to be spent? Success online doesn't come from racing to the finish line — take your time, evaluate your campaign's performance, make adjustments, and then, after you get a good feel for what your campaigns are doing, increase your daily budget.

You'll obviously want to test your new landing pages to ensure that they work from a technical standpoint. If there's a form on the landing page, make sure that a visitor can fill it out successfully (and without a lot of hassle). If there are links or banners, make some test clicks before launching your AdWords campaign. Play any video or rich media that your new landing page may have on it to make sure it functions properly. You get the idea — stress-test your new landing pages before turning on your new AdWords campaign.

Website Optimizer is all about conversions and improving your conversion rate. After your new AdWords campaign has been running for a week or two, and after you've launched your Website Optimizer experiments, evaluate which landing page or experiment combination is the highest-converting one. As you know from Chapter 11, the highest-converting landing page or combination is the one that you should permanently go with on your website. When your Website Optimizer experiment is complete, you can still improve your conversion rate by evaluating your best-performing ads, keywords, and settings. You can continue to test and refine your new AdWords campaign, even after your first Website Optimizer experiment is complete. And I say your first Website Optimizer experiment because, as you know by now, I'm a proponent of implementing a culture of continual testing and experimentation.

Specifically, you'll want to ensure you do all the following when launching both a new AdWords campaign and a new landing page:

- Before anything gets activated online, you need to sit down with your web designer and webmaster to tag your landing pages and other website pages with both Google Website Optimizer tracking codes and the Google AdWords conversion tracking tool. This ensures that conversion-oriented metrics will appear in both AdWords and Website Optimizer, which in turn will give you a good idea of what adjustments to make.

- You'll also want to work closely with your webmaster or web designer to ensure that your new landing pages have a strong, visible, and enticing call to action. Remember that your landing pages are tools for your website, either for generating leads and revenue or for having visitors contact you. There will need to be a prominent image, headline, or other means of persuading visitors to perform the desired action that you've set forth for them.

- When creating a new AdWords campaign, keep it simple. Create a few ad groups at maximum (no more than three), run up to three ads within each ad group, and bid on no more than 10 keywords per ad group. Keep the default AdWords campaign settings as they are and allocate a conservative daily budget to the new campaign. This way you have a strong grasp on your campaign and can identify areas of potential optimization much faster than you could with a huge campaign. Once the Google Website Optimizer experiment on your landing pages is complete (and before the follow-up experiment), you can allocate more money and create more ad groups if desired.

- While your Google Website Optimizer experiment is running, try not to change anything (settings, ads, keywords). Your changes will affect the Google Website Optimizer experiment process and will create a situation in which your experiment will not be pure. Let your experiment run naturally.

- After Google Website Optimizer has declared an experiment winner, and before you run a follow-up experiment, make the changes to your AdWords campaign that you couldn't make before. Pause poorly performing ads, raise bids on high-converting keywords, and try settings like position preference and ad delivery.

Experiment: New AdWords, Existing Landing Pages

In this situation you already have established website pages that you've been using for pay-per-click advertising or other marketing initiatives. But this time you've created a new campaign or possibly a new AdWords account (if this is your first time running a pay-per-click campaign).

While I always recommend experimenting on your landing pages, you should focus more on your new AdWords campaigns and focus less on your landing pages. Be conservative and start small, as you would if you had a new landing page, but be confident that your landing page works. I am working on the assumption that you've done your due diligence and have analyzed your landing page's performance over time, using Google Analytics and running experiments using Google Website Optimizer.

You really don't need to spend too much money on AdWords in the first few weeks, because your existing landing page has been live for a while and has built up some SEO weight. Organic, non-paid search engine traffic is going to come to this landing page already, so you don't have to ramp up your AdWords budget — at least for the time being. Then after a few weeks, as you learn how your AdWords campaigns perform, allocate more budget as you would in the first situation described.

Experiment: Existing AdWords, New Landing Pages

The dream situation for anyone wishing to run an experiment using Google Website Optimizer is an existing, established AdWords account sending refined traffic to a new landing page. It makes the experiment run more smoothly and allows the website owner to collect experiment data much faster than is possible with an experiment on an existing page.

New landing pages haven't been indexed by the search engines and are probably receiving most of their traffic from new visitors generated by your AdWords campaigns. Even though this is a "dream" situation from an experimental standpoint, you are completely dependent upon your online marketing to bring visibility to your new landing page.

Here, as in the first situation, you want to ensure that the new landing page has the necessary tracking codes from Google Website Optimizer and that you've worked with your design team to come up with a good experiment to run. In AdWords you'll want to make sure that you switch out your destination URLs to the new landing page. Download Google AdWords Editor and make an account-wide update to all destination URLs to make your life easier, rather than log in to the AdWords interface to switch out URLs manually.

Experiment: Existing AdWords, Existing Landing Pages

In this fourth situation you already have existing AdWords campaigns sending traffic to existing landing pages. You have the necessary tagging, coding, and query parameters enabled, and you have lots of experiment history and traffic to base decisions on.

All I can recommend to you in this situation is to keep doing what you've been doing — find new, creative ways to experiment with your AdWords campaigns and your landing pages. If you're fresh out of landing-page experiment ideas, check out the next section in this chapter.

Ideas for Landing-Page Experiments

Anyone can design a landing page. Yes, even you — without any experience in graphic design or web development — can install Photoshop or visit a free website-creation service like www.webs.com. In no time you can have a working landing page to use for your site. However, as I mentioned in the previous section, there are sizeable differences between designing a landing page for usability, for aesthetic pleasure, and for conversions. Designing for conversions is not easy to do, as you must design for all three factors (usability, aesthetics, and conversions). As a business or site owner, your primary goal is optimizing your website for conversions. The tools that can help you optimize your website are Google AdWords and Google Website Optimizer.

This section focuses more on Google Website Optimizer, as I share some ideas for things to experiment with on your landing pages. First, let me illustrate the difference between designing for usability and designing for conversions.

Designing for Usability vs. Designing for Conversions

A critical part of designing your website or your landing pages successfully is to create a navigational system on your website that makes sense, is easy to use, and is clean. Your website visitors should not have any problems — technical or otherwise — using your website. The visitor's browser shouldn't crash, clicks on links should execute instantly, images should load immediately, text and pictures should be easy to read and see, and the visitor should have a clear, concise understanding of what it is you do or what it is you're selling. It sounds a lot easier than it actually is to put all this together on one landing page. I always advise hiring a professional design firm to help you in this process, but I know that hiring a company isn't always financially feasible. Perhaps the next few examples will at least give you a glimmer of insight into what you should be looking at in the landing-page design process.

Figure 15-1 is the website for www.fifa.com during the 2010 World Cup. There are some great elements on this page — it's well organized, it's extremely clear what the page is all about, and it's very easy to find things. (Matches, teams, and statistics are just some of the easy-to-see options on the top navigational menu.) While it's impossible to predict visitor intent (what visitors want to do when they land on a page of a site), what is it that www.fifa.com wants visitors to do? See game summaries? View photos? Register on the site (do you see the Register link tucked away on the top right of the page, to the left of the Login link)? Subscribe to the RSS feed? While www.fifa.com has a great site and one that's very easy to use, it is not designed for conversions (at least not what we think of as conversions in the traditional sense, such as purchasing something from an online store or filling out an inquiry form).

Figure 15-1: The www.fifa.com website

Figure 15-2 is the website for www.soccer.com. Unlike www.fifa.com, this is an Internet business, focusing on selling soccer-related products. For web merchants like www.soccer.com, the 2010 World Cup is the equivalent of four holiday seasons during one month in terms of business. It's probably not a reach to say that www.soccer.com does well during the World Cup. However, websites still need to be designed for conversions, while engaging in experiments to continually improve their business. The www.soccer.com site is not only designed for usability and aesthetic pleasure, it's also very clear where the site is pointing visitors to. It wants to convert visitors by getting them to click anywhere on that huge splash image titled "10 Fan Essentials." It also offers an enticing value proposition below the splash image, informing you that you can get free shipping on orders of $99 or more by using the provided coupon code.

Figure 15-2: The www.soccer.com website

The www.fifa.com site is designed only for usability, information, aesthetics, and brand-name recognition. There's nothing wrong with that, but as a website owner running a business, you need to design for conversions the way www.soccer.com has been designed in Figure 15-2.

Calls to Action

Think back to Chapter 11, where I showed an image of nine different buttons that www.twitter.com could experiment with on its homepage. Those buttons are examples of different calls to action, which are the most critical element in the conversion process. It's what can make or break a conversion from one of your website's visitors. Sure, many other things are in play, like website usability and ease of use of a shopping cart, but the call to action that a visitor sees is the biggest influence on that visitor's decision-making process.

The actual text that a call to action contains is clearly the most important factor of a button or image, but you can also get creative by experimenting with Google Website Optimizer and creating different shapes and sizes for your call-to-action buttons. And — though you might not have thought of this — arrows, plus signs, checkmarks, and other shapes integrated within your calls to action can also influence the conversion process.

Figure 15-3 is a sample from `www.freebuttons.org`, where a vast quantity of button shapes, sizes, colors, texts, and integrated images can be found.

Figure 15-3: Call-to-action button ideas

You don't necessarily *need* to use an image for your call to action. It can be plain HTML text that is hyperlinked to the page or section where you want the visitor to go. But you can still apply some of the principles of the call-to-action buttons (different text, emoticons like smiley faces, and other text symbols) to entice your visitors to convert on your website. Figure 15-4 shows the homepage for `www.aol.com` — notice the use of the text call to action on the left-hand side (where it reads "Get Free Mail" — that's actually text with a background color).

Savvy Internet marketers use Google AdWords alongside their Google Website Optimizer experiments to further assist their landing pages by sending traffic from text ads that echo and pick up on what the landing pages are trying to accomplish. If the call to action on a landing page is for a free trial, the ads in rotation that send traffic to the landing page should mirror the call to action and also strongly mention the free trial being offered.

Figure 15-4: Text call to action on www.aol.com

Landing-Page Headlines

The first thing that a visitor may see when entering a landing page is the headline of the page. This is usually at the top of a page, and it's usually in concert with the headline of the ad that a visitor clicked to reach the page. This is a very intelligent tactic used by seasoned online professionals. They realize that ads and landing pages working together increase the chances that a visitor will engage with the site — and convert.

In AdWords, you're limited to 25 characters of headline text to entice your potential website visitors. On your landing pages you can get more creative. With Google Website Optimizer you can perform experiments on your landing-page headlines to see which one performs the best.

Here are a few landing-page headline ideas:

- **Short vs. long titles:** Since there's no limit to headline sizes on your own web pages, why not test their lengths to see which one converts? Will the headline "The Fan's Store" convert better than "The Ultimate Store for Fans Everywhere!"? Use Google Website Optimizer to test and send traffic to your site with an ad that mentions the title with Google AdWords.

- **Questions vs. statements:** How you approach your visitors in both your landing pages and your ads can have a strong influence on what your visitors ultimately do. Try an experiment with both your ads and your landing pages by asking visitors a question one week (like "Want to Save Money?") and making a statement the following week (like "Start Saving Money!"). The results may surprise you.

- **Formality vs. informality:** Each person likes to be talked to differently. Some visitors prefer a refined approach and formal language — other visitors respond well to shouts, screams, and exclamation points. Which type of language do your visitors respond to? Do they like to be called *sir* or *ma'am*, or do they prefer a less formal approach? Test the approach that your headlines use on both AdWords and Website Optimizer and find what's successful for your site.

Selling/Value Propositions

There's an old adage in sales: "When they ask how much it is, tell them how great it is." This speaks to the fact that selling something offline or online isn't just about the sticker price; it's about how you sell it. What features, benefits, or rewards will a visitor receive when he or she purchases an item from your store? How fast, strong, or aggressive can your potential customers expect your service to be if they fill out your online Request for Proposal (RFP)? Your selling or value propositions can make or break a deal in the online world, just as they can in the offline world.

Normally, advertisers using Google AdWords will experiment with different value propositions in the two description lines that appear underneath the headline of the ad. Those same value propositions will appear again on the landing page, reinforcing the deal or value for your prospective client or customer.

Here are some ideas that you could experiment with on your own ads and landing pages:

- **Quality vs. convenience:** Your product or service has more than one selling point. But which of those selling points will make the difference between a visitor who browses and a visitor who converts? Is telling visitors that your product is "A+ rated" going to work better than telling them that your product will "last a lifetime"?

- **Features vs. service:** Some visitors will want to know about all the bells and whistles that come with whatever you're selling or offering. Others will want to know what types of services they can expect when engaging with your business. Test both of them to see what your visitors respond well to.

- **Making money vs. saving money:** Who doesn't like making money? Who doesn't like saving money? Believe it or not, some of your website audience will respond better to value propositions highlighting the money they'll save, rather than the money they'll make.

- **50 percent off vs. buy one, get one free:** This classic proposition is tested in stores, supermarkets, and basically everywhere in the world. Do your visitors respond better to ads and landing pages offering 50 percent off on a product, or to ads and landing pages that offer buy one, get one free? Only experimentation in AdWords and Website Optimizer will answer that question for you.

NOTE Throughout this chapter you've noticed the repeated use of phrases like "how your visitors respond" and "what your visitors like." It's impossible to predict the intent of a visitor, and it's nearly impossible to predict what visitors will do once they are on your website. Therefore, it's up to you to experiment continually to home in as closely as possible on what your visitors are doing. Google AdWords, Analytics, and Website Optimizer are the tools that will help you determine what your visitors are doing on your website, and Website Optimizer is the tool that will help you continue to improve on it.

Short, Medium, and Long Forms

Advertisers will often ask their web developers and/or graphic designers to integrate a form into a page. This way their potential visitors have an opportunity to quickly interact with a site and provide information to start the customer relationship.

You as a website owner or marketer can experiment with the size and shape of the forms on your landing pages. You can even apply the experiment methodology to pages that follow the landing page (after a visitor clicks a call to action). Figure 15-5 shows a nice-sized form on Equifax's website for a new customer.

It's not very long, but also not too short. For Equifax's customers-to-be, this form is most likely the right combination — one that has proven to work the best for Equifax. For your website, a shorter form may perform well, or maybe a long form will do better. Again, experimentation is the key to your success online. I really cannot stress that enough.

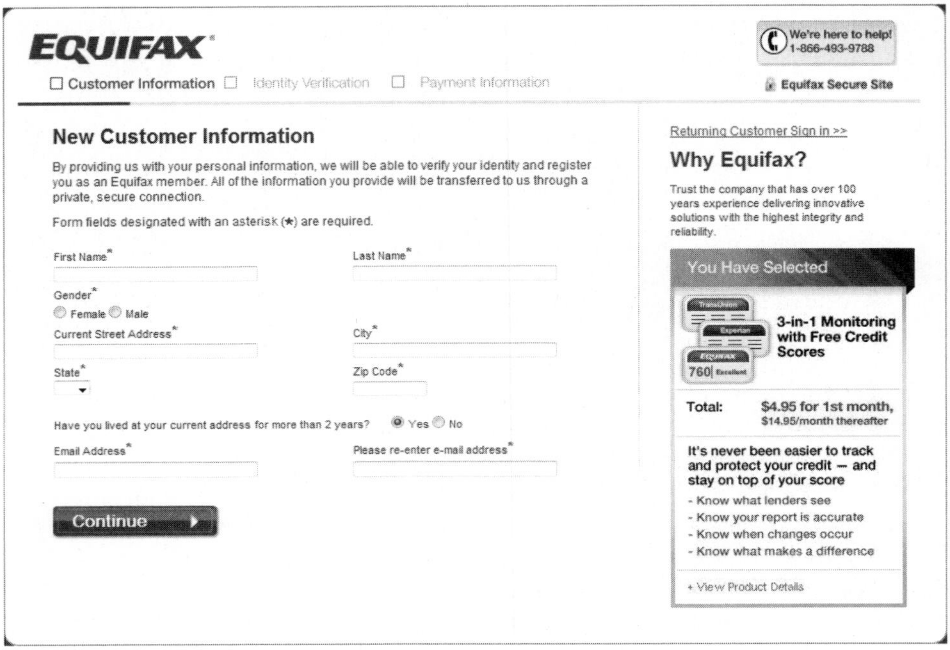

Figure 15-5: Equifax's New Customer Information form

People, Places, and Things

You see images of these three elements on web pages all the time — so much so that you probably don't even realize it when you see them. Savvy website owners who experiment using Google Website Optimizer (or another A/B or multivariate experiment tool) evaluate the performance of their AdWords campaigns and landing pages when they use photos of people, places, or items (things).

Each type of website does it differently. Pictures of people are prominent on service- or location-oriented websites, like the one in Figure 15-6, which is the homepage of Palm Beach State College.

Figure 15-6: Palm Beach State College's homepage

Places are used on destination and travel sites like cruise-line websites. Things are almost always used on shopping websites. Often, smart website managers use people wearing articles of clothing or at a location to combine elements into one image.

CHAPTER 16

Google Analytics and Google Website Optimizer

The final chapter in Part V of *Your Google Game Plan for Success* will discuss the merging of Google Analytics and Google Website Optimizer (GWO). These two programs naturally go together — so much so that Google has released code-compatibility fixes for users running experiments with Google Website Optimizer and tracking website traffic with Google Analytics.

The two foci of this chapter are ensuring that your Google Website Optimizer Tracking Code isn't interfering with your Google Analytics Tracking Code, and interpreting report data in Google Analytics to augment your experiment data from Google Website Optimizer. As you learned in Chapter 11, Google Website Optimizer provides a limited (but powerful) amount of data. You know only how many people visited the experiment page(s) and how many of those visitors converted. With Google Analytics you'll be able to add powerful layers of data on top of what you already know from Google Website Optimizer.

Before you can start analyzing your data, you need to ensure that your tracking codes are working together, and not interfering with each other. First, let's review the tracking code compatibility.

Tracking Code Compatibility

As I mentioned in Chapter 13, you'll need to ensure that your Google Website Optimizer code is not interfering with your Google Analytics code. In the early days of Google Website Optimizer the `pageTracker` function was a part of the code snippet, which caused problems with the Google Analytics Tracking Code (which also uses `pageTracker`). Now Google Website Optimizer uses a `gwoTracker` command, which does not interfere with Google Analytics.

Using GA and GWO on One Domain

If you're running a Google Website Optimizer experiment while tracking your website with Google Analytics, you'll need to ensure that the Google Website Optimizer Tracking Code appears after (below) the Google Analytics Tracking Code. That's all that you'll need to make sure of if you're using the ga.js version of the Google Analytics Tracking Code. If you're using the async version this shouldn't be an issue at all, as the async tracking code is to be installed within the `<head>` section of your page's source code.

The following code snippets show a quick example of what the code should look like on your page, with the Google Analytics Tracking Code placed above the Google Website Optimizer Tracking Code.

```
<script type="text/javascript">
var gaJsHost = (("https:" == document.location.protocol)
? " https://ssl." : "http://www.");
document.write(unescape("%3Cscript src='" + gaJsHost +
"google-analytics.com/ga.js '
type='text/javascript'%3E%3C/script%3E"));
</script>
<script type="text/javascript">
try {
var pageTracker = _gat._getTracker("UA-1234567-1");
pageTracker._trackPageview();
} catch(err) {}
</script>

<script type="text/javascript">
if(typeof(_gat)!='object')document.write('<sc'+'ript src="http'+
(document.location.protocol=='https:'?'s://ssl':'://www')+ '.google
analytics.com/ga.js"></sc'+'ript>')</script>
<script type="text/javascript">
try {
var gwoTracker=_gat._getTracker("UA-1234567-2");
gwoTracker._trackPageview("/123456789/test");
}catch(err){}
</script>
```

Make sure that you use this order for your original page, your variation page(s), and your experiment conversion page. For more detail about where to install the Google Website Optimizer Tracking Code, flip back to Chapter 13. Remember that you can't simply copy the code examples shown from this book — you'll actually have to log in to your Google Website Optimizer account and grab the code from there (as it includes your UA account number).

Using GA and GWO on Sub-Domains

Not everyone who wishes to run a Google Website Optimizer experiment uses only one domain for his or her website efforts. Many people — especially those with shopping carts — use separate sub-domains that visitors must travel across in order to complete their purchases or other important actions. Google Website Optimizer does offer an officially supported work-around that gives you an alternative to using its product across sub-domains (there are some unofficial work-arounds posted online that may or may not work).

Whether you're running the new async code, the older ga.js model, or the legacy urchin.js version of the Google Analytics Tracking Code, you'll need to add an "urchin-style" customization before the Google Website Optimizer control script on any page that contains the Google Website Optimizer Tracking Code. You're also going to need to update the tracking and conversion scripts to include a call to setDomainName, as you would in order to track sub-domains with Google Analytics.

First, here's the addition to the control script featuring the _udn function. This example shows the _udn function immediately above a control script.

```
<script>
_udn = ".example.com";
</script>
<!-- Google Website Optimizer Control Script -->
<script>
function utmx_section(){}function utmx(){}
(function(){var k='123456123456',d=document,l=d.location
c=d.cookie;function f(n){if(c){var i=c.indexOf(n+'=');
if(i>-1){var j=c.indexOf(';',i);return c.substring(i+n.
length+1,j<0?c.length:j)}}}var
x=f('__utmx'),xx=f('__utmxx'),h=l.hash;
d.write('<sc'+'ript src="'+
'http'+(l.protocol=='https:'?'s://ssl':'://www')+
'.google-analytics.com'+'/siteopt.js?v=1&utmxkey='+k+'&utmx='+(x?x:'')
+'&utmxx='+(xx?xx:'')+'&utmxtime='
+new Date().valueOf()+(h?'&utmxhash='+escape(h.substr(1)):'')+
'" type="text/javascript" charset="utf-8"></sc'+'ript>')})();
</script><script>utmx("url",'A/B');</script>
<!-- End of Google Website Optimizer Control Script -->
```

Next, on the Google Website Optimizer tracking snippet and conversion snippet, you'll need to add the call to setDomainName to tell Google Website Optimizer that your experiment involves separate sub-domains:

```
gwoTracker._setDomainName(".example.com");
```

Here's an example of a Google Website Optimizer tracking snippet using `setDomainName`:

```html
<!-- Google Website Optimizer tracking script -->
<script type="text/javascript">
if(typeof(_gat)!='object')document.write('<sc'+'ript src="http'+
(document.location.protocol=='https:'?'s://ssl':'://www')+ '.google
analytics.com/ga.js"></sc'+'ript>')</script>
<script type="text/javascript">
try {
var gwoTracker=_gat._getTracker("UA-1234567-2");
gwoTracker._setDomainName(".example.com");
gwoTracker._trackPageview("/123456789/test");
}catch(err){}
</script>
<!-- End of Google Website Optimizer Tracking Script -->
```

And here's an example of the Google Website Optimizer conversion code using `setDomainName`:

```html
<!-- Google Website Optimizer conversion script -->
<script type="text/javascript">
if(typeof(_gat)!='object')document.write('<sc'+'ript src="http'+
(document.location.protocol=='https:'?'s://ssl':'://www')+ '.google
analytics.com/ga.js"></sc'+'ript>')</script>
<script type="text/javascript">
try {
var gwoTracker=_gat._getTracker("UA-1234567-2");
gwoTracker._setDomainName(".example.com");
gwoTracker._trackPageview("/123456789/goal");
}catch(err){}
</script>
<!-- End of Google Website Optimizer conversion Script -->
```

Once you're finished, re-upload your experiment pages live, and you'll be all set for tracking Google Analytics and Google Website Optimizer across sub-domains.

Now that you're receiving experiment data in Google Website Optimizer, let's take a deeper look at what data Google Analytics has to offer to augment your analysis and website improvement efforts.

Analyzing Google Website Optimizer Data in Google Analytics

Google Analytics has more than 100 reports, dozens upon dozens of options for users (including views, segments, menus, and filters), and leading-edge advanced features like Advanced Segments and Intelligence. You can leverage the power of Google Analytics to augment your Google Website Optimizer data. Once you know where to go and what you're looking for, you'll readily use Google Analytics to evaluate your test pages and your visitor behavior for each experiment that you run. You'll rediscover Google Analytics and reignite that spark that you had when you discovered it for the very first time.

Annotations

In Part III of *Your Google Game Plan for Success* you learned about the ability for users to insert annotations — small, informational, 160-character sentences — to add what Google Analytics calls "tribal data" to the system, allowing you to match offline knowledge with online traffic statistics. Naturally, you'll want to make use of annotations for every important action involved in your Google Website Optimizer experiments. When your experiment launches, insert an annotation into Google Analytics. When Google Website Optimizer finds a winning combination, make a note of it using annotations. When you run your follow-up experiment, be sure to insert a note into Google Analytics using annotations. When a combination receives its 50th conversion, denote that by creating an annotation. You get the idea — when something significant happens with Google Website Optimizer, use annotations in Google Analytics. Figure 16-1 shows an example of what it could look like to do this in your account. I've added several annotations to this particular account, denoting important tidbits of information about Google Website Optimizer and a new Google AdWords campaign that I launched to run concurrently with my experiment and my subsequent follow-up experiments.

Remember that annotations do not appear only on your dashboard's trending graph; they appear on every trending graph throughout Google Analytics. Also remember that you can set annotations as private (so that only you can see them) or as public (so that any user with access to your profile can see them). Refer to Chapter 9 for more information about creating annotations.

Advanced Segments

Chapter 9 introduced you to Advanced Segments — default or custom options that you can enable "on the fly" that allow you to slice and dice data to obtain a deeper understanding of it. While Google Analytics comes equipped with some very useful default segments like Visits with Conversions and Paid Search Traffic, you can create your own segments for your needs.

An obviously useful Advanced Segment that you can create is one where the dimension is the landing page that matches the name of the experiment page(s) you're running in Google Website Optimizer. An Advanced Segment landing page for Google Website Optimizer is shown being edited in Figure 16-2.

Figure 16-1: Annotations including information about Google Website Optimizer

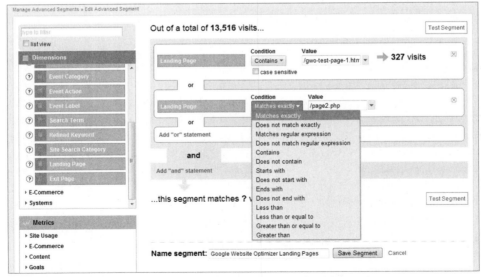

Figure 16-2: Creating Google Website Optimizer–friendly Advanced Segments

Custom Reports

As you also know from Chapter 9, custom reports are powerful, customizable views for your data. With them you can organize your data in ways that are meaningful and valuable to you, without having to rely upon the default reports that Google Analytics provides. In Figure 16-3 I've created a custom report that will help me analyze my Google Website Optimizer data, taking my understanding of the experiment far beyond what's possible within the Google Website Optimizer interface.

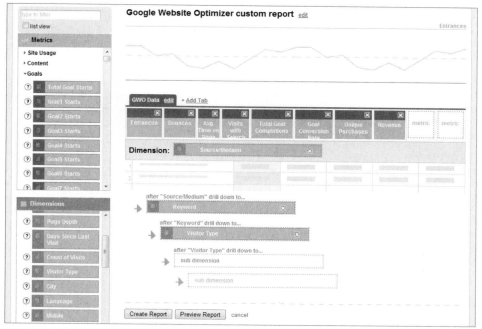

Figure 16-3: Creating a custom report for Google Website Optimizer data

In Figure 16-3 my metrics going across the scorecard horizontally are (from left to right) Entrances, Bounces, Average Time on Page, Visits with Search, Total Goal Completions, Goal Conversion Rate, Unique Purchases, and Revenue. My dimensions going down the report (from top to bottom) are Source/Medium, Keyword, and Visitor Type.

When I save and apply this report within my Google Analytics profile, I'll be able to take it a step further and apply the Google Website Optimizer Advanced Segment that I created a few pages ago. This way I'm looking at Google Website Optimizer landing-page data in a report that I built specifically for Google Website Optimizer. It doesn't get any sweeter than that.

All Traffic Sources

From this point forward you could theoretically use any report with Google Analytics to view your Google Website Optimizer data, once you've created Advanced Segments and custom reports to match. One of my favorites to use for such analysis is the All Traffic Sources report, shown in Figure 16-4. I once again have applied my Google Website Optimizer Advanced Segment, and I used the standard table filter to view only organic traffic sources.

Figure 16-4: The All Traffic Sources report with my Google Website Optimizer Advanced Segment applied

Map Overlay

The Map Overlay report (segmented by landing page or your own Google Website Optimizer–style Advanced Segment) can be a great source of information for you. Perhaps geo-targeted Google AdWords campaigns drive a lot of traffic to your Google Website Optimizer experiment pages; depending on any campaign's regional performance and experiment results, you can optimize your paid search campaigns accordingly. Figure 16-5 shows an example of the Map Overlay report with my Google Website Optimizer Advanced Segment enabled. I am looking at city-level detail for the United States, and my metric is set to goal-conversion rate in the report.

New vs. Returning

You can use the New vs. Returning report to see the difference in website statistics and performance metrics between first-time (new) visitors and repeat (returning) visitors. This is actually a very useful report because Google Website Optimizer does not report on returning visitors. The reports in Google Website Optimizer show you only visit and conversion data from new unique visitors. This report can help identify how experiments affect the returning visitors who were previously exposed to your Google Website Optimizer experiment. New vs. Returning is also an Advanced Segment, so you can apply it as an Advanced Segment and compare it to a Google Website Optimizer–style Advanced Segment. Figure 16-6 shows my New vs. Returning visitors report with the Comparison to Site Average Table view enabled.

Figure 16-5: The Map Overlay report, with city-level detail and the goal-conversion rate metric applied

Mobile Devices

If you're like me, you're obsessed with mobile traffic on your site. If you're *really* like me, you want to know how many people use mobile devices and what those people do on your site. Are they engaging with your Google Website Optimizer experiment and visiting key pages? The Mobile Devices report shown in Figure 16-7 can give you an idea of what types of mobile devices are being used during your Google Website Optimizer experiments (hint: most of the traffic will come from iPhones, by far the most popular mobile device). Here I'm analyzing the pages-per-visit metric in the Performance Table view.

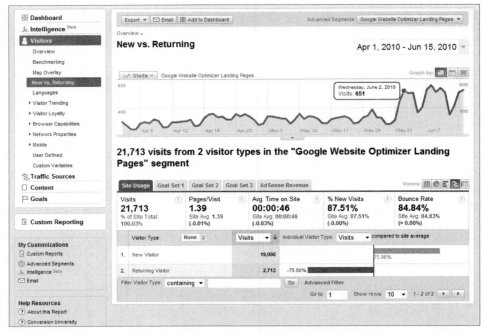

Figure 16-6: The New vs. Returning report with a Google Website Optimizer Advanced Segment enabled

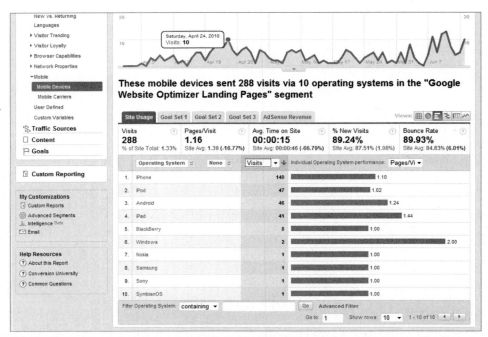

Figure 16-7: The Mobile Devices report with the Performance Table view applied

Goals Overview

As you know from Chapter 11, when you run an experiment using Google Website Optimizer, you choose experiment pages and one conversion page. However, for a lot of websites, there are multiple touch points that a visitor can reach in order to have what the website owner will consider a successful visit. Just because Google Website Optimizer shows you data for only one conversion point doesn't mean that you can't augment your understanding of your visitor's behavior by analyzing that behavior against all your site's goals. Figure 16-8 shows the Goals Overview report, with my Google Website Optimizer segment applied. Now, you can really get a deep understanding of the true impact of your Google Website Optimizer experiments by viewing what goals the visitors actually converted on, and not only the goal that you defined within the Google Website Optimizer interface.

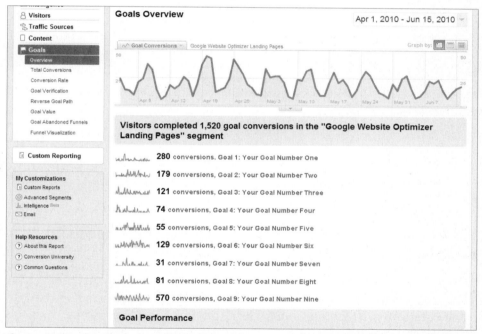

Figure 16-8: The Goals Overview report with a Google Website Optimizer Advanced Segment enabled

Reverse Goal Path

Quite a few of my fellow web-analytics colleagues dislike the Reverse Goal Path report in Google Analytics. They think it is very limited and unusable in its current state. Personally, I think it does serve its purpose and can be useful, especially for using Google Website Optimizer data to understand the paths that visitors take before they convert. As you know from Chapter 7, the Reverse Goal Path report shows you the last four pages viewed by a visitor before converting. Applying an Advanced Segment designed with Google Website Optimizer in mind, you can get an even deeper understanding of the ways in which your experiments are affecting visitors. See Figure 16-9 for an example of this report.

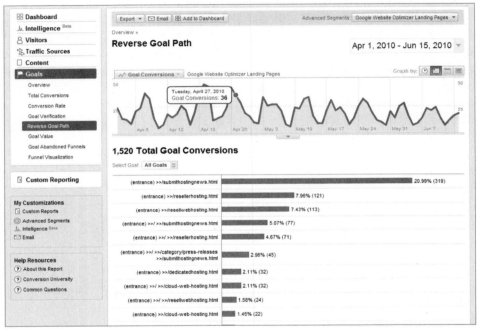

Figure 16-9: The Reverse Goal Path report

Creating a Duplicate Profile for Your Google Website Optimizer Data

If you have a keen eye (which I know you do — you're reading this book!), you will have noticed at the beginning of this chapter (and Chapter 11) that the Google Website Optimizer Tracking Code's UA number is slightly different from the Google Analytics Tracking Code's UA number. When you create an experiment with Google Website Optimizer, you create a placeholder for a future profile in Google Analytics (you actually create much more than that — basically, Google needs a place to store and process your experiment data as it collects that data, so it reserves a profile number specifically for Google Website Optimizer). After creating an experiment, click Create New Profile from within your Google Analytics account, and you should notice within the URL selection drop-down menu an entry for Google Website Optimizer. Creating the profile with this as the selected URL will allow you to store all Google Analytics data from visitors who were exposed to your experiment.

You should consider creating this duplicate profile because not every report in Google Analytics can use Advanced Segments. Reports like the Keyword Positions report in the AdWords section, Funnel Visualization, and Unique Visitors cannot be segmented by an Advanced Segment. When you view your data through this new profile, it's as if you're pre-segmenting your visitors (because they came from your Google Website Optimizer experiment). You can use this second profile for regular analysis efforts as well.

The *Your Google Game Plan for Success* experience is winding down into the final two chapters and an appendix. In those chapters I'm going to discuss additional tools, resources, and programs (within the Google ecosystem and outside of it) that you can take advantage of, and some other interesting things like ways to contact me, blogs to read, and Twitter accounts to follow. I hope you saved room for the proverbial dessert!

Wrapping It Up

In This Part

Google Programs to Add to Your Game Plan

The last couple of chapters in *Your Google Game Plan for Success* are dedicated to broadening your horizons to include programs and tools that you can use within the Google ecosystem and outside the Google network. Google AdWords, Google Analytics, Google Website Optimizer, and the combination of those three platforms will take you places, but will only take you so far. You really need a wide-ranging variety of programs, tools, and knowledge at your disposal to truly distance yourself from the competition.

My experience in the search-marketing/web-analytics industry tells me that when you've read and understood the next two chapters, you're going to be in a better position than most of your competitors. There are simply *not* a lot of website owners and online advertisers using these tools and actively engaging in these programs. Quite a number of website owners and online advertisers aren't even aware that these programs exist. Even if you don't try every one of the programs in the next two chapters, you'll at least be exposed to them and understand how they work and what they're trying to show and tell you, which is more than can be said for most people (unfortunately for our industry, but fortunately for you).

First, let's take a look in this chapter at some Google-based programs that can be great additional resources for you to use. These programs all carry the Google brand, and simply searching for their names on Google will quickly bring up their respective URLs. I've separated this chapter into three categories:

- **Programs for analysis:** These programs can add to your understanding of trends happening online that you can take advantage of.

- **Programs for your website:** These online sites offer beneficial snippets of code and software that you can integrate with your website, enhancing the online experience for your website's visitors.

- **Programs for advertising:** Google offers additional avenues not only for promoting your products and services on Google, but also for running ads on your own website.

Let's start by taking a look at some programs for analyzing what's happening online.

Programs for Analysis

Google Analytics and other traditional web-analytics programs are designed to tell you what has happened on your website. Anything that happens outside your website (e.g., any developing trends or fast-rising searches) isn't going to be reported by your web-analytics package of choice. You may be able to get by for a while on simply analyzing the data from your own website, but eventually you'll have to evaluate developing trends in your industry and what other searches and websites your visitors are also using and visiting. Instead of being reactive by analyzing only your website's data, you'll become more proactive and spot outside trends and insights before they necessarily reach your website. Even an ostrich has to come up for air once in a while.

Two great, powerful programs within the Google ecosystem and available completely for free are Google Insights for Search (www.google.com/insights/search) and Google Trends (www.google.com/trends).

Google Insights for Search

At the Insights for Search site you'll be able to compare search-volume patterns across search terms, locations, and time ranges to better understand the trends that are developing online. It's critical to be able to spot these trends and predict what will happen next; otherwise, your competitors may have a leg up on you and take advantage of an opportunity before you have the chance.

Let's walk through some examples of setting up your comparative data so that you can get a better idea of what you should expect to see. You'll need to build your comparison and specify certain criteria before seeing your data. At the top of the Google Insights for Search homepage you'll be able to select one of three different options by which to compare data. First, you can compare multiple search terms — up to five at any one time. As shown in Figure 17-1, you can enter your search terms in the boxes provided (you'll need to click Add Search Term, which is a text link that appears below the first box, to add more search terms to compare). Then, to its right, apply the filter conditions by which you want to compare your data. The first drop-down menu is defaulted to Web Search, but this can be changed to compare data by Image Search, News Search, or Product Search. The second drop-down menu allows you to select the countries or territories that you want to compare. By default, this is set to Worldwide. When you select an individual country (I've chosen the United States), you can further refine your data by subregion and even further by metro area.

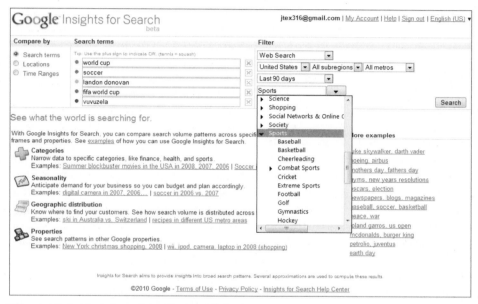

Figure 17-1: Google Insights for Search homepage

The third drop-down menu, which defaults to "2004–present," is the date range. You can select any individual year since 2004 or choose options like "Last seven days" or "Last 30 days"; you can even specify your own custom date range. Finally, the fourth drop-down menu allows you to select the specific category by which you want to view your data.

Please be aware that the more you refine your filters, the less data will be available. When you are finished putting together your search terms and filter criteria, click Search and prepare to see some very interesting stuff! Don't worry — you can edit your search terms and filters on the fly on the next screen.

After you click Search, the page will refresh and data will be presented to you. The next two screenshots come from the same page, but I've broken them into two halves. The first (top) half of your Google Insights for Search results is shown in Figure 17-2. At the top of the figure you can see the five search terms that I used and my filter options, as well as some related categories. To the right of this, the averages for each line on the graph are displayed and color-coded (sorry, folks — you can't make it out in the black-and-white screenshots). Below the averages appears a trending graph, showing the volume of searches for my chosen search terms during the chosen date range, which in this example was the last 90 days. The largest spike shown here is for the term World Cup, and the date is Saturday, June 12, 2010. This coincides with the United States's first World Cup match against the United Kingdom, which happened the afternoon of June 12, 2010. Clearly you can begin to deduce how online search behavior is affected by offline events, such as the World Cup.

Figure 17-2: Search term interest data (top half)

Below the trending graph is a regional interest breakdown, showing the top 10 search regions for the first keyword term (click the Regional Interest drop-down menu to view regional interest for other search terms). Below and to the right of the trending graph is a Map Overlay feature that displays the interest in a particular keyword over the selected date range. You can modify this map to show the interest at the metro and city levels, which will also update the regional interest data on the left of the map.

The second (bottom) half, which appears below the Regional Interest and Map Overlay breakdown, is shown in the bottom half of Figure 17-3. At the bottom left you can view the top 10 search terms related to the selected search term, based upon the search term that you have selected from the drop-down menu directly above the list. To the right you are shown the top 10 rising search terms. These are search terms that, in your date range, have been climbing in popularity, based on your filter and search criteria.

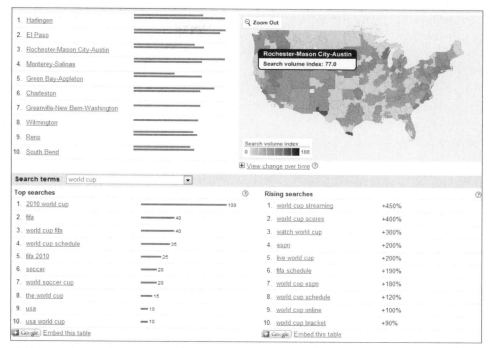

Figure 17-3: Search term interest data (bottom half)

My World Cup example shows what happens when an offline event affects the online search world. But much of the time offline events aren't influencing online behavior.

A great advantage for you, the business and website owner, is your ability to use this information for research on your AdWords campaigns. Discover search terms related to your queries that are rising in popularity and those that people search for online. If you run geo-targeted campaigns you can really harness the power of Google Insights for Search by drilling down through country, subregion, metro, and even city levels to view top search keywords and fast-rising keywords that you can bid for within your own campaigns. You can also get an idea about competitor penetration on your brand and keywords that you're bidding for. Are there competitor search phrases appearing for keywords you're bidding on? This could be a sign that a competitor is penetrating your market and creating enough interest online to influence the data you see.

Here's one more example of Google Insights for Search, in Figure 17-4. By applying the Time Ranges comparison for the last 12 months with a filter of Image Search in the United States, I can see the top 10 search terms and rising searches that U.S. users are performing on Google Images. The term "justin bieber" is considered a *breakout* search term by Google because that search term has experienced a change in growth of more than 5,000 percent! Two other fast-rising search terms on Google Images within the United States in the last 12 months were "michael jackson" and "lady gaga."

Figure 17-4: Image search interest, last 12 months in the United States

NOTE In a few of the previous figures you may have noticed that I was signed in with my Google account to Google Insights for Search. You do not have to be logged in to your Google account, or even have one, to use Google Insights for Search.

Google Trends

Google Trends, the URL of which was given earlier, is another great Google-based program that can augment your analysis efforts. While Google Insights for Search provides refined, detailed, and specific data, Google Trends specializes in the analysis of broad search patterns. There are also a few data points within Google Trends that are not available in Google Insights for Search, such as website trends and visited sites.

Let's start with Figure 17-5, which is the Google Trends homepage. Here, you can enter comma-separated search terms for which you want to view trending data. Below the search bar are hot topics on the bottom left and hot searches on the bottom right. In Figure 17-5 I entered "chocolate, vanilla, strawberry" into the search bar.

Figure 17-6 is the search results page showing you the data from the search phrases that you entered on the homepage. On the top right, you can filter your results by region and subregion (it defaults to show you data for all regions). You can also filter your results by time period (the default of "All years" includes all data since 2004, but as with Google Insights for Search, you have multiple options here). In the middle of the screen two color-coded trending graphs are provided. The first shows the search volume index, and the second (the small one) displays the news reference volume. The higher trending-graph line in the Search Volume Index graph in Figure 17-6 represents my chocolate search term; the higher of the bottom two lines represents the strawberry search term; the almost flat trending-graph line represents vanilla.

Figure 17-5: Google Trends homepage

To the right of the trending graphs you can see the related news articles that correspond to the annotations in the trending graphs. Click any news article to be taken directly to it (you'll be taken to the website where the article appears). On the bottom half of Figure 17-6 you can view the interest for each search term you entered in terms of region, city, and language. These are also color-coded, and each search term's color corresponds to the color of these smaller graphing lines. Obviously, people search for chocolate a lot more than they do for the other Neapolitan flavors!

You may have noticed something in Figure 17-6 — the words Searches and Websites at the upper left of the screen. With Google Trends you can analyze trends not only by comma-separated search terms but also by websites. Clicking the Websites link on the upper left of the Google Trends website will generate a message telling you there is no data to display to you. This is because your comma-separated search terms are not domain names. So enter at least one domain name to obtain website trend data. In Figure 17-7 I've decided that I'd like to compare three websites similar in nature: www.target.com, www.kmart.com, and www.kohls.com.

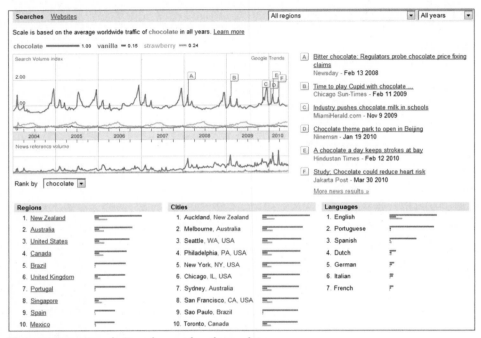

Figure 17-6: Google Trends search volume data

First, near the top of the page, you can view a trending graph comparing search volume for the three websites. That lift in traffic that you see for all three sites coincides with the holiday season (specifically, around the time of "Black Friday," the biggest offline shopping day of the year). Naturally, online shopping activity picks up dramatically at that time. The trending line with the largest volume is www.target.com, followed by www.kohls.com in a very distant second and leading www.kmart.com by a small amount.

The three columns of information below the trending graph are what savvy online analysts and marketers dream of. This data offers an insight that is not easy to find online. Companies like Hitwise (www.hitwise.com) can offer this type of competitive intelligence and website trend data, but be prepared to pay a substantial amount for it.

The first column on the left-hand side breaks down the website trends by subregion. This could be valuable information for any pay-per-click advertiser considering (or running) geo-targeted campaigns. Naturally, you'll want to point your ads to the geographic areas that are generating the most interest. However, in the United States most of the interest for national advertisers usually comes from the top five regions listed in Figure 17-7 (California, New York, Florida, Texas, and Illinois). Most businesses that sell online nationally and most websites that generate any type of significant volume will get most of their traffic from these five states.

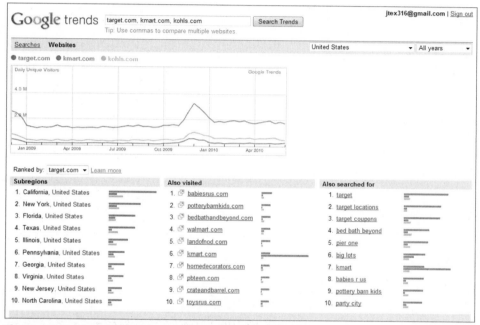

Figure 17-7: Google Trends website comparison data

The middle column shows the top 10 sites that visitors visit before or after they visit the site being analyzed. This is excellent competitive research data, as you can see if your visitors are also viewing your competition's websites. For example, in Figure 17-7, visitors viewing the www.target.com website are also viewing sites like www.babiesrus.com and www.potterybarnkids.com. These sites may indicate areas in which www.target.com is not very strong, leading visitors to try to find products elsewhere. Luckily for www.target. com, there doesn't seem to be too much direct-competitor penetration. Study this column for your own website to see what other websites your visitors are viewing.

The column on the far right shows you search terms that visitors to your website are using online. This can give you great ideas for search terms to bid for in your pay-per-click campaigns or keywords to optimize for in your SEO efforts. In the previous example users searched for brand-oriented words, as well as some competitor search terms like *pier one* and *bed bath beyond*.

Google Trends data is available for export in a CSV file. When you are using this interface, look at the very bottom of the page: you'll see a link enabling you to download your data in a CSV file.

Both Google Insights for Search and Google Trends offer great additional insight into what people are doing outside your website. Once again, this data isn't available in Google Analytics or any web-analytics package.

Programs for Your Website

The second category of free programs at your disposal from Google includes programs you can use to improve or add to your website. Tools like Google Webmaster Tools are necessary for search engine optimization (SEO) work, and can provide insight into what search engine spiders/robots are doing (knowing how search engine spiders crawl your website's pages is key to understanding how your website is working from a technical point of view). In recent years Google acquired FeedBurner, which manages your RSS feeds and provides reports and information on your feed's subscribers and what feed readers they are using.

Google Webmaster Tools

Google Webmaster Tools comes very highly recommended by webmasters. It's a program that provides you with detailed instructions not only for verifying your site with Google, but also for providing Google with what is known as a *site map* — a roadmap to your site's pages that Google can index, adding your site's pages to its ever-growing database. Using Google Webmaster Tools helps your website get listed on Google, which allows visitors to find your site without having to click on a pay-per-click advertisement.

The first thing you'll need to do is sign in to the Google account that you created in order to use a Google AdWords, Google Analytics, or Google Website Optimizer account. Then visit www.google.com/webmaster/tools and sign in to Google Webmaster Tools. From there you can find the link to Webmaster Tools under My Products, as shown in Figure 17-8.

When you arrive at your Google Webmaster Tools homepage, the first thing you'll need to do is add your site for verification. This process involves a couple of steps, and at this point it's important that you obtain the assistance of your web developer or IT person, because you'll need to add a bit of HTML code to your website's homepage.

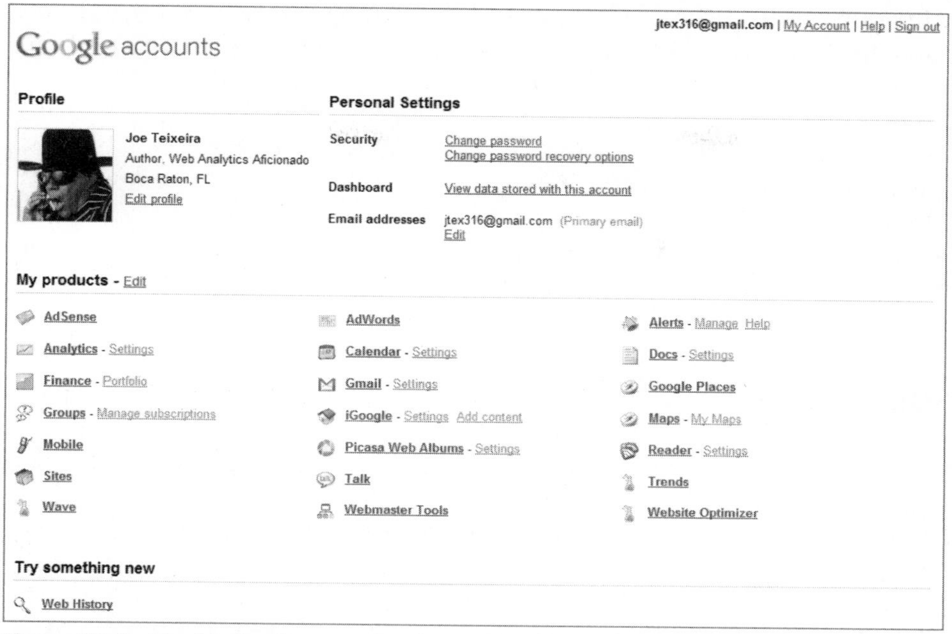

Figure 17-8: The My Products section in your Google Account Settings page

First, at the Google Webmaster Tools homepage, click Add to Site, which is a silver button on the bottom of the page (it should be a very empty-looking page if this is your first time in this program). Once you do so, a text field should pop up, in which you can insert the URL of your website. Google Webmaster Tools allows you to add up to 1,000 sites, and Google recommends adding any sub-domains and other versions of your domain (such as www.yoursite.com and yoursite.com without the www prefix).

Once you click Continue you'll be taken to the screen that you see in Figure 17-9, where you can view the status of your verification and choose your website-verification options. Google provides you with three different ways to verify your site. You can add a verification meta-tag on your website's homepage in the <head> portion of the code; you can download a verification file in HTML to upload to your web server (step-by-step instructions are provided on the page); or you can add a domain name system (DNS) record. This page also provides you with additional information on the three verification options. Once you have implemented one of them, revisit this page in your Google Webmaster Tools account and click Verify, which will be at the bottom of the page. The webpage will inform you whether your verification was successful.

After you verify your site you'll be able to update your preferred domain and geo-targeting settings. Both of these settings help Google understand more about your website, and help the Google search algorithm deliver better organic search engine results to your visitors.

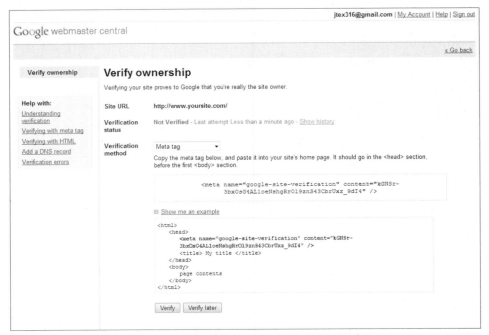

Figure 17-9: Verifying your website with Google Webmaster Tools

After updating your settings you can view lots of reports about the technical aspects of your website and how your website is found and ranked by Google. Crawl Errors is a report found within Google Webmaster Tools that will show you any URLs on your site that Google tried and failed to crawl. The Links to Your Site report shows you the web pages on the Internet that have links pointing to your website (as long as they have also been verified by Google Webmaster Tools). The Search Queries report shows you the number of times your web pages have come up in search results, including how many impressions and clicks they received and their click-through rates. This report is great for diagnosing whether your site is appearing in irrelevant searches (if it is, you have some SEO optimization work to do that's beyond the scope of this book). Google Webmaster Tools can also give you HTML advice for your site and notify you if your website has been hacked. Figure 17-10 shows the Overview screen of a Google Webmaster Tools account.

Check Appendix A at the end of this book for some links to more information about Google Webmaster Tools.

Google FeedBurner

Another great tool for your website is Google Feedburner (`http://feedburner .google.com/`). If you have a blog and want to make it easy for readers to receive, read, and understand updates as you publish them, you can use Really Simple Syndication (RSS) powered by Google Feedburner.

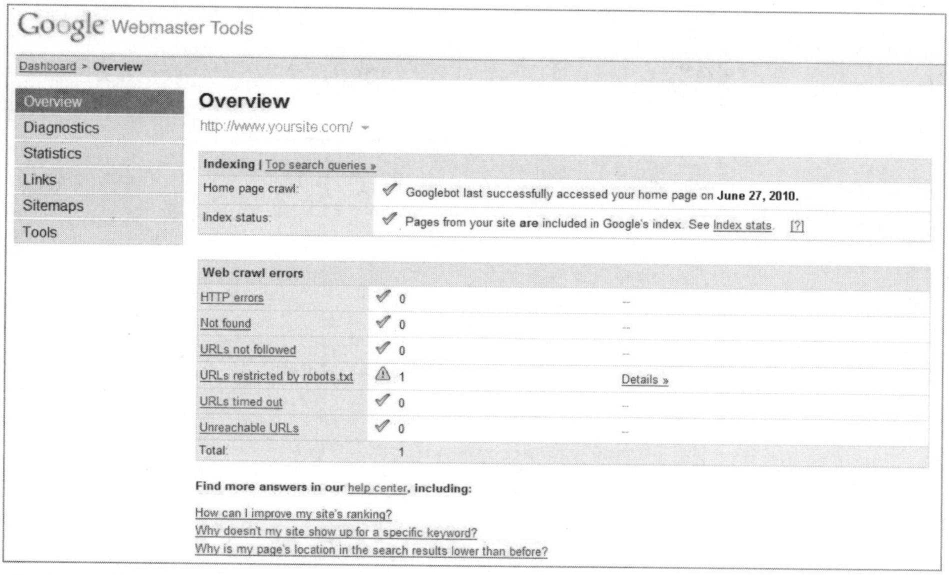

Figure 17-10: Google Webmaster Tools Overview report

You (or your webmaster) have most likely set up an XML, RSS, or ATOM feed for your blog. The universal feed subscription icon has probably also been added to your site so your blog's readers can subscribe to your updates and read your updates in such feed-reader programs as Google Reader, NewsGator, and My Yahoo!. Google Feedburner is essentially a one-stop shop for feed management, diagnostics, traffic reports, add-ons, and a host of other tools.

Figure 17-11 shows the Google Feedburner homepage. From here you can analyze and view traffic-statistic information, the number of subscribers to your feed, and the reach (clicks) on your feed items from feed readers. You can also optimize your feed's delivery by enabling browser-friendly options, page-friendly options, and photo- and video-friendly options. Within the interface you can also troubleshoot technical problems and set up programs like Google AdSense for blogs.

Again, please consult your webmaster or IT person to help you with Google Feedburner.

Programs for Advertising

Google offers some neat advertising-based programs that allow you to further promote your products and services, or to promote yourself. Using Google AdWords you're already advertising to an audience of potential customers on Google's search engine and Content Network Partners. Using a few other Google-based programs, like Google TV Ads and Google Merchant Center, you can reach a whole new base of potential customers and further spread your message. You can become a member of the Google Content Network yourself and earn revenue for running ads on your own site by signing up for Google AdSense.

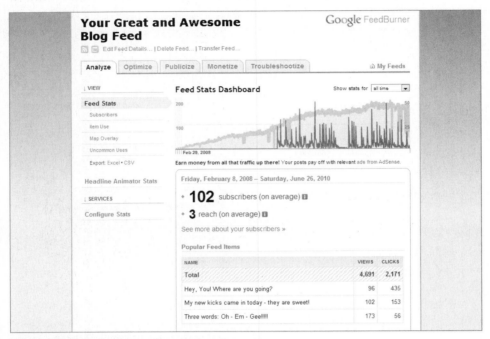

Figure 17-11: Google Feedburner homepage

Google TV Ads

In Chapter 14 you saw a TV Ads report within the AdWords report subsection of Google Analytics. When you run TV ads with Google, your data will appear not only in AdWords but also in this report section in Google Analytics. TV ads are exactly what they sound like — your video ads running on select television stations across the country! As you can imagine, Google puts you, the advertiser, in full control of where, when, and how your ads run on television. There's even a marketplace for finding and negotiating with media companies to create TV ads for you if you aren't equipped to do that yourself.

Google TV Ads are much more expensive than text, image, or online video ads, so you'll definitely need to have the budget for them. I can't tell you how much such ads will cost, because a lot of factors play into the total cost of running (and possibly creating) an ad with Google. It depends on what you're looking to do, in what markets you're willing to advertise, and what times of day you want your ads to run.

To begin your Google TV Ads adventure, sign in to your Google AdWords account and navigate to your Campaigns tab. Scroll to the bottom of the Campaigns sub-tab to find a text link for creating your TV campaign. Clicking that link will send you to a page that looks pretty much like the screenshot in Figure 17-12. Click Start Now on the upper left to begin creating your TV campaign (or click the video or other links to learn more about the program and how it works, which I recommend).

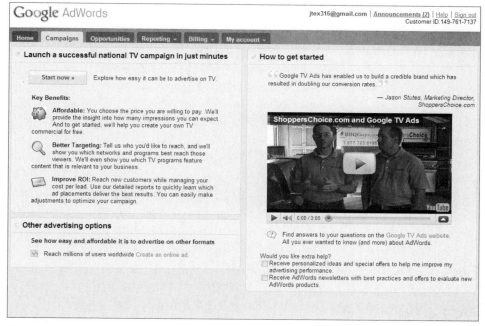

Figure 17-12: Google TV Ads homepage

Once you click Start Now you'll see a campaign-creation screen, as shown in Figure 17-13. First, name your campaign, set a default bid, and create a daily budget. The default bid is the maximum cost-per-thousand-impressions bid that you're willing to make (do understand that a thousand impressions is not all that many when it comes to television advertising). Then select whether or not you want to create a TV ad using Google's Ad Creation Marketplace (more on that in a minute), or using SpotMixer, a third-party TV ad-creation tool (not free, and you must first agree to terms and conditions before leaving to SpotMixer's website). You can also upload your own TV ad, provided that you own your TV ad in a digital file that you can upload through the Google TV Ads interface.

After reviewing these options you can enable some advanced settings for your TV ads. First, you can specify active date ranges, which are good if you are running sales or promotions within a certain window of time. Then you can edit your audience, distribution, days, and times, and specify whether or not you want your ads to run during paid programming. Paid-programming spots are generally less expensive than regular spots, but understand that paid programming essentially consists of very long advertisements (so you'd be advertising during an advertising spot).

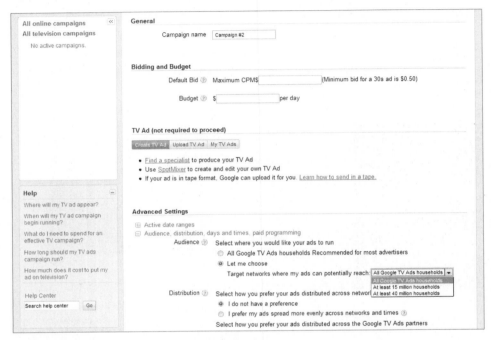

Figure 17-13: Google TV Ads campaign settings

Finally, you have reporting options for traffic and billing. Hit Save and Continue on the bottom of the campaign settings screen to save your work and view your TV campaign reports.

A few paragraphs ago I mentioned Google's Ad Creation Marketplace. Suppose that you want to advertise with Google's TV Ads and you don't have a TV ad ready to upload. Using this marketplace you can seek out media companies or individuals who can help you create a TV ad. You can view what they are charging and samples of their work, and interact with them through this secure interface. You can also pay for services rendered within the marketplace. These media companies or individual contractors cannot do any of the marketing for you, but they can create a TV ad that will promote your product or service.

After examining Figure 17-14, where I show the Google Ad Creation Marketplace homepage, start to think about whether or not Google TV Ads is something you can comfortably afford to get involved in. You're probably looking at five-figure spending as an absolute bare minimum to create and run a TV ad for a couple of weeks. The viewers of your TV ads do not have the luxury of clicking them to be taken directly to your website; you're going to have to urge the viewer to visit (probably more than once), and your domain name will have to be easy to remember. TV advertising is a whole different ball game from online advertising, and even with all the great data Google can provide, it's still not easy to determine how effective your TV spots were.

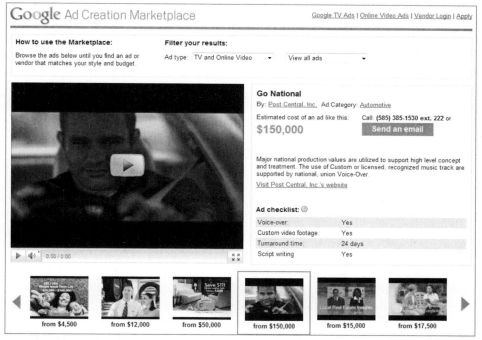

Figure 17-14: Google Ad Creation Marketplace homepage

Google Merchant Center

A far more affordable form of advertising than Google TV Ads is Google's Merchant Center, which allows you to upload product feeds that can appear on Google shopping and www.google.com organic and paid search results. This Google product is designed specifically with the e-commerce merchant in mind. Visit www.google.com/merchants and sign in to your Google account to find file specifications; then download a template of a product feed, insert your data into the template, and upload your product feed in a tab-separated text file (the instructions are very clear on the Google Merchant Center). Chances are pretty good that you already have a product feed or database file that you can export into a spreadsheet program like Microsoft Excel.

As you learned in Chapter 2, if you do have an active feed on Google's Merchant Center and are using product thumbnail images, those images can appear on your pay-per-click ads, as well as your organic search engine results. This can greatly enhance the strength of your brand for potential customers and make it more appealing for search engine users to click on your ads. In a recent search for the phrase "pencil sharpener" on Google, I saw an ad from `www.shoplet.com` that had product images, prices, and links from within its pay-per-click ad, as shown in Figure 17-15. Other Google Merchant Center shopping results can be seen partially at the bottom of Figure 17-15, and a few national-brand conglomerates like Walmart and Staples are shown toward the right-hand side.

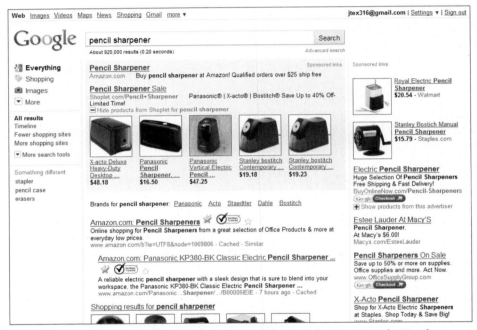

Figure 17-15: Search results page on www.google.com showing Google Merchant Center listings

Google AdSense

A Google program you may want to think about for your own website is Google AdSense. You've read about it already in a few previous chapters, and you know that you have a section of reports in Google Analytics dedicated to this product. Basically, Google AdSense allows website owners to earn revenue by allowing Google to serve up Content Network text, image, video, and rich media ads on their sites, which results in Google paying website owners for clicks on those ads.

Log in with your Google account at www.google.com/adsense/home and set up your AdSense account by following the very simple on-screen instructions. Google handles the payment for your generated clicks through the online interface, so you'll need to enter in banking information (like check-routing numbers). After you set that up, you will have an entire interface at your disposal, as shown in Figure 17-16. Unfortunately, no one has clicked on any ads on my website; because of this there's no estimate of any earnings from Google.

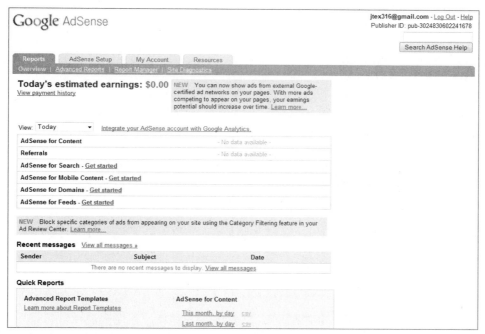

Figure 17-16: The Google AdSense account interface

If the e-mail address that you use to log in to AdSense is the same address that's an administrator on your Google Analytics account, you'll be able to see reports within the Content section. Figure 17-17 shows the AdSense report section in Google Analytics. Again, there's no actual data to display, but you can get a sense of the types of metrics and reports Google Analytics provides for your AdSense analysis. Revenue, click-through rate, impressions, top referrers, and top content are just some of the data that this subsection of reports provides. Now if you, unlike me, collect some of that data, you'll be loving this section!

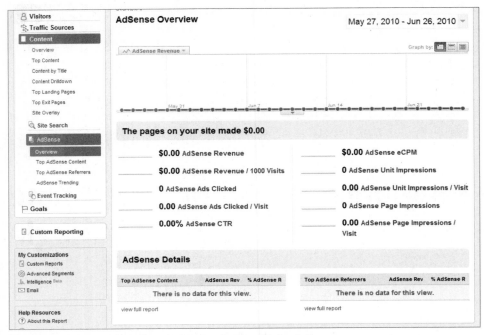

Figure 17-17: Google AdSense reports in Google Analytics

I hope this chapter gave you some good ideas about the possibilities that exist in the seemingly endless ecosystem called Google. But there are other tools out there on the Web that don't belong to Google, and that's what this book's final chapter will cover.

CHAPTER 18

Programs to Add to Your Game Plan Outside Google

The online world isn't closed to anything non-Google. Yes, Google is great and provides incredible advertising and analysis tools at a bare minimum of expense. However, some tools, programs, and applications that live outside the Google ecosystem are also great and very cost-effective. This final chapter of *Your Google Game Plan for Success* is dedicated to talking about programs that are not under the Google umbrella.

Since you're most likely using Google Analytics (or heavily considering it after reading through this book), you're going to need to know how to integrate other marketing programs into Google Analytics. Google AdWords can sync with your Google Analytics account and export data for your analysis and segmenting (something you learned about in Chapter 14). For other advertising platforms, like MSN AdCenter, or any newsletter promotions sent out to your subscriber base, or any links that you've shared with other website owners, you'll have to do a bit of work and build links that will pass referral information from the visitor to Google Analytics. I call this "manual URL tagging," and we'll kick this chapter off by showing you how to build your URLs for Google Analytics.

Manual URL Tagging

Manual URL tagging is the process of building your links in your non-Google advertising efforts, so that Google Analytics can organize your data in a clean and concise manner. The most important places where you'll most definitely have to use manual URL tagging are the search engine advertising platforms like MSN AdCenter. Other places where you should use manual URL tagging include any links in e-mail newsletters sent out weekly, monthly, or quarterly to your subscriber base, and any links that you share with other website owners. You might also use manual URL tagging when writing a blog post or participating in a message board. However, manual URL tagging shouldn't be used if the message board or blog resides on your own website. Also, most blogs using FeedBurner and other RSS aggregator programs have automatic Google Analytics URL tagging, which means that you may not need to do anything at all. For this section of the chapter, we'll talk about URL tagging for non-Google advertising programs and e-mail initiatives.

> **NOTE** Even if you don't use Google Analytics, you should still read through these next few pages. A client or colleague of yours may use Google Analytics and may need help with it, or your web analytics program may have its own query parameters that need to get built into destination URLs in your marketing efforts. The query parameters themselves may be different, but a lot of the technical aspects of how it works are the same.

The Five Query Parameters

As you learned in Chapter 14, when your Google AdWords account is synced with your Google Analytics account, a `gclid` query string parameter is added to the end of the destination URL by Google, as in this example:

```
www.americanlegacyfishing.com/gloomis?gclid=COPEnOKy1KICFQ5c2god
cRJOwQ
```

This `gclid` parameter, combined with the Google Analytics Tracking Code that is on every page of your site, sends data from Google AdWords to Google Analytics, so that you can tell what source, medium, campaign, ad, and keyword sent you website visitors. This example, from a pay-per-click ad on Google AdWords from American Legacy Fishing, is properly set up to track pay-per-click visits on Google.

But what about being set up to track pay-per-click traffic from Yahoo! Search Marketing, MSN AdCenter, Ask Sponsored Listings, or another pay-per-click search engine? There isn't a `gclid` parameter in MSN AdCenter that allows you to import data directly into Google Analytics, nor is there a Google Analytics account syncing option in Yahoo! Search Marketing. By default, any clicks from a search result page in any search engine, like www.bing.com (MSN) or www.ask.com will appear in Google Analytics with a medium of organic (not cpc). So how do we set up our destination URLs to allow Google Analytics to differentiate organic medium clicks from paid (cpc) medium clicks? Enter manual URL tagging, of course!

Let's pretend for the moment that American Legacy Fishing is advertising on www.bing.com's pay-per-click advertising platform, which is MSN AdCenter. A destination URL that could be used for a hypothetical search term in a make-believe campaign on MSN AdCenter could look something like the following:

www.americanlegacyfishing.com/gloomis?utm_source=bing&utm_medium=
cpc&utm_campaign=Fishing+Rods&utm_term=black+fishing+rods&utm_content=
Save+$50+Off!

In the previous URL, everything after the question-mark symbol in the first line of the URL comprises the manual tagging components that an advertiser would need to use as a destination URL. For Google Analytics, there are up to five different query parameters that can be used in a destination URL, three of which are required in order for Google Analytics to collect this data.

The five query parameters are as follows:

- **Source:** The source query parameter is represented in the previous URL as utm_source. It is one of the three required query parameters, and utm_source must also be the first query parameter in the string. The source is naturally the original source that was responsible for sending a visitor to your site. In the example URL I just used, the value of the utm_source query parameter is "bing," and it will appear as such in the All Traffic Sources report and the Search Engines report in Google Analytics. If you're advertising in Yahoo!, ASK, or sending out links within an e-mail newsletter, you would obviously change the value of utm_source to "yahoo," "ask," or "newsletter."

- **Medium:** The medium query parameter is the second parameter that follows source, and it is the means by which a visitor arrives at your site. It's represented by the utm_medium query parameter, and in the example URL the value for utm_medium is "cpc." If you're doing an e-mail newsletter, you could make the medium "e-mail." If you're doing a media buy and have a banner ad running, the medium could be "banner." The medium query parameter is required.

- **Campaign:** The campaign query parameter is represented by utm_campaign in the example destination URL, and it is the third required query parameter. This campaign query parameter will let you know what campaign was responsible for bringing you traffic. For pay-per-click efforts, the campaign could simply be the name that you assign your campaign in your marketing efforts. If you're doing something like an e-mail newsletter, it could be the name of the month and year, like "September, 2010." In the example URL, I used "Fishing Rods."

- **Term:** The term query parameter is an optional query parameter that does not have to be used in order for manual URL tagging to work with Google Analytics. It's represented by utm_term in the example URL, and it is used for the search term (or keyword) that a visitor types into a search engine to find your pay-per-click ad. For all keyword-based pay-per-click efforts, you'll really miss out on valuable keyword-level data by not using `utm_term`, so I highly recommend it. However, for e-mail initiatives or media buys, it's unnecessary to use `utm_term` because there is no search term that a user types in. In the example URL I used "black fishing rods" as my term.

▪ **Content:** `utm_content` is the fifth query parameter that you can use. Like `utm_term`, `utm_content` is optional and can be used to identify the ad that was clicked on. The data from `utm_content` will appear in the Ad Content report in Google Analytics. It can be used in both pay-per-click efforts and non-cpc initiatives. In my previous example URL, I used "Save $50 Off!" which will appear as such in my reports.

A great online tool that you can use to build your URLs is the Tool: URL Builder from the Google Analytics Help section. You plug in your URL and fill in the query parameter values, and the output is the fully built URL, like my example URL. Figure 18-1 shows the Tool: URL Builder page (which is located at `www.google.com/support/analytics/bin/answer.py?hl=en&answer=55578`), Additionally, you can search for Tool URL Builder in Google.

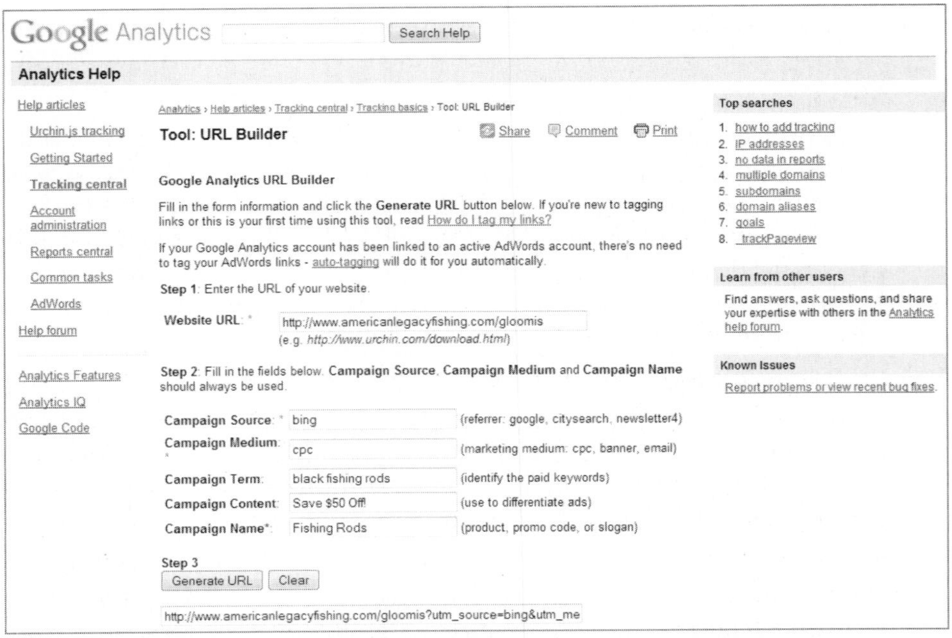

Figure 18-1: The Tool: URL Builder from the Google Analytics Help Center

Tips to Ensure Your Query Parameters Work Properly

Manually tagging your URLs and implementing them in your advertising efforts is only half the battle. There are quite a number of tips, pitfalls, and things to watch out for to ensure that your manually tagged URLs collect your data properly. Let's review some of them.

- **Google Analytics Tracking Code:** You'll be surprised how often this gets overlooked. If the page to which you're sending the visitor does not have the Google Analytics Tracking Code installed, you won't be able to collect any data, even if you have successfully tagged your URLs manually. This means that you can't perform manual URL tagging on outbound links (from your site to another site that you don't control) and collect data for it in your Google Analytics account.

- **Redirects:** Redirects are usually not very friendly when it comes to any kind of query parameters at the end of a destination URL. Your destination URL must retain the query parameters in the address bar of a visitor's browser in order for you to collect data. If there are redirects in place or some other technology that strips the query parameters out of the URL, then you won't be able to track the visitor's data in Google Analytics.

- **Order of operations:** Remember that the `utm_source` parameter must come before any other Google Analytics query parameter.

- **Compatible:** The Google Analytics manual URL tagging query parameters are compatible with any other query parameters from other web-analytics tools and other tracking methodologies.

- **Question-mark symbol:** In any URL on the Web, there can be only one question-mark symbol in the URL string. If there is more than one question-mark symbol, the URL won't resolve. If your destination URL already has a question-mark symbol and you want to add Google Analytics URL tagging to it, simply replace the question-mark symbol (`?utm_source=`) with an ampersand symbol (`&utm_source=`), and your URL will work properly.

- **Plus-sign symbols:** In the example URL, you may have noticed that I used `utm_term=black+fishing+rods` with plus signs where there would be regular spaces. Plus signs will translate into spaces in Google Analytics reports (and technically any other software program or web-analytics platform), so that your data appears cleanly and legibly.

- **Spaces:** As the follow-up to the last bullet point, don't use any blank spaces in your query-parameter values. These may render your URL broken, or they can add garbled characters in your Google Analytics reports, making report data harder to read.

- **Lowercase sources or mediums:** Something not a lot of people know is that a lowercase source or medium is different than an uppercase source or medium in Google Analytics. Google Analytics expects a lowercase medium of "cpc" for any pay-per-click marketing traffic. If you use an uppercase "CPC" instead, this will not count as cost-per-click in your reports, and you'll be missing data in key reports, like the Keywords and Search Engines reports. To be safe, I highly recommend using lowercase letters on all sources and mediums, across the board.

A great tip for you is to perform a test click on your URL before activating it. If you're taken to the correct landing page and your URL query parameters remain in the URL in the address bar, then you're most likely all set.

Pay-per-Click Programs

Google AdWords dominates the search market with about 65 percent of the U. S. search market share (source: comScore, www.comscore.com/). That means you're missing out on roughly 35 percent of the market if you're only advertising with Google AdWords. You're missing www.yahoo.com, www.msn.com, and www.ask.com, among others.

During the writing of this book, an interesting development has been occurring with respect to Yahoo!'s pay-per-click advertising program (called Yahoo! Search Marketing) and www.bing.com's pay-per-click advertising program (called MSN AdCenter). It's known as the Search Alliance, and it's the end result of a search agreement between Yahoo! and Microsoft that will allow Microsoft to serve results to Yahoo!'s search engine. As of now, advertisers running pay-per-click ads in Yahoo! will eventually be merged into the MSN AdCenter platform; advertising with the new Search Alliance means that an advertiser's ads will then appear on both www.yahoo.com and www.bing.com search results.

The Yahoo!/Microsoft Search Alliance

Figure 18-2 shows the homepage of the Yahoo!/Microsoft Search Alliance, which is the place for all the information you'll need to know concerning details of this merger. When the Search Alliance platform merging is complete, advertisers will use the MSN AdCenter platform to manage and run their campaigns. Marketers' ads will appear on both www.bing.com and www.yahoo.com search results. As of this time, there is no way to tell the MSN AdCenter platform not to show ads on Yahoo!, making advertising with the Search Alliance all-inclusive. This includes the Application Programming Interface (API) that IT developers use to download and incorporate paid search data within their own platforms.

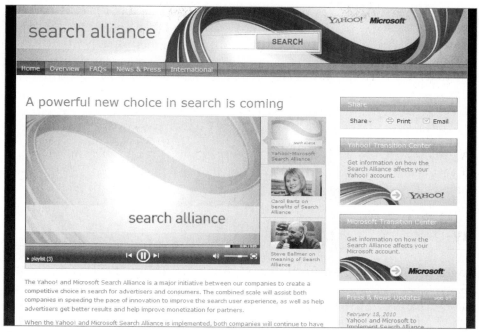

Figure 18-2: Search Alliance website

This Search Alliance only realistically covers paid search and regular, non-paid search results. It isn't a merger that includes instant messaging, e-mail, or display advertising. Its web address is www.searchalliance.com/.

Ask Sponsored Listings

ASK.com also has a pay-per-click engine called ASK Sponsored Listings. ASK does not have much market share (2 percent or a little less), but it can bring in some decent ancillary paid traffic to your site. ASK.com does have some partnerships (with NASCAR, among others), so there could be some future potential for a higher volume of traffic.

Figure 18-3 shows a search result for soccer equipment on ASK.com's search engine. The sponsored results appear near the middle of the page, versus Google or Yahoo!, where the sponsored search results appear at the very top of the page. There are also some other links on the right-hand side of the page showing related searches and your recent search history (as it shows mine on the bottom right of Figure 18-3, where I misspelled *soccer*). And sometimes, depending on your search query, you are presented with either three sponsored listings or four.

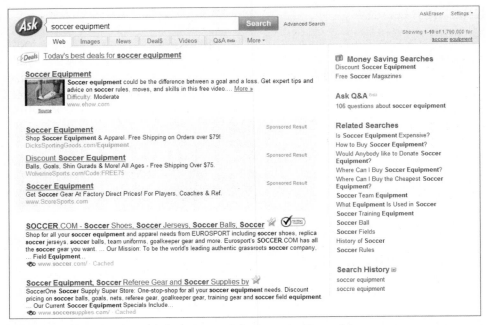

Figure 18-3: A search result for soccer equipment on www.ask.com

Quite a number of other websites out there offer some model of pay-per-click advertising that can bring some ancillary traffic to your site. However, don't expect much in terms of quality from this second-tier traffic. Usually, advertisers use ancillary paid networks if they have a certain volume of traffic they need to reach, but very rarely does that traffic convert or turn into a qualified lead for the website owner.

Some Other Tools to Add

Perhaps you don't care to advertise on any platform other than Google AdWords (perhaps, you simply can't afford to). That's OK — but before you put down *Your Google Game Plan for Success* and find a spot for it on your bookshelf or your desk at work, take a look at some other tools that you can add to your game plan that don't cost you anything more than a little of your time. If you do turn a profit on Google, however, chances are you may be able to do the same on some of the other platforms mentioned.

With the explosion of social media in the last few years, I'd be remiss if I didn't talk about some websites and tools that you'll need to fortify your social-media strategy. As you probably know, you are allowed only up to 140 characters per tweet on Twitter, and there are similar restrictions on other social-media sites. This means that you'll need to use a URL shortener to share links on social-media sites with strict character limits.

URL Shorteners

Figure 18-4 is a screenshot of bit.ly, one of the most popular URL-shortening tools online. Bit.ly is a free service into which you insert your normal URL that you want to share. Once you hit Shorten, you'll receive a very small URL that you can use on Twitter and other social media. You can also use this for your e-mail marketing campaigns to reduce the ugliness of long URLs with seemingly never-ending query parameters.

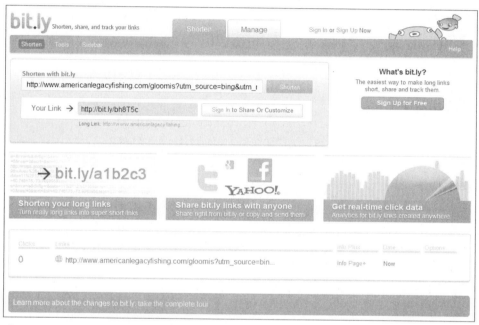

Figure 18-4: Bit.ly, a URL shortener

One of the reasons I like to use bit.ly so much is that you get some fairly comprehensive reporting on your shortened URL activity. Figure 18-5 gives you some examples of the types of reports you'll receive for free simply by using the bit.ly service.

Klout

In Google Analytics (and other web analytics tools) you can track clicks to your site from social-media efforts like Twitter by using the manual URL tagging technique I discussed at the beginning of the chapter, and then running the tagged URL through a URL shortener like bit.ly. But tracking visits to your site from Twitter isn't the only way you can measure your social-media efforts or your influence in the social-media landscape.

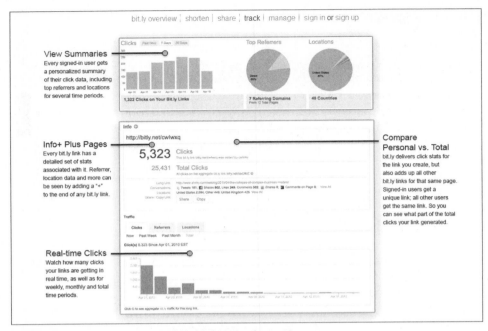

Figure 18-5: Reports provided by bit.ly URL shortening

Programs like Klout (www.klout.com/), displayed in Figure 18-6, are free programs that are specifically designed to measure one's influence on social media, particularly Twitter. Klout has created a scoring algorithm based on your activity on Twitter, which follows you and how your tweets are being read and shared across the Twitter universe. The score ranges from 0–100, with 100 being the highest score you can get. When you create your free profile and enter in your Twitter username, you'll have access to some insightful details that aren't provided by your web-analytics tool. I'm not very active on Twitter (but feel free to reach me via Twitter; it's always open in the background in a separate browser window). Therefore, I have a low Twitter score of 8 (out of 100). Perhaps we can engage on Twitter and raise my score?

Twitalyzer

Another great Twitter influence-tracking program is called Twitalyzer (www.twitalyzer.com/). Twitalyzer differentiates itself from Klout by providing more in-depth reporting features, providing benchmark statistics, and allowing you to define goals. It's also a free service, and setting up an account is very easy to do. (Twitalyzer will ask your permission and redirect you to Twitter to authenticate your username so you can view your stats.) Figure 18-7 shows my Twitalyzer homepage; if you thought my Klout score was bad, it's miles better than what my Impact Score shows. I really need help on Twitter, people.

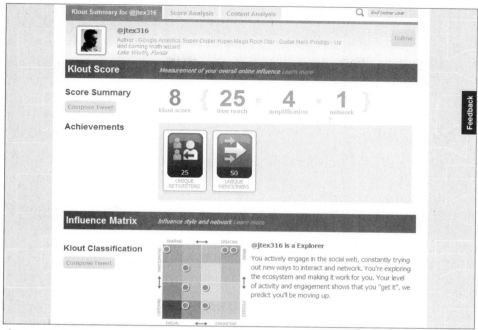

Figure 18-6: My personal Klout profile summary page

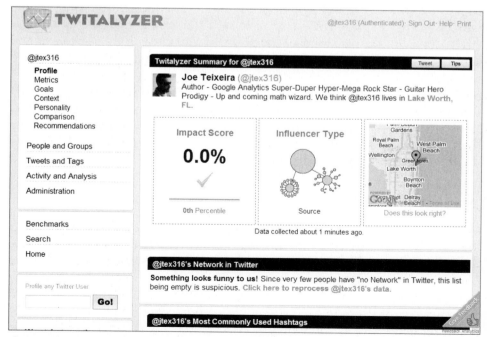

Figure 18-7: My own Twitalyzer account homepage

The point of tools like Klout and Twitalyzer is to be able to diagnose the health and impact of your Twitter feed and obtain feedback on things that you can do to become more influential in the social-media world. My takeaway for my own Twitter account is that I need to really step up my level of engagement and participate in conversations on Twitter much more than I have if I want to improve my Klout and Twitalyzer scores. What are yours?

PercentMobile

PercentMobile is a free tool that allows you to set up a profile and track the mobile activity on your website. You can sign up for a free account at www.percentmobile .com/ and grab a very small piece of JavaScript code that will be placed on the pages of your website. Then, as your website collects mobile data, PercentMobile will display incredibly interesting data for you that no web-analytics vendor is currently doing. You can find out what devices were used, how many devices had a touchscreen, what operating system the devices had, and everything else you ever wanted to know about the mobile demographic of visitors to your website. PercentMobile also shows you full images of each mobile phone, as shown in the example in Figure 18-8. PercentMobile is a company that "gets it," and you should get a PercentMobile account.

Figure 18-8: PercentMobile report on the "Rise of the Experience Phone in 2010"

There are a few other (paid) mobile tools out there like Bango Mobile Analytics (`www.bango.com/`), and these can also provide rich insights into your mobile traffic. Bango comes with a 30-day free trial, but then you'll have to pay for its mobile-analytics service. Paid mobile analytics are probably a good idea if you're heavily into mobile, but try out PercentMobile first.

CrazyEgg

Google Analytics has the Site Overlay report that will show you click data on top of your website; you learned about this in Chapter 7. However, the Site Overlay report is limited in its functionality and depth of data. If you really like heat maps and visualizations, give CrazyEgg (`www.crazyegg.com/`) a try.

CrazyEgg is not a free program — its basic package starts at $9 per month. For about $120 a year, you'll receive excellent heat map data and be able to use that information to drive the optimization changes that you make on your site. It's also an excellent complement to your Google Website Optimizer experiments, since you'll be able to see where on your landing pages people are gravitating. Figure 18-9 shows the heat map example from the CrazyEgg website overview page.

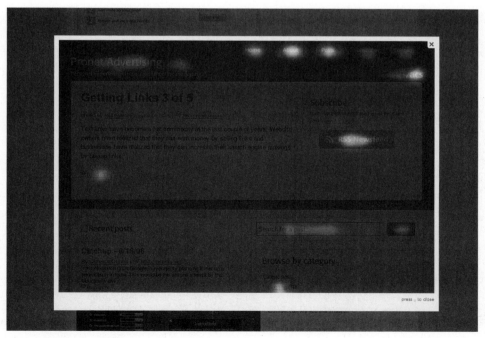

Figure 18-9: CrazyEgg's heat map example

This is only a handful of the great programs outside the Google ecosystem that you can incorporate into your marketing and analysis efforts. There are many solid products out there that can help you achieve the level of success you deserve. The third and final thing that I want you to get out of *Your Google Game Plan for Success* is the incentive to try a non-Google program, like Klout or CrazyEgg, and incorporate it into your own game plan. I hope you found this book a useful and informative guide. However, I'm not done quite yet — check out the appendix that follows this chapter, where I list links and resources for you, and also offer personal thanks to you, the reader and soon-to-be successful online businessperson!

Resources and a Thank-You!

I didn't want to end *Your Google Game Plan for Success* without providing you wonderful readers with some resources to the tools I've been showing you throughout this book. As you know, I've made many references to this section in virtually every chapter. Some friends tell me that the appendix of a book is a favorite section because of the sheer volume of collected links and resources that an author organizes. I've always remembered that, and I'm happy to be able to collect these references for you.

Getting in Touch with the Author

I want you to reach out to me. Why? Because as I wrote in the introduction of this book, I feel that the author-to-reader connection is something of a lost art, regardless of what type of book (technical, science fiction, thriller, etc.) a reader owns.

You can feel free to get in touch with me at any time. If you have comments, suggestions, questions, thoughts, or corrections, you can let me know, and I'll get back to you as soon as I can. If you completely disagree with something you've read and have a better, easier way to do it, I'm all ears.

The two best ways to contact me are via e-mail and via my Twitter account. I also have a LinkedIn account, which I invite you to use. I'm very responsive to both e-mail and Twitter, so if you send me a message, you will be responded to (not necessarily at once, but I'll eventually reply to you).

My e-mail address is
`jtex316@gmail.com`
My Twitter account ID is
`@jtex316`
My LinkedIn profile page is
`http://www.linkedin.com/in/joeteixeira`
I eagerly await your communication!

Thank You, Reader!

Far too often I see manuals, magazines, newspapers, blogs, and books that don't take time to thank their readers not only for purchasing the author's content, but also for taking the time out of their busy lives to actually read it. I promised myself that if I ever authored a book I would make sure there is a personal "Thank You" message from me to you. And here it is!

Thank you so very much for opening the pages of this book, whether you have ordered it online, bought it in your local bookstore, or borrowed it from an office colleague. I truly am honored that you have chosen this book for your library — or that you are simply spending a few minutes flipping through the pages as you wait for someone. It means a lot to me.

Let's get to some resources, shall we? Most of the following links are shortened URLs for your convenience — using a service like bit.ly. They save you from having to use long and ugly URLs for your links. The ones that aren't shortened URLs are self-explanatory. If you don't feel like typing any of these URLs in by hand, simply search for the title of the link on Google. (If you do type them in, be sure to distinguish a character like a lowercase "l" from a number 1. There's not a lot of difference in the printing font.)

Google Resources

The following resources are all under the Google umbrella. In a way, they are "official" resources from the 800-pound gorilla that is Google. If it's on any of these resources, it's the official word.

AdWords Help Forum:

`http://bit.ly/9YfqTs`

AdWords Online Classroom:

`http://bit.ly/9O93WD`

Google AdSense:

`http://bit.ly/9raB5v`

Google AdWords API:

http://bit.ly/bcgMsw

Google AdWords:

http://www.google.com/adwords

Google Analytics Application Gallery:

http://bit.ly/dyz4nJ

Google Analytics Certified Partners (GACP):

http://bit.ly/awgKs6

Google Analytics Developer Docs (Google Code):

http://bit.ly/cBRQAi

Google Analytics Help Center:

http://bit.ly/cOnfvI

Google Analytics Help Forum:

http://bit.ly/beKKaF

Google Analytics IQ Lessons:

http://bit.ly/bLkoAf

Google Analytics Setup Checklist:

http://bit.ly/bzva9f

Google Analytics Tool: URL Builder:

http://bit.ly/djxtoE

Google Analytics YouTube Channel:

http://bit.ly/as2Wf3

Google Analytics:

http://www.google.com/analytics

Google DoubleClick Ad Planner:

http://bit.ly/cD96Za

Google FeedBurner:

http://bit.ly/9H1JHr

Google for Advertisers:

http://bit.ly/b7ulty

Google Insights for Search:

http://bit.ly/axMjXH

Google Labs:

http://bit.ly/aGAMuO

Google Partner Search:

http://bit.ly/dzFoAD

Google Places:

http://bit.ly/9hPt6X

Google Product Search:

http://bit.ly/dfmwbX

Google Search-Based Keyword Tool:

http://bit.ly/9TmZUc

Google Trends:

http://bit.ly/bDeEOJ

Google URL Shortener (Goo.gl):

http://goo.gl/

Google Webmaster Central Help Forum:

http://bit.ly/cUSIqd

Google Webmaster Central Webmaster Guidelines:

http://bit.ly/bsfjr6

Google Webmaster Central:

http://bit.ly/aE7vrs

Google Webmaster Tools API:

http://bit.ly/dBP5Kv

Google Webmaster Tools:

http://bit.ly/9qXrlb

Google Website Optimizer API:

http://bit.ly/d35JMI

Google Website Optimizer Articles on Website Optimization:

http://bit.ly/ato8Vu

Google Website Optimizer Authorized Consultants:

http://bit.ly/c6e4aQ

Google Website Optimizer Help Forum:

http://bit.ly/d5oYC9

Google Website Optimizer Help:

http://bit.ly/dcnLaL

Google Website Optimizer Technology Partners:

http://bit.ly/aXkkFB

Google Website Optimizer Tutorials & Videos:

http://bit.ly/96ZoO5

Google Website Optimizer:

http://www.google.com/websiteoptimizer

Google YouTube Business Channel:

http://bit.ly/dCS0Ii

Google YouTube Webmaster Central Channel:

http://bit.ly/aGfvyo

Seminars for Success:

http://bit.ly/c0H0AF

Non-Google Resources

There are plenty of non-Google resources out there, from marketing platforms to tools to social-media measurement websites. Bookmark some of these great resources for future use.

4Q Online Survey:

http://www.4qsurvey.com/

Acquisio:

http://bit.ly/bUySSu

Alterian:

http://www.alterian.com/

AppClix:

http://www.mobilytics.net/

Ask Sponsored Listings:

http://sponsoredlistings.ask.com/

Atlas:

http://bit.ly/9Tf351

AWStats:

http://bit.ly/bW1Zvu

Bango Mobile Analytics:

http://www.bango.com/mobileanalytics

BidRank:

http://bit.ly/9sHL3p

Bit.ly:

http://bit.ly

Business.com Ad Center:

http://bit.ly/bW2r1D

clickdensity:

http://www.clickdensity.com/

ClickTale:

http://www.clicktale.com/

Compete:

http://www.compete.com/

Coremetrics:

http://www.coremetrics.com/

CrazyEgg:

http://www.crazyegg.com/

ForeSee Results:

http://www.foreseeresults.com/

Free Online Surveys:

http://www.freeonlinesurveys.com/

GoStats:

http://gostats.com/

HitsLink:

http://www.hitslink.com/

Hitwise:

http://www.hitwise.com/

Kampyle:

http://www.kampyle.com/

Keyword Spy:

http://bit.ly/bAzUJA

Klout:

http://www.klout.com/

Lyris (ClickTracks):

http://bit.ly/9zVP5k

MailChimp:

http://www.mailchimp.com/

MetaSun:

http://www.metasun.com/

Microsoft AdCenter:

https://adcenter.microsoft.com/

NetSuite:

http://bit.ly/cpG5Jt

Omniture Test&Target:

http://bit.ly/a1e7Xd

Omniture:

http://www.omniture.com/

OneStat:

http://www.onestat.net/

Opentracker:

http://www.opentracker.net/

Ow.ly:

http://ow.ly

PercentMobile:

http://www.percentmobile.com/

Piwik:

http://piwik.org/

PowerMapper:

http://www.powermapper.com/

RexSwain:

http://www.rexswain.com/

Sales Force:

http://bit.ly/9wmXUO

SearchForce:

http://bit.ly/bhPn7r

SiteScan:

http://bit.ly/aH32J0

SiteSpect:

http://www.sitespect.com/

Splunk:

http://www.splunk.com/

StatCounter:

http://www.statcounter.com/

SurveyMonkey:

http://www.surveymonkey.com/

Tiny:

http://tiny.cc/

Trellian Keyword Discovery:

http://bit.ly/9ASMPV

Twitalyzer:

http://www.twitalyzer.com/

Unica:

http://www.unica.com/

VisiStat:

http://www.visistat.com/

Web Analytics Solution Profiler (WASP):

http://bit.ly/cYSNMA

Webtrends:

http://www.webtrends.com/

Woopra:

http://www.woopra.com/

Yahoo! Advertising:

http://advertising.yahoo.com/

Yahoo! Web Analytics:

http://bit.ly/aqtTbT

Zoho:

http://www.zoho.com/

Zoomerang:

http://www.zoomerang.com/

Blogs to Subscribe To

There are a lot of great, influential, and intelligent people in our industry who have taken the time to share their thoughts to the world about all things concerning online marketing, web analytics, site optimization, and more. You should subscribe to as many of these blogs as you possibly can to expand your knowledge and learn all about what the leaders of our industry are doing.

Actionable Analytics:

http://bit.ly/9sm8r0

AdWords API Blog:

http://bit.ly/dhjZrP

Analytics Advice:

http://bit.ly/d5XDVe

Analytics Talk:

http://bit.ly/cmkGW5

BG Theory:

http://bit.ly/afAbpm

Blast Advanced Media:

http://bit.ly/a4jxHK

ClickTale Blog:

http://bit.ly/bbS6gk

ClickZ:

http://bit.ly/dtXw45

Copy Blogger:

http://bit.ly/aIhATe

Duct Tape Marketing:

http://bit.ly/bY6Bwr

Econsultancy:

http://bit.ly/aKYEkt

E-Nor Blog:

http://bit.ly/ah2uZt

Google Analytics Blog:

http://analytics.blogspot.com/

Google Analytics Results:

http://bit.ly/aWz4Rt

Google Conversion Room Blog:

http://bit.ly/aycaf0

Google Website Optimizer Tricks:

http://bit.ly/d4JR3X

Grok Dot Com (FutureNow):

http://bit.ly/a7iPTj

I ❤ Split Testing:

http://bit.ly/aJi0Yz

Immeria:

http://bit.ly/dyLGig

Inside AdWords:

http://adwords.blogspot.com/

Juice Analytics:

http://bit.ly/cnnGHC

Junk Charts:

http://bit.ly/99h6FR

KISSmetrics:

http://bit.ly/dxotjj

LunaMetrics:

http://bit.ly/dnZNIC

Marketing Pilgrim:

http://bit.ly/aJtujP

Measuring Success:

http://bit.ly/cbvCvx

Michael Whitaker's Web Analytics Blog:

http://bit.ly/a0Uf4P

Mobile Analytics Today:

http://bit.ly/dnAH9T

Occam's Razor by Avinash Kaushik:

http://www.kaushik.net/avinash/

Omniture Industry Insights:

http://bit.ly/bsU7m4

Online-Behavior:

http://bit.ly/9SQevL

Pay Per Click Universe:

http://bit.ly/durjRG

PPC Blog:

http://bit.ly/cT57E8

PPC Blog (UK):

http://bit.ly/cZDidK

Rich Page:

http://bit.ly/bfrukl

ROI Revolution:

http://bit.ly/cfHTkz

Search Engine Guide:

http://bit.ly/cU20pa

Search Engine Land:

http://searchengineland.com/

The Official Google Website Optimizer Blog:

http://bit.ly/caRP1V

Visual Revenue:

http://bit.ly/9hjVX8

VKI Studios:

http://bit.ly/9JVQWh

Web Analytics Demystified:

http://bit.ly/aATkJS

Web Analytics World:

http://bit.ly/aEm6PP

Web Analytics, Behavioral Targeting and Optimization:

http://bit.ly/9uMNmd

WebShare:

http://bit.ly/9wt6rc

Webtrends:

http://bit.ly/dnJ2I0

Yahoo! Web Analytics:

http://bit.ly/ar6HgI

Most if not all of the companies and people who are in charge of and write content for these resources have Twitter accounts. Simply go to www.google.com and search for these resources with the word "Twitter" in your search query to find the resources' Twitter accounts.